5-6-74

Introduction to
Quantitative Methods in Economics

INTRODUCTION TO QUANTITATIVE METHODS IN ECONOMICS

D. E. James
Senior Lecturer in Economics
Macquarie University

C. D. Throsby
Associate Professor in Economics
Macquarie University

John Wiley & Sons Australasia Pty Ltd
Sydney
New York　　　　　London　　　　　Toronto

ISBN: Cloth: 0 471 43917-7
       Paper (WIE): 0 471 43918-5
Library of Congress Catalog Card Number: 72-5462

Registered at the General Post Office, Sydney, for
transmission through the post as a book

Printed at The Griffin Press, Adelaide

10 9 8 7 6 5 4 3 2 1

1805001

Table of Contents

Page

Preface   xi

Part I: Simple Functions and Economic Relationships   I

1. Introduction   3

2. Algebraic Functions and Economic Relationships   8

     2.1   Some Examples of Economic Interdependence............8
     2.2   Use of Symbols......................................10
     2.3   What is a Function? 12
     2.4   Symbolic Representation of Functions.................12
     2.5   The Value of a Function..............................13
     2.6   Inverse Functions and the Problem of Causality..........14
     2.7   Implicit and Explicit Functions........................15

3. Representation of Simple Functions   17

     3.1   Algebraic Representation.............................17
     3.2   Graphical Representation............................17
     3.3   Linear and Nonlinear Functions......................21
     3.4   Continuity and Discontinuity........................22
     3.5   Further Examples of Functions.......................25
     3.6   General Algebraic Statements........................26
     3.7   Prediction from Simple Functions....................27

4. Models Based on Linear Functions   30

     4.1   Properties of Linear Functions.......................30
     4.2   An Example of a Linear Model: Supply and Demand.......35
     4.3   Equilibrium in the Linear Supply and Demand Model......38
     4.4   A Linear Income Determination Model.................40
     4.5   Addition of Functions...............................43

5. *Nonlinear Economic Relationships*   47

    5.1 Introduction 47
    5.2 Polynomials...47
    5.3 Power Functions...51
    5.4 Exponential Functions...............................52
    5.5 Logarithmic Functions...............................54
    5.6 The Rectangular Hyperbola 58
    5.7 Equilibrium in Nonlinear Models....................60

Part II: Elementary Calculus in Economics   63

6. *The Derivative of a Function*   65

    6.1 Slope of Nonlinear Functions 65
    6.2 Derivative of a Linear Function 72
    6.3 Some Simple Rules for Derivation.....................72
    6.4 Differentiation of Functions Containing Several Terms 76
    6.5 Differentiation of Logarithmic Functions................77

7. *The Economic Significance of Derivatives*   79

    7.1 Elasticity 79
    7.2 Derivatives in Production and Cost Theory.............85
    7.3 Derivatives in the Theory of Consumer Behaviour.......92
    7.4 Derivatives in Aggregate Models.....................94

8. *Maximisation and Minimisation*   96

    8.1 Maxima and Minima in Economics.....................96
    8.2 A Maximisation Example..............................96
    8.3 A Minimisation Example..............................98
    8.4 Distinguishing Between Maximum and Minimum 99
    8.5 A More Complicated Example........................101
    8.6 Local and Global Extrema...........................102
    8.7 Functions Without a Maximum and/or Minimum........104
    8.8 Summary 105

9. *The Use of Simple Derivatives in Economic Optimisation* 107

    9.1 Economic Optimisation..............................107
    9.2 Some Examples of Unconstrained Optimisation.........110
    9.3 Some Examples of Constrained Optimisation..........114

**Part III: Functions of Several Variables in Economic
Analysis**   125

10. *Functions of Several Variables*   127

    10.1 Introduction 127
    10.2 Linear Relationships Involving Three Variables..........128
    10.3 Linear Equations Involving More than Three Variables....133
    10.4 Implicit and Explicit Functions Involving Several Variables 134

10.5 Higher-Degree Polynomial Functions of Several Variables 135
10.6 The Cobb-Douglas Production Function with Two Inputs 135
10.7 Production Functions with More than Two Inputs 148
10.8 Utility Functions 149

11. Partial Derivatives   152
11.1 Marginal Products in the Two-Input Cobb-Douglas
     Production Function 152
11.2 Partial Derivatives of Cobb-Douglas Functions with More
     than Two Inputs. 157
11.3 Some Further Examples of Partial Derivation 158
11.4 Second-Order Partial Derivatives. 159

12. Homogeneous Functions and Euler's Theorem   162
12.1 Homogeneous and Nonhomogeneous Functions. 162
12.2 Homogeneous Production Functions 165
12.3 Euler's Theorem and Income Distribution. 166

13. Optimisation of Functions of Several Variables   170
13.1 Introduction 170
13.2 Unconstrained Optimisation 171
13.3 Constrained Optimisation and Lagrange Multipliers 176

Part IV: Linear Economic Models and Matrix Algebra 189

14. Linear Models in Matrix Form   191
14.1 The Role of Linear Algebra in Economics. 191
14.2 Elementary Matrix Notation 194
14.3 Further Linear Macromodels 196
14.4 The Linear Supply and Demand Model in Matrix Terms. . . 198
14.5 Some Properties of Matrices. 198
14.6 Subscript Notation 200
14.7 Sigma Notation 202

15. Matrix Multiplication   205
15.1 Multiplying a Matrix by a Vector 205
15.2 Multiplying a Matrix by a Matrix 209
15.3 Aspects of Matrix Multiplication 213
15.4 Some Important Special Matrices. 215

16. Economic Equilibrium and the Matrix Inverse   218
16.1 The Concept of the Matrix Inverse 218
16.2 Computing the Inverse Matrix. 219
16.3 Macroeconomic Equilibrium Once Again 224

17. Multiplier Analysis   227
17.1 The Concept of Macroeconomic Multipliers. 227
17.2 The Simple Investment Multiplier 228

17.3   The Impact of Changes in Autonomous Investment on
       Consumption Expenditure........................230
17.4   Changes in Autonomous Consumption Expenditure.....231
17.5   Summary of Results 232
17.6   The Matrix Approach to Multiplier Analysis 233

18. *Input-Output Analysis*   237
18.1   An Example..237
18.2   Addition and Subtraction of Matrices 240
18.3   Solving the Input-Output System 241
18.4   Application to Larger Systems 244
18.5   Some Further Ramifications of Input-Output Analysis....245

19. *Linear Programming*   250
19.1   An Example..250
19.2   Solving the Linear Programming Example 255
19.3   Larger Problems...................................259
19.4   Linear Programming Solutions in Matrix Terms 260
19.5   Some Further Ramifications of Linear Programming......263

Part V: Elementary Econometric Method   267

20. *Econometric Method and Simple Regression*   269
20.1   Introduction 269
20.2   The Methodology of Econometrics 269
20.3   The Simple Regression Model.......................274
20.4   An Alternative Way of Finding the Regression
       Coefficients 279
20.5   The Applicability of the Regression Model.............280

21. *Assumptions and Significance of the Simple Regression
    Model*   283
21.1   Assumptions of Linear Regression....................283
21.2   The Correlation Coefficient 289
21.3   Significance Tests on α and β.........................292
21.4   Significance Tests in Numerical Example..............292

Appendix A: Revision of Some Basic Algebra   295
A.1   Solving Simultaneous Equations 295
A.2   Solution of Quadratic Equations 296
A.3   Indices...297
A.4   Logarithms.......................................298
A.5   Expansion of $(x + y)^2$ and $(x + y)^3$ 298

Appendix B: Extensions of the Calculus   300
B.1   Maximisation and Minimisation of Functions of Several
       Variables...300

B.2 Constrained Maximisation and Minimisation: First-order
Conditions in the General Case........................301

Appendix C: Extensions of Matrix Algebra 303

C.1 Some Special Types of Matrices.......................303
C.2 Cramer's Rule for Solving a Set of Linear Simultaneous
Equations 305
C.3 A Method for Finding Third-Order Determinants 306
C.4 Determinants in the General Case 307
C.5 The Adjoint Matrix in the General Case 310
C.6 The Inverse Matrix in the General Case................310

Appendix D: The Linear Regression Model in Matrix Terms 312

D.1 The Two-Variable Case 312
D.2 The m-Variable Case...............................314
D.3 Assumptions of the General Linear Model..............314

Answers to Exercises 316

Further Reading 326

Index 329

Preface

This preface is not just another sermon on the virtues of using mathematics in economic analysis. In our view, that subject is important enough to warrant a chapter on its own (see Chapter 1). Here we wish simply to explain how this book differs from others in the field of quantitative economics and to indicate ways in which the student may use the book to his maximum advantage.

In Chapter 1 we point out that mathematics has become an indispensable tool in modern economic analysis, and hence that any student seeking a sound education in economics must gain a proper understanding of the mathematical and statistical techniques upon which the discipline has increasingly come to depend. There do exist several excellent texts dealing with mathematics for students of economics. But almost without exception these books teach mathematics followed by economic applications, and even at the "introductory" level adopt a level of rigour in exposition which frequently tends to frighten off students who are nervous about forced contact with "advanced" mathematics.

The present book, which is designed for use in conjunction with standard economics textbooks in mainstream economics courses in universities, colleges, other tertiary institutions, and even at advanced secondary school level, aims at developing the student's appreciation of the role of quantitative methods through a mixture of accepted economic theory, mathematical technique and ordinary intuition. The book has grown out of lectures we have given over several years to first-year and second-year economics students at Macquarie University. It is not a text in pure mathematics, or even mathematics for economists, though it does provide the average student with most of the mathematical equipment he will require up to intermediate level (that is, up to about the end of the second year of most university economics courses). Rather than presenting abstract axiomatic mathematical principles which are subsequently applied to economic problems, we adopt the strategy of teaching by way of example, of putting forward the mathematical apparatus in recognisable economic form, and of drawing out the economic and mathematical implications simultaneously. Herein lies one of the main differences between this book and others in the field. Students typically are eager to know *why* they are learning a particular technique and tend to lose interest if mathematical methods are presented in purely abstract terms lacking practical application. The use of familiar illustrations as the means of exposition, on the other hand, provides a practical basis, yet still allows the power of logic and generalisation to emerge.

Thus this book should be seen as a precursor to more advanced works in the field, including some of the so-called "introductory" texts. The student who masters the material presented herein should be able to tackle more rigorous works with much greater confidence. We hasten to stress that we do not disapprove of a rigorous approach to quantitative economics; on the contrary, we hope that when the initial groundwork has been laid and the student feels at home with basic mathematical reasoning in economics, he will be stimulated to improve his expertise in both pure and applied mathematics. The highest levels of achievement in mathematical economics can be reached only through a mutual development of economic theory and mathematical analysis.

Examples have been drawn from both microeconomic and macro-economic theory, with one or two from the pure theory of international trade. On the micro side, the text deals with such topics as production and cost theory, supply and demand analysis, consumer behaviour, and the theory of the firm under different market structures. The main macro-economic topics are the construction of linear aggregative models, equilibrium analysis, and impact multipliers. Input-output economics and linear programming are also treated at an introductory level. Important attention is devoted to a discussion of economic optimisation and its relationship with mathematical theory. Although this is not a textbook in statistics, the fundamental role of econometric method is emphasised throughout, and two chapters are included that introduce the student to the logic of econometric analysis and the linear regression model. Thus, overall the book touches on most of the economic subject matter to which quantitative methods are relevant that is encountered by the student during his first two years of study at the tertiary level.

Students approach their tertiary studies in economics with a wide variety of mathematical backgrounds. Some students have learned little or no mathematics, or studied maths so long ago that they have since become rather rusty. Others have been exposed to a sound mathematical education, occasionally at quite a high level. However, students in the latter categories have generally learned mathematics in conjunction with the physical rather than the social sciences; and one frequently comes across the student with an impeccable mathematical training who nonetheless finds it difficult to make the transition from abstract mathematics to economic application. We have accordingly structured this book in such a way that the reader may choose a point of entry which is appropriate to his own level of mathematical attainment. This is explained further in the following paragraphs, which briefly survey the contents of the volume.

The complete novice, or the student who has forgotten all the maths he ever learned, should begin with Part I, covering Chapters 1 to 5, which deals with simple functions and economic relationships. Chapter 1 provides an introduction to the role of quantitative methods in economics, and could in fact be read profitably by all students as a means of orientation. In Chapters 2 and 3, basic algebraic and geometric concepts used in economic analysis are explained. Chapters 4 and 5 examine linear and nonlinear economic relationships respectively. The student with a relatively weak mathematical background should commence his study at least with Chapter 5 and preferably with Chapter 4.

Part II deals with the role of elementary calculus in economics in the context of functions of a single variable. The technique of differentiation is explained from first principles in Chapter 6, and the importance of derivatives is discussed in Chapter 7. Methods of maximisation and minimisation using the calculus are considered in Chapter 8, and in Chapter 9 we proceed to a detailed study of constrained and unconstrained optimisation in economics.

Some students are adept at ordinary algebra but have not previously encountered the calculus. They should begin reading this book at Chapter 6. A student who has studied the calculus but is new to economics should commence with Chapter 7 but may omit Chapter 8. A student who has previously studied both mathematics and economics up to relatively high levels at school will probably find it useful to skim through Chapters 7 and 9 before plunging into Part III.

Under the general heading of "Functions of Several Variables in Economic Analysis", Part III considers the nature of functions of several variables (Chapter 10), partial derivatives (Chapter 11), homogeneity (Chapter 12) and optimisation problems (Chapter 13). Production theory is the main medium of analysis and special attention is paid to the Cobb-Douglas production function. Most students will not have studied much of this material before, though the more mathematically mature student can easily skip the first parts of Chapter 10 and most of Chapter 11.

Part IV is concerned with linear algebra, developing the techniques of matrix analysis mainly in terms of static macroeconomic models. The usefulness of linear algebra in setting up such models is stressed in Chapter 14. Chapter 15 looks at matrix multiplication by way of some specific economic examples, and in Chapter 16 we turn to the problem of solving linear systems. The calculation of impact multipliers from static linear systems is treated in Chapter 17. Input-output analysis and linear programming are seen as important applications of matrix methods to the study of economic problems; these topics are introduced in Chapters 18 and 19 respectively.

Our treatment of linear algebra exemplifies the expositional approach used throughout this book. Rather than discussing matrix operations in isolation, we introduce the relevant techniques when demanded by the analysis of the economic problems under study. Thus, for example, matrix inversion, which is essential to the solution of linear systems, is introduced in Chapter 16 in the context of equilibrium analysis in macromodels, while addition and subtraction of matrices is not encountered until required for input-output analysis in Chapter 19.

Because of the importance of econometrics in putting empirical flesh on the bones of economic theory, we have included in Part V an introductory treatment of the basic linear regression model. It is impossible to venture far into this area without calling on the concepts and methodology of statistics. However, an attempt is made in Chapter 20 to introduce the student to the methodology of empirical economic study and to the ideas behind simple regression in a way which does not presume any statistical expertise. All students are urged to read this chapter at some stage; in particular, Sections 20.1 and 20.2 do not depend on preceding chapters, and could therefore be read quite early in the student's study programme.

In Chapter 21 the basic assumptions and tests of significance in linear regression are considered. Stress is laid on building up the student's intuitive understanding of the distributional properties of the least-squares estimators. In writing this chapter it was impossible to avoid presupposing some elementary statistical knowledge. However, since most economics students take at least a first course in statistics at an early stage in their undergraduate programme, this chapter should eventually be accessible to most readers.

Exercises are provided to enable the student to test his progress and to fix in his mind the concepts studied. Some exercises are scattered through the text and further problems are grouped at the end of each chapter. Answers to the latter exercises are given at the end of the book.

A few students have problems with the basic operations of ordinary algebra—such as solving simultaneous equations, operations with indices, logarithms and so on. To enable such students to review these fundamentals, Appendix A lists in summary form some useful principles of basic algebra. At the other extreme, there are some extensions and generalisations of methods studied in the text which, for convenience of exposition, have also been placed in appendices. Appendices B, C and D include further development of the calculus, linear algebra and econometrics respectively. These three appendices, which are written in a terser style than the main text, are not essential for an understanding of the body of the book, and are provided mainly for the sake of completeness and to meet the needs of keener and more advanced students. For the further benefit of such students, an annotated Bibliography is given at the end of the book.

We wish to acknowledge the assistance provided by several people. Our colleagues David Rutledge, Graham Madden and Jose Lanz read the manuscript and made a number of useful suggestions. Various drafts were cheerfully and competently typed by Jacqueline Taylor, Helen Knight and Suzanne Lyon. Much as we might like to, we cannot implicate any of the above in any shortcomings this book may still have.

North Ryde, New South Wales   D. E. JAMES
June 1972   C. D. THROSBY

Part 1: Simple Functions and Economic Relationships

Chapter I

Introduction

Economics in the twentieth century has been characterised by a continually increasing use of the techniques of quantitative analysis. To the student beginning a first course in economics, the thought of being caught up in the world of what is referred to often derisively as "higher mathematics" looms as a frightening prospect. In fact, such fears are frequently based on a misunderstanding of the role of quantitative methods in economics. Thus it is important at the outset for the reader to appreciate what is meant by the term "quantitative economics".

Firstly, it should be emphasised that adopting a quantitative approach to economics does *not* mean merely playing with numbers. Economic theory has suffered enough from attempts to "prove" general principles by way of tedious arithmetic examples. Nor does quantitative economics involve simply the introduction of mathematical notation as a highbrow alternative to ordinary language as a means of communication. Certainly these aspects—numbers and notation—play a part in quantitative economics, but to see them as the sole characteristics of this field is to see but the tip of the iceberg.

A mathematical approach to economics has become important because, practically speaking, it is possible to formulate in quantitative terms almost all of the questions economists ask. Just about everything that economists analyse can be quantified in one way or another: the rates at which inputs are fed into production processes, the transformation of resources into commodities, the prices paid for goods and services in a market economy, the shadow prices of factors of production in a centrally-planned system, rates of consumption, levels of employment, quantities of savings, gross national product—all are capable of measurement. Moreover, not only can questions be *posed* in quantitative terms, they can also be analysed and solved using mathematical methods.

Essentially, quantitative economics refers to the application of mathematical *logic* to problems of economic theory. If a piece of economic investigation is to mean anything at all, it is imperative that it have a sound theoretical basis. Economists study their theories in the form of *models*, that is, formal logical structures which contain the essence of the real-world problem under study. In the construction of economic models, mathematics plays a crucial role. Mathematics is a powerful and rigorous tool of thought; it forces the analyst to specify his problems in a careful and unambiguous fashion, and it provides him with techniques of analysis through which his theoretical ideas may be readily brought to fruition and eventually given empirical substance.

The traditional marginalist principles on which a great deal of economic theory now rests represented, in the beginning, merely the discovery of the calculus in terms of economic equilibrium analysis. Joseph Schumpeter, in making this point, had the following to say in praise of the calculus as a technique of economic reasoning:

> The logic of the calculus may be expressed in terms of a small number of concepts such as variables, functions, limits, continuity, derivatives and differentials, maxima and minima. Familiarity with these concepts— and with such notions as systems of equations, determinateness, stability, all of which admit of simple explanations—changes one's whole attitude to the problems that arise from theoretical schemata of quantitative relations between things: problems acquire a new definiteness; the points at which they lose it stand out clearly; new methods of proof and disproof emerge; the maximum of return may be distilled from the little we know about the form of the relations between our variables; and the logic of infinitesimals disposes automatically of much controversial matter that, without its help, clogs the wheels of analytic advance.†

In surveying the development of economics over the period 1870 to 1914, Schumpeter noted that

> It was during [this] period . . . that the inevitable happened: mathematical methods began to play a significant and indeed decisive role *in the pure theory of our science.* Numerical or algebraic formulations and numerical calculations had occurred of course in the earlier stages of economic analysis. . . . But the use of figures—Ricardo made ample use of numerical illustrations—or of formulae—such as we find in Marx—or even the restatement in algebraic form of some result of non-mathematical reasoning does not constitute mathematical economics: a distinctive element enters only when the reasoning itself that produces the result is explicitly mathematical.‡

This "inevitable" growth in the use of mathematics in economics has continued to the present day. Indeed, so central have systems of mathematical reasoning become in modern economics that it is scarcely meaningful any longer to talk of "quantitative economics" as if it were distinguishable from a separate field of endeavour, "nonquantitative economics".

---

† JOSEPH A. SCHUMPETER, *History of Economic Analysis*, Oxford University Press, New York (George Allen and Unwin, London), 1959, pp. 955–56.
‡ Ibid., pp. 954–55.

A more valid distinction is between the use of quantitative and non-quantitative *tools* for presentation and analysis of economic argument. But even so these tools should not be regarded as competitive; rather, mathematical and other methods should be thought of as complementary, to be called upon as appropriate. It just happens that, as suggested earlier, the majority of the problems that economists analyse are quantitative in nature, and hence it is inevitable that mathematical methods must figure prominently in most aspects of economic analysis.

Of course the particular sorts of questions studied in economics often depend on the structure of the economic system in which the economist is working, be it a free market economy, or a centrally planned system. But quantitative method in economics is useful regardless of political ideology. Mathematical logic is just as valuable in the study of, say, monopoly pricing or output control in a multinational corporation as it is in the analysis of government supply of factors of production to state-owned enterprises in a socialist economy.† Even the fervent radical who advocates the overthrow of all existing economic institutions stands in need of quantitative methods of economic analysis if he is to erect something in their place.

It is sometimes suggested that the "general" student of economics, one who takes a degree in order to get a job in government or industry, has no need of sophisticated mathematics. This is perhaps true. But it is difficult to argue that he has no need of mathematics whatsoever. In this book, in covering the requirement for quantitative methods of the average student up to about intermediate university standard, we make use of only basic mathematical concepts and techniques. Yet an understanding of these methods is essential for any student who is to gain an adequate insight into the postulates and conclusions of economic theory. For the general student, this will probably be sufficient. The "specialist" student of mathematical economics or econometrics, however, will go much further into areas of advanced mathematics and statistics in his study of the quantitative aspects of his subject.

We have argued earlier that the increasing use of mathematics in economics in this century has been due to the fact that the problems confronting the economist are particularly amenable to quantitative analysis. Accepting this, we may list three further reasons for this trend.

Firstly, in the current technological environment, most economic problems are no longer simple. What is the optimum output position for a firm which produces a range of thirty different products? How much of each commodity should a country produce and exchange on international markets so as to maximise social welfare? What is the effect of budgetary policy on national income, consumption, employment, and on different industries or regions within the economy? How much of each commodity

---

† In fact in recent years some of the most important advances in the application of mathematical methods to large scale economic planning have been made in Eastern Europe.

should a consumer buy to maximise his utility? Questions such as these are so complicated that they cannot be effectively attacked in anything other than quantitative terms. In most areas of economic decision making, strong demands are constantly being made for analytical techniques capable of accommodating the complexities of the issues which typically arise.

Secondly, there has been a growing appreciation of the *practical* value of the quantitative approach. Mathematics offers notational systems and methods of reasoning through which large numbers of interacting economic variables can be handled with comparative ease. Through appropriate statistical procedures, greater realism can be achieved in the use and interpretation of raw economic data. The combination of mathematics and statistics in economics has led to a much clearer specification of problems, to the development of more powerful theories, and above all to the derivation of principles and policy recommendations that do lend themselves to empirical testing in real-world conditions.

The third factor responsible for the ever-growing emphasis on quantitative analysis is the electronic computer. With the aid of a large-scale modern computer, economists can confidently tackle problems which hitherto would have been considered impossible to solve. Recent macro-econometric models, for example, have contained many hundreds of equations, and it is quite common to find interindustry models with tens of thousands of input coefficients. The calculations involved with such models would, in earlier times, have taken years to carry out; now they can be performed on a computer in a matter of seconds. Thus the student of modern economics should not feel enslaved by the techniques used, but liberated. Computer technology will now leave him free to concentrate on ideas rather than preoccupying himself with laborious calculations and worrying about the need to "get his sums right". In any practical problem, all his sums will be done for him.

So far we have concentrated our attention mainly on the role of mathematics in economics. But there is a further aspect of the quantitative approach to economics, namely, statistical method. Over the years it has been found that a great deal of classical statistical analysis, relating mainly to the physical and biological sciences, is inappropriate in economic applications. Economists have accordingly found it necessary to develop a new blend of mathematical theory and statistical procedures leading to the comparatively new discipline of *econometrics*. Economic theory is of very little value if it cannot be tried in practice. Through econometric techniques, economic models can be tested against actual data. Quantitative relations between variables can be given more definite form, and conclusions can be drawn that have a positive connection with reality. The field of econometrics is an important one, and it is expanding rapidly. Indeed, it may be safely said that all economic theory will ultimately meet its fate in the econometrician's laboratory. Although the main emphasis in this book is placed on quantitative methods as a system of logical thought, the reader is urged to bear in mind that theorising is only one of the functions economists are called upon to perform. The other chief responsibility is to ensure that economic model building does eventually reflect real conditions. If not, solving economic problems becomes a pastime similar to solving chess problems: an elegant intellectual exercise and nothing more.

Exercises

1. There is one obvious sense in which economics is a conservative discipline—namely that it helps those currently responsible for running the economy to make more rational decisions and hence presumably to stay in power for longer. But this is as true of those Communist elites who choose to avail themselves of bourgeois economic know-how as it is of capitalist ones. I understand that Che Guevara introduced linear programming to Cuba. In this case an accepted part of the bourgeois economic tool-kit may have helped to keep a Marxist regime in power.

    (F. H. GRUEN, "The Radical Challenge to Bourgeois Economics", *Australian Quarterly*, March 1971, **43**, No. 1, p. 63.)

    Discuss.

2. Write an essay on the role of the electronic computer in modern economic analysis.

3. An economist with mathematical training is subject to the dual temptations of (1) limiting himself to problems that *can* be solved mathematically and (2) adopting inappropriate economic assumptions for the sake of mathematical convenience. Unless he is careful, therefore, he may become preoccupied with, and engulfed in, *mathematical techniques* instead of *economic principles*. In other words, one may unwittingly let mathematics assume the status of master rather than servant. Should this happen, though, it represents the failing not so much of mathematical economics as of the economist himself.

    (A. C. CHIANG, *Fundamental Methods of Mathematical Economics*, McGraw-Hill, New York, 1967, p. 4.)

    Discuss.

Chapter 2

Algebraic Functions and Economic Relationships

2.1. Some Examples of Economic Interdependence
2.1.1 EXAMPLE A: A DEMAND SCHEDULE

Imagine a housewife buying the weekly supply of potatoes for her family. The quantity she buys will depend, among other things, upon the price the greengrocer charges. As a rule, the higher the price, the smaller the quantity she buys. Suppose we observe her purchasing behaviour over a series of weeks, recording the price of potatoes and the corresponding number of kilograms she purchases. Observations over six weeks might give us the data shown in Table 2.1.

TABLE 2.1

Quantity of Potatoes Purchased by Housewife in Various Weeks

Date	Price of Potatoes (cents/kg)	Quantity Purchased (kg)
March 7	6	2
14	4	3
21	0	5
28	2	4
April 4	10	0
11	8	1

The quantity of any item purchased in any market at a given price at a given time is called the *quantity demanded*. The relationship between quantity demanded and price can be studied via a so-called *demand schedule*. Such a schedule might be expressed simply as a list of price-quantity observations as shown in Table 2.1, or as arranged in more orderly fashion in Table 2.2.

More generally, we note from Table 2.2 that the price of potatoes has *varied* over a range of numerical values from 0 to 10. For this set of prices the quantity demanded also *varies* over a range of values from 5 to 0.

TABLE 2.2

Housewife's Demand Schedule for Potatoes

Price of Potatoes (p) (cents/kg)	Weekly Quantity Demanded (q) (kg)
0	5
2	4
4	3
6	2
8	1
10	0

The two items of immediate interest—price and quantity demanded—can accordingly be referred to as *economic variables*. They are both quantifiable, in the sense that each may take on certain numerical values, and they are linked by a definite relation, such that for each price there is a unique quantity demanded.

The quantity demanded, being dependent upon price, may be described as a *dependent variable*. Price itself, which causes a certain quantity to be bought, is referred to as an *independent variable*. Table 2.2 reveals that variation in the independent variable (price) leads to variation in the dependent variable (quantity demanded).

2.1.2 EXAMPLE B: A PRODUCTION FUNCTION

Consider a wheat farmer who can obtain higher yields of wheat from a given area of land by applying more fertiliser to the soil. Suppose some research is undertaken showing the response of wheat production to various inputs of fertiliser. The results are shown in Table 2.3. Output of wheat increases in response to the input of fertiliser and reaches a maximum output of 70 centals when 5 to 6 kg of fertiliser are applied to each hectare.

TABLE 2.3

Output of Wheat in Response to Input of Fertiliser

Amount of Fertiliser Used (x) (kg/hectare)	Quantity of Wheat Produced (y) (centals/hectare)
0	40
1	50
2	58
3	64
4	68
5	70
6	70
7	68

It is possible for the farmer to use too much fertiliser. If he applies 7 kg per hectare, some of the plants are poisoned and total output declines.

A relationship between input and output such as that shown in Table 2.3 is called a *production function*. In this function, variations in the independent variable (fertiliser) cause variations in the dependent variable (total output of wheat).

2.1.3 EXAMPLE C: A CONSUMPTION FUNCTION

A man earns a salary of $10 thousand per year. Of this he has to pay $2 thousand to the government in income tax, he puts $3 thousand into the savings bank, and the remaining $5 thousand he spends on consumption (food and clothing for himself and his family, the education of his children, holidays, and so on). What would happen to his consumption expenditure if his income were to change? If he were to take a lower paid job, earning, say, $7 thousand per year, he might have to economise on some items of consumption, and his total consumption expenditure might fall to perhaps $4 thousand per year. On the other hand, suppose he were promoted to a salary of $16 thousand. He could now afford more expensive food, clothes, holidays, etc., and his consumption expenditure might increase to, say, $7 thousand.

It would be possible to draw up for this family a table showing the levels of consumption expenditure corresponding to a variety of likely family incomes. Table 2.4 shows the consumption expenditure corresponding to income levels from $4 thousand to $19 thousand per year for this hypothetical family.

TABLE 2.4

Consumption Expenditure per Year of a Given Family at Various Income Levels

Annual Family Income (Y) ($ '000)	Annual Consumption Expenditure (C) ($ '000)
4	3
7	4
10	5
13	6
16	7
19	8

A relationship between consumption and income such as that shown in Table 2.4 is called a *consumption function*. As in the preceding examples, we may designate income as an independent variable and consumption expenditure as a dependent variable.

2.2 Use of Symbols

2.2.1 WHAT SYMBOLS MEAN

To streamline the description of variables, we may designate them by symbols; a unique symbol may be chosen to represent any variable we wish to talk about. We may, for instance, use the symbol "q" to denote "the weekly quantity of potatoes demanded by the housewife, expressed in kg".

Let us introduce further symbols to represent the variables in our above examples.

Example A: Let q = weekly quantity of potatoes demanded in kg;
                p = price of potatoes in cents per kg.

Example B: Let y = output of wheat in centals per hectare;
                  x = quantity of fertiliser applied in kg per hectare.

Example C: Let C = family consumption expenditure in $'000 per year;
                  Y = family income in $'000 per year.

2.2.2 CHOICE OF NOTATION

We may choose our symbols from an almost inexhaustible supply. The basic building blocks are lower case and capital letters from the Roman and Greek alphabets, which contain twenty-six and twenty-four characters respectively.

Subscripts are a useful way of extending the range of a single symbol; for example, the prices of apples, bananas and carrots might be indicated by p_a, p_b and p_c respectively. Subscripts are also commonly used to designate particular items in a group. For example, net imports in a given month may be given the symbol M_i, where the subscript i refers to the particular month in question. We could let the subscript i take values of $1,2,3, \ldots, 12$ to indicate January through December; then M_5 would stand for the value of imports in the month of May.

Again, a single letter may be employed to represent different things merely by the introduction of apostrophes, asterisks, dashes and the like. Thus, for example, p^* may refer to the price of eggs in 1971 and p^{**} to the price in 1972.

Some symbols conventionally have a special meaning, such as the following:

Σ (Greek capital sigma): used to indicate sum of;
π (Greek lower case pi): used to indicate the constant $3.14159 \ldots$;
Δ (Greek capital delta): used to indicate a finite change;
δ (Greek lower case delta): used to indicate an infinitesimal change;
d (Roman lower case D): used to indicate differentiation;
e (Roman lower case E): used to indicate the constant $2.71828. \ldots$

In economics, one finds particular symbols that are used fairly generally to indicate specific variables. For example the following symbols are often (but by no means always) used:

C = consumption
I = investment
G = government expenditure
S = savings
Y = income
p = price
q = quantity.

However, in particular contexts, we are at liberty to define any symbol, including the above "special" ones, in any way we please, provided we make our definitions perfectly clear.

2.3 What is a Function?

The three Examples A,B and C discussed previously have several properties in common. In each case a dependent variable is determined by a single independent variable. Moreover, for a given numerical value of the independent variable, there corresponds a single value for the dependent variable. And in each example we observe some kind of rule or pattern governing the quantitative interdependence of the variables. In fact, the relations contained in Tables 2.1 to 2.4 may be stated as follows:

Example A: the quantity of potatoes demanded by the housewife *is a function of* the price of potatoes;

Example B: the quantity of wheat produced by the farmer *is a function of* the amount of fertiliser used;

Example C: the level of consumption expenditure of the family *is a function of* the family's annual income.

These are all verbal statements of functions. In economics, the term "function" is used mainly to indicate a *causal* relationship, such that variation in one or more variables will *cause* variation in some other variable, as in the examples above. In mathematics, on the other hand, the term "function" has a wider connotation, as we shall see in Section 2.6 below.

2.4 Symbolic Representation of Functions

Verbal statements of functions such as we made in the preceding section are very cumbersome, and it is highly desirable to use a more compact way to write them down. We have already seen that the variables in a function may be represented by symbols. Thus, our only requirement for a complete symbolic representation of functions is a substitute for the expression "is a function of". Here again we make use of symbols. For instance, in the case of Example A we might write

$$q = h(p) \tag{2.1}$$

which reads: "the variable q (kg of potatoes demanded) is a function of the variable p (the price of potatoes)".
Similarly, we might have, for Example B,

$$y = f(x), \tag{2.2}$$

which reads: "the variable y (total output of wheat) is a function of the variable x (input of fertiliser)".
And for Example C, we might have

$$C = \phi(Y), \tag{2.3}$$

which reads: "the variable C (consumption expenditure) is a function of the variable Y (family income)".

Notice that in each case an equation has been established, expressing the fact that, for a given value of the independent variable, some value for the dependent variable is implied. The independent variable is enclosed in brackets, and an appropriate symbol (such as h, f or ϕ) is placed in front of the brackets to indicate that the two variables are linked in some definite way. In Equations (2.1) to (2.3), the three function symbols (h, f and ϕ) are different in order to show that quite different functional relationships are implied between the dependent and independent variables in each of the three cases.

Though certain symbols are very common ones for representing functions (particularly the symbol "f"), a host of others may be used. Appropriately defined, any of the following examples may be employed to represent, say, the farmer's production function:

$$y = k(x), \qquad y = Z^*(x), \qquad y = \beta(x), \qquad y = zap(x),$$
$$y = f_n(x), \qquad y = g^i(x), \qquad \text{etc., etc.}$$

2.5 The Value of a Function

General functional statements such as those in Equations (2.1) to (2.3) indicate that a quantitative relationship exists between certain variables, but in themselves do not tell us anything about the nature of that relationship. How are we to know, when looking at Equation (2.1), for example, whether the quantity demanded goes up or down as the price of potatoes is raised? Hence, the above functions are purely *qualitative* in nature.

Consider a further example relating net government revenue (R) to a country's net imports (M). Net imports can be defined as total imports minus total exports. (It is thus possible for net imports to be negative, if in any year exports exceed imports.) Further, let us suppose the government pays a subsidy on export production and raises customs revenue on imports. The government will accordingly experience an outflow of its funds as exports increase and an inflow as imports increase. We take R to measure the net difference between these two flows—that is, customs revenue minus subsidy payments.

A function relating net revenue to net imports might be written as

$$R = r(M). \tag{2.4}$$

Now this equation is, again, merely a qualitative statement, telling us that R is some function of M. It is clear that a general statement such as this is only of very limited use. We are likely to want to answer questions along the lines of: "For a given level of M, what value does R take?" and "If M changes by a certain amount, by how much does R change?" For this purpose an *exact* mathematical relationship is essential.

Suppose we are able to write instead,

$$R = 0.25M. \tag{2.5}$$

We now have a precise quantitative statement telling us that if net imports are, say, \$10 million, net revenue will be one-quarter of this amount, or \$2.5 million. In other words, for a given numerical value of the independent variable, we are able to find the *value of the function*—that is, the corresponding numerical value that the dependent variable takes.

Observe that for any given value of M there corresponds a single unique value of R. The function (2.5) is thus an example of a *single-valued function*. Look at Tables 2.2 to 2.4 and confirm that the functions (2.1) to (2.3) respectively are also single-valued.

2.6 Inverse Functions and the Problem of Causality

So far, in all the functions we have studied, the dependent variable has been written on the left-hand side of the equality sign and the independent variable on the right. In economic terms, the causal relationship between the variables has been assumed to run in one direction only, from right to left.

In more general mathematical usage, however, the term "function" is used without any implied logical causality. The function merely specifies the relationship that exists between the variables. Mathematically, there is nothing to stop us, for example, from rearranging Equation (2.5) into the form

$$M = \frac{R}{0.25} \tag{2.6}$$

where M clearly emerges as a function of R. Although this rearrangement of the original equation is quite legitimate in terms of mathematical logic, it would obviously be nonsensical from an economic viewpoint to suggest that the causal link between the two variables still runs from right to left. A net revenue of $2.5 million no more causes a level of $10 million in net imports to be reached than having an upset stomach causes you to eat green apples.

In mathematical terms, the function (2.6) is known as the *inverse* of the original function (2.5). With a clear understanding of the true causal relationship between R and M in the Equation (2.6) we can use the inverse function to answer a variety of questions of economic significance. For example, we could use Equation (2.6) to calculate that for net revenue to equal, say, $5 million, net imports would need to equal $20 million.

More generally, if we begin with the function

$$R = r(M), \tag{2.7}$$

we can write the corresponding inverse function as

$$M = r^{-1}(R) \tag{2.8}$$

where the notation "r^{-1}" indicates "the inverse of the function r". The functions (2.5) and (2.6) are merely specific instances of the functions (2.7) and (2.8) respectively.

The same concepts may be applied to the farmer's production function,

$$y = f(x). \tag{2.9}$$

By writing the inverse as

$$x = f^{-1}(y), \tag{2.10}$$

we derive an equation which will indicate the quantity of fertiliser x that must be applied to achieve a given level of total output y. As Table 2.3 shows, however, in the inverse function (2.10) there is no guarantee that for a given value of the variable y on the right-hand side (RHS), there will exist a unique value for the variable x on the left-hand side (LHS). For example, Table 2.3 shows that when total output is 68 centals per hectare, the corresponding input level may be 4 kg or 7 kg per hectare. In this instance, the function $f^{-1}(x)$ is said to be *multiple-valued* or simply *multivalued*.

To reiterate, a function $z = \gamma(w)$ is said to be single-valued if one and only one value of z corresponds to any given value of w; it is said to be multivalued if more than one value of z exists for any given value of w.

2.7 Implicit and Explicit Functions

Equations (2.5) and (2.6) can both be written in the form

$$R - 0.25M = 0. \tag{2.11}$$

Equation (2.11) is an example of an *implicit function*. It tells us that, implicitly, there exists a relationship between R and M.

Equations (2.5) and (2.6), on the other hand, are examples of *explicit functions*. In each case, the variable on the LHS of each equation is an explicit function of the variable on the RHS.

Hence in looking at an implicit function containing two variables, we should bear in mind that one variable may be taken as the dependent variable and considered as a function of the remaining independent variable. In our example above, for instance, even though Equation (2.11) is an implicit function of the variables R and M, we know that R is dependent, M is independent and that R can be written as an explicit function of M as in Equation (2.5).

More generally, we define an implicit function of the variables x and y as

$$F(x, y) = 0 \tag{2.12}$$

where again one variable may be taken as independent, and the other dependent. Note that we use a special symbol, "F", to indicate an implicit function, although any symbol would suffice.

In the next chapter we shall investigate further the properties of functional relationships between economic variables.

Exercises

1. It is postulated that a relationship exists between the monthly volume of savings bank deposits and the rate of interest paid on such deposits. Choosing appropriate symbols to define the two variables (savings and rate of interest), write down this general relationship in symbolic form.

2. Write down in general form the inverse of the function in Exercise 1 above.

3. Suppose quantity supplied (q) of a particular good is related to its price (p) by the following equation:

$$q = 5p.$$

Is this function single-valued or multivalued?

4. (a) Write the supply equation from Exercise 3 above in implicit form.
   (b) How many explicit functions can we make from this implicit function?
   (c) What are these explicit functions?

5. The supply of men's shoes from a manufacturer to his retail outlets over a series of months is recorded. Also known is the price the retailers pay for the shoes. The data are shown below.

Month	Supply of Men's Shoes (pairs)	Wholesale Price of Shoes ($/pair)
Jan.	880	11
Feb.	740	10
Mar.	550	8
Apr.	150	5
May	510	9
June	610	10
July	920	14
Aug.	800	13
Sept.	1,100	15
Oct.	840	12
Nov.	629	10
Dec.	590	10

(a) Express in words the functional relationship implied in this table.
(b) Devise symbols to represent the variables in this function, and express the function in symbolic terms in its most general form.
(c) Explain the terminology "dependent and independent variables" in the context of this example.
(d) What other influences might affect the supply of shoes in this situation?

Chapter 3

Representation of Simple Functions

3.1 Algebraic Representation

At the end of the last chapter, we postulated a functional relationship existing between net revenue (R) and net imports (M), both variables measured in millions of dollars. This function was written in general algebraic form as

$$R = r(M), \qquad (3.1)$$

indicating simply that R is some function of M. But as we have already seen, to progress further we require a *specific* algebraic form for this function. What specific forms could Equation (3.1) take? In the previous chapter we saw one simple example,

$$R = 0.25M, \qquad (3.2)$$

which tells us that for any particular value of M, the corresponding value of R would be that value of M multiplied by 0.25. Equation (3.2) is an *algebraic* representation of this function.

3.2 Graphical Representation

Another way in which we may represent a simple function is by means of a *graph*. The use of graphs is limited by the number of dimensions at our disposal. Since we require one dimension for each variable in our relationship, and since there are only two dimensions available on a flat page, graphs are largely confined to illustrating two-variable relationships. Furthermore, it is clear that a graph can only represent a *specific* algebraic function; it is not possible, for instance, to draw a graph of Equation (3.1). We can illustrate the procedure for drawing graphs by using Equation (3.2).

3.2.1 CHOICE OF AXES

The axes or reference lines are used to indicate which variable is measured in which dimension, and to mark out the scale of measurement for each

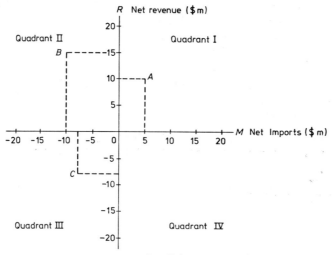

Fig. 3.1

variable. It is customary to show the *independent* variable on the *horizontal* axis, and the *dependent* variable on the *vertical* axis. Fig. 3.1 shows the axes in position. They are placed so that they cross at the point where both variables are zero; this point is called the *origin*. Any point on the *vertical* axis *above* 0 signifies a *positive* value for R, while any point on the *horizontal* axis to the *right* of 0 indicates a *positive* value for M. Points on the vertical axis *below* 0 or on the horizontal axis to the *left* of 0 signify *negative* values for R and M respectively. In fact, the diagram in Fig. 3.1 is divided by its two axes into four zones, called *quadrants*. Imagine the outermost points on each axis to represent the four points of the compass. Then we can identify the "northeast" quadrant as Quadrant I, where both variables are positive. In Quadrant II, to the northwest, R is positive and M is negative. In Quadrant III to the southwest, both R and M are negative, while in the southeast Quadrant IV, R is negative and M positive.

Next we can specify the scale of our figure. Suppose we want to show this relationship for a range of values of M from − $20 million to + $20 million. Then we can mark off the horizontal axis leftwards and rightwards from 0 at any convenient scale, let us say eight divisions of $5 million each as shown in Fig. 3.1. Similarly, we could use the same scale for the vertical axis to measure R, as illustrated on the diagram. But, of course, we are not obliged to use the same scale on vertical and horizontal axes; we are free to choose whatever scales we wish.

3.2.2 PLOTTING POINTS

Any point on Fig. 3.1 represents a specific combination of R and M. For example, the point A indicates a combination of $R = 10$, $M = 5$; B shows the point where $R = 15$, $M = -10$ and the point C indicates a level of -8 for both R and M.

We refer to the values of the two variables at any point on such a graph as the *coordinates* of that point. Thus the coordinates of the point A, for instance, are 5 and 10, sometimes written (5,10). Note the order in which the values are written: the first number in the brackets refers to measurement along the horizontal axis, which is also called the *abscissa*, and the second number indicates measurement on the vertical axis, or *ordinate*. Hence we can write the coordinates of the points B and C in Fig. 3.1 as $(-10,15)$ and $(-8,-8)$ respectively.

3.2.3 THE COORDINATES OF A SPECIFIC FUNCTION

Let us now determine a series of coordinates corresponding to the revenue function (3.2). To do this we need to specify a range of values for M, and then calculate the corresponding values of R. This will give a series of coordinate pairs.

Assuming that the relationship in Equation (3.2) holds for all positive and negative values of the independent variable, let us take M ranging from -20 to $+20$ in jumps of ten. The calculation of the corresponding R values is shown in Table 3.1. The points from Table 3.1 are plotted on Fig. 3.2. Make sure you understand the calculations in Table 3.1 and the transfer of the points to Fig. 3.2.

TABLE 3.1

Calculation of Coordinates for the Graph of Equation (3.2)

If M equals	then R equals	Coordinates
-20	$0.25 \times -20 = -5$	$(-20, -5)$
-10	$0.25 \times -10 = -2.5$	$(-10, -2.5)$
0	$0.25 \times \quad 0 = \quad 0$	$(0, 0)$
10	$0.25 \times \quad 10 = \quad 2.5$	$(10, 2.5)$
20	$0.25 \times \quad 20 = \quad 5$	$(20, 5)$

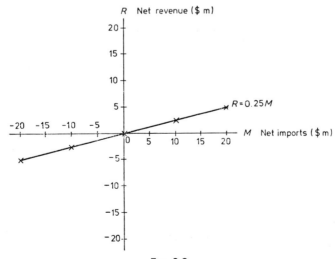

Fig. 3.2

3.2.4 DRAWING THE GRAPH

The five points plotted on Fig. 3.2 clearly lie along a straight line, and it is a simple matter to draw in the line as shown. This line represents the graph of the function $R = 0.25M$.

3.2.5 ANOTHER EXAMPLE

Consider the case of a Pitt Street farmer with an investment in a rural property. If he makes a profit on his investment he pays tax to the government. If he sustains a loss, he writes off the loss against the rest of his income, is obliged to pay less tax to the government and is effectively subsidised by the Treasury on his loss. Let us imagine that the tax-cum-profit situation for his investment can be represented by the function

$$T = (0.4 - 0.01P)P \equiv 0.4P - 0.01P^2, \qquad (3.3)\dagger$$

where T = net tax paid in $'000 per year; and

$\quad P$ = net operating profit in $'000 per year.

Note that where P becomes negative a loss is implied. Similarly, a negative value of T implies a tax refund (or subsidy) from the government.

Let us draw a graph of this function. Taking values of P ranging from -20 to $+20$ and calculating the relevant values of T, we obtain the results shown in Table 3.2. The coordinates are next plotted in Fig. 3.3 (a) and the curve joining the points drawn in. In practice, when drawing curved graphs, we may have to do some further calculations to establish the position of intermediate points more exactly. For instance, if we did not feel confident about drawing the graph in Fig. 3.3 (a) using only the five points calculated in Table 3.2, we could compute the positions of intermediate points for, say, $P = -15, -5, 5, 15$.

TABLE 3.2
Calculation of Coordinates for the Graph of Equation (3.3)

If P equals	then T equals	Coordinates
-20	$(0.4 \times -20) - (0.01 \times -20 \times -20) = -8-4 = -12$	$(-20, -12)$
-10	$(0.4 \times -10) - (0.01 \times -10 \times -10) = -4-1 = -5$	$(-10, -5)$
0	$(0.4 \times 0) - (0.01 \times 0 \times 0) \qquad = 0-0 = 0$	$(0, 0)$
10	$(0.4 \times 10) - (0.01 \times 10 \times 10) \qquad = 4-1 = 3$	$(10, 3)$
20	$(0.4 \times 20) - (0.01 \times 20 \times 20) \qquad = 8-4 = 4$	$(20, 4)$

In economics, the variables we deal with more often than not take only positive values. In drawing graphs for such variables, we need consider only Quadrant I. So, for example, if we were concerned only about the relationship between T and P generated by Equation (3.3) at levels equal to or greater than zero, we could redraw Fig. 3.3 (a) as in Fig. 3.3 (b),

---

† The three-bar equals sign means "is equivalent to" or "is identical to". We use it here to indicate that the expression $0.4P - 0.01P^2$ is simply an alternative way of writing down the expression $(0.4 - 0.01P)P$. Make sure you understand *why* these two expressions are identical.

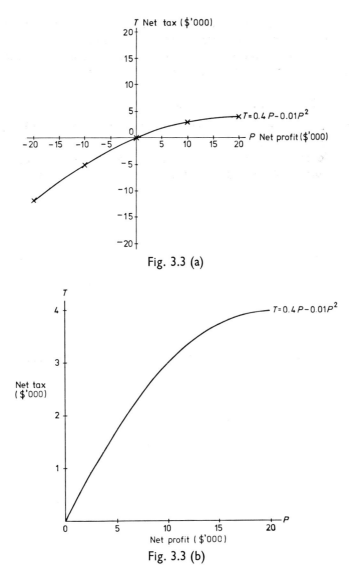

Fig. 3.3 (a)

Fig. 3.3 (b)

excluding the negative zone of both axes. (Notice that the scale of the vertical axis in Fig. 3.3 (b) has been changed. The function represented is identical with that drawn in Fig. 3.3 (a), the only difference between the two figures being the scale of measurement of one of the axes.)

3.3 Linear and Nonlinear Functions

The graph in Fig. 3.2 is a straight line. It is called *linear*, and the function from which it is drawn, Equation (3.2), is called a *linear function*. Contrast this with the graph in Figs 3.3 (a) and (b) where we see curved lines. These are *nonlinear* graphs, derived from a *nonlinear function*, Equation (3.3).

The distinction between linear and nonlinear relationships in economics is a very important one. In the next chapter we shall be studying the properties of linear functions and then, in Chapter 5, we shall be looking at some characteristic nonlinear economic relationships.

3.4 Continuity and Discontinuity

The graphs we have looked at so far do not have any vertical or horizontal gaps or jumps, and are therefore called *continuous*. This description is also applicable to the functions themselves, from which the graphs were derived. Figure 3.4 shows some further examples of continuous functions.

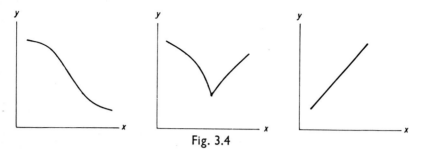

Fig. 3.4

Functions or graphs which do contain gaps are called *discontinuous*; some examples are illustrated in Fig. 3.5.

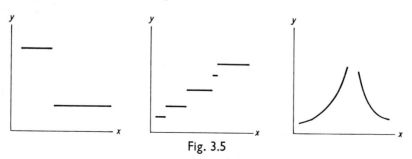

Fig. 3.5

In our examples above, all the variables are capable in principle of continuous variation; that is, they are not restricted to whole-number (*integer*) values like 3 or 7, but may take on any value, such as $3\frac{1}{2}$ or 7.81259. Furthermore the relationship between R and M in Equation (3.2), and between T and P in Equation (3.3), shows no breaks or discontinuities. In general, in order to produce a continuous function, the following two conditions are required:

(a) the variables in the function must be capable of continuous variation; and

(b) the relationship between them must also be continuous.

In economic analysis, functions that are strictly discontinuous are often approximated by a continuous relationship. For example, we might postulate an equation showing household income as a function of family size. Now a variable representing family size would be strictly an integer variable, since it can only assume whole-number values; there can only be 0, 1, 2, . . . children in a single family. Thus a function relating income to family size would be strictly discontinuous. However, for the purpose of economic analysis, it would be perfectly permissible for us to assume that family size is a continuous variable, and thus to hypothesise a continuous function relating it to other genuinely continuous variables.

Discontinuities also arise quite often in empirical data. For instance, data on Gross National Product may be obtainable only on an annual basis, as in the following example:

Year	Australian GNP at Current Price ($ m)
1960–61	14,686
1961–62	14,999
1962–63	16,242
1963–64	18,001
1964–65	19,845
1965–66	20,822
1966–67	22,737
1967–68	24,152

Nevertheless, we could draw a graph of these data that appears to show GNP growing continuously over time. If we plot each observation as if it were the level of GNP obtaining at the exact middle of each financial year (January 1, 1961 for the financial year 1960–61, etc.), and join up the resulting points, we would obtain the continuous graph shown in Fig. 3.6.

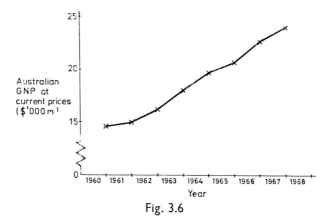

Fig. 3.6

(Notice the broken vertical axis in this figure, indicating that some part of its length has been omitted in order to make the graph a manageable size.)

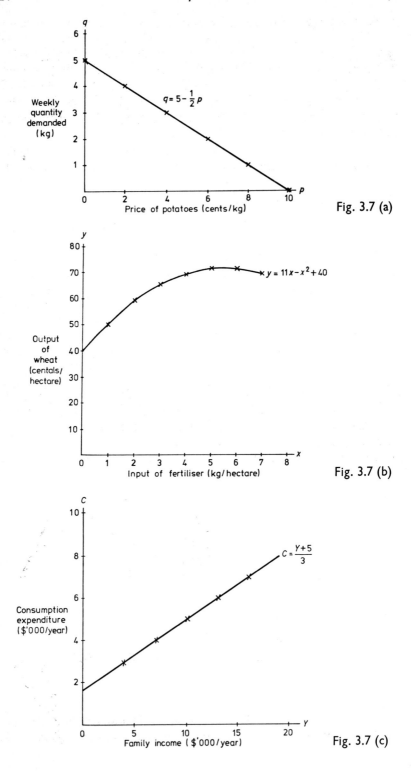

Fig. 3.7 (a)

Fig. 3.7 (b)

Fig. 3.7 (c)

3.5 Further Examples of Functions

Let us turn back to the three examples—of a demand function, a production function and a consumption function—that we introduced in Chapter 2. It so happens that each of the sets of data for these functions, shown in Tables 2.2, 2.3 and 2.4, exactly fits a specific algebraic form shown in Equations (3.4), (3.5) and (3.6) respectively:

Example A: *a demand function*
$$q = 5 - \tfrac{1}{2}p. \qquad (3.4)$$
Example B: *a production function*
$$y = 11x - x^2 + 40. \qquad (3.5)$$
Example C: *a consumption function*
$$C = \frac{Y + 5}{3}. \qquad (3.6)$$

These three functions are graphed in the three parts of Fig. 3.7. The reader should verify that the functions above describe the data in Chapter 2 by drawing them himself in graphical form. In terms of our earlier discussions, the reader will find that all of these three functions are continuous, and that Examples A and C are linear while B is nonlinear.

The data tabulated in Tables 2.2 to 2.4 happen to coincide exactly with functions (3.4) to (3.6) because we arranged it this way for purposes of exposition. In reality, of course, we would be rather surprised if data collected from observation of real-world behaviour happened to fit some precise functional form exactly. For example, if we tabulated the purchases of potatoes by a housewife over a series of weeks, we are more likely to get a scattered set of observations like that shown in Table 3.3, and plotted in Fig. 3.8 (a).

TABLE 3.3

Quantity of Potatoes Purchased by Housewife in Various Weeks

Date	Price (p) (cents/kg)	Quantity Purchased (q) (kg)
March 7	6	3
14	4	2
21	0	5
28	2	2
April 4	10	0
11	8	3
18	3	4
25	9	1

It would be impossible to find one simple function whose graph passed through every point on Fig. 3.8. Nor would we require such a function. What we might seek is a simple mathematical function giving a *reasonably good* description of this set of data. For example the points on Fig. 3.8 (a) suggest a downward sloping relationship between q and p, and we could

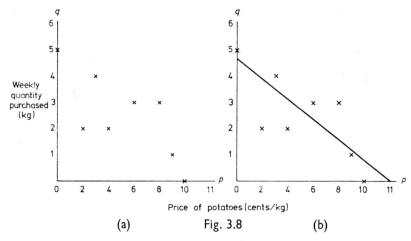

Price of potatoes (cents/kg)

(a)   Fig. 3.8   (b)

draw in a freehand line such as that shown in Fig. 3.8 (b) to represent this function. In doing this we have guessed the position of a linear function that *approximately* describes the data in Table 3.3.

The finding of specific mathematical functions to represent relationships contained in sets of empirical data is one of the tasks of *econometrics*, to which we have already made reference in Chapter 1. We shall be returning to this subject later (see Chapters 20 and 21).

3.6 General Algebraic Statements

The functions we have been studying in this chapter are specific mathematical statements of functional relationships existing for a particular housewife, a particular country, a particular farmer, and so on. How far can we go towards stating these functions in terms which could apply to any housewife, any country, any farmer? How far

Suppose all housewives have linear demand functions for potatoes. We might unearth three more housewives (numbered 2, 3 and 4) whose particular demand functions take the following forms:

Housewife 2:
$$q_2 = 6 - \tfrac{2}{3}p. \tag{3.7}$$
Housewife 3:
$$q_3 = 15 - 2p. \tag{3.8}$$
Housewife 4:
$$q_4 = 2 - 0p. \tag{3.9}$$

Similarly, suppose all farmers have production functions for wheat that are of the same general form as (3.5), though with different numbers in them. The functions for two such farmers might be:

Farmer 2:
$$y_2 = 9x - 2x^2 + 115. \tag{3.10}$$
Farmer 3:
$$y_3 = 25.2x - 1.8x^2 + 92. \tag{3.11}$$

Since these functions are clearly of similar nature, we could replace the numbers by symbols, in order to represent the *general* form that is common to these demand functions and production functions. Let us replace the two numbers in the demand functions by α and β, and the three numbers in the production functions by the symbols a, b, and c. Then we can write the general form of our linear demand function as

$$q = \alpha + \beta p, \tag{3.12}$$

and the general form of our nonlinear production function, with some rearrangement of the order of the variables, as

$$y = ax^2 + bx + c. \tag{3.13}$$

Thus, Equation (3.12) shows a general linear demand function for potatoes. For our original housewife, we can see that $\alpha = 5$ and $\beta = -\frac{1}{2}$. For housewife 2, $\alpha = 6$ and $\beta = -\frac{2}{3}$. Similarly, in the general production function shown in (3.13), our original farmer has $a = -1$, $b = 11$, and $c = 40$ (remember the order of variables has been rearranged). Likewise, the production function (3.11) contains $a = -1.8$, $b = 25.2$ and $c = 92$.

In Equations (3.12) and (3.13), the symbols α, β and a, b, c and the numbers they represent are loosely called *coefficients*. If we were considering just one housewife or one farmer, so that these coefficients had just one value each, we could call them *constants*. If we were considering many demand schedules or production functions of the same basic form as Equations (3.12) and (3.13), but where α, β, etc. could take on different values in different cases, these coefficients would be called *parameters*.

3.7 Prediction from Simple Functions

One immediate use of a function, whether represented in graphical or algebraic terms, is for "predicting" the value of the dependent variable for a given value or values of the independent variable. We use the word "predict" here, not in the sense of foretelling the future, but in the logical sense of a result following on from a set of conditions or assumptions. For example, if we assume that a particular housewife's demand schedule for potatoes is as shown in Equation (3.4), then it follows as a logical consequence that if the price of potatoes is 7 cents per kg the quantity demanded will be:

$$q = 5 - \tfrac{1}{2} \times 7 = 1\tfrac{1}{2} \text{ kg.}$$

In other words, we could use this function to "predict" that the housewife will purchase $1\frac{1}{2}$ kg if the price is 7 cents.

Similarly we could use Equation (3.5) to predict that if this particular farmer uses a fertiliser input of, say $1\frac{2}{3}$ kg per hectare, his yield will be 55.55 centals. Check this for yourself.

An identical process of prediction can be employed using graphs. The graph of the demand schedule from Equation (3.4) is redrawn in Fig. 3.9. Let us use this graph to predict the housewife's demand, again at a price of 7 cents. Find the required value of the independent variable on the horizontal axis (point *A*), and erect a perpendicular line *AB*. At the point

where this perpendicular cuts the graph (point *B*), draw a horizontal line
to the vertical axis. The point where this line cuts the vertical axis (point
C) is the required prediction. It is apparent that the function drawn in this
graph "predicts" a demand of $1\frac{1}{2}$ kg when the price is 7 cents.

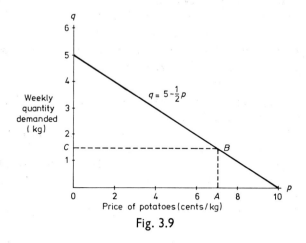

Fig. 3.9

Exercises

1. Draw a graph of the supply equation from Exercise 3, Chapter 2.
   Assume *q* is measured as the number of units sold per week, and *p* is
   measured in cents per unit.

2. The average costs of a particular firm are expressed by the following
   function:
$$AC = 2y^2 - 25y + 150$$
   where AC = average cost per unit of output in dollars; and
              y = level of output in units.
   Calculate the level of AC for values of y ranging from 0 to 8 in jumps
   of 2.

3. Draw a graph of the function in Exercise 2 above.

4. Is the graph drawn in Exercise 3 above:
   (a) continuous or discontinuous?
   (b) linear or nonlinear?

5. Draw on the same diagram graphs of the two production functions
   from Equations (3.10) and (3.11).

6. A general form of the average cost equation in Exercise 2 might be
   written:
$$AC = \alpha_1 + \alpha_2 y + \alpha_3 y^2$$
   What are the values of the parameters α_1, α_2 and α_3 in our specific
   example of this function in Exercise 2?

7. What level of average costs does the function in Exercise 2 above predict will be incurred by the firm, if output is 5 units?

8. Use a graph to determine whether or not there seems to be a relationship between the gross value of imports into Australia, and gross personal consumption expenditure, as detailed in the following table.

Year	Value of Imports ($ m)	Personal Consumption Expenditure ($ m)
1957–58	1,584	7,611
1958–59	1,593	8,011
1959–60	1,854	8,781
1960–61	2,175	9,302
1961–62	1,769	9,591
1962–63	2,163	10,281
1963–64	2,373	11,077
1964–65	2,905	11,943
1965–66	2,939	12,621
1966–67	3,045	13,504

Chapter 4

Models Based on Linear Functions

4.1 Properties of Linear Functions

To study some properties of linear functions, let us take a simple example. Imagine a steel-producing plant whose total annual costs may be expressed as a linear function of the annual quantity of steel produced.

Let TC = total annual costs incurred by the plant, expressed in dollars; and

$\quad\quad y$ = annual output of steel, in metric tons.

It is known from experience that the relationship between costs and output for this factory may be expressed by the following equation:

$$TC = 400 + 3y. \quad\quad\quad (4.1)$$

Since this cost function is linear, its graph will be a straight line. It is shown in Fig. 4.1.

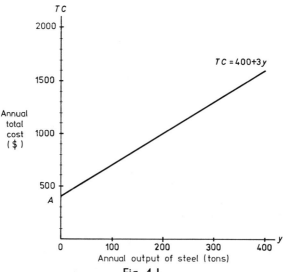

Fig. 4.1

Let us look at the significance of the two numerical coefficients in Equation (4.1).

4.1.1 THE INTERCEPT TERM

It is clear that the term "400" in Equation (4.1) represents the value that *TC* would take if *y* were zero, i.e., the amount of total costs if the firm produced no output whatsoever. In other words, if $y = 0$, we can calculate that $TC = 400 + (3 \times 0) = 400$.

In Fig. 4.1 this position is represented by the point where the graph intercepts the axis of the dependent variable, namely, point *A*. Thus the coefficient 400 in Equation (4.1) is called the *intercept term*, or occasionally the *constant term*.

An intercept term may be zero. For example, suppose that for the same factory the total annual contract cost (*t*) of transporting steel from plant to railway siding depends only on the volume of output. If there is no output, there is nothing to transport, and hence no transport cost. In other words, the intercept term is zero, as shown in Equation (4.2):

$$t = 0 + 1.5y \text{ or } t = 1.5y. \tag{4.2}$$

Figure 4.2 shows this function. You can see that when the intercept is zero, the function passes through the origin of the graph.

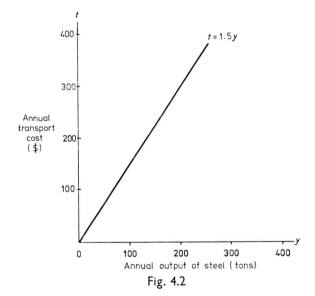

Fig. 4.2

It is also possible for an intercept term to be negative. For instance, a person's consumption of scotch whisky might be expressed as a function of his income. Figure 4.3 illustrates this situation. If the man's income

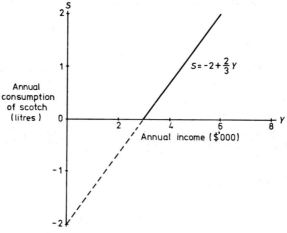

Fig. 4.3

were $6 thousand per year, he would consume 2 litres per year, but if it fell to $3 thousand per year the graph shows he would give up scotch altogether. The equation for the function in Fig. 4.3 is

$$S = -2 + \tfrac{2}{3}Y, \qquad (4.3)$$

where S = consumption of scotch in litres per year; and
      Y = annual income in $'000.

The intercept term is negative because the function cuts the axis of the dependent variable (S) at a point where this variable is negative, namely where $S = -2$. The broken segment of this function (i.e., below $Y = 3$) has no meaning in practical terms, since negative consumption in this example is impossible.

4.1.2 THE GRADIENT OF A LINEAR FUNCTION

When we say a stretch of railway track has a "slope of 1 in 15" we mean that for every fifteen units of horizontal distance, the track rises through a vertical distance of one unit, as shown in Fig. 4.4.

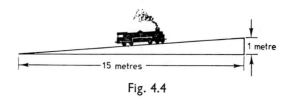

Fig. 4.4

Alternatively we could say that this stretch of track has a slope of $\frac{1}{15}$ or, more generally:

$$\text{Slope} = \frac{\text{vertical distance}}{\text{horizontal distance}}.$$

Sometimes "vertical distance over horizontal distance" is expressed by the easily remembered phrase, "rise over run".

Figure 4.5 shows the cost function from Fig. 4.1 redrawn with two new

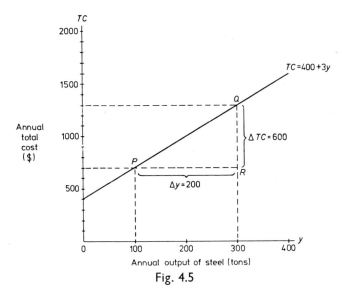

Fig. 4.5

arbitrary points, P and Q. At P, $y = 100$ tons, $TC = \$700$; at Q, $y = 300$, $TC = 1300$. Let us measure the slope of the graph between P and Q. Moving from P to Q we traverse a horizontal distance PR and a vertical distance QR. By inspection of Fig. 4.5 we can see that PR represents a horizontal distance of 200 tons and QR a vertical distance of \$600. Immediately we can calculate the slope of PQ as:

$$\frac{\text{vertical distance}}{\text{horizontal distance}} = \frac{600}{200} = 3 \text{ or "3 in 1".}$$

More formally, we can express these distances as the differences between the respective coordinates at Q and those at P. Thus, for instance, the vertical distance between P and Q is measured by the difference between the value of TC at Q $(= \$1300)$ and the value of TC at P $(= \$700)$. This difference, $\$(1300 - 700) = \$600$ represents the change in TC between the points P and Q. If we let the symbol Δ (a capital Greek delta) stand for "a finite change in", then we can write "the change in TC between P and Q" simply as ΔTC. Likewise Δy represents the change in y between P and Q, measured as the difference between the value of y at Q and its value at P. Thus we calculate:

$$\text{Slope of } PQ = \frac{\Delta TC}{\Delta y} = \frac{1300 - 700}{300 - 100} = \frac{600}{200} = 3.$$

In this example the number 3 representing the slope of PQ is measured in dollars per ton; that is, for every ton increase in output, total costs rise by \$3.

It is apparent from the very nature of a straight line that a linear function must have the same slope throughout its whole length. We could choose *any* two points on a given linear function and we would always find the same ratio of vertical to horizontal distances between them. Check for yourself that the slope of the function in Figs 4.1 and 4.5 is always 3, by taking another pair of points on the function and measuring the ratio of vertical to horizontal distance between them.

Now look back to Equation (4.1) from which Fig. 4.5 was derived. You will see that the coefficient of y is 3. This coefficient in the equation tells us that if y were to increase by 1 ton, TC would rise by \$3. For example, by substitution we can see that if y were increased from, say, 10 to 11 tons, TC would increase from \$430 to \$433, a rise of \$3. It is clear that the coefficient 3 in this equation is identical with the *slope* of this same function as calculated in Fig. 4.5. In fact the coefficient 3 in Equation (4.1) is called the *slope* or *gradient* of this linear function.

4.1.3 NEGATIVE GRADIENT

Figure 4.6 shows a linear function which slopes *downhill* from left to right. In this figure the number of houses built per year (H) is shown as a function of the home loan interest rate (i).

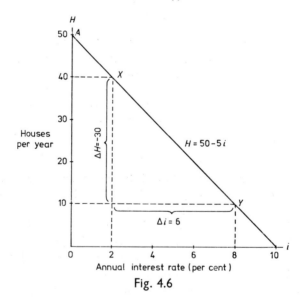

Fig. 4.6

The slope of this function between the points X and Y (coordinates (2, 40) and (8, 10) respectively) is given as:

$$\frac{\Delta H}{\Delta i} = \frac{10 - 40}{8 - 2} = \frac{-30}{6} = -5.$$

From the graph we see the intercept is where $H = 50$ (point A).

Thus if we denote the general form of this function by

$$H = a + bi, \tag{4.4}$$

we have calculated the intercept term $a = 50$, and the slope term $b = -5$. Hence the function may be written:

$$H = 50 - 5i. \qquad (4.5)$$

4.1.4 SUMMARY

In summary, in the general linear equation

$$y = a + bx \qquad (4.6)$$

where y and x are variables, the coefficient a is the *intercept* of the function and the coefficient b is the *slope* or *gradient* of the function.

4.2 An Example of a Linear Model: Supply and Demand

4.2.1 MARKET DEMAND CURVE

The demand schedules we examined in Chapters 2 and 3 related to individual units in the market, that is, to individual housewives. As such, they are termed *individual demand schedules*. We may also be interested in the aggregate quantities demanded by *all* buyers in a market in response to various prices. For example, we might consider the city wholesale vegetable markets, where many retailers and selling agents meet every day to buy and sell potatoes.

Just as we were able to identify a function showing the quantities of potatoes an individual housewife will demand at various prices, so also can we imagine a function showing the total quantities of potatoes that *all* buyers will demand at the wholesale markets at different prices prevailing over a given day, week, month or year. Since it refers to the operation of a whole market (for potatoes), such a function would be termed a *market demand schedule*.

TABLE 4.1

Wholesale Demand for Potatoes

Price (p) (cents/kg)	Quantity Demanded (q_d) ('000 kg)
0	20
1	17
2	14
3	11
4	8
5	5
6	2

Table 4.1 gives an example of a market demand schedule. Observation over a period of time has shown that the total daily demand for potatoes in this particular market is 20 thousand kg if the average price on that day is 0 cents per kg, 17 thousand kg if the price is 1 cent per kg, and so on.

It so happens that the set of observations in Table 4.1 conforms to a simple linear function. The points shown in the table are plotted on Fig. 4.7. Using the methods studied in Section 4.1 above, we can verify that the table corresponds to the following linear demand equation

$$q_d = 20 - 3p \qquad (4.7)$$

where q_d = quantity of potatoes demanded per day in '000 kg; and
       p = average daily price of potatoes in cents per kg.
Check this equation with Table 4.1 and Fig. 4.7 to ensure that you understand what the equation signifies.

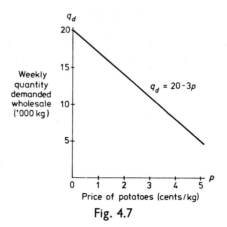

Fig. 4.7

4.2.2 MARKET SUPPLY CURVE

The suppliers of a good to a particular market are also likely to adjust the
quantities they will supply according to the price they receive. Generally
we would expect that the higher the price, the greater the quantity the
suppliers are willing to offer for sale. A relationship between quantity
supplied and price for a given good or goods being supplied to a given
market over a given period is called a *market supply schedule*. An example
is given in Table 4.2, where, for the same market considered in the previous
section, the quantities of potatoes that sellers are willing to supply at
different prices are tabulated.

TABLE 4.2

Wholesale Supply of Potatoes

Price (p) (cents/kg)	Quantity Supplied (q_s) ('000 kg)
0	0
1	$2\frac{1}{2}$
2	5
3	$7\frac{1}{2}$
4	10
5	$12\frac{1}{2}$
6	15

Again, it so happens that our set of supply observations conforms
exactly to a simple linear equation. With q_s denoting quantity of potatoes
supplied per day in '000 kg, and p as defined above, this equation takes
the form

$$q_s = \tfrac{5}{2}p. \tag{4.8}$$

It is graphed in Fig. 4.8. Make sure that you understand that Equation (4.8) is a linear equation in which the intercept term is zero and the slope is $+ \frac{5}{2}$. Again, you should substitute one or two values for p into Equation (4.8) to verify the figures in Table 4.2.

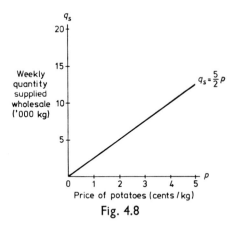

Fig. 4.8

4.2.3 THE LINEAR MODEL OF SUPPLY AND DEMAND

Combining Equations (4.7) and (4.8) allows us to construct a complete representation of supply and demand conditions in this potato market, as follows:

$$q_d = 20 - 3p \qquad (4.9a)$$
$$q_s = \tfrac{5}{2}p. \qquad (4.9b)$$

When one constructs a set of equations such as these, one may use them to see how they behave in different circumstances. For example, as we shall see in the following section, one may determine the price level and the volume of goods traded that will tend to prevail on a given day in this market if these equations hold. This procedure of construction and manipulation of equations is very similar to the building of, say, a model of an aircraft, followed by the use of the model in a wind tunnel to study the reaction of the real plane to different environmental conditions. In fact economists use the word *model* to describe just such a set of equations.

An economic model is simply a representation of some set of economic circumstances that exists in the real world, framed in such a way that it can be manipulated or analysed so as to tell us something about the phenomena it represents. It may consist of verbal and/or mathematical statements. If the principal components of an economic model are mathematical statements (such as in the supply and demand model above) it is called a *quantitative model*. Generally an economic model involves some simplification, containing only those elements considered most important to the problem under study.

The above supply and demand model related to a specific location, commodity, time, etc. A *general* linear model of supply and demand could be written as:

$$q_d = \alpha + \beta p \tag{4.10a}$$
$$q_s = \gamma + \varepsilon p. \tag{4.10b}$$

You can see that Equations (4.9) are a specific form of this general model, in which

$$\alpha = 20,$$
$$\beta = -3,$$
$$\gamma = 0,$$
$$\varepsilon = 2\tfrac{1}{2}.$$

4.3 Equilibrium in the Linear Supply and Demand Model

4.3.1 GRAPHICAL DETERMINATION OF MARKET EQUILIBRIUM

Let us now examine how the simple linear model of supply and demand can be used to determine what will happen to prices and to quantities bought and sold in this potato market. As a first approach, we shall consider this question by using graphs.

The graphs of the two Equations (4.9) are shown in Fig. 4.9, where it is important to note that price (the independent variable) is now shown on the *vertical* axis, and quantity (the dependent variable) is on the *horizontal* axis. As we have already seen in Section 3.2.1, the usual designation of the independent and dependent variables is to the horizontal and vertical axes respectively. The switching of the axes in Fig. 4.9 (and henceforth in supply and demand graphs) is in deference to a long tradition in economic analysis of depicting supply and demand schedules with the roles of the axes reversed.

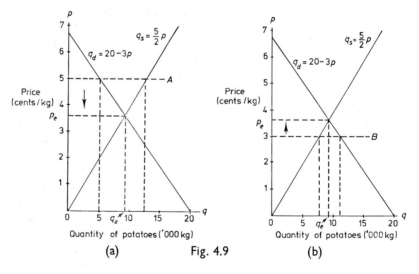

(a)   Fig. 4.9   (b)

Let us suppose that the schedules shown in Fig. 4.9 are the true and unchanging picture of demand and supply conditions in this market. Then we can determine what will happen to the price of potatoes on any particular day.

Suppose the price opens at the start of trading at 5 cents per kg, shown by the horizontal line A in Fig. 4.9 (a). At this price sellers are willing to offer $12\frac{1}{2}$ thousand kg of potatoes but buyers will only buy 5 thousand kg. When some sellers realise the weakness of demand they will reduce their price and the quantity demanded will correspondingly increase. This process will tend to drive the price down towards p_e.

Likewise, suppose the initial price were 3 cents per kg (line B in Fig. 4.9(b)). At this price buyers would like to obtain 11 thousand kg, but sellers are only prepared to offer $7\frac{1}{2}$ thousand. When buyers find they cannot satisfy their demands at this price, they will offer to pay a higher price in order to get what they want. This will tend to force the price upwards towards p_e.

Thus it is apparent that in the market the price will tend towards a single *equilibrium price* shown at p_e in Fig. 4.9. At this price, quantities supplied and demanded will be exactly matched at an *equilibrium quantity*, q_e. The position where price p_e rules, and the market is just cleared at a quantity q_e bought and sold, is called *market equilibrium*.

4.3.2 ALGEBRAIC DETERMINATION OF MARKET EQUILIBRIUM

The graphical analysis in Fig. 4.9 gives only an approximate reading of the values of p_e and q_e. Knowing the demand and supply equations for this market (Equations (4.9)), we can calculate the equilibrium price and quantity exactly.

We know that at equilibrium the quantities demanded and supplied must be equal at a level q_e, i.e.,

$$q_d = q_s = q_e. \tag{4.11}$$

Hence, by writing q_e in place of q_d and q_s in both Equations (4.9) we can say that at equilibrium the following two equations must hold:

$$q_e = 20 - 3p_e \tag{4.12a}$$
$$q_e = \tfrac{5}{2}p_e . \tag{4.12b}$$

In this pair of equations, a single value of q_e and a single value of p_e must be determined that will satisfy both equations *simultaneously*. Thus they are called *simultaneous equations*.

The solution of simultaneous equations is discussed in Appendix A. These methods may be applied to Equations (4.12) to determine p_e and q_e. However, in this case a solution can be found more quickly by recognising that since the LHS of Equation (4.12a) and (4.12b) are identical, their RHS may be equated. So setting the RHS of (4.12a) equal to that of (4.12b), we obtain

$$20 - 3p_e = \tfrac{5}{2}p_e$$

whence
$$20 = 3p_e + \tfrac{5}{2}p_e ,$$
$$40 = 11p_e$$

and we obtain $p_e = 3\frac{7}{11}$, or 3.6363 cents per kg. Substituting this value for p_e in either (4.12a) or (4.12b) will enable us to calculate the value of q_e. Performing the substitution in (4.12a) gives:

$$q_e + \frac{3 \times 40}{11} = 20$$

whence

$$11q_e + 120 = 220,$$

$$q_e = \frac{100}{11} = 9\frac{1}{11} \text{ or } 9.0909 \text{ thousand kg.}$$

Thus for this market, the equilibrium price for potatoes is 3.64 cents per kg, at which price sellers will offer, and buyers will purchase, 9.09 thousand kg.

4.4 A Linear Income Determination Model
4.4.1 CONSTRUCTION OF THE MODEL

As another illustration of a linear model, let us take a very simple Keynesian income determination system.

Suppose that national income (Y) for the economy is entirely spent on either consumption (C) or investment (I). Then we can write as a definition:

$$Y = C + I. \tag{4.13}$$

Note that this is not a functional relationship in the usual sense used earlier; rather it is simply a statement that the LHS and RHS are identical. In fact the name for a definitional equation such as (4.13) is an *identity*.

Now suppose the level of consumption expenditure is a function of the level of income. For simplicity, imagine that there is a linear relationship between consumption and income, so that we can write it down in the familiar form:

$$C = a + cY. \tag{4.14}$$

This is an example of a *consumption function* for the economy as a whole, and is a counterpart at the national level of the individual family man's consumption function that we encountered in Chapters 2 and 3. Note that the economy is assumed to spend a fixed amount, a, on consumption, irrespective of income levels. The intercept term of Equation (4.14) thus represents *autonomous* consumption expenditure. The coefficient c, which represents the proportion of *extra* income spent on consumption, is known as the *marginal propensity to consume (MPC)*.

We can assume, finally, that a given level of investment expenditure I^* is undertaken. Investment demand is accordingly deemed to be entirely autonomous—that is, it remains unaffected by anything else in the model. Putting this in equation form, we have

$$I = I^* \tag{4.15}$$

Combining Equations (4.13), (4.14) and (4.15) we obtain our complete linear macroeconomic model as:

$$Y = C + I^* \tag{4.16a}$$

$$C = a + cY. \tag{4.16b}$$

These equations together represent the workings of the national economy by means of linear equations. As we expect with a model, the set of equations can be manipulated in order to study the way this economy behaves. In particular, we can use the model to determine the equilibrium level of national income under certain assumptions.

4.4.2 ALGEBRAIC DETERMINATION OF THE EQUILIBRIUM LEVEL OF NATIONAL INCOME

At equilibrium, national income and national expenditure must be equal. In other words, in terms of our model we can look upon the identity in Equation (4.13) as an *equilibrium condition*. Thus we may derive an expression for the equilibrium level of income by substituting the RHS of (4.14) for the variable C in (4.16a):

$$Y = a + cY + I^*.$$

Rearranging, we obtain:

$$(1 - c)Y = a + I^*$$

and hence

$$Y = \frac{a + I^*}{1 - c}. \tag{4.17}$$

Equation (4.17) thus provides an expression for the equilibrium level of income in terms of the autonomous components of the model (a and I^*) and the *MPC* (c).

As a numerical example, let us suppose that autonomous consumption expenditure (a) is \$100 million, autonomous investment (I^*) is \$50 million, and the marginal propensity to consume (c) is 0.8. Then the equilibrium level of income is calculated from (4.17) as:

$$
\begin{aligned}
Y &= \frac{100 + 50}{1 - 0.8} \\
&= 5\,(100 + 50) \\
&= \$750 \text{ million.}
\end{aligned}
$$

While the preceding method provides a value for equilibrium income, it disguises many properties of the model that are evident in larger, more general macro systems. First, we may observe that the model contains not just one unknown, but two—namely, income and consumption expenditure. For a fuller account of macro-equilibrium the system should be solved for equilibrium consumption expenditure as well as for equilibrium income. In an elementary model such as this, equilibrium consumption may be found through simple substitution. We substitute the expression for equilibrium income (4.17) in the consumption Equation (4.16b):

$$C = a + c\left(\frac{a + I^*}{1 - c}\right). \tag{4.18}$$

Completing our numerical example:

$$
\begin{aligned}
C &= 100 + 0.8\,(750) \\
&= \$700 \text{ million.}
\end{aligned}
$$

This simple linear model consists of two independent Equations (4.16a) and (4.16b). We used it to determine the levels of two variables, C and Y, for a given level of the third variable I. In other words the values of C and Y are determined *within* the model, whereas the value of I is given from *outside* of the model. We use the term *endogenous variable* to describe a variable whose level is determined within a given system, such as C and Y in this model. On the other hand a variable such as I whose value is determined outside of the system is called an *exogenous variable*. Autonomous consumption (a), too, is determined outside the model and therefore can also be thought of as an exogenous expenditure component.

It is apparent that in solving the system to study the properties of equilibrium, the values of the endogenous variables satisfying the simultaneous equations emerge as functions of the exogenous components of the model. In the solution to our simple $C + I$ system, equilibrium income and equilibrium consumption both appear as linear functions of autonomous investment and autonomous consumption expenditure as shown in Equations (4.17) and (4.18) respectively.

The typical static linear economic model accordingly has a "feed-in" of exogenous elements; it has a set of simultaneous linear equations that define the structural form of the model and describe the way in which the relevant endogenous and exogenous components of the system are interrelated, and it possesses a set of equilibrium values for the endogenous variables. These equilibrium values may be found by solving the system and deriving a series of expressions for the unknowns in terms of the model's exogenous elements. In later chapters (Chapters 14–17) we shall see how mathematics provides systematic methods of writing down and exploring these characteristics more fully. We shall also see how the above simple two-equation model may be expanded to provide more realistic descriptions of the workings of macroeconomic systems.

4.4.3 GRAPHICAL DETERMINATION OF THE EQUILIBRIUM LEVEL OF NATIONAL INCOME

To complete our treatment of this simple Keynesian system, let us solve the same problem by graphical means. First we draw the axes, with expenditure (C and I) on the vertical and income (Y) on the horizontal, as shown in Fig. 4.10. In this sort of graph it is convenient to use the same scale on both axes, for reasons which will become clear.

Next we may draw in our consumption function, which is of the form

$$C = 100 + 0.8Y. \qquad (4.19)$$

Check that you understand how this equation is constructed on Fig. 4.10. Since I is constant at \$50 million, it will appear as a horizontal straight line in Fig. 4.10 at a height of 50 units above the horizontal axis. It does not vary with income. Check that whatever level of Y you choose on the horizontal axis, you always obtain a reading of \$50 million as the value of I.

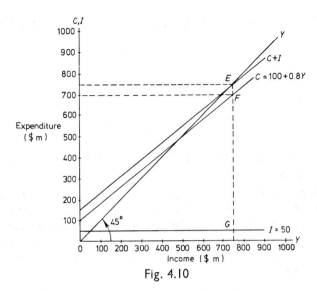

Fig. 4.10

To obtain the graph for total expenditure, $C + I$, we may simply raise every point on the consumption schedule by the constant amount of I, $50 million. This produces a graph of $C + I$ which is parallel to the graph of C and 50 units higher, as shown in Fig. 4.10.

We are now ready to read off the equilibrium level of national income. According to our condition (4.13), the levels of income and expenditure are equal in equilibrium. Given that the two axes in Fig. 4.10 are measured on the same scale, all points on the diagram where income (horizontal axis) and expenditure (vertical axis) are equal will lie along a line drawn at 45° to the origin. Check that you understand the significance of the 45° line by reference to Fig. 4.10.

The expenditure schedule $C + I$ cuts the 45° line at the point E. This is the only point along the $C + I$ line that satisfies the equilibrium condition (4.13), i.e., that equates national income and expenditure. E is thus the point of equilibrium. It gives a reading on either axis of $750 million. Thus this result verifies that found in the previous section. Notice that we may also read from Fig. 4.10 the levels of C and I at the equilibrium point. These are given as the values on the vertical axis corresponding to the points F and G respectively, where we verify that $C = \$700$ million and $I = \$50$ million.

4.5 Addition of Functions

Often in economics we wish to aggregate or combine functions. In the previous section we saw an example of this, the combining of C and I to give total national expenditure. As we know (see further in Appendix A), if $a = b$, and $c = d$, then it follows that the addition (or subtraction) of the LHS of these two equations must equal the addition (or subtraction) of their RHS, i.e., $a + c = b + d$, and $a - c = b - d$. Thus in our example, given

$$C = 100 + 0.8\,Y$$

and

$$I = 50,$$

we can obtain

$$C + I = 100 + 50 + 0.8\,Y$$
$$= 150 + 0.8\,Y.$$

Check for yourself that the $C + I$ schedule in Fig. 4.10 is in fact a graph of the expression $150 + 0.8\,Y$.

Another area where combining functions may be important is in the derivation of market demand and supply schedules from the individual demand and supply schedules of every participant in a given market. For large markets, it is most unlikely that we could identify *every* buyer's demand schedule or every seller's supply schedule. But for a small market this may be possible.

For example, suppose that there are only four housewives who patronise a particular greengrocer and that every Saturday they all turn up to buy their weekly potato order. Imagine that we know their individual demand schedules. Denote $q_1, \ldots, q_4$ as the quantity of potatoes demanded by housewife $1, \ldots, 4$. Their demand equations are as follows:

$$q_1 = 5 - \tfrac{1}{2}p \qquad\qquad\qquad (4.20\text{a})$$
$$q_2 = 6 - \tfrac{2}{3}p \qquad\qquad\qquad (4.20\text{b})$$
$$q_3 = 15 - 2p \qquad\qquad\qquad (4.20\text{c})$$
$$q_4 = 2 - 0p. \qquad\qquad\qquad (4.20\text{d})$$

Now, at any price level the total quantity of potatoes demanded in this market is simply the sum of the individual housewives' demands at that price. For example, at 3 cents per kg:

Housewife 1 buys $5 - (\tfrac{1}{2} \times 3) = 5 - 1\tfrac{1}{2} = 3\tfrac{1}{2}$ kg,
Housewife 2 buys $6 - (\tfrac{2}{3} \times 3) = 6 - 2 = 4$ kg,
Housewife 3 buys $15 - (2 \times 3) = 15 - 6 = 9$ kg,
Housewife 4 buys $2 - (0 \times 3) = 2 - 0 = 2$ kg.

Thus, at 3 cents per kg a total of $3\tfrac{1}{2} + 4 + 9 + 2$ kg is purchased, equalling $18\tfrac{1}{2}$ kg.

Table 4.3 shows the quantities demanded by each housewife at prices ranging from 0 to 6 cents per kg. The first and last columns of this table represent a schedule relating the total quantity of potatoes demanded *in the whole market* to price. It is in fact the *market demand schedule* for this small market. Inspection of Table 4.3 shows that this schedule is linear, and we could use the data in the table to calculate the equation of the market demand schedule. However, let us determine this equation more formally, using the information we have from the individual demand Equations (4.20).

TABLE 4.3

Empirical Determination of Market Demand

Price (p) cents/kg	Individual Quantities Demanded				Total Quantity Demanded (kg)
	Housewife 1 (kg)	Housewife 2 (kg)	Housewife 3 (kg)	Housewife 4 (kg)	
0	5	6	15	2	28
1	$4\frac{1}{2}$	$5\frac{1}{3}$	13	2	$24\frac{5}{6}$
2	4	$4\frac{2}{3}$	11	2	$21\frac{2}{3}$
3	$3\frac{1}{2}$	4	9	2	$18\frac{1}{2}$
4	3	$3\frac{1}{3}$	7	2	$15\frac{1}{3}$
5	$2\frac{1}{2}$	$2\frac{2}{3}$	5	2	$12\frac{1}{6}$
6	2	2	3	2	9

Let Q = the total quantity of potatoes demanded on a given day. Then for any given price:

$$Q = q_1 + q_2 + q_3 + q_4, \tag{4.21}$$

and hence, from Equations (4.20a to d):

$$Q = (5 - \tfrac{1}{2}p) + (6 - \tfrac{2}{3}p) + (15 - 2p) + (2 - 0p)$$
$$= 5 + 6 + 15 + 2 - \tfrac{1}{2}p - \tfrac{2}{3}p - 2p - 0p.$$

Thus

$$Q = 28 - 3\tfrac{1}{6}p. \tag{4.22}$$

As an exercise the reader may verify that the market demand schedule in (4.22) "predicts", for a given price level, the total quantity demanded as shown in Table 4.3.

Exercises

1. The price of sausages is p cents per kg and it is found that the market demand is q thousand kg per week as in the following table:

p (cents/kg)	q ('000 kg)
20	82.5
24	70.8
28	63.1
30	60.7
32	55.0
36	48.9
40	39.8

Draw a graph of the demand schedule suggested by these observations. Show that the relationship approximates to the linear form $q = 120 - 2p$ by plotting q for several values of p according to this equation.

2. Write a formula for the equilibrium price p_e in the general linear supply and demand model in Equations (4.10).

3. Use algebraic methods to find the equilibrium price and quantity in a market characterised by the following linear demand and supply functions:

$$q_d = 2(60 - p)$$
$$q_s = 5 + 3p.$$

4. Confirm the result from Exercise 3 above using graphical methods.

5. Consider the simple income determination model shown in Equations (4.16). Suppose autonomous consumption is $25 million, the marginal propensity to consume is 0.7, and exogenous aggregate investment is given as $80 million. Determine algebraically the equilibrium level of national income. What is the equilibrium level of consumption expenditure?

6. Confirm the results from Exercise 5 above using graphical methods.

7. Write down the equations which describe the following graphs:

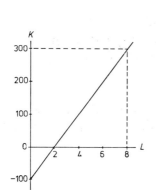 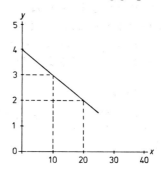

Fig. 4.11

8. Four firms supply a particular market, the market supply equation being

$$Q = 4p^2 + 7p + 2.$$

The individual supply equations of the first three firms are:

$$q_1 = 3 + 2p^2,$$
$$q_2 = 2p^2 + \tfrac{2}{3}p,$$
$$q_3 = \frac{p - 3}{3}.$$

What is the supply equation for the fourth firm?

9. Describe in words the effect on the graph of the total cost equation in Fig. 4.1 if:
   (a) the intercept term in Equation (4.1) is increased to 800, the slope term remaining at 3;
   (b) the intercept term remains at 400 but the slope term reduces to 2.

Chapter 5

Nonlinear Economic Relationships

5.1 Introduction

In the preceding chapter we saw how any function $y = f(x)$ whose graph is a perfectly straight line will have the general algebraic form of a linear function, namely,

$$y = a + bx. \tag{5.1}$$

The converse is also true, that is, any function $y = f(x)$ whose graph is *not* a perfectly straight line will be expressible only in an algebraic form *other than* that of Equation (5.1). This general class of functions of real variables† comprising all functions other than linear ones is called simply *nonlinear*.

In this chapter we shall examine some examples of nonlinear functions that are commonly used in economic analysis.

5.2 Polynomials

5.2.1 SOME EXAMPLES

The example of a production function which we first examined in Chapter 3 was

$$y = 40 + 11x - x^2 \tag{5.2}$$

where y and x measure units of output and input respectively. Notice that the order of the terms on the RHS is different in Equation (5.2) from the order originally used, but this of course makes no difference to the value of the function.

The RHS of (5.2) represents the sum of three terms involving increasing powers of x. Remembering that $x^0 \equiv 1$ and $x^1 \equiv x$ (see further in

---

† We restrict our consideration to "real variables", that is, variables whose values lie in the domain of the system of *real numbers*. For a precise definition of the latter term the interested reader may refer to one of the books listed in Section 1 of Further Reading, page 326.

Appendix A), we can write the RHS of Equation (5.2) more fully as:
$$40 \times x^0 + 11 \times x^1 - 1 \times x^2.$$
That is, the first term involves x raised to the power of zero, the second involves x raised to the power one, and the third involves x raised to the power two.

Now let us look at another example. Suppose the total costs of a firm may be expressed as a function of the output of the firm, by means of the following equation:
$$TC = 30 + 15y - 5y^2 + \tfrac{2}{3}y^3 \qquad (5.3)$$
where TC = total costs in dollars per year; and
$\qquad y$ = units of output per year.

Again, we may write the RHS of Equation (5.3) in greater detail as:
$$30 \times y^0 + 15 \times y^1 - 5 \times y^2 + \tfrac{2}{3} \times y^3,$$
and once more we observe an expression containing the sum of terms involving successively higher integer powers of the independent variable.

Such expressions are called *polynomials* (literally "many terms"). This word does service as an adjective as well as a noun; thus we may speak of *polynomial functions* (as in Equations (5.2) and (5.3)), *polynomial expressions* (such as the RHS of these two functions), *polynomial equations*, and so on.

In any polynomial, the highest power determines its *degree*. Thus in (5.2) the highest power of x is two, hence this is called a *polynomial of the second degree*. An alternative name for a second-degree polynomial is a *quadratic*, a word that also serves both as a noun and an adjective. (Again, we speak of quadratic expressions, equations and functions.)

In the cost function (5.3) the highest power of y is three, hence this is a *third-degree polynomial function*. A polynomial of degree three is also called a *cubic*.

Higher-degree polynomials, in which the greatest power to which the variable is raised is four, five, six, . . . , may be constructed, but they are more complicated to handle, and are not widely encountered in economics.

It should now be apparent that a linear function such as in Equation (5.1) is also a polynomial, since it too contains terms involving successive powers of x. That is, the RHS of Equation (5.1) can be written:
$$a \times x^0 + b \times x^1$$
and we see that this is a polynomial expression of the *first degree*.

Furthermore, if we were to lop off the last term from the RHS of (5.1) we would have a *polynomial of degree zero*:
$$y = ax^0, \text{ or } y = a \qquad (5.4)$$
in which y is simply equal to the constant a. The special name for this type of function is a *constant function*. We have already seen an example of such a function in Chapter 4, where, in the simple national income model, we encountered the investment function
$$I = 50. \qquad (5.5)$$
This function indicates that investment in this model, being exogenously determined, is independent of the level of income, and is therefore constant.

5.2.2 THE GENERAL POLYNOMIAL FORM

Let us draw together the examples of the previous section and set down the general form of the various polynomials we have studied. Denote the coefficients $a_0, a_1, \ldots, a_n$, to attach to the terms $x^0, x^1, \ldots, x^n$. Then, in ascending order of degree, we may write the various polynomial functions $y = f(x)$ as follows:

Degree	Function	Common Name
0	$y = a_0$	Constant
1	$y = a_0 + a_1 x$	Linear
2	$y = a_0 + a_1 x + a_2 x^2$	Quadratic
3	$y = a_0 + a_1 x + a_2 x^2 + a_3 x^3$	Cubic
4	$y = a_0 + a_1 x + a_2 x^2 + a_3 x^3 + a_4 x^4$	Quartic
n	$y = a_0 + a_1 x + a_2 x^2 + a_3 x^3 + a_4 x^4 + \ldots + a_n x^n$	nth degree polynomial.

Notice that only *whole-number* or *integer* powers of x are involved in polynomial expressions. A function containing x raised to the power, say, $\frac{1}{2}$ or $2\frac{1}{4}$ would not fall into the category of a polynomial function. Note also that the coefficients $a_0, \ldots, a_n$ may be positive, negative or zero. In the latter event, for instance, we could regard the function, say, $y = x^3$ as a polynomial in which $a_0, a_1, a_2 = 0$ and $a_3 = 1$.

5.2.3 GRAPHS OF SOME POLYNOMIAL FUNCTIONS

The graphs of polynomial functions vary in shape, of course, depending on the numerical size and sign of their coefficients, a_0, a_1, a_2, etc.

(a) The graph of a *constant function* is a horizontal straight line at a distance up the vertical axis of a_0 units. For example, the graph of the function in Equation (5.5) is seen in Fig. 4.10, where we see the level of I given as \$50 million regardless of the level of Y.

(b) The graph of a *linear function* is a straight line with intercept a_0 and gradient a_1, as studied in Chapter 4.

(c) The graph of a *quadratic function* is an example of a *parabola*, which appears as a graph symmetrical about a line called the *axis* passing through the highest or lowest point on the curve, as illustrated in Fig. 5.1 for two arbitrarily chosen quadratic functions. In the two examples shown, the axis is indicated as *PQ*. The actual shapes of these graphs depend on the nature of the coefficients in the specific quadratic functions from which they are generated. In particular, whether the graph rises to a maximum as in Fig. 5.1 (a) or falls to a minimum as in Fig. 5.1 (b), depends on the *sign of the coefficient* a_2, the coefficient of the x^2 term. When this coefficient is negative, as in Fig. 5.1 (a), the graph depicts a hill; when it is positive, as in Fig. 5.1 (b), the graph appears as a valley.

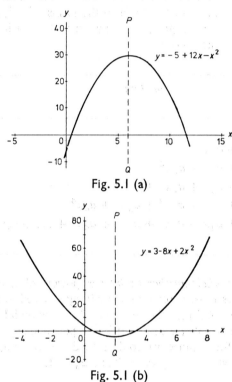

Fig. 5.1 (a)

Fig. 5.1 (b)

Note in passing that we often use the words "concave" and "convex" to describe the curvature of nonlinear graphs. The application of these terms is conditional on our specifying the vantage point from which we view the graph. For example, when viewed from above, the graph in Fig. 5.1 (a) is *convex* (similar to the shape of a convex lens or mirror). The same graph would be described as *concave* from below. If a curve is described simply as "convex" or "concave" *without* qualification, it is usually understood to imply a viewpoint *from below*.

(d) A *cubic function* may take a variety of shapes, again depending on the size and sign of the numerical coefficients. The particular example used above (Equation (5.3)) has the characteristic shape of a total cost curve. Its graph may be seen if you turn over to Fig. 7.4. Another specific cubic function with a different shape may be seen in Equation (8.4) and is graphed in Fig. 8.3.

(e) *Higher-degree polynomials* may have even more complicated shapes, but since we shall not be dealing graphically with such functions, we shall not pursue them further here.

5.3 Power Functions

5.3.1 AN EXAMPLE

In the theory of production, a widely used mathematical form for the production function is illustrated by the following case of a single variable factor:

$$y = 280L^{0.85} \qquad (5.6)$$

where y = output of an industry in \$ millions; and

 L = employment of labour in the industry expressed in number of workers over a given time period.

(More realistic production functions involving more than one variable factor of production will be treated in Chapter 10.)

The coefficient 0.85 in Equation (5.6) is called the *exponent* or *power* to which L is raised. In the area of two-variable relationships, the term *power function* is used to indicate a function, such as (5.6), where the exponent is a *constant*. (Compare this with *variable exponent* functions treated in Section 5.4 below.) In the specific field of production theory, the power function when used to express a relationship between output and input(s) is frequently referred to as the *Cobb-Douglas function*, after C. W. Cobb and P. H. Douglas who first developed its empirical use in this context.

5.3.2 GENERAL FORM OF THE POWER FUNCTION

Stated in general terms, the power function involving two variables may be written

$$y = ax^b \qquad (5.7)$$

where y and x are variables, and a and b are constants. We shall consider only cases where $a,b > 0$.† It is clear that if $b = 0$, Equation (5.7) degenerates to the constant function $y = a$. Furthermore, in the special cases where b is a positive whole number, the set of power functions intersects with the set of polynomials. For example, if $b = 1$, Equation (5.7) becomes a linear function with a zero intercept and slope of a; if $b = 2$, it becomes the quadratic $y = ax^2$, and so on.

Graphically, the shape of Equation (5.7) depends on the size of the coefficients, particularly on whether b is less than, equal to, or greater than unity. Figure 5.2 shows the general shape of the power function in these three cases. In the terminology of production theory, we would say that a production function of the form of Equation (5.7) shows diminishing returns to the use of the variable input when $0 < b < 1$,‡ constant returns when $b = 1$, and increasing returns when $b > 1$. (See further in Sections 7.2.1, 10.6.3 and 11.1.)

---

† The sign $>$ indicates "is/are greater than"; hence the expression $a, b > 0$ reads "a and b are greater than zero".

‡ The sign $<$ indicates "is/are less than"; hence the expression $0 < b < 1$ reads literally "zero is less than b is less than 1", or in other words "b is greater than zero and less than 1" or alternatively "b lies between zero and 1". Note that this expression specifically *disallows* either $b = 0$ or $b = 1$.

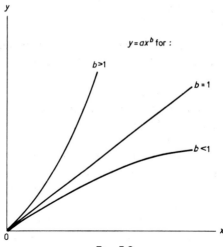

Fig. 5.2

A significant mathematical property of the power function is seen if we express it in logarithms. Taking logs of Equation (5.7) (see further in Appendix A) gives:

$$\log y = \log a + b \log x. \tag{5.8}$$

Denote $y' = \log y$
$\qquad a' = \log a$
$\qquad x' = \log x.$

Then Equation (5.8) may be written

$$y' = a' + bx' \tag{5.9}$$

which is immediately apparent as a linear equation. Thus we see that while the relationship between the variables in Equation (5.7) is nonlinear (when $b \neq 1$)†, the relationship between the *logarithms* of the variables is linear. Thus we say that the power function is *linear in logarithms*. Further examples of functions containing logs will be met later in this chapter.

5.4 Exponential Functions

5.4.1 AN EXAMPLE

As hinted in the previous section, in an *exponential function* the independent variable itself appears *as part of an exponent* in the RHS. Such functions are frequently used to express the ways in which certain variables grow over time. For example, if one invests $50 at 8 per cent per year where the interest is added once yearly, the amount (A) to which the sum has grown after t years may be expressed as a function of t. The specific form of $A = f(t)$ in this case is

$$A = 50(1.08)^t, \tag{5.10}$$

where we see the independent variable t appearing as an exponent on the

_____

† The sign $\neq$ indicates "is/are not equal to"; hence the expression $b \neq 1$ reads "b is not equal to 1".

RHS. So, for example, after four years, the $50 will have grown to $68.02, ascertained by substituting 4 for t in (5.10) as follows:
$$A = 50(1.08)^4 = 50(1.3605) = \$68.02.$$
The function in Equation (5.10) is graphed in Fig. 5.3. Since t must be an integer (interest being added only once per year), the graph in Fig. 5.3 is discontinuous. It shows the characteristic upward trend of this type of growth function. In fact, this kind of trend, rising by an increasing amount as time passes, is frequently described as "exponential" growth.

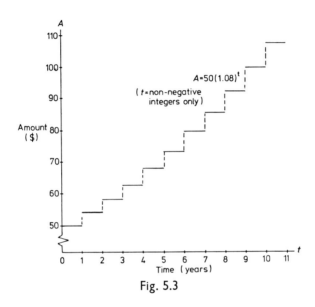

Fig. 5.3

5.4.2 GENERAL FORMS OF EXPONENTIAL FUNCTIONS

In general terms, an exponential function $y = f(x)$ can be written as:
$$y = ab^{cx} \qquad (5.11)$$
where y and x are variables and a, b, c are parameters. Certain restrictions need to be placed on the numerical values of these parameters to prevent us from straying into the world of imaginary and complex numbers. In particular, in growth situations it is generally convenient to consider only $b > 1$.

A specific case of an exponential function of considerable use in economics is where the coefficient b in Equation (5.11) is replaced with the constant $e = 2.71828 \ldots$, the base of natural logarithms, giving:
$$y = ae^{cx}. \qquad (5.12)$$
Such a function is called a *natural exponential function*, and is of considerable use in describing continuous (or quasi-continuous) growth processes.

A particular form of (5.12) is the following:
$$y = ae^{rt} \qquad (5.13)$$
where y = level of some variable (e.g., value of an asset) after t periods of *continuous* growth at a rate r, beginning from a level of a in the first period.

This type of function could be used to describe the above compound interest problem if the interest, calculated at a nominal rate of 8 per cent per year, were added *continuously* to the principal, instead of only once per year. Under this minute-by-minute compounding arrangement, our \$50 would grow to $\$50(e^{0.08 \times 4}) = \$68.86$ in four years according to Equation (5.13)† instead of the \$68.02 calculated for the discrete once-a-year interest case of Equation (5.10).

In practice, however, interest usually does not accrue continuously. A better example of the use of Equation (5.13) is some more nearly continuous growth process, such as that of population. For instance, suppose the population of a country is currently 8 million, and is growing continuously at a rate of 3 per cent per year. Then its level P after t years can be expressed as a natural exponential function as in (5.13). Specifically, we have:

$$P = 8e^{0.03t}. \tag{5.14}$$

So, for example, after five years we calculate the population level as:

$$P = 8(e^{0.03 \times 5}) = 8(1.1618) = 9.29 \text{ million.}$$

5.5 Logarithmic Functions

5.5.I SOME EXAMPLES

When a variable y is expressed as a function of the logarithm of another variable x we have a *logarithmic function*. For example, take the continuous population growth illustration in Equation (5.14). Suppose we wish to determine the number of years that would be required for the population to grow from its present level of 8 million, at the given rate of increase of 3 per cent per year, to a new level of P million. In order to calculate this we must find an expression showing t as a function of P, in other words, we must find the inverse of the function in Equation (5.14). Taking natural logs of (5.14) we get:

$$\log_e P = \log_e 8 + 0.03t \log_e e,$$

and since $\log_e e = 1$, and $\log_e 8$ (from tables) $= 2.0794$, we may write this as

$$\log_e P = 2.0794 + 0.03t. \tag{5.15}$$

Now, rearranging so that t is on the LHS gives

$$t = \frac{-2.0794 + \log_e P}{0.03},$$

hence

$$t = -69.31 + 33.33 \log_e P. \tag{5.16}$$

Equation (5.16) allows us to calculate t for any required level of P. So, for example, we would calculate the number of years required to reach a population of, say, 10 million as:

$$t = -69.31 + 33.33(2.0326) = 7.44 \text{ years.}$$

---

† To evaluate the quantity $e^{0.32}$ in this example, the simplest and most convenient method is to consult any standard volume of mathematical tables where powers of e are tabulated. Alternatively, the calculation may be made "longhand" with the aid of natural or base-10 log tables.

But our point in developing Equation (5.16) is to illustrate a logarithmic function. We observe that this equation shows the variable t as a function of the log of the variable P, thereby complying with the definition of a logarithmic function given at the beginning of this section. Notice the close tie between exponential and logarithmic functions. In general, if y is an exponential function of x then x can be expressed as a logarithmic function of y.

In economics, the term "logarithmic function" is frequently used to refer in general terms to any function containing the logs of any or all of the variables involved. An example is Equation (5.8), in which $\log y$ is shown as a function of $\log x$. This function is simply a logarithmic expression of a power function.

Another example of a two-variable relation containing logarithms is one in which the log of one variable is expressed as a function of the other variable. We met an example of such a function earlier in Equation (5.15), which is a logarithmic expression of the exponential function in Equation (5.14). Likewise, if we were to take logs of the discontinuous growth process in Equation (5.10), we would also obtain a relationship showing the logarithm of one variable (A) as a function of another variable (t). Taking logs, this time to base 10, of Equation (5.10) gives:

$$\log_{10} A = \log_{10} 50 + t \log_{10} 1.08 = 1.6990 + 0.0334t. \qquad (5.17)$$

Notice that Equation (5.15) and (5.17) show the log of the variables P and A to be *linear* functions of time. This is because a constant *proportional* increase in a variable is equivalent to a constant *absolute* increase in its logarithm (to whatever base the log is taken). To illustrate, some values of the variables in Equations (5.10) and (5.17) are:

t	A	$\log_{10} A$
0	50.00	1.6990
1	54.00	1.7324
2	58.32	1.7658
3	62.99	1.7992
4	68.02	1.8326

Hence we see A increasing by 8 per cent for each unit increase in t, whereas $\log_{10} A$, increases by a constant *absolute* amount of 0.0334 for each unit of t.

This fact is frequently exploited when considering the growth of such economic variables as consumption, exports, employment, GNP, etc. If the log of such a variable, say Y, is expressible as a linear function of time t, that is, as an equation

$$\log Y = a + bt, \qquad (5.18)$$

then a constant percentage growth rate is indicated. If the growth process is continuous and the LHS of Equation (5.18) is expressed in natural logarithms, the coefficient b directly measures the rate of growth. Thus, for example, in Equation (5.15) the coefficient b is seen to be 0.03, immediately indicating a growth rate of 3 per cent per year for this process.

We have dealt in this section mainly with time-related processes, since this is the most common area in which exponential and logarithmic functions are used in economics. However, the general functional forms containing logarithms that we have discussed—namely, $y = f(\log x)$, $\log y = f(x)$, and $\log y = f(\log x)$—may occur throughout economic analysis when it so happens that they provide appropriate representations of the particular relationships under study.

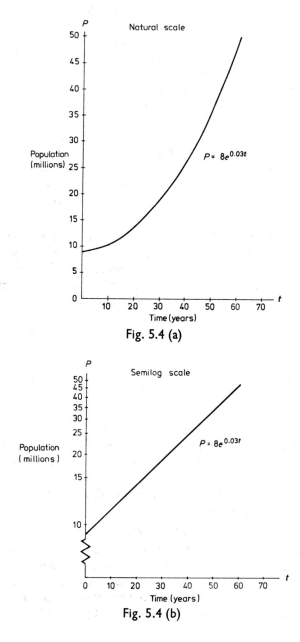

Fig. 5.4 (a)

Fig. 5.4 (b)

5.5.2 GRAPHS OF FUNCTIONS CONTAINING LOGARITHMS

The graphing of functions containing logarithms may be illustrated by using the continuous population growth process depicted in Equations (5.14) and (5.15). If we were to graph Equation (5.15) with log P on the vertical axis and t on the horizontal, the result would clearly be a straight line with intercept 2.0794 and slope 0.03. But if we are more interested in the relationship between t and the variable P itself rather than with the log of P, we simply graph the original function (5.14). This is shown in Fig. 5.4 (a).

Alternatively, instead of marking out the vertical axis in the "natural" units of P, we may use a *logarithmic scale*. The result will be a picture of Equation (5.15) but with P still identified in terms of its original units. This graph is shown in Fig. 5.4 (b). A graph such as this, in which one of the axes is measured on a logarithmic scale and the other on a "natural" scale, is called a *semilogarithmic graph*.

A widespread application of semilog graphs in economics is the plotting of economic time series. If we take, say, the quantity of imports (M) into a certain country over a period of years (t), and plot the dependent variable (M) on a logarithmic scale with t on a natural scale, we can graph log $M = f(t)$ directly without recourse to log tables. If the plotted points lie approximately along a straight line, then a roughly constant rate of growth in imports is indicated.

To illustrate, Table 5.1 shows the level of imports M into a hypothetical country over a period of ten years. The coordinates of the two variables M and t are plotted on a natural scale in Fig. 5.5 (a) and in semilog fashion in Fig. 5.5 (b) where the M axis is measured in logarithmic units. It is apparent from the roughly linear patterns that appear

TABLE 5.1
Imports into Hypothetical Country 1960–69

Year	t	M ($ m)
1960	0	110
1961	1	139
1962	2	185
1963	3	248
1964	4	320
1965	5	331
1966	6	290
1967	7	255
1968	8	225
1969	9	198

in Fig. 5.5 (b) that imports have shown an approximately constant percentage growth over the first five years of the period studied, followed by a smaller percentage decline over the latter half of the period.

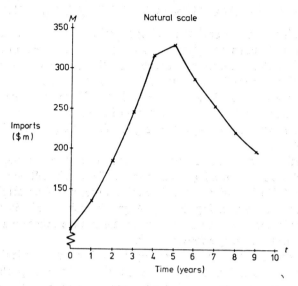

Fig. 5.5 (a)

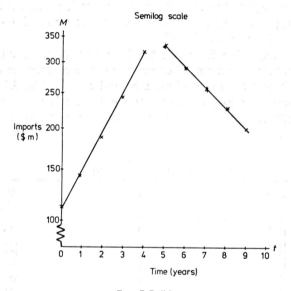

Fig. 5.5 (b)

5.6 The Rectangular Hyperbola

5.6.1 AN EXAMPLE

Suppose a man is so well aware of his preferences for two consumption goods, champagne and oysters, that he can express his attitudes in the form of a series of equations. Imagine that he can specify all combinations

of these two goods which bring him one particular level of satisfaction as
follows:

$$m = \frac{10}{s} \qquad (5.19)$$

where m = quantity of champagne consumed per day in numbers of
            glasses; and
      s = quantity of oysters eaten per day in dozens.

Plotting this relationship gives us the curve shown in Fig. 5.6, which has
the characteristic convex shape of an *indifference curve*. All points on the
curve represent the same level of satisfaction, so we observe that this
consumer would be indifferent between a combination of, say, 10 glasses
of champagne and 1 dozen oysters (point A in Fig. 5.6) and, say, 5 glasses
of champagne and 2 dozen oysters (point B). To put it another way, if he
habitually consumed the combination at point B and his oyster supply
were cut to 1 dozen (point E) he would require an extra 5 glasses of
champagne per day (point C) as compensation—that is, he would have to
move to the combination at point A to keep his total utility level the same.

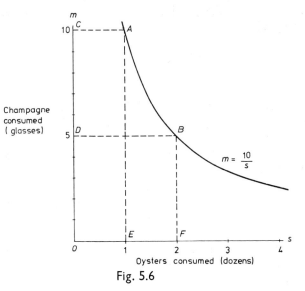

Fig. 5.6

Equation (5.19) is an example of a *rectangular hyperbola*. The curve
derives its name from the fact that rectangles drawn from all points on the
curve and bounded by the two axes are equal in area. Thus, for example,
the rectangles $OCAE$ and $ODBF$ in Fig. 5.6 have the same area.

5.6.2 GENERAL FORM OF THE RECTANGULAR HYPERBOLA

In general, the rectangular hyperbola is obtained when the product of two
variables is a constant, that is,

$$xy = a \qquad (5.20)$$

where x and y are variables and a a constant. Confirm that Equation (5.19) can be rearranged to show the product of the two variables m and s as equal to the constant 10.

For positive values of the two variables, the rectangular hyperbola always exhibits the characterictic convex shape shown in Fig. 5.6. If the curve were extended indefinitely upwards, it would never quite reach the vertical axis; Equation (5.19) indicates this when it shows that $m =$ infinity for $s =$ zero. Similarly, if the curve were extended indefinitely to the right, it would never meet the horizontal axis.

5.7 Equilibrium in Nonlinear Models

If a quantitative economic model contains nonlinear equations—perhaps conforming to one or more of the functional forms discussed above—it may be referred to as a *nonlinear model*. In the previous chapter we illustrated the process of equilibrium analysis in linear models. Now, to round off our introduction to nonlinear functions, let us examine the calculation of an equilibrium solution for a simple nonlinear model.

Suppose that in a particular market it is known that the demand and supply schedules for the good under study conform to the following nonlinear equations:

$$q_d = \frac{16}{p} \tag{5.21a}$$

$$q_s = 2p^2 \tag{5.21b}$$

where $q_d =$ quantity of good demanded per time period;
$q_s =$ quantity of good supplied per time period; and
$p \;\; =$ price of the good.

The demand equation is an example of a rectangular hyperbola, and the supply equation is a simple quadratic.

The determination of equilibrium price and quantity for this market proceeds in the same way as discussed in connection with the linear supply and demand model in Chapter 4. Firstly, a graphical solution may be found as shown in Fig. 5.7. The point of intersection of demand and supply curves gives the price/quantity equilibrium as $q_e = 8$, $p_e = 2$. Alternatively, an algebraic solution may be determined by substituting q_e for both q_d and q_s in Equations (5.21). This yields two equations in two unknowns, p_e, and q_e, which may be solved using whatever solution procedures are appropriate. In this case the simplest method is to equate the RHS of (5.21a) and (5.21b) giving:

$$\frac{16}{p_e} = 2p_e^2 \tag{5.22}$$

whence $p_e^3 = 8$ so that $p_e = 2$. Substitution of 2 for p in, say, (5.21a) immediately gives the equilibrium value of q_e as 8.

It so happened that in this example the equation we were required to solve, Equation (5.22), was particularly simple. It is clear that different numerical or algebraic forms for the demand and supply equations could

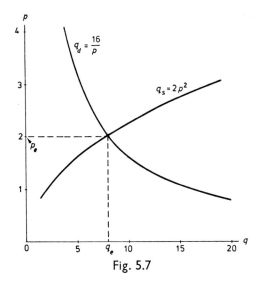

Fig. 5.7

make Equation (5.22) more complicated and therefore more difficult to solve.

Thus we may conclude that in theory the procedures for determining equilibrium solutions in nonlinear models are much the same as those in similar models containing only linear functions. However, the difference is that in practical terms the calculation of solutions in nonlinear cases is usually likely to be rather more difficult.

Exercises

1. The following table shows the monthly market supply of a certain type of soap at various prices.

p (cents per cake)	s ('000 cakes)
3	20
5	40
7	68
9	104
11	148

Plot these points on a graph. Verify that they conform to the quadratic polynomial $s = p^2 + 2p + 5$.

2. Use the supply equation from Exercise 1 to predict the quantity of soap supplied when the price is (a) $2\frac{1}{2}$ cents, (b) 6 cents, (c) 15 cents.

3. Of what form are the following functions:

(a) $p = \dfrac{\alpha + 5}{q}$,

(b) $y = 3x^4 + 5$,
(c) $C = Y - I$,
(d) $q = p[p(p - 2)]$,
(e) $z = 4^w$.

4. A man invests $200 at an interest rate of 2 per cent per month, where the interest is added monthly. What will his investment be worth at the end of one year?

5. Suppose inflation is proceeding in the economy at a continuous rate of 6 per cent per quarter. How much will I have to pay in exactly one year's time for a bundle of goods whose total cost at present prices is $100?

6. Over a period of six successive years a certain man's annual income increases as follows:

Year	Income per year
1	$1,600
2	$2,500
3	$4,000
4	$6,300
5	$10,000
6	$15,800

Use a semilogarithmic graph to show that his income has grown at a constant rate over this period. Make a rough estimate from your graph of the annual growth rate in his income.

7. A given market is characterised by a linear demand function and a quadratic supply function as follows:

$$q_d = 20 - 6p$$
$$q_s = p^2 + 4.$$

Given that negative prices and quantities are infeasible, at what price and quantity will equilibrium be reached in this market?

Part II: Elementary Calculus in Economics

Chapter 6

The Derivative of a Function

6.1 Slope of Nonlinear Functions
6.1.1 INTRODUCTION

An important characteristic of linear functions, which we studied in Chapter 4, was their *slope* or *gradient*. Now, in the context of nonlinear functions, the notion of slope is again significant. Recall that one property of a linear function is that its slope is constant at all points along its length. If we look at the graph of a *nonlinear* function, it is obvious that its slope is *not* constant, but changes as we move along the graph. For example, suppose we are travelling along a road which climbs up an undulating hill, as shown in cross-section in Fig. 6.1. At some points the road is quite steep, at others it is flatter, and at one point it even runs downhill for a little way. In other words the slope of this curved "function" is not constant, but varies at different points; sometimes it is large and positive

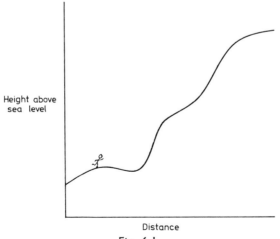

Height above
sea level

Distance

Fig. 6.1

(in the steep uphill bits), and over one stretch it becomes negative (where the road runs downhill).

How could we measure the slope of a curved function? When we studied linear functions, we used the formula "vertical over horizontal distance" to measure slope, and arrived at a single unique answer. But as we have just observed, the slope of a nonlinear function is not unique.

One approach to measuring the slope of a nonlinear function is to break it up into small linear bits and use our "rise-over-run" formula to calculate the slope of each individual bit. For example, consider the quadratic function which we have discussed in previous chapters.

$$y = 11x - x^2 + 40 \qquad (6.1)$$

where y = output of wheat in centals; and
$\quad\quad\;\; x$ = input of fertiliser in kg per hectare.

Let us draw this graph not as a smooth curve, but as a series of linear segments, each segment corresponding to one unit of x. The resulting graph is shown in Fig. 6.2.

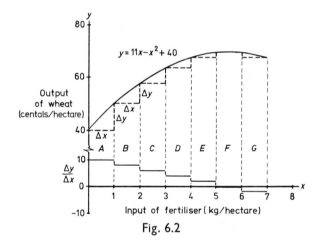

Fig. 6.2

The slope of each individual linear segment may be measured using the methods studied in Chapter 4, i.e., by applying the simple formula that calculates slope, $\Delta y/\Delta x$. Table 6.1 shows the calculations of the slope of each segment marked A through G on Fig. 6.2. Since the graph gets flatter as we move rightwards from segment A, it is obvious that the slope of each successive segment should become smaller. This is confirmed by Table 6.1, where we see that Δx is constant and Δy declines as x increases, hence $\Delta y/\Delta x$, the slope, declines as x increases, from a value of 10 for segment A, through zero at segment F, to -2 at segment G.

TABLE 6.1

Slope of Quadratic Production Function

x	y	Segment on Fig. 6.2	Δx	Δy	$\dfrac{\Delta y}{\Delta x}$
0	40				
		A	1	10	10
1	50				
		B	1	8	8
2	58				
		C	1	6	6
3	64				
		D	1	4	4
4	68				
		E	1	2	2
5	70				
		F	1	0	0
6	70				
		G	1	-2	-2
7	68				

We can write the last statement in the previous paragraph as a formal functional relationship, i.e., the slope of each linear segment, $\Delta y/\Delta x$, is a function of the level of x:

$$\frac{\Delta y}{\Delta x} = f(x). \tag{6.2}$$

Our procedure has yielded a *discontinuous* functional relationship between the slope of function (6.1) and x. This arises from the fact that we have treated the slope as a discrete variable. The graph of $\Delta y/\Delta x$ as a discontinuous function of x is shown in the lower section of Fig. 6.2.

6.1.2 SLOPE AT A PARTICULAR POINT ON THE SMOOTH-CURVED PRODUCTION FUNCTION

The above method of calculating the slope of a curved function clearly provides only an approximation. We want a more accurate way of pinpointing the *exact* slope at a point on the function. In this section, we shall consider a graphical way of doing this, then in the next section a more general algebraic means will be derived.

Suppose we wish to measure the slope at a particular point on the outside of the dome of St Paul's Cathedral (or, in the case of Catholics, St Peter's). This can be achieved by holding a long straight piece of wood so that it just touches the dome at the desired point. In Fig. 6.3, PQ represents the dome, A the required point and BC the piece of wood. The axes y and x measure vertical and horizontal distances respectively. Now the slope of the dome at point A may be ascertained by measuring the slope of BC, given as $\Delta y/\Delta x$. BC is called a *tangent* to the curve PQ at point A. The word "tangent" comes from the Latin word meaning "to touch".

Similarly, if PQ in Fig. 6.3 were instead the graph of a particular function $y = f(x)$, the slope of this function at point A could be measured graphically by drawing the tangent BC and measuring its slope, again as

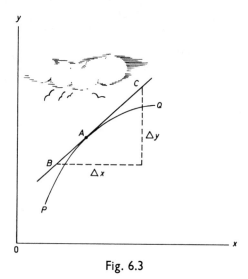

Fig. 6.3

$\Delta y/\Delta x$. Notice that there is only *one* tangent to a curve at any point and hence the curve has a unique slope at that particular point. If you don't believe this, try and draw a line with a slope different from that of *BC* which is also a tangent to *PQ* at *A*. Remember that a tangent only *touches* a curve at the required point, it does not cut it.

Now let us use this method to calculate the slope of our smooth-curved production function example at some point, for example, where $x = 3$. The graphical analysis is shown in Fig. 6.4. The required point is *S*, and the tangent at *S* is *PQ*. Let us measure the slope of the tangent, say between

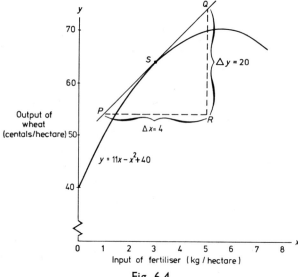

Fig. 6.4

the points where $x = 1$ and $x = 5$. The corresponding values of y at these points, as read from the graph, are 54 and 74 respectively. Thus the slope of PQ is:

$$\frac{\Delta y}{\Delta x} = \frac{QR}{PR} = \frac{74 - 54}{5 - 1} = \frac{20}{4} = 5.$$

Thus our production function at point S where $x = 3$ has a slope of 5.

6.1.3 SLOPE AT ANY POINT ON THE SMOOTH-CURVED PRODUCTION FUNCTION

The graphical method for calculating slope outlined in the previous section is both cumbersome and liable to error if the graph is inexactly drawn. Suppose we wish to know, for our production function (6.1), what form the "slope" Equation (6.2) takes when it indicates the *exact* slope of the production function at a given point.

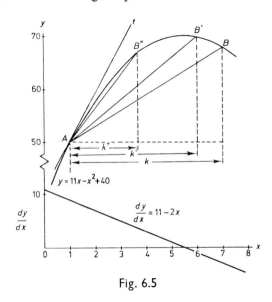

Fig. 6.5

Take any point on the function, say A in Fig. 6.5. We are not concerned with the numerical values of x and y at this point, since we want it to represent *any* point on the function. Let us simply denote the values of x and y at A as x_0 and y_0 respectively. Then by substituting of x_0 and y_0 into Equation (6.1) we have:

$$y_0 = 11x_0 - x_0^2 + 40. \tag{6.3}$$

Now look at another point B on the function where x has increased by k units to $(x_0 + k)$. If we let (x_1, y_1) be the coordinates of point B, we can write:

$$x_1 = x_0 + k \tag{6.4}$$

and

$$y_1 = 11x_1 - x_1^2 + 40 \tag{6.5}$$

or, putting (6.4) into (6.5),

$$y_1 = 11(x_0 + k) - (x_0 + k)^2 + 40. \tag{6.6}$$

Let us calculate the slope of the straight line AB which we may take as representing the *average slope of the arc AB*. We have:

$$\text{Slope } AB = \frac{\Delta y}{\Delta x} = \frac{y_1 - y_0}{x_1 - x_0}. \tag{6.7}$$

Now, in Equation (6.7) substitute Equation (6.6) for y_1, Equation (6.3) for y_0, and k, from Equation (6.4), for $x_1 - x_0$. This gives:†

$$\frac{\Delta y}{\Delta x} = \frac{11(x_0 + k) - (x_0 + k)^2 + 40 - (11x_0 - x_0^2 + 40)}{k}$$

$$= \frac{11k - 2x_0 k - k^2}{k}$$

$$= 11 - 2x_0 - k$$

and since we said A could be anywhere on the function we can drop the specific subscript from x and write in general terms:

$$\frac{\Delta y}{\Delta x} = 11 - 2x - k. \tag{6.8}$$

Consider what happens as k gets smaller, that is, changes to k' and k'' in Fig. 6.5. The arc AB gets smaller (changes to AB' and AB'') and the slope of the line AB (AB', AB'') gets steeper.

In other words, as k (i.e., Δx) gets smaller (i.e., approaches zero), the arc AB gets smaller and the straight line AB gets closer and closer to being the tangent (t) to the curve at A. Finally the "arc AB" is simply the point A, and the "line AB" is the tangent to the curve at the point A. Since k has reached a limiting value of zero, it disappears from Equation (6.8) and thus the slope of the line AB, which is now the tangent at A, has a value $11 - 2x$.

Symbolically this may be written:

$$\lim_{\Delta x \to 0} \frac{\Delta y}{\Delta x} = 11 - 2x \tag{6.9}$$

which reads "the limit of the value $\Delta y/\Delta x$ as Δx approaches zero is $11 - 2x$".

This expression gives the slope or rate of change of the function at any point. It is called the *derivative* of the function with respect to x, and is written dy/dx. Thus for our production function we may write:

$$\frac{dy}{dx} = 11 - 2x. \tag{6.10}$$

The LHS of (6.10) is pronounced "dee y dee x" or "dee y by dee x". The study of derivatives forms part of that branch of mathematics called the *calculus*.

---

† Some of the algebra required to understand the following steps is contained in Appendix A.

Equation (6.10) is the specific form we have been seeking for the general functional statement in Equation (6.2). It is clear from Equation (6.10) that the slope of the original function (6.1) is a continuous linear function of the independent variable x. This is graphed in the lower part of Fig. 6.5.

Let us use Equation (6.10) to calculate the slope of the production function (6.1) at several points along its length. First, recall our earlier graphical analysis, which showed that the function's slope at the point where $x = 3$ is 5. This result is confirmed algebraically by substituting $x = 3$ into (6.10) as follows:

$$\frac{dy}{dx} = 11 - (2 \times 3) = 5.$$

Now let us use Equation (6.10) to calculate dy/dx at some further points, say where $x = 1, 5, 5\frac{1}{2}, 7$ and 12. We find:

when $x = 1$, $\dfrac{dy}{dx} = 11 - (2 \times 1) = 9$

$x = 5$, $\dfrac{dy}{dx} = 11 - (2 \times 5) = 1$

$x = 5\frac{1}{2}$, $\dfrac{dy}{dx} = 11 - (2 \times 5\frac{1}{2}) = 0$

$x = 7$, $\dfrac{dy}{dx} = 11 - (2 \times 7) = -3$

$x = 12$, $\dfrac{dy}{dx} = 11 - (2 \times 12) = -13.$

By comparing these results with the graph of this function in Fig. 6.5, the following general facts are illustrated.

- If at a given point a function slopes *upwards*, its *derivative* (slope) at that point is *positive*.
- If at a given point a function slopes *downwards*, its *derivative* (slope) at that point is negative.
- If at a given point a function is *flat* (horizontal), its *derivative* (slope) at that point is zero.

It also follows, although not illustrated in Fig. 6.5, that:

- If at a given point a function is *vertical*, its *derivative* (slope) at that point is infinite.

6.1.4 COMPARISON OF $\dfrac{\Delta y}{\Delta x}$ AND $\dfrac{dy}{dx}$

The quantity $\Delta y/\Delta x$ represents the ratio between finite measurable quantities Δy and Δx. However, dy/dx is *not* a ratio. Any particular value of the derivative relates to a specific point, and a point has no dimensions, i.e., there is no actual measurable change in y and x at that point. But there is a *rate of change*, or slope, which the function exhibits at that point, and that is what dy/dx measures. You might compare this with a single frame from a movie film of a car travelling at 80 km/h. The frame "freezes" the car's motion in the same way as the derivative gives us a "snapshot" of the function's rate of change at a specific point.

6.2 Derivative of a Linear Function

The linear cost function studied in Chapter 4 (Equation (4.1), Figs 4.1 and 4.5) was

$$TC = 400 + 3y \qquad (6.11)$$

where TC = total annual costs in dollars; and
$\qquad\quad y$ = annual output in tons.

In Section 4.1 we observed that the slope of this function $\Delta TC/\Delta y$ was constant, having a value of 3 no matter how large or how small Δy was taken to be. In other words, if Δy were to become smaller and smaller (approach zero) the slope of the function would still remain at 3. Using the notation of Equation (6.9) we can write:

$$\lim_{\Delta y \to 0} \frac{\Delta TC}{\Delta y} = 3, \qquad (6.12)$$

that is, the limiting value of $\Delta TC/\Delta y$ as Δy approaches zero is 3. Hence we may write directly the derivative of Equation (6.11) as:

$$\frac{dTC}{dy} = 3.$$

This derivative is graphed in the lower section of Fig. 6.6.

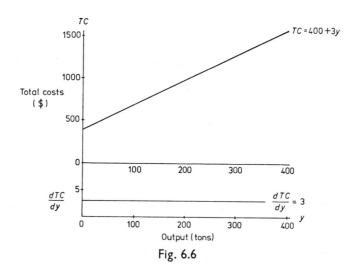

Fig. 6.6

6.3 Some Simple Rules for Derivation

6.3.1 NOTATION FOR DERIVATIVE

Given any function, say $z = f(t)$, the process of finding the derivative dz/dt is called *derivation* or *differentiation*. In performing this task, think of the notation d/dt as an "operator", that is as an indication of an operation to be performed, just as "$\times$" indicates "multiply by", or "Σ" denotes "take the sum of" (see Section 14.7). Thus we interpret d/dt as saying "differentiate with respect to t". Applying this to the function

$z = f(t)$, we have $\frac{d}{dt}(z)$ or simply $\frac{dz}{dt}$ indicating "differentiate z with respect to t". Equivalently, we may apply the operator $\frac{d}{dt}$ to $f(t)$ and thus write $\frac{d}{dt}f(t)$ which indicates the same differentiation process by saying "differentiate the function $f(t)$ with respect to t". Yet another way of writing the derivative of the function $z = f(t)$ is $f'(t)$.

Summarising, for the function $z = f(t)$ we may indicate the operation of differentiation by any of the following equivalent expressions:

$$\frac{dz}{dt}, \quad \frac{d}{dt}f(t), \quad f'(t).$$

6.3.2 THE DERIVATIVE OF $y = x^2$

We may now begin to formulate some rules for differentiation applicable to a wide range of numerical functions. We shall approach this in terms of some simple examples. First let us find the equation for the derivative of the function $y = x^2$ using the same technique as we used in Section 6.1.3 above.

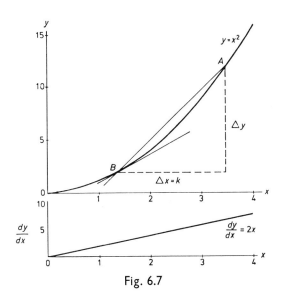

Fig. 6.7

Initially, we wish to measure the average slope of any arc AB on this function as shown in Fig. 6.7. This is done by measuring the slope of the chord AB. The coordinates of A are (x_0, y_0) and those of B are $(x_0 + k, y_1)$. Thus at A, $y_0 = x_0^2$ and at B, $y_1 = (x_0 + k)^2$. Hence, dropping the subscripts straight away we have:

74

Elementary Calculus

$$\text{Slope } AB = \frac{\Delta y}{\Delta x} = \frac{(x + k)^2 - x^2}{k}$$

$$= \frac{x^2 + 2xk + k^2 - x^2}{k} = \frac{2xk + k^2}{k}$$

$$= 2x + k.$$

As we make k (i.e., Δx) smaller and smaller, the point B moves nearer and nearer to A. When k disappears, the line AB becomes the tangent at A, and its slope is the slope of the function at that point. We write this as:

$$\lim_{\Delta x \to 0} \frac{\Delta y}{\Delta x} = 2x \tag{6.13}$$

since k vanishes from the expression $2x + k$ above. Thus we can write:

$$\frac{dy}{dx} = 2x, \tag{6.14}$$

which is an equation giving the slope of the original function $y = x^2$ at any point. This derivative is graphed in the lower part of Fig. 6.7.

Now let us calculate the slope of this function using both (a) the graphical method (measuring the slope of the tangent at the point in question) and (b) the algebraic method (using Equation (6.14)), for a particular point, say where $x = 3$.

(a) The use of a tangent to find the slope of the function at the point Q where $x = 3$ is shown in Fig. 6.8. We find that the slope at this point equals 6.

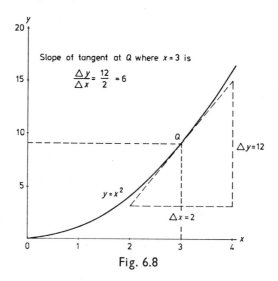

Fig. 6.8

(b) The value of the derivative at $x = 3$ yields the same result, that is, substituting 3 for x in Equation (6.14) gives:

$$\frac{dy}{dx} = 2 \times 3 = 6.$$

6.3.3 THE DERIVATIVE OF $y = x^3$

Following through the same procedure for the function $y = x^3$ (see Fig. 6.9) we find:†

Slope $AB = \dfrac{\Delta y}{\Delta x} = \dfrac{(x + k)^3 - x^3}{k} = 3x^2 + 3xk + k^2.$

Hence when $k\ (= \Delta x)$ becomes zero,

$$\lim_{\Delta x \to 0} \frac{\Delta y}{\Delta x} = 3x^2$$

and thus

$$\frac{dy}{dx} = 3x^2. \tag{6.15}$$

This derivative is graphed in the lower section of Fig. 6.9.

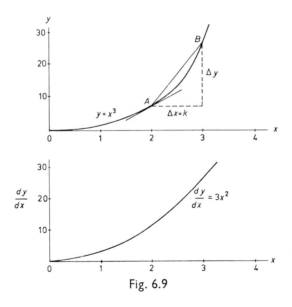

Fig. 6.9

Let us again evaluate the slope of $y = x^3$ by both methods for a particular point, say where $x = 2$. The graphical method as shown in Fig. 6.10 yields a slope $\Delta y / \Delta x = 12$ at the relevant point Q.

Evaluation of the derivative for $x = 2$ gives the same result. That is, by substitution in Equation (6.15) we get:

$$\frac{dy}{dx} = 3 \times 2^2 = 12.$$

† Appendix A outlines some of the algebra involved in the following analysis.

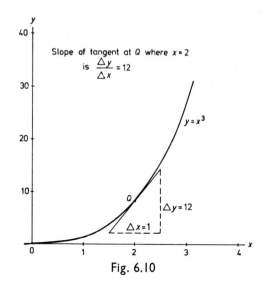

Fig. 6.10

6.3.4 THE DERIVATIVE OF THE GENERAL POWER FUNCTION

We have now seen that if $y = x^2$, $dy/dx = 2x$, and if $y = x^3$, $dy/dx = 3x^2$. These are specific examples of a general rule which may be used in the differentiation of functions containing a variable raised to any power. This rule is:

• if $y = x^n$, then $\dfrac{dy}{dx} = nx^{n-1}$.

• Thus for example, if $p = q^6$, $\dfrac{dp}{dq} = 6q^{6-1} = 6q^5$.

Again if $u = \dfrac{1}{t^2} \equiv t^{-2}$, the same rule may be applied to give

$$\frac{du}{dt} = -2t^{-2-1} = -2t^{-3} = \frac{-2}{t^3}.$$

We may generalise the formula to include a coefficient a in front of the RHS variable as follows:

• if $y = ax^n$, then $\dfrac{dy}{dx} = nax^{n-1}$.

For example, if $y = 10x^4$, $\dfrac{dy}{dx} = 4 \times 10x^{4-1} = 40x^3$.

6.4 Differentiation of Functions Containing Several Terms

Consider the function

$$S = 5Y^2 - 13jY^5 - 14 + 7Y. \tag{6.16}$$

This is indeed a complicated function, yet finding its derivative is quite easy if one applies piecemeal the rule from the previous section. Before doing so, we should note that:

• if a function $y = f(x)$ contains on its RHS the sum of several terms, the derivative dy/dx is simply the sum of the separate derivatives of each term.
• if a term on the RHS of such a function does not contain the variable x, it disappears in the process of differentiation.

Now turning our attention to the equation $S = f(Y)$ in (6.16) above, we wish to determine dS/dY. The derivative of the first term on the RHS is found by application of the rule from Section 6.3.4. The result is:

$$2 \times 5 \times Y^{2-1} = 10Y^1 \equiv 10Y.$$

In the second term on the RHS of Equation (6.16), the expression $13j$ is regarded as a constant. Hence reapplying the above rule we can calculate the derivative of this term as:

$$-5 \times 13j \times Y^{5-1} = -65jY^4.$$

Likewise, we can find the component of the derivative corresponding to the fourth term on the RHS of (6.16). This component is 7. Finally, the third term, being a constant and independent of Y, disappears.

Thus, putting all these results together:

$$\frac{dS}{dY} = 10Y - 65jY^4 + 7. \tag{6.17}$$

Check that you understand this process. The derivative in Equation (6.17) would allow us to calculate the slope of the function in (6.16) for any particular level of Y.

Finally, let us illustrate this process once more by formally calculating the derivative of the production function $y = 11x - x^2 + 40$ used in Section 6.1 above. We have

$$\frac{dy}{dx} = 1 \times 11 \times x^{1-1} - 2 \times 1 \times x^{2-1}$$
$$= 11 - 2x \text{ as before.}$$

6.5 Differentiation of Logarithmic Functions

The basic rules for differentiation of log functions are stated here without derivation or proof (y and x are variables, and a and b are constants).

• If $y = \log_e x$, then $\dfrac{dy}{dx} = \dfrac{1}{x}$.

• If $y = \log_e ax$, then $\dfrac{dy}{dx} = \dfrac{1}{x}$.

• If $y = \log_e x^b$, then $\dfrac{dy}{dx} = \dfrac{b}{x}$.

The basic rules for differentiation of exponential functions are:

• If $y = e^x$, then $\dfrac{dy}{dx} = e^x$.

• If $y = e^{ax}$, then $\dfrac{dy}{dx} = ae^{ax}$.

Exercises

1. Draw a graph of the demand schedule

$$q = \frac{2}{p^2}$$

over the interval $p = 0$ to 6, where p is measured in dollars per unit. Use the graph to calculate the slope of the function at the point where price is $2, by drawing a tangent at this point and measuring its slope.

2. For the function in Exercise 1 above, evaluate dq/dp at the level $p = 2$. Compare your answer with that from Exercise 1.

3. A firm's total cost function is given by the equation
$$TC = 3y^3 - y^2 + 2y + 5$$
where $y = $ level of output. What is the slope of this function at the point where $y = 1$?

4. Determine the equation for the derivative of the utility function
$$U = 5y^2 - \tfrac{1}{2}y^3$$
where y is the quantity of a consumption good.

5. Find the slope of the indifference curve in Equation (5.19) where the daily intake of oysters is $2\tfrac{1}{2}$ dozen.

6. Derive an equation to calculate the slope at any point on the Cobb-Douglas production function in Equation (5.6).

7. Prove that the following supply equation is upward sloping:
$$q = \alpha p^3 + \beta p - \gamma$$
where α, β, γ are positive constants.

Chapter 7

The Economic Significance
of Derivatives

7.1 Elasticity
7.1.1 CONCEPT OF ELASTICITY

A familiar problem in economics is the determination of the response of demand to changes in price. Consider the following demand function:

$$q = 40 - 3p \qquad (7.1)$$

where q = the quantity of hamburger buns demanded per week; and
p = the price per bun in cents.

Now one way of studying the effect of a change in price upon the quantity demanded is simply to differentiate the function:

$$\frac{dq}{dp} = -3. \qquad (7.2)$$

The slope of the demand curve is -3. Thus, when the price per bun is raised by 1 cent the quantity demanded will decline by 3 buns.

But looking at the slope alone may be quite misleading. Suppose, for example, we expressed the price of buns in dollars. Then our demand function would become:

$$q = 40 - 300p. \qquad (7.3)$$

Differentiating this function, we see that

$$\frac{dq}{dp} = -300. \qquad (7.4)$$

The slope of the function (7.3) is much greater in absolute numerical terms than that of (7.1), yet the economic relationship is still the same: Equation (7.4) shows that if the price per bun is raised by \$1, demand will decline by 300 buns, or equivalently if price is raised by 1 cent, demand will decline by 3 buns, as found in (7.1). Hence the concept of slope as a measure of response has one important disadvantage: it is dependent on the units of measurement.

One of the most common methods of freeing changes in variables from units in which they are measured is by means of percentages. Thus we could express a change in p in Equation (7.1) from 4 to 5 cents as being the following percentage change:

$$\frac{5 - 4}{4} \times 100 = 25\%. \tag{7.5}$$

The equivalent change in p in Equation (7.3) is from 0.04 to 0.05, also a change of 25 per cent.

Thus, in considering any function $q = h(p)$, instead of dealing with ratios of absolute changes, it is more useful to think of the ratio of percentage changes. Such a ratio is called *elasticity*.

For a demand function we can define the percentage change in price as $\Delta p/p \times 100$ (compare Equation (7.5)). Similarly, we have for the percentage change in quantity demanded $\Delta q/q \times 100$.

We may thus write:

$$\text{Elasticity} = E_p = \frac{\dfrac{\Delta q}{q} \times 100}{\dfrac{\Delta p}{p} \times 100} = \frac{\Delta q}{\Delta p} \times \frac{p}{q} \tag{7.6}$$

Note that we are referring to the elasticity of the quantity demanded (the dependent variable in the demand function) with respect to price (the independent variable). A subscript p has accordingly been appended to the symbol E to indicate the *price elasticity of demand*.

In general, given any function $y = f(x)$, the elasticity of y with respect to x over a given interval can be written:

$$\text{Elasticity} = E = \frac{\Delta y}{\Delta x} \times \frac{x}{y} \tag{7.7}$$

The ratio $\Delta y/\Delta x$ may be interpreted as a measure of the average slope of $y = f(x)$ over the given interval.

7.1.2 POINT ELASTICITY

In Chapter 6 it was explained that, for any function $y = f(x)$, the limit of $\Delta y/\Delta x$ as $\Delta x \to 0$ is in fact the derivative of the function. This in turn, when interpreted graphically, can be conceived as the slope of the function at a given point. It should be apparent, then, that if we wish to calculate the elasticity of any function at a given point, the ratio $\Delta y/\Delta x$ in the general definition of elasticity provided by formula (7.7) may be replaced by the appropriate derivative. Thus, to define *point elasticity* we simply substitute dy/dx for $\Delta y/\Delta x$ in Equation (7.7). The formula for point elasticity is thus:

$$E = \frac{dy}{dx} \times \frac{x}{y} \tag{7.8}$$

The values that we substitute for x and y in Equation (7.8) are those obtained at the point we have chosen—that is, the coordinates of the point.

Of course, Equation (7.7) may be used as a point elasticity formula if $\Delta y/\Delta x$ is interpreted as measuring the slope of the *tangent* to the curve at the point (x, y).

7.1.3 SOME EXAMPLES OF ELASTICITY

Given the general algebraic form of our demand function to be $q = h(p)$, we saw in Section 7.1.1 that demand elasticity with respect to price can be written as in Equation (7.6). To use this equation to measure elasticity at a given point, we could substitute dq/dp for $\Delta q/\Delta p$.

We might also take the quantity demanded as a function of income, all other things remaining constant. Let us suppose $q = \phi(Y)$, where $Y = $ annual consumer income. We can then define the elasticity of demand with respect to income, or the *income elasticity of demand*, as

$$E_Y = \frac{\Delta q}{\Delta Y} \times \frac{Y}{q} \text{ or } \frac{dq}{dY} \times \frac{Y}{q} \quad (7.9)$$

As explained earlier, we would prefer the formula containing the derivative when $q = \phi(Y)$ is differentiable.

Further, we may think of the quantity demanded being affected, all other things held constant, by the price of some other commodity. For example, the quantity of hamburger buns demanded can be taken as a function of the price of bread rolls, which serve as a close substitute. Accordingly, we might have $q = u(z)$, where q is the quantity of hamburger buns demanded per time period, and z is the price of bread rolls. We could then define the *cross-elasticity of demand* for buns with respect to the price of bread rolls as:

$$E_z = \frac{\Delta q}{\Delta z} \times \frac{z}{q} \text{ or } \frac{dq}{dz} \times \frac{z}{q} \quad (7.10)$$

Elasticity of supply is obtained along similar lines. If the quantity offered for sale (q) is a function of market price (p), the *elasticity of supply* is:

$$E_s = \frac{\Delta q}{\Delta p} \times \frac{p}{q} \text{ or } \frac{dq}{dp} \times \frac{p}{q} \quad (7.11)$$

Note the similarity between Equation (7.11) and the expression for demand elasticity in Equation (7.6). The difference between them shows up, of course, in the fact that the functions connecting q and p will be quite distinct for the demand and supply situations. As a rule, we expect demand curves to slope downwards and supply curves to slope upwards. Hence we expect $\Delta q/\Delta p$ (and dq/dp) to be negative in the case of demand, but positive for supply.

Finally, let us again look at our farmer's production function $y = f(x)$, where y is the output of wheat and x is the input of fertiliser. We define the *elasticity of output* with respect to fertiliser as

$$E_y = \frac{\Delta y}{\Delta x} \times \frac{x}{y} \text{ or } \frac{dy}{dx} \times \frac{x}{y} \quad (7.12)$$

7.1.4 ARC ELASTICITY

In some cases we are interested in calculating elasticity over a range or arc of a function rather than at a single point. To illustrate the concept, let us refer to our production function $y = 11x - x^2 + 40$. A portion of the graph of this function is shown in Fig. 7.1. Suppose we wish to know the average elasticity of the arc AB in Fig. 7.1. Direct application of Equation (7.7) is possible but, although Δy and Δx are clearly measurable, what level of x and y should we use? It seems reasonable to let x in Equation (7.7) be the average or midpoint value between the two extremes that the arc covers. In this example the arc runs from $x = 2$ to $x = 5$, so let us take x in (7.7) to be the mean of these two values, $3\frac{1}{2}$. Similarly, define y in (7.7) as the midpoint between $y = 58$ and $y = 70$, that is $y = 64$.

Thus we may calculate:

$$\text{Arc elasticity between } A \text{ and } B = \frac{\Delta y}{\Delta x} \times \frac{x}{y}$$
$$= \frac{70 - 58}{5 - 2} \times \frac{3\frac{1}{2}}{64}$$
$$= 0.219.$$

In general, if we define the range of variation of x as being between levels x_0 and x_1, and the corresponding variation in y as being between y_0 and y_1, then a general formula for arc elasticity may be derived as follows:

$$\text{Arc elasticity} = \frac{y_1 - y_0}{x_1 - x_0} \times \frac{(x_0 + x_1)/2}{(y_0 + y_1)/2}$$
$$= \frac{y_1 - y_0}{x_1 - x_0} \times \frac{x_0 + x_1}{y_0 + y_1}. \tag{7.13}$$

The levels y_0, y_1, x_0, and x_1 in our example are marked in Fig. 7.1. Calculate the arc elasticity between A and B again, this time by direct substitution into Equation (7.13).

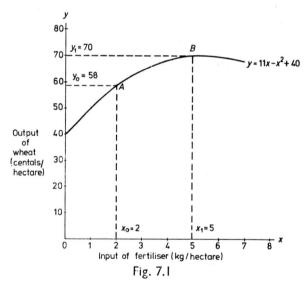

Fig. 7.1

Now let us compare the arc elasticity for the arc AB in Fig. 7.1, with the elasticities at the separate points A and B found by applying the point elasticity formula (7.8). The derivative of this production function was found in Equation (6.10) to be $11 - 2x$. Substituting this for dy/dx in our definition Equation (7.8), we find that for any point on the function in Fig. 7.1 the elasticity is calculated as:

$$E_y = (11 - 2x)\frac{x}{y}. \tag{7.14}$$

Now, at point A, $x = 2$ and $y = 58$. Putting these values in Equation (7.14), we get:

$$E_y = [11 - (2 \times 2)]\frac{2}{58} = 0.241.$$

The same procedure is followed to calculate the point elasticity at B, where $x = 5$ and $y = 70$. Substitution into (7.14) yields:

$$E_y = [11 - (2 \times 5)]\frac{5}{70} = 0.071.$$

Compare these two results with the arc elasticity of 0.219 calculated above. Notice in particular that the arc elasticity for this function is *not* equal to the average of the two point elasticities at each end of the arc.

7.1.5 ELASTICITY OF LINEAR FUNCTIONS

Take our earlier example of a linear cost function relating total costs (TC) to output of a firm (y):

$$TC = 400 + 3y. \tag{7.15}$$

The point elasticity formula when applied to Equation (7.15) reduces to:

$$E_c = 3 \times \frac{y}{TC} \tag{7.16}$$

where the subscript c is used to indicate that we are measuring the elasticity of a cost function. Applying this formula to three arbitrarily chosen points on this function, where $y = 0$, 200 and 400 respectively, we obtain the values for E_c shown in Table 7.1. The three points chosen are indicated A, B and C respectively on the graph of Equation (7.15), which is shown in Fig. 7.2.

TABLE 7.I

Elasticity of Linear Cost Function

Point on Fig. 7.2	y	TC	$\frac{y}{TC}$	E_c (from (7.16))
A	0	400	0	0
B	200	1000	0.20	0.60
C	400	1600	0.25	0.75

It is clear from Table 7.1 that the elasticity of this linear function (7.15) varies at different points on the function. In fact, it is true that the elasticity of the general linear function $y = a + bx$ varies as you move along it. Note that this result does not apply if the intercept term is zero (see next section).

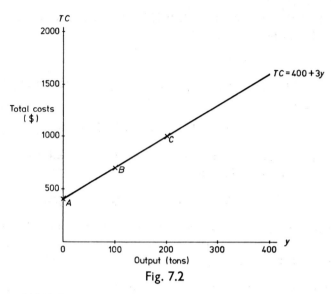

Fig. 7.2

7.1.6 UNITARY ELASTICITY

Certain functions exhibit constant elasticity, that is, they have the same level of elasticity throughout their whole length. A special case of constant elasticity is where elasticity always equals unity. A rectangular hyperbola is one example. Suppose demand for a good is given as the following function of its price:

$$q = \frac{25}{p}. \tag{7.17}$$

The elasticity of this rectangular hyperbola may be calculated by applying the formula (7.6) as follows (substituting the derivative dq/dp for the ratio $\Delta q/\Delta p$):

$$E_p = \frac{dq}{dp} \times \frac{p}{q} = \frac{-25}{p^2} \times \frac{p}{q} = \frac{-25}{pq}. \tag{7.18}$$

Substitute Equation (7.17) for q in (7.18):

$$E_p = \frac{-25 \times p}{p \times 25} = -1.$$

So the elasticity of (7.17) is (minus) unity at all points along its length. Equation (7.17) is an example of a *unitary elastic demand curve*.

A further example is given by the linear upward sloping supply curve:

$$q = cp \tag{7.19}$$

where q = quantity supplied;
p = price; and
c = constant.

The elasticity of this function is

$$E_s = \frac{dq}{dp} \times \frac{p}{q} = c\left(\frac{p}{q}\right)$$

But $q = cp$ from Equation (7.19). Hence:

$$E_s = \frac{cp}{cp} = 1.$$

Thus, Equation (7.19) is an example of a *unitary elastic supply curve*. Note that the intercept term in the linear function (7.19) is zero.

A summary comparison of these characteristics of linear and nonlinear functions is presented in Table 7.2.

TABLE 7.2
Comparison of Linear and Nonlinear Functions

	Linear Function $y = a + bx$	Nonlinear Function
Slope	Constant	Varies
Elasticity	Varies if $a \neq 0$ Unity if $a = 0$	May vary May be constant

7.2 Derivatives in Production and Cost Theory

7.2.I MARGINAL PRODUCT

What is the economic interpretation of the derivative of a production function? Take again our quadratic function $y = 11x - x^2 + 40$, whose derivative is:

$$\frac{dy}{dx} = 11 - 2x. \qquad (7.20)$$

In Chapter 6 we formulated this derivative as a limiting value of the expression $\Delta y/\Delta x$ (specifically, the limit as $\Delta x \to 0$). Now the ratio $\Delta y/\Delta x$ measures the change in output y per unit change in input x, or the *extra* output achieved per unit of *extra* input. This is the *marginal product* (*MP*) of the factor x. For example, if x is increased by 1 kg from 4 to 5 kg, then y rises by 2 centals from 68 to 70 centals (see Table 6.1). Thus for this finite change we measure *MP* as $\Delta y/\Delta x = 2$ centals per kg.

But, although the ratio of finite changes in y and x is an easily understood rough measure of *MP*, it is only a discontinuous approximation to the *continuous* rate of change of the original function. For a more accurate measure we must turn to the derivative, Equation (7.20), which shows how *MP* varies *continuously* with the level of input. So, for instance, the exact marginal product of the factor x at a level of, say, 4 kg, is calculated by substitution into (7.20) as:

$$MP = \frac{dy}{dx} = 11 - (2 \times 4) = 3 \text{ kg per cental.}$$

The graph of a marginal product equation, as shown for this example in the lower part of Fig. 6.5 is simply a picture of the *marginal product curve*.

The *shape* of a marginal product curve, of course, depends on the shape of the production function from which it is derived, which in turn depends on the *mathematical nature* of the production function. If it happens to be a quadratic, as in the above example, its marginal product curve will be a straight line since, as we have seen, the derivative of a quadratic is a linear function.

Let us now look at a slightly more complicated example. Suppose the output S of a steel manufacturing enterprise can be represented as a cubic function of the input of capital K, according to the following empirically determined relationship:

$$S = 30K + 3K^2 - \tfrac{1}{3}K^3. \tag{7.21}$$

An expression for the *MP* of capital may immediately be found by differentiating Equation (7.21) with respect to K, as follows:

$$MP \text{ of capital} = \frac{dS}{dK} = 30 + 6K - K^2. \tag{7.22}$$

Let us also find an expression for the *average product* (*AP*) of capital. Since this is defined as the volume of output per unit input of capital, i.e., S/K, the required *AP* equation may be found by dividing both sides of Equation (7.21) by K, as follows:

$$AP \text{ of capital} = \frac{S}{K} = 30 + 3K - \tfrac{1}{3}K^2. \tag{7.23}$$

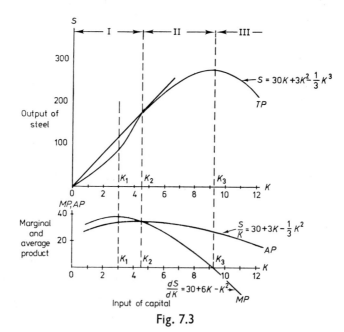

Fig. 7.3

The production function or total product (*TP*) curve, the *AP* curve and the *MP* curve for this example are drawn in Fig. 7.3. Observe the various properties of the relationship between S and K as K increases from zero:

- as the level of capital increases from 0 to K_1, *TP* increases at an increasing rate; that is, *MP* is rising;

- as K increases beyond K_1, the law of diminishing returns begins to operate; that is, MP declines;
- at the level K_2, AP reaches a maximum; at this point, MP is declining and cuts AP at its maximum;
- at the level K_3, TP reaches a maximum; that is, MP is zero;
- beyond K_3, TP declines; that is, MP is negative.

Frequently, three phases of the production function are distinguished, as follows:

- Phase I, for levels of K from 0 to K_2;
- Phase II, for levels of K from K_2 to K_3;
- Phase III, for levels of K beyond K_3.

These phases are marked on Fig. 7.3.

7.2.2 MARGINAL COST

In Section 5.2 we studied a total cost equation of the form

$$TC = 30 + 15y - 5y^2 + \tfrac{2}{3}y^3 \tag{7.24}$$

where TC = total costs of a particular firm per year; and
$\quad\quad\;\, y$ = level of output of the firm in units per year.

Given this information, we may immediately derive the equation for all the cost curves of this firm.

First, we see that TC can be divided into a fixed component which is constant regardless of the level of output, and a variable component which changes as y changes. Inspection of Equation (7.24) shows that the first term on the RHS is constant and the remaining terms are variable. Thus we can write expressions for total fixed costs (TFC) and total variable costs (TVC) as follows:

$$TFC = 30, \tag{7.25}$$
$$TVC = 15y - 5y^2 + \tfrac{2}{3}y^3. \tag{7.26}$$

Confirm that by adding Equation (7.25) to (7.26) we obtain Equation (7.24).

Average fixed costs (AFC) and average variable costs (AVC), defined as the level of fixed and variable costs respectively per unit of output, are obtained by dividing both sides of Equations (7.25) and of (7.26) by the level of output y, as follows:

$$AFC = \frac{TFC}{y} = \frac{30}{y}, \tag{7.27}$$

$$AVC = \frac{TVC}{y} = 15 - 5y + \tfrac{2}{3}y^2. \tag{7.28}$$

We notice in passing that the AFC equation is a rectangular hyperbola, and that, in this example, AVC is a quadratic.

Similarly, average total costs (ATC or simply AC) are found by dividing

Equation (7.24) by y, or alternatively by adding Equations (7.27) and (7.28). Either way we get

$$AC = \frac{TC}{y} = \frac{30}{y} + 15 - 5y + \tfrac{2}{3}y^2. \tag{7.29}$$

Now marginal cost (MC) is defined as the addition to total costs resulting from the expansion of the firm's output by one unit. As in the case of MP earlier, we may imagine this in finite terms as the change in total costs per unit change in output, that is, as $\Delta TC/\Delta y$. However, more accurately we take MC as a *continuous* function of y and calculate it as the derivative of the TC equation. Differentiating Equation (7.24) with respect to y gives

$$MC = \frac{dTC}{dy} = 15 - 10y + 2y^2. \tag{7.30}$$

All the above cost functions are graphed in Fig. 7.4.

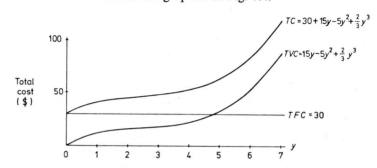

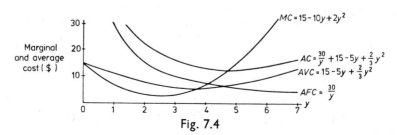

Fig. 7.4

7.2.3 MARGINAL REVENUE

Let us take the case of a firm operating under perfect competition. The volume of its output cannot affect the market price of its product. Suppose the prevailing market price for the firm's product is, say, $9 per unit. Consider, then, the various revenue functions faced by the firm.

First, total revenue (TR) is simply the number of units of quantity of output sold, (y), multiplied by the selling price per unit. Thus

$$TR = 9y. \tag{7.31}$$

Next, we have average revenue (AR) which is found by dividing total revenue by the number of units sold:

$$AR = \frac{TR}{y} = 9. \tag{7.32}$$

The firm's marginal revenue (MR) is defined as the increase in total revenue per unit increase in output, which may be calculated as the derivative of the TR function:

$$MR = \frac{dTR}{dy} = 9. \tag{7.33}$$

We see that Equations (7.32) and (7.33) are identical constant functions, showing that for the perfectly competitive firm $AR = MR = $ price of product.

The firm's revenue curves are graphed in Fig. 7.5.

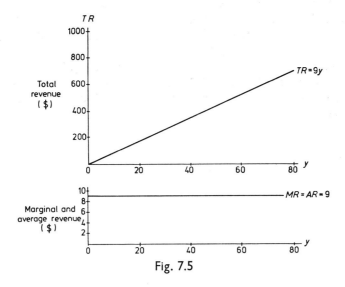

Fig. 7.5

A firm operating under imperfect competition, however, does have some control over its selling price. Let us consider the example of a monopolist who faces a demand curve for his product as follows:

$$y = 5 - \tfrac{1}{3}p \tag{7.34}$$

where y represents the volume of output demanded and p is the selling price he is able to charge.

Again, total revenue is given as output multiplied by price. However, unlike the perfect competitor whose selling price is fixed, the monopolist has a variable selling price dependent upon the quantity he supplies to the market. Rearranging Equation (7.34) we see that:

$$p = 15 - 3y. \tag{7.35}$$

Hence total revenue becomes

$$TR = py = (15 - 3y)y \equiv 15y - 3y^2. \tag{7.36}$$

The monopolist's total revenue function, in other words, is a quadratic for this particular example.

Now marginal revenue is found by taking the derivative of the total revenue function. Differentiating Equation (7.36) we get

$$MR = \frac{dTR}{dy} = 15 - 6y. \tag{7.37}$$

Finally, we obtain the monopolist's average revenue function as

$$AR = \frac{TR}{y} = 15 - 3y. \tag{7.38}$$

Notice that Equation (7.38) is identical to Equation (7.35), illustrating that the monopolist's average revenue function is the same as the demand function for his product. Further, observe that as he expands the volume of sales, the monopolist's marginal revenue falls twice as fast as his average revenue. The rate of decrease of revenue in Equation (7.37) is 6, whereas for Equation (7.38) it is 3.

The monopolist's revenue curves are graphed in Fig. 7.6. The diagram shows quite clearly that when TR is rising MR will be positive; when TR reaches a peak MR will equal zero; and when TR is declining MR will be negative.

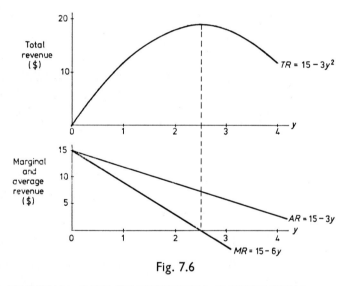

Fig. 7.6

7.2.4 MARGINAL RATE OF TECHNICAL SUBSTITUTION

Suppose a newspaper publisher has a fixed demand for a certain number of newspapers per day. He employs two variable factors of production, labour (L) and capital (K). From experience gained from varying the relative inputs of these two factors, he has been able to construct an empirical picture of the way in which labour and capital may be substituted for each other in the production of the fixed level of output. Suppose this relationship is characterised by the following equation:

$$K = \frac{100}{L^2} + 30. \tag{7.39}$$

The function $K = f(L)$ represented here is in fact a ratio between the two quadratic expressions $100 + 30L^2$ and L^2. Being a *ratio* between two polynomials it is an example of a *rational function*. It is graphed in the upper section of Fig. 7.7. The graph shows all combinations of the two factors K and L which will produce the given level of output, and is thus an example of an *isoquant*.

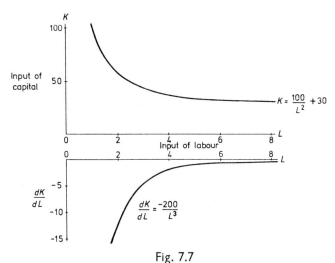

Fig. 7.7

The rate at which L may be substituted for K at any point on the isoquant is given by the derivative of Equation (7.39). It is called the *marginal rate of technical substitution* or simply the rate of technical substitution (*RTS*) of L for K. We have

$$RTS \text{ of } L \text{ for } K = \frac{dK}{dL} = -\frac{200}{L^3}. \tag{7.40}$$

Equation (7.40) is graphed in the lower part of Fig. 7.7. Thus we see that the *RTS* at any point on the isoquant is simply the slope of the isoquant at that point as measured by the derivative.

7.2.5 MARGINAL RATE OF TRANSFORMATION

Imagine a firm producing cigars and cigarettes using fixed supplies of resources. Suppose all combinations of the two products which may be produced from various allocations of this bundle of factors are given by the following equation:

$$u = 32 - \tfrac{1}{2}v^3 \tag{7.41}$$

where u = output of cigarettes in thousands per day; and
$\quad\quad v$ = output of cigars in thousands per day.

This equation is graphed in the upper part of Fig. 7.8. The resulting curve is called a *production possibility curve* or *product transformation curve*†

---

† Also known as a production possibilities *frontier* or *boundary*.

since it shows how one product may be "transformed" into the other by shifting resources from production of the first into production of the second. The *rate* at which, say, u is transformed into v in this example, is called the *marginal rate of transformation (MRT)* and is measured by the derivative of Equation (7.41). Thus we obtain:

$$MRT \text{ of } u \text{ into } v = \frac{du}{dv} = -\tfrac{3}{2}v^2. \qquad (7.42)$$

Equation (7.42) is graphed in the lower section of Fig. 7.8.

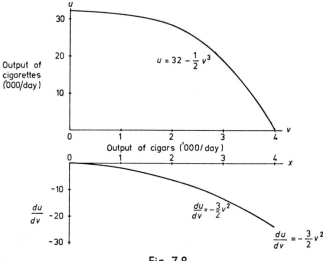

Fig. 7.8

7.2.6 SUMMARY

In this section we have seen how derivatives, which in purely mathematical terms indicate the slopes of functions, have special economic significance. In particular we have seen how *marginal* quantities are simply derivatives of the functions for corresponding *total* quantities. Thus, for example, the derivative of a *total* product, revenue or cost function measures *marginal* product, revenue or cost.

7.3 Derivatives in the Theory of Consumer Behaviour
7.3.1 MARGINAL UTILITY

If we make the heroic assumption that the satisfaction which a person receives from consumption of a certain good or goods is numerically measurable, we may specify a utility function for him in respect of the commodities he consumes. For instance, suppose the satisfaction a man derives from consumption of bananas can be expressed by the following power function:

$$U = 3b^{0.8} \qquad (7.43)$$

where U = level of utility achieved, measured in "utils"; and
  b = number of bananas consumed per day.

This function is graphed in the upper part of Fig. 7.9. From the diagram we read, for example, that if he eats 2 bananas in a given day, his total utility level will be a little over 5 utils.

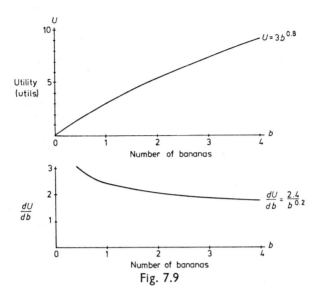

Fig. 7.9

The curve describing the utility function in Fig. 7.9 is concave, due to the fact that the exponent of b is less than unity (see Section 5.3.2). Thus each extra banana consumed on a given day adds slightly less to total utility than the previous banana did. The addition to total utility from each additional banana may be measured approximately by the finite quantity $\Delta U/\Delta b$. This quantity is *marginal utility* (*MU*)—that is, the extra utility per extra unit of the good consumed. An exact measure is provided by the derivative dU/db.

From Equation (7.43) we can derive the function $MU = f(b)$ by differentiation:

$$MU = \frac{dU}{db} = 0.8 \times 3 \times b^{0.8-1} = \frac{2.4}{b^{0.2}}. \qquad (7.44)$$

This marginal utility function is graphed in the lower portion of Fig. 7.9. As we would expect, the slope of $U = f(b)$ (that is, MU) declines as b increases, indicating the operation of the *law of diminishing marginal utility*.

7.3.2 MARGINAL RATE OF SUBSTITUTION

In Section 5.6.1 we met an example of an indifference curve showing all combinations of champagne (m) and oysters (s) yielding a certain consumer a given level of satisfaction or utility. The equation

$$m = \frac{10}{s} \qquad (7.45)$$

described the indifference curve, which was also illustrated in Fig. 5.6.

The slope of the indifference curve between two points (say A and B in Fig. 5.6) indicates the increase in the amount of one good that would be required to make up for a given loss in the other. In the champagne and oysters case, we could designate the quantity $\Delta m/\Delta s$ as the number of lost glasses of champagne for which a dozen oysters will substitute in order to maintain the given level of utility. The ratio $\Delta m/\Delta s$ is an approximation of the *marginal rate of substitution (MRS)* of oysters for champagne, which is measured exactly in the continuous case by the derivative dm/ds. In other words, the slope of an indifference curve as measured by its derivative indicates the MRS of one good for the other at every point along the curve.

In our example, the MRS of oysters for champagne changes as we move along the indifference curve. We calculate:

$$MRS \text{ of } s \text{ for } m = \frac{dm}{ds} = -\frac{10}{s^2}. \qquad (7.46)$$

Thus at point B in Fig. 5.6, for example, where a consumption of 5 glasses of champagne and 2 dozen oysters is indicated, the MRS of oysters for champagne is calculated from Equation (7.46) as

$$-\frac{10}{2^2} = -2.5.$$

That is, *at this point* an extra dozen oysters would just compensate him for the loss of $2\frac{1}{2}$ glasses of champagne.

7.4 Derivatives in Aggregate Models

As a prelude to a more detailed treatment later in this book (see Chapter 14), we shall consider the significance of the first derivative of a typical equation from an aggregate model such as a national income determination system. For the purpose of illustration, consider the model discussed in Section 4.4. This model contained the consumption function

$$C = 100 + 0.8Y \qquad (7.47)$$

where C = aggregate consumption in \$ millions; and
Y = national income in \$ millions.

This equation shows us that when income rises by \$1 million, consumption will rise by \$0.8 million, since the slope of the function is given by the derivative:

$$\frac{dC}{dY} = 0.8. \qquad (7.48)$$

As we have already noted, the derivative of a consumption function represents the *marginal propensity to consume (MPC)*, that is, the proportion of any rise in income which is spent on consumption. In this example, the MPC is constant because the consumption function is linear, but in a more complicated model, where the consumption function is nonlinear, we would find MPC varying with the level of Y.

Likewise, where particular savings functions, import functions and so forth are specified, their derivatives represent the corresponding marginal propensities to save, import and so on.

Exercises

1. For the demand function given in Exercise 1, Chapter 6:
   (a) What is the point elasticity of demand at a price of $2?
   (b) What is the arc elasticity of demand between prices of $2 and $3?

2. What is the marginal cost at an output of 5 units of the firm whose total cost equation is given in Exercise 3, Chapter 6?

3. Derive an equation to calculate the income elasticity of demand at any point on the following function:
$$q = 40 - Y^{\frac{3}{4}},$$
where q = quantity demanded in units; and
Y = purchaser's income in $'000.

4. (a) Use the elasticity formula from Exercise 3 above to calculate income elasticity of demand at an income of $4 thousand.
   (b) Why is this an "inferior good"?

5. A person's consumption of meat per year is related to his income by the function
$$C = 0.004 \ Y^{0.29}.$$
Use your knowledge about elasticities to calculate the percentage change in his consumption of meat if his income falls from $6,000 to $5,500 per year.

6. The total cost equation for a firm has the form
$$TC = \tfrac{1}{2}y^2$$
where y = units of output.
If the firm employs only one input, x, whose cost is constant at $4 per unit, show that the firm's production function $y = f(x)$ conforms to the law of diminishing returns.

7. The average output (AP) of a brick factory at various levels of labour input (L) is described by the following average product equation:
$$AP = 500L^{-1} + 5L - \frac{L^2}{6}.$$
   (a) What is the form of this firm's production function?
   (b) Calculate the firm's marginal product at a labour input of 10 units.

8. For the isoquant Equation (7.39), determine the combination of labour and capital at which the rate of technical substitution of labour for capital is -0.2.

9. Given the indifference curve in Equation (7.45), calculate the marginal rate of substitution of champagne for oysters, at the point where oyster consumption is 3 dozen per day.

Chapter 8

Maximisation and Minimisation

8.1 Maxima and Minima in Economics

One of the main tasks of economic analysis is to find the *best* possible means of attaining a given objective or range of objectives. The search for an optimum for a consumer, firm, industry or whole economy entails the formulation of plans to achieve *greatest* possible utility, *least* possible cost, *most efficient* possible operation, *highest* possible rate of growth, and so on. The concepts of maximisation and minimisation, meaning "attaining the greatest" and "attaining the least" respectively, are thus of great importance in economic optimisation. For the present, let us concentrate on the mathematical properties of maxima and minima. Application of these concepts to optimisation problems in economics will be treated in Chapter 9.

In mathematical usage, the word *extremum* is often used to refer to a maximum or a minimum; and *extremisation* is sometimes used instead of the terms *maximisation* and *minimisation*. As examples of extrema we may think of, say, the highest and lowest points on a graph. Maxima and minima of algebraic functions, however, require a rather fuller explanation. Let us explore this topic with the aid of some specific examples.

8.2 A Maximisation Example

Suppose we wish to determine the maximum physical output which is yielded by the production function example first examined in Chapter 3. That is, we wish to determine what level of input x maximises the function $y = 11x - x^2 + 40$, and what level of output y is produced at that point.

We know the slope of any function can be calculated from its derivative. The derivative of this function is

$$\frac{dy}{dx} = 11 - 2x. \qquad (8.1)$$

Thus we can tabulate the value of the function, and its slope for various discrete values of x, as in Fig. 8.1, which shows the graphs of the production function and its derivative.

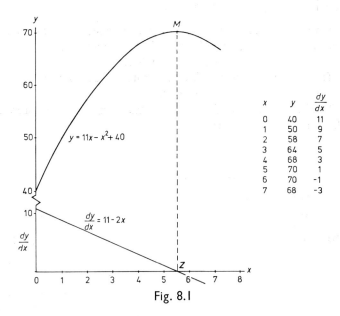

x	y	$\dfrac{dy}{dx}$
0	40	11
1	50	9
2	58	7
3	64	5
4	68	3
5	70	1
6	70	-1
7	68	-3

Fig. 8.1

As we have already seen, as x is increased, the corresponding value of y at first increases rapidly, that is, the function is steep (has a large slope) for low values of x. As x increases further, the slope of the function declines. At the top of the hill (i.e., at the maximum point) the function is perfectly flat (i.e., has a zero slope). Thereafter it slopes downhill, and its gradient, as shown by the derivative, is negative.

It is thus clear that the characteristic of the maximum point of the function is that *its slope at this point is zero*. The point Z, where the graph of the derivative crosses the horizontal axis in Fig. 8.1 (i.e., the point where $dy/dx = 0$), is clearly identical with the point M, where the function $y = f(x)$ reaches its maximum.

Let us actually calculate the point at which this maximum is reached. Noting that the slope (or derivative) of the function is zero at the maximum point, we simply equate dy/dx in Equation (8.1) to zero. Accordingly we obtain $11 - 2x = 0$, so that $x = 5\frac{1}{2}$. In other words, our production function reaches its maximum value at the point where $x = 5\frac{1}{2}$.

It is also evident, by substituting $x = 5\frac{1}{2}$ into the production function, that the corresponding level of y is: $y = 11(5\frac{1}{2}) - (5\frac{1}{2})^2 + 40 = 70\frac{1}{4}$. The coordinates of the maximum point are thus $x = 5\frac{1}{2}; y = 70\frac{1}{4}$, or $(5\frac{1}{2}, 70\frac{1}{4})$. Check these results in Fig. 8.1.

In general, for any "smooth" function possessing a maximum point, we can find this maximum by differentiating the function, equating the derivative to zero and solving the resulting equation. For the example we have just been discussing, the maximum level of total output obtainable is $70\frac{1}{4}$ centals of grain, achieved with a fertiliser input of $5\frac{1}{2}$ kg per hectare.

8.3 A Minimisation Example

Suppose we know that, for a particular firm, average total costs are a function of output as expressed by the following equation:

$$AC = 2y^2 - 25y + 150 \qquad (8.2)$$

where AC = average costs in dollars per unit of output; and
$\quad\quad\quad y$ = level of output in units.

Fig. 8.2 shows the curve derived from this average cost equation. The curve has the familiar U-shape.

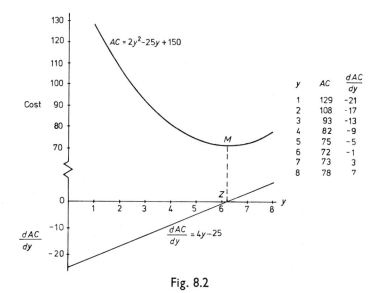

y	AC	$\dfrac{dAC}{dy}$
1	129	-21
2	108	-17
3	93	-13
4	82	-9
5	75	-5
6	72	-1
7	73	3
8	78	7

Fig. 8.2

Suppose we wish to determine at what level of the firm's output average costs are minimised. From the graph we can see that the lowest point on the AC curve is at M, and the level of output at this point (read from the horizontal axis) is a little over 6 units.

Now consider the derivative of Equation (8.2) which, using the usual rules, we calculate as:

$$\frac{dAC}{dy} = 4y - 25. \qquad (8.3)$$

This derivative is graphed in the lower section of Fig. 8.2. Notice that the derivative is negative at first, indicating that the AC curve is sloping downhill. As AC approaches its minimum it gets flatter, that is, its slope gets smaller and dAC/dy approaches zero. At M the AC curve is perfectly flat, with zero slope and therefore zero derivative as shown by point Z. Rightwards from M, the AC curve begins to climb uphill and dAC/dy therefore becomes positive.

Thus again we have a "turning point", in this case a minimum point, where the derivative of the function is zero. For our example, we may calculate the exact point where AC reaches its minimum by determining the value of y which makes dAC/dy equal to zero. Equating (8.3) to zero, we have

$$4y - 25 = 0,$$
$$y = 6\tfrac{1}{4} \text{ units.}$$

At this output, the level of AC is determined by substitution into Equation (8.2):

$$AC = 2(6\tfrac{1}{4})^2 - 25(6\tfrac{1}{4}) + 150$$
$$= 71\tfrac{7}{8} = \$71.88.$$

Check these results with Fig. 8.2.

8.4 Distinguishing Between Maximum and Minimum

8.4.1 SECOND DERIVATIVES: AN INTUITIVE EXPLANATION

The previous sections used the same technique for finding a minimum of a function as for finding a maximum, namely, equating the derivative to zero. How is one to know whether it is a maximum or a minimum which one has found by this method? The answer is to look at the behaviour of the derivative.

(a) In our first example, as we move from the origin along the horizontal axis of Fig. 8.1 taking successively larger values of the variable x, the derivative of the function is *positive* and *decreasing* in absolute value. Now we know that, because the derivative is positive, the function at first must slope "uphill". But consider the significance of the fact that the derivative is also decreasing in absolute value: this means that the hill becomes less steep. If we are walking up a hill that is continually getting flatter, we must be approaching a summit, i.e., a maximum.

(b) In our second example, the derivative at first is *negative* and *decreasing* in absolute value for successively larger values of x. Again, in simpler language, we know (because the derivative is negative) that the function must slope "downhill". But once more the derivative is also decreasing in absolute value, indicating that the function is simultaneously becoming less steep. If we are walking down a hill that is continually getting flatter, we must be approaching the floor of a valley, i.e., a minimum.

8.4.2 SECOND DERIVATIVES: A MORE RIGOROUS EXPLANATION

How could these criteria for judging a maximum or minimum be stated in more formal terms?

As may be clearly observed in Fig. 8.1, in the case of a *maximum* the function is increasing before the maximum point and decreasing after, so that the *derivative* of the function must be *positive before and negative after* passing through zero. The graph of the derivative slopes *downwards* as it passes through zero. Thus the *slope* of the *derivative* itself must be *negative* as it passes through zero.

In the case of a *minimum*, as in Fig. 8.2, the original AC function is decreasing before the minimum point and increasing after. Hence the *derivative* of the function must be *negative before and positive after* passing through zero. The graph of the derivative slopes *upwards* as it passes through zero. That is to say, the *slope* of the *derivative* itself must be positive as it passes through zero.

As we have already seen, the slope of a function is given by its derivative. Now a derivative itself is a function. In the case of our two examples we have:

$$\text{derivative of Equation (8.1)} = \frac{dy}{dx} = 11 - 2x;$$

$$\text{derivative of Equation (8.3)} = \frac{dAC}{dy} = 4y - 25.$$

These are referred to as *first derivatives* of the original functions.

In each example the *slope of the derivative* can be found by differentiating the derivative function itself. Taking the derivatives of the derivatives we get:

derivative of $11 - 2x = -2$ (negative, hence a maximum has been reached where $dy/dx = 0$);

derivative of $4y - 25 = 4$ (positive, hence a minimum has been reached where $dAC/dy = 0$).

These results, obtained by twice differentiating the original functions, are called *second-order derivatives*, or simply *second derivatives*.

Second derivatives can be represented by a variety of symbolic forms. Because the second derivatives of Equations (8.1) and (8.3) are equivalent to the operations $\frac{d(dy)}{dx(dx)}$ and $\frac{d(dAC)}{dy(dy)}$ respectively, we can "remove brackets" so to speak, and write them quite compactly as $\frac{d^2y}{dx^2}$ and $\frac{d^2AC}{dy^2}$.

Applying these expressions, we have for our examples:

$$\frac{d^2y}{dx^2} = -2; \qquad \frac{d^2AC}{dy^2} = 4.$$

Alternatively, since the first derivative of $y = f(x)$ is sometimes written as $f'(x)$, the second derivative is sometimes referred to as $f''(x)$. We use exactly the same differentiation rules to determine second derivatives as we have already studied in the case of first derivatives.

Statements of maximum and minimum conditions in terms of the signs of the second derivatives are called *second-order* conditions.

8.5 A More Complicated Example

Suppose that over a period of years a certain firm has observed that output per man day is a function of the number of men employed. It has been found that if there is only one employee, efficiency is fairly low. It is even lower if there are two or three workmen, because they spend too much time talking. Further increases in the workforce enable economies in machinery usage to be achieved and, therefore, improvements in labour productivity; but beyond a certain point diseconomies prevail and average output per man again begins to decline.

Suppose that the relationship between output per man-day and labour input can be expressed by the function

$$v = -\tfrac{1}{3}m^3 + 6m^2 - 27m + 50 \qquad (8.4)$$

where v = efficiency of labour measured in units of output per man-day; and

m = number of men employed.

The graph of this function is shown in the upper part of Fig. 8.3. Observe that the function has *both* a minimum *and* a maximum point within the range plotted on the figure. Let us work out the values of m which maximise and minimise the function.

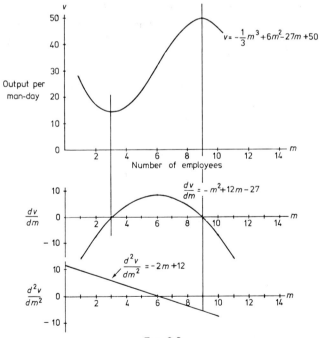

Fig. 8.3

Firstly, determine the *first derivative* of the function. We obtain:

$$\frac{dv}{dm} = -1m^2 + 12m - 27. \qquad (8.5)$$

Thus, the first derivative is a quadratic. It is graphed in the middle part of Fig. 8.3.

Next, in order to find either a minimum and/or maximum point on the function (8.4) we equate its first derivative to zero. Setting Equation (8.5) to zero gives:

$$-1m^2 + 12m - 27 = 0, \qquad (8.6)$$

which has two solutions, $m = 3$ and $m = 9$.†

Thus we can say that the function has two turning points, one where $m = 3$ and the other where $m = 9$. Are they maxima or minima? To find out, we evaluate the *second derivative* of Equation (8.5), by taking the derivative of Equation (8.6). Differentiating (8.6) with respect to m gives:

$$\frac{d^2v}{dm^2} = -2m + 12. \qquad (8.7)$$

What is the sign of the second derivative at each of our calculated extreme points? By substitution into Equation (8.7) we obtain:

When $m = 3$, $\dfrac{d^2v}{dm^2} = (-2 \times 3) + 12 = +6$;

When $m = 9$, $\dfrac{d^2v}{dm^2} = (-2 \times 9) + 12 = -6$.

Thus, at the extreme point where $m = 3$, $d^2v/dm^2 > 0$ (is positive), indicating that this extreme point is a minimum. Similarly at the extreme point where $m = 9$, $d^2v/dm^2 < 0$ (is negative), indicating that this extreme point is a maximum. The second derivative is graphed in the third part of Fig. 8.3.

Verify this result in Fig. 8.3, and as an exercise calculate the minimum and maximum levels of output per man that the firm could expect to achieve if it employed 3 and 9 men respectively.

8.6 Local and Global Extrema

In defining the maximum or minimum of a given function, we may need to ask the question: is a particular extremum the highest or lowest point over the *whole range* of variation of the two variables? For instance, look at the function $y = f(x)$ depicted in the top part of Fig. 8.4. It rises to a peak at point A, then falls away, rising to a higher peak at point C. The peak at point A is called a *local* or *relative maximum* because it is a maximum of the function $y = f(x)$ only over a limited range of variation of x (say for x in the range OD). On the other hand, suppose we know from the nature of $y = f(x)$ that C is the highest point the function reaches, whatever the size of x. Then we call the maximum at point C a *global* or *absolute maximum* since it is the highest point on $y = f(x)$ for the whole range of variation of x (that is, for x in the range of $-\infty$ to $+\infty$).

---

† The solution of quadratic equations is considered in Appendix A, Section 2.

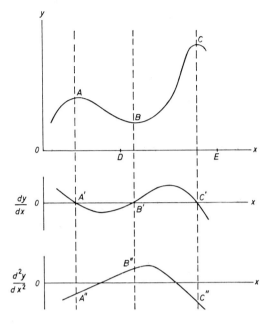

Fig. 8.4

Now look at dy/dx plotted in the middle section of Fig. 8.4. Observe that the conditions for the existence of an extreme point are fulfilled in the case of both local and global extrema. In other words, $dy/dx = 0$ at the points A', B' and C' corresponding to the extrema A, B, and C respectively. Furthermore, the second-order conditions are also all fulfilled, as can be seen from the graph of the second derivative at the bottom of Fig. 8.4. We see $d^2y/dx^2 < 0$ at the points A'' and C'' corresponding to the maxima A and C, and $d^2y/dx^2 > 0$ at B'' corresponding to the minimum B.

It is therefore apparent that the first- and second-order conditions for the existence of an extreme point, which we have outlined in this chapter, are incapable of distinguishing between local and global extrema. In fact, it is obvious that all maxima (minima) are local maxima (minima) and the global maximum (minimum) just happens to be the highest (lowest) out of all the local maxima (minima). Thus the first- and second-order conditions discussed above may be regarded as applying to the search for local or relative extrema.

The problem remains, however, of identifying a global extremum. One simple way is to compare all the local maxima (minima) and take the highest (lowest). Thus, in terms of Fig. 8.4, if we knew that A and C were the only relative maxima, we could determine C as the global maximum by showing that the value of $f(x)$ at C is greater than its value at A. Alternatively, more complicated mathematical methods may be used in the search for global extrema; they are, however, beyond our present scope.

8.7 Functions Without a Maximum and/or Minimum

Earlier we examined a firm's total cost function, which happened to be linear. It was of the form

$$TC = 400 + 3y \qquad (8.8)$$

where TC = total costs; and
$\qquad y$ = level of output.

The first and second derivatives of this function are respectively:

$$\frac{dTC}{dy} = 3 \qquad (8.9a)$$

$$\frac{d^2TC}{dy^2} = 0. \qquad (8.9b)$$

To find a maximum or minimum of Equation (8.8), we need to equate its first derivative (Equation (8.9a)) to zero. But this is impossible. Hence, as is intuitively obvious, a linear function has no maximum or minimum if the variables are allowed to vary over an indefinitely large range.

In practice, however, there may be limits placed on the variables. For example, negative output is infeasible for this firm, hence we are only interested in the values of Equation (8.8) for $y \geqslant 0$.† Similarly, the firm's short-run output might be constrained by size of plant to, say, 500 units of output. If so, for practical purposes values of y in excess of 500 are also infeasible.

We could therefore define *relative* maxima and minima for Equation (8.8) for the range $0 \leqslant y \leqslant 500$ as being the *end points* of the function in this range. In Fig. 8.5, where the function (8.8) is graphed, the segment AB

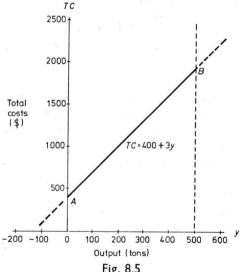

Fig. 8.5

---

† The sign $\geqslant$ indicates "is equal to or greater than"; thus $y \geqslant 0$ reads "y is equal to or greater than zero". Similarly, the sign $\leqslant$ indicates "is equal to or less than".

is the area of interest. The end points of $TC = f(y)$ over the range $0 \leqslant y \leqslant 500$ are A, which is a relative minimum, and B, which is a relative maximum.

Now look at the quadratic production function discussed above in Section 8.2. Its first and second derivatives are as follows:

$$\frac{dy}{dx} = 11 - 2x \qquad (8.10\text{a})$$

$$\frac{d^2 y}{dx^2} = -2. \qquad (8.10\text{b})$$

The second derivative (8.10b) is a *negative* constant. Since the second-order condition for the existence of a *minimum* of a function is that the second derivative be *positive*, we can see that the original production function can never have a minimum turning point. It has a single maximum turning point. As discovered earlier, this occurs where $x = 5\frac{1}{2}$.

Nevertheless, if we wished to restrict our consideration to, say, non-negative levels of output (i.e., $y \geqslant 0$), a relative minimum could be defined at an end point of this function for the range of non-negative input levels $0 \leqslant x \leqslant x^*$. It is left as an exercise for the reader to calculate that $x^* = 13.88$ in this particular case. At this point, the production curve cuts the horizontal axis.

8.8 Summary

The condition for the existence of a local extreme turning point for a function $y = f(x)$ is

$$\frac{dy}{dx} = 0.$$

This turning point is:

• a maximum if $\dfrac{d^2 y}{dx^2} < 0$;

• a minimum if $\dfrac{d^2 y}{dx^2} > 0$.

A local maximum or minimum of a function may possibly exist at an end point of the function if a restricted range of variation of the variables is specified.

Exercises

1. A consumer's utility function for beer is given by the function:
$$U = 150 + 35b - 2b^2$$
   where $b =$ daily consumption in litres. What level of intake of beer per day will maximise this consumer's utility?

2. Show that the extreme point found in Exercise 1 above is a maximum and not a minimum.

3. Suppose a firm's total cost equation is
$$TC = y^3 - 10y^2 - 40y$$
where $y =$ units of output. Use this example to demonstrate the general fact that the MC curve cuts the AC curve at the latter's minimum point.

4. Show that the Cobb-Douglas function in Equation (5.6) continues to increase while L increases without reaching a maximum point for finite L.

5. Prove that the firm considered in Exercise 6, Chapter 7, can never attain a global minimum point on its average cost curve.

6. Calculate the level of output at which average product is maximised for a firm whose production function is

$$y = 5L^2 - \frac{L^3}{6}$$

where $y =$ level of output in units; and
$\quad\quad L =$ labour input in units.

Check the second-order conditions to ensure a maximum has been found.

7. For the example in the previous exercise, show that the MP curve passes through the maximum point on the AP curve.

Chapter 9

The Use of Simple Derivatives in Economic Optimisation

9.1 Economic Optimisation

9.1.1 THE OBJECTIVE FUNCTION

At the beginning of the last chapter, mention was made of the link between mathematical extremisation and economic optimisation. Problems frequently arise in economics whereby the maximisation or minimisation of some objective is required.

What exactly should be maximised or minimised in a particular piece of economic analysis? In practice, this is often an exceedingly difficult question to answer. A great deal depends on the context of the analysis. Should a firm maximise its short-run profits or should it operate at a loss by lowering its selling price, driving off potential competitors and perhaps strengthening its long-run monopoly powers? What should the community maximise in its production—cars, guns, or solely those products which do not lead to pollution of the environment? Should a government minimise inflation or minimise unemployment?

Quite frequently, the objective to be maximised or minimised can be specified only in terms of *value judgments*, that is, *opinions* as to what is "best". Suppose, for example, we all agree that society is better off when it minimises environmental pollution. The economist can then study all the factors related to pollution and subsequently describe the pattern of resource utilisation that fulfils this objective, thereby spelling out (according to the above value judgment) the necessary conditions for society's economic optimum. Again, if we are prepared to accept profit maximisation as a social objective, then the economist can proceed to analyse the cost and revenue functions of firms and state the conditions under which an economic optimum (i.e., maximum profit) occurs. On the other hand, if we think that society is in the best situation when output is sold at minimum average cost, then the minimisation of average cost would become the "proper" objective to pursue.

The economist, like everybody else, has his own personal value judgments about what is "good" and "bad" in the area of economic policy at micro or macro levels. In certain circumstances he may be free to incorporate his own value judgments in a particular piece of research or analysis, although he should always be sure to emphasise the premises upon which he specifies an optimum. In other circumstances the economist cannot commit himself to any particular set of doctrinal beliefs, but must accept the value judgments provided for him by an appropriate higher institution. For example, an economist engaged in studying policy problems for a government or large corporation is usually obliged to accept those criteria of what is "best" for the country or the firm that are handed down to him by his employers.

In quantitative terms, the maximisation or minimisation of some objective can be interpreted to mean the maximisation or minimisation of a function involving economic variables. This function may be referred to as the *objective function*. Thus, for example, the objective function of a firm may be the maximisation of profits. A consumer's objective function will usually be the maximisation of utility. And society itself will undoubtedly try, in one way or another, to maximise its economic welfare.†

9.1.2 UNCONSTRAINED OPTIMISATION

In simple cases, the function to be maximised or minimised itself possesses a maximum or minimum, and is subject to no other restrictions over the range of variation in its value. By way of illustration, let us reconsider the average cost function for the firm discussed in Section 8.3. Suppose we wish to maximise the social efficiency of the firm's production, taking this to be the minimisation of average cost. Hence our problem is to minimise average cost (the objective function) which itself is a function of output. We do not impose any other restrictions over the solution. We do not, for example, insist that average cost must not fall below a certain value, such as \$85. As calculated in Section 8.3, the average cost function possesses a minimum value of \$71.88, which is arrived at when output is $6\frac{1}{4}$ units. Hence the necessary mathematical conditions for the firm's production to be socially optimal are that $AC = \$71.88$ and $y = 6\frac{1}{4}$.

In this example, the optimal solution is obtained merely by calculating the maximum or minimum value of the objective function, without any restrictions or constraints on the variables. Any problem of this kind is referred to as an *unconstrained optimisation problem*. It will be appreciated that, where such problems lend themselves to solution via the methods of the calculus, the mathematical theory of first and second derivatives outlined in the preceding chapter becomes an invaluable aid in discovering the necessary conditions for an optimum. We shall consider further examples of unconstrained optimisation problems in Section 9.2.

---

† There is a supposedly true account of a distinguished economist who visited an underdeveloped country and, in proffering advice on resource allocation, demanded of the authorities: "Describe your social welfare function"!

9.1.3 CONSTRAINED OPTIMISATION

One characteristic of extremisation in practical problems is that it can usually be achieved in only one direction at a time. For example, suppose I wish to travel from the university to the city centre by the *quickest* and *cheapest* means. Here we have an objective involving two "dimensions" of optimisation: speed and cost. Now it is unlikely (though in some cases not impossible) that a single mode of transport could optimise with respect to both of these objectives simultaneously. That is, the *quickest* method of getting to town might be by hiring a taxi or helicopter, but this is unlikely to be the cheapest solution. Likewise, the *cheapest* means of transport might be to walk, but this would be slower than other methods. It is just possible that hitchhiking, for instance, might prove to be *both* quickest *and* cheapest, but this will not necessarily be so, and in general it is unlikely that a single mode of transport will be able to optimise in respect of both objectives at once.

Similar problems arise in economics. Minimising inflation, for example, generally conflicts with the objective of minimising unemployment; it is most unlikely that a given package of monetary and fiscal policies will be able *both* to minimise unemployment *and* minimise the rate of inflation. Yet how often do we hear of politicians promising to do just this, and possibly also to maximise the rate of growth as well!

This dilemma involves what is often called a *tradeoff situation*. That is, in order to arrive at a resolution of the problem, we have to trade one objective off against another. For example, in getting to town on foot we may swap some speed for extra cheapness. Similarly, in choosing economic policies, there is a tradeoff between keeping the rate of inflation down and preventing the level of unemployment from rising too far.

One way of resolving a tradeoff problem is to specify a given acceptable level for one or more objectives such that only one is left to be optimised. For example, we could rephrase the transport problem as "I want the quickest means of getting to town provided it does not cost more than 50 cents", or "I want the cheapest means of getting to town which will get me there in less than a half-hour". Again, a policy-maker may determine, say, a permissible upper level of unemployment, and attempt to formulate a strategy which will minimise inflation within this constraint.

With problems of this kind, so-called *side conditions* or *constraints* are introduced that restrict the range of possible values the objective function may take. To find the optimal solution we must accordingly maximise or minimise the objective function subject to whatever constraints are relevant. We refer to any problem of this variety as a *constrained optimisation* problem.

Economics abounds in constrained optimisation problems. The community as a whole endeavours to maximise the satisfaction of economic wants, subject to the limitations of given resources and technology. Producers aim to minimise costs, subject to certain factor-price and output considerations. And consumers try to maximise utility subject to their budget allowances. We shall consider some numerical examples of constrained optimisation problems in Sections 9.3 and 9.4.

9.2 Some Examples of Unconstrained Optimisation
9.2.1 REVENUE MAXIMISATION OF A MONOPOLIST

Take the problem of a monopolist who has a large stockpile of eggs and whose objective is to maximise total sales revenue. His economic optimum will be reached when he sells just that quantity at which his total revenue is as great as possible; we assume he is quite unconcerned if some eggs must be dumped, rather than "spoil the market". Here we have a simple example of an unconstrained optimisation problem: find the volume of sales which maximises the monopolist's total revenue function.

Assume the market price the monopolist is able to charge is given by the linear market demand function:

$$p = 500 - 2q \qquad (9.1)$$

where p = price of eggs in cents per hundred; and
       q = the quantity of eggs offered for sale in hundreds.

Total revenue is thus

$$TR = pq. \qquad (9.2)$$

Substituting for p we get:

$$TR = (500 - 2q)q$$
$$= 500q - 2q^2. \qquad (9.3)$$

To maximise total revenue we differentiate Equation (9.3) and equate the result to zero:

$$\frac{dTR}{dq} = 500 - 4q = 0 \qquad (9.4)$$

so that

$$q = 125.$$

The quantity which the monopolist should sell to achieve his economic optimum is thus 125 hundred eggs.

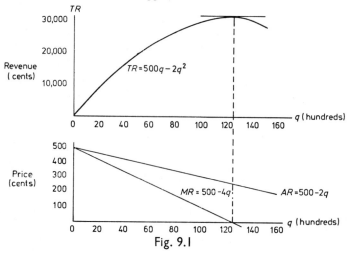

Fig. 9.1

This problem is described in graphical form in Fig. 9.1. Diagrammatically, we may think of the above optimisation process as bringing us to the top of the monopolist's total revenue "hill". Note that if we take the second derivative of the function (9.3), that is, differentiate the first derivative (9.4), we get:

$$\frac{d^2 TR}{dq^2} = -4.$$

The second derivative is negative, proving that in fact a maximum has been reached.

9.2.2 PROFIT MAXIMISATION UNDER PERFECT COMPETITION

Let us consider the case of a firm operating under perfect competition that faces a cost function described by Equation (7.24), which was of the form:

$$TC = 30 + 15y - 5y^2 + \tfrac{2}{3}y^3. \tag{9.5}$$

Suppose also that the firm's total revenue function is given by the following:

$$TR = 14y. \tag{9.6}$$

Under the usual assumption that the firm's objective is to maximise profits, we again have an unconstrained optimisation problem and can proceed to determine the short-run equilibrium output level. We define profit or net revenue (NR) as the difference between TR and TC. Writing Equation (9.6) *minus* Equation (9.5), we get:

$$NR = TR - TC = 14y - (30 + 15y - 5y^2 + \tfrac{2}{3}y^3) \tag{9.7}$$

which simplifies to:

$$NR = -30 - y + 5y^2 - \tfrac{2}{3}y^3. \tag{9.8}$$

To maximise NR, we set its first derivative to zero. Differentiating Equation (9.8) with respect to y gives:

$$\frac{dNR}{dy} = -1 + 10y - 2y^2. \tag{9.9}$$

Setting the RHS of Equation (9.9) to zero and rearranging, yields the quadratic equation

$$2y^2 - 10y + 1 = 0 \tag{9.10}$$

which we shall solve presently.

First, however, we must note the alternative means of determining the profit-maximising position by using the *equimarginal* principle. This principle states that output of the firm should be expanded (contracted) as long as each extra unit of output is bringing in a return which is greater (less) than the extra cost incurred. That is, while $MR > MC$, output should be expanded, and while $MR < MC$, output should be contracted. The point of maximum profit is given where $MR = MC$, that is, where the revenue from the last unit of output just covers the extra cost. For our example, equating MR with MC involves equating the derivatives of Equations (9.5) and (9.6). Thus we find the profit-maximising position where

$$14 = 15 - 10y + 2y^2, \qquad (9.11)$$

which simplifies to the same quadratic equation as we obtained above, namely, Equation (9.10).

The two solutions to Equation (9.10) are $y = 0.102$ and $y = 4.898$, indicating that the NR function reaches an extremum at both of these levels of output.† At which point is profit *maximised*? By evaluating the second derivative of Equation (9.8) we obtain:

$$\frac{d^2 NR}{dy^2} = 10 - 4y \qquad (9.12)$$

which, we can easily see, has a positive value when $y = 0.102$, and a negative value when $y = 4.898$. Thus, at the former point NR reaches a *minimum*, and at the latter attains a *maximum*. Hence, for this firm the short-run equilibrium position where profits are maximised is at an output of 4.898 units.

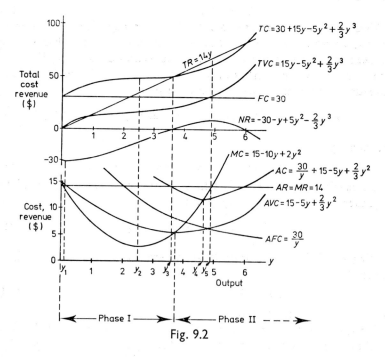

Fig. 9.2

These results are confirmed graphically in Fig. 9.2 where the cost and revenue curves are superimposed. The short-run profit-maximising output level (shown as the point y_5) is given where:

---

† The solution of quadratic equations is discussed in Appendix A, Section 2.

- the vertical distance between TR and TC is greatest;
- the NR curve is at a maximum; and
- $MR = MC$ when MC is rising (the latter is a statement of the second-order condition for profit maximisation, which is equivalent to that attaching to the NR function).

Notice, in addition to the above, the following points about Fig. 9.2:

- when $MC = MR$ and the MC curve is *falling*, NR is minimised (point y_1);
- when MC reaches a minimum, TC and TVC pass through an inflection point and their slopes start increasing (point y_2);
- when $TC = TR$, NR is zero and $AC = AR$ (point y_3);
- MC cuts AC at its minimum point (point y_4); according to the theory of perfect competition, this point will be the equilibrium level of output of the firm in the long run;
- Phases I and II, corresponding to Phases I and II of the underlying production function given constant input prices, are marked on the diagram.

9.2.3 PROFIT MAXIMISATION UNDER IMPERFECT COMPETITION

Suppose a producer in a market exhibiting imperfect competition faces a demand curve for his product given by

$$q = 5 - \tfrac{1}{3}p. \tag{9.13}$$

Since the quantity demanded (q) is equivalent to output (y), we can write y for q and rearrange Equation (9.13) to get

$$p = 15 - 3y. \tag{9.14}$$

Suppose also that the producer has an upward-sloping linear average total cost curve given by the equation

$$AC = 2y. \tag{9.15}$$

Figure 9.3 shows these two functions.

The producer's optimum output point can be found as the solution to an unconstrained maximisation problem.

The firm's net revenue equation is calculated as follows:

$$TR = py = (15 - 3y)y = 15y - 3y^2, \tag{9.16}$$
$$TC = (AC)y = (2y)y = 2y^2, \tag{9.17}$$
$$\text{Hence } NR = TR - TC = (15y - 3y^2) - 2y^2$$
$$= 15y - 5y^2. \tag{9.18}$$

To maximise profit (NR), we must equate the derivative of the NR function to zero. We determine

$$\frac{dNR}{dy} = 15 - 10y \tag{9.19}$$

and set this to zero, which yields $y = 1\tfrac{1}{2}$. Thus the output level at which the producer maximises profit is $1\tfrac{1}{2}$ units.

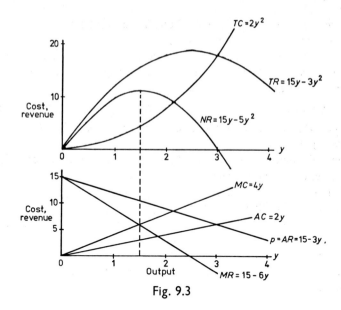

Fig. 9.3

This result may be confirmed by calculating the point at which $MC = MR$.

$$\text{From } TC \text{ we get } MC = \frac{dTC}{dy} = 4y, \qquad (9.20)$$

$$\text{From } TR \text{ we get } MR = \frac{dTR}{dy} = 15 - 6y. \qquad (9.21)$$

Hence maximum profit is achieved where

$$4y = 15 - 6y,$$

which gives $y = 1\frac{1}{2}$ as before. This result is verified graphically in Fig. 9.3.

The price charged by the producer is found by substituting $y = 1\frac{1}{2}$ into Equation (9.14):

$$p = 15 - (3 \times 1\frac{1}{2}) = \$10\frac{1}{2}.$$

By a similar process the reader may, as an exercise, work out the equilibrium levels of AC ($\$3$), TR ($\$15\frac{3}{4}$), TC ($\$4\frac{1}{2}$) and NR ($\$11\frac{1}{4}$).

9.3 Some Examples of Constrained Optimisation
9.3.1 COST MINIMISATION

We now encounter our first example of a constrained optimisation problem. In Section 7.2.4 we considered the case of a newspaper publisher employing inputs of labour (L) and capital (K). To produce a given volume of output, labour and capital may be substituted for each other according to the isoquant equation

$$K = \frac{100}{L^2} + 30. \qquad (9.22)$$

Let us imagine that the costs per unit of the two inputs, labour and capital, are w and r respectively. Then we can write the total costs of the newspaper publisher, for any input levels of L and K, as

$$TC = wL + rK. \tag{9.23}$$

Suppose that in this example a unit of labour costs $6 and a unit of capital costs $3. The TC function thus becomes

$$TC = 6L + 3K. \tag{9.24}$$

Equation (9.24) is called an *isocost equation*. To see why it commands this title, let us rearrange (9.24) to obtain K in terms of L:

$$K = \frac{TC}{3} - 2L. \tag{9.25}$$

For a given level of total cost we get a unique linear relationship between K and L. This is shown in Fig. 9.4. The graph of Equation (9.25) (or equivalently, of Equation (9.24)) for a given value of TC yields a straight line with intercept $TC/3$ and slope -2. Isocost lines for TC levels of $240 and $180 are indicated on the diagram. It is apparent that the smaller the value of TC, the closer the isocost line to the origin.

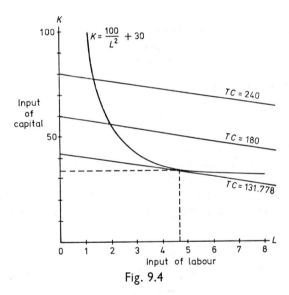

Fig. 9.4

Now the entrepreneur's short-run decision problem may be seen as one of minimising total cost, subject to the condition that the output volume described by the isoquant Equation (9.22) be met. Algebraically, our objective function is thus Equation (9.24) and the relevant side condition or constraint is Equation (9.22). Graphically, in minimising total cost we must try to find the isocost line nearest to the origin. Without the isoquant constraint, of course, the lowest possible isocost line (given $K,L \geqslant 0$) would be that passing *through* the origin, which implies no production of newspapers at all! To meet the required output target and simultaneously minimise total cost, we seek the isocost line that is nearest to the origin but that still touches the isoquant. It is clear that the required isocost line is the one which is a tangent to the isoquant.

The variables in the objective function, L and K, are the same as those in the side condition. What the newspaper publisher must determine, in establishing his economic optimum, are the quantities of labour and capital he should purchase so that his total cost is minimised and his target level of output fulfilled. In other words, the solution of our constrained optimisation problem involves calculating the values of L and K at the tangency point of the isoquant and isocost lines.

We know that at the tangency point the slopes of the isoquant and isocost lines are equal. Now the slope of the isoquant is given by the derivative of Equation (9.22) and that of the isocost line by the derivative of (9.25). Thus, by differentiating K with respect to L in both the objective function and the isocost function, and equating the results, we obtain the required solution.

The first derivative of Equation (9.25) is

$$\frac{dK}{dL} = -2. \tag{9.26}$$

The first derivative of Equation (9.22) is

$$\frac{dK}{dL} = -\frac{200}{L^3}. \tag{9.27}$$

Equating these we see that:

$$-\frac{200}{L^3} = -2 \tag{9.28}$$

whence $L^3 = 100$ so that $L = 4.642$. The corresponding level of K is calculated, by substitution into Equation (9.22), as 34.642.

The tangency solution is illustrated in Fig. 9.4.

By substituting these values for L and K into the isocost Equation (9.24), we can calculate the minimum permissible value of the objective function, as follows:

$$TC = 6(4.642) + 3(34.642)$$
$$= \$131.778.$$

More generally, observe that Equation (9.23) may be rearranged to give:

$$K = \frac{TC}{r} - \frac{wL}{r}. \tag{9.29}$$

Hence the slope of the isocost line can be expressed as the derivative of Equation (9.29),

$$\frac{dK}{dL} = -\frac{w}{r}, \tag{9.30}$$

that is, the negative ratio of input prices.

In Section 7.2.4, however, we saw that dK/dL also represents the slope of the isoquant, or the marginal rate of technical substitution (RTS) of

L for K. Hence the necessary condition for any firm facing the above constrained optimisation problem may be stated as the equilibrium condition

$$RTS = \frac{dK}{dL} = -\frac{w}{r}. \tag{9.31}$$

To reach an economic optimum:

- if $RTS > \frac{w}{r}$ in absolute terms, increase L and decrease K;

- if $R\ \ TS < \frac{w}{r}$ in absolute terms, decrease L and expand K;

- if $RTS = -\frac{w}{r}$, equilibrium is obtained.

9.3.2 THE MULTIPRODUCT FIRM

Let us refer again to the firm producing cigarettes (u) and cigars (v) from a fixed bundle of resources, as described in Section 7.2.5. The firm's product transformation curve, or production possibility curve, is given as:

$$u = 32 - \tfrac{1}{2}v^3. \tag{9.32}$$

By differentiating the function (9.32) we obtain the slope of the curve, that is, the marginal rate of transformation (MRT) of u into v:

$$MRT = \frac{du}{dv} = -\tfrac{3}{2}v^2. \tag{9.33}$$

Let us assume the firm supplies each product to a perfectly competitive market, and is thus a price taker. We can represent the fixed prices of cigarettes and cigars as p_u and p_v respectively.

Now the firm's daily revenue is simply the sum of the separate revenues earned by selling the two products; that is,

$$TR = p_u u + p_v v. \tag{9.34}$$

On the assumption that the price of cigarettes is $15 per thousand and the price of cigars is $150 per thousand, the firm's total revenue function becomes

$$TR = 15u + 150v. \tag{9.35}$$

Since the firm's factors of production are fixed in supply, we can take total cost as being constant. Therefore, if the firm's aim is to maximise profit, all we need to do is determine the conditions under which total revenue is maximised. The objective function to be maximised is thus Equation (9.35).

Equation (9.35) describes all combinations of u and v yielding a given level of total revenue, and is called an *isorevenue equation*. Rearranging, we obtain u in terms of v as follows:

$$u = \frac{TR}{15} - 10v. \tag{9.36}$$

For a particular value of TR, Equation (9.36) gives rise to a single *isorevenue line* when plotted as a graph. So, for example, if $TR = \$150$, we get $u = 10 - 10v$; if $TR = \$300$, the isorevenue equation becomes $u = 20 - 10v$; and so on. The two isorevenue lines corresponding to $TR = \$150$ and $\$300$ are shown in Fig. 9.5.

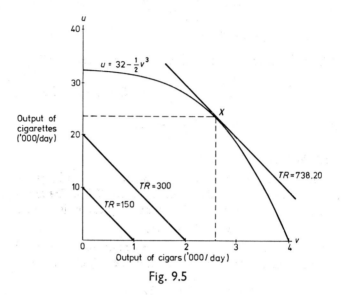

Fig. 9.5

It is clear that, as total revenue increases, the isorevenue line moves outwards from the origin of Fig. 9.5. In order to maximise revenue we must move it outwards as far as possible. How far can this be? The limit is set by the production possibility curve. Hence, once again we have a constrained optimisation problem. Specifically, it is of the form: maximise the total revenue function (9.35) subject to the product transformation constraint (9.32).

The isorevenue line furthest from the origin is that which is a tangent to the production possibility curve, as shown at point X in Fig. 9.5. We know that the tangent to a curve at any point has the same slope as the curve at that point. So if we wish to find where the isorevenue line is a tangent to the production possibility curve, we simply equate their slopes. The slope of any isorevenue line, for our given product prices, is immediately seen from Equation (9.36) to be -10. The slope of the production possibility curve has already been calculated in Equation (9.33). Therefore, the point of tangency is given where these slopes are equal:

$$-\tfrac{3}{2}v^2 = -10$$

from which we obtain

$$v^2 = \frac{20}{3},$$

$$v = 2.583.$$

(Obviously we may ignore the negative root, -2.583, since it represents an infeasible output level.)

We have thus determined the equilibrium level of output of cigars for this firm to be 2.583 thousand per day, and by substitution into Equation (9.32) we find the optimum level of cigarette production to be 23.383 thousand. Finally, substitution into (9.35) enables us to calculate the total revenue of the firm at this combination of outputs as \$738.20.

To arrive at a more general summary of our conclusions, let us rearrange the total revenue Equation (9.34) to obtain

$$u = \frac{TR}{p_u} - \frac{p_v v}{p_u}. \tag{9.37}$$

The slope of this isorevenue equation can be calculated as

$$\frac{du}{dv} = -\frac{p_v}{p_u}. \tag{9.38}$$

Remembering that du/dv is the marginal rate of transformation (MRT), we see that for this model an economic optimum will be attained when MRT is equal to the negative ratio of product prices. The firm will accordingly discover that it is worth producing an extra unit of v if the gain from doing so is greater than the loss from those extra units of u that have to be sacrificed. In other words,

- if $MRT > \dfrac{p_v}{p_u}$, in absolute terms, expand v, contract u;

- if $MRT < \dfrac{p_v}{p_u}$, in absolute terms, contract v, expand u;

- if $MRT = -\dfrac{p_v}{p_u}$, equilibrium is obtained.

9.3.3 LONG-RUN EQUILIBRIUM IN MONOPOLISTIC COMPETITION

Suppose a firm in an industry featuring monopolistic competition has an average cost curve given by

$$AC = y^2 - 10y + 40 \tag{9.39}$$

where y is the volume of output.

In the short run, let us assume the demand curve of the firm takes the form

$$q = 14 - \frac{p}{3} \tag{9.40}$$

or, equivalently,

$$p = 42 - 3q \tag{9.41}$$

where $q = $ quantity demanded; and
$p = $ selling price.

Since q and y are identical, and since in any imperfectly competitive situation the firm's demand function is identical to its average revenue function, we can rewrite Equation (9.41) as

$$AR = 42 - 3y. \tag{9.42}$$

Total revenue in the short run is thus

$$TR = (AR)y$$
$$= (42 - 3y)y$$
$$= 42y - 3y^2. \tag{9.43}$$

Total cost is

$$TC = (AC)y$$
$$= (y^2 - 10y + 40)y$$
$$= y^3 - 10y^2 + 40y. \tag{9.44}$$

Hence total profit or net revenue becomes:

$$NR = TR - TC = 2y + 7y^2 - y^3. \tag{9.45}$$

The firm's *short-run* equilibrium can be found as the solution to an *unconstrained* optimisation problem. To maximise short-run profit we differentiate Equation (9.45) and equate the result to zero. Thus

$$2 + 14y - 3y^2 = 0. \tag{9.46}$$

From Equation (9.46) we discover that the firm's optimum short-run output level is 4.8 units.

This solution is illustrated in Fig. 9.6 where the short-run demand curve is DD. It is clear that at the short-run equilibrium output level, above-normal profits are received by the firm.†

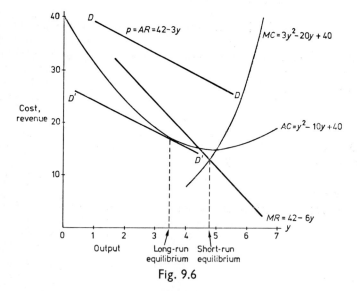

Fig. 9.6

In the long run, however, we may imagine new firms entering the industry, attracted by the excess profits being earned. Our firm's demand curve can therefore be expected to move leftwards as the firm gradually

---

† In the diagram, the short-run optimum has been determined in terms of the firm's marginal cost and marginal revenue curves, rather than a net profit curve. The reader should verify that the same result is obtained in either case.

loses its share of the market to other competitors. How far can this process continue? To simplify affairs, let us assume that the firm's demand curve shifts in parallel to the short-run curve DD. Imagine furthermore that the firm's cost curves remain constant. For the firm to stay in business, average revenue must not fall below average cost.

The firm's *long-run* equilibrium is thus the solution to a *constrained* optimisation problem. We must minimise the level of the average revenue curve subject to the side condition that $AR = AC$ where AC is given by Equation (9.39).

The solution emerges at a point on the AC curve where the demand curve $D'D'$ and the AC curve are tangential. Since, by assumption, the demand curve moves parallel to itself, its slope remains the same. Hence, long-run equilibrium will be found where the slope of the average revenue function is equal to the slope of the AC function.

Slope of AR is $\dfrac{dAR}{dy} = -3$.

Slope of AC is $\dfrac{dAC}{dy} = 2y - 10$.

Equilibrium arises where $2y - 10 = -3$ or $y = 3\frac{1}{2}$.

This solution is confirmed graphically in Fig. 9.6.

9.3.4 CONSUMER EQUILIBRIUM

In Section 7.3.2 we considered a consumer's indifference curve for oysters (s) and champagne (m) described by the equation

$$m = \frac{10}{s}. \tag{9.47}$$

Suppose the consumer wishes to determine the combination of oysters and champagne which will yield this constant level of satisfaction at least cost.

Taking the fixed prices of oysters and champagne as p_s and p_m respectively, we can write the consumer's required total outlay, for any purchases of s and m, as:

$$z = p_s s + p_m m. \tag{9.48}$$

The consumer's economic problem, an example of constrained optimisation, is to minimise the total outlay function (9.48), subject to a given level of satisfaction being attained as expressed by Equation (9.47).

By reasoning analogous to that used in Section 9.3.1 above, we can show that a tangency solution yields the minimum cost point, that is, the point where a line with the slope $-(p_s/p_m)$ just touches the indifference curve. To find this point we differentiate Equation (9.47) to get the slope of the indifference curve, i.e., the MRS of oysters for champagne:

$$MRS = \frac{dm}{ds} = -\frac{10}{s^2}. \tag{9.49}$$

We then equate the MRS with the price ratio $-(p_s/p_m)$.

For example, suppose a dozen oysters costs $1.20 and a glass of champagne (vintage) is priced at 90 cents. Then the price ratio is calculated as $-(1.2/0.9)$. Hence we can determine the optimum by solving:

$$-\frac{10}{s^2} = -\frac{1.2}{0.9} \tag{9.50}$$

which gives $s^2 = 7.5$, so that $s = 2.74$ (ignoring the negative root). By substitution back into Equation (9.47) we calculate the corresponding level of m to be 3.65.

Thus for the given price ratio, this consumer can achieve his required utility level at minimum cost by consuming 2.74 dozen oysters and 3.65 glasses of champagne per day.

The solution to this problem is presented in graphical form in Fig. 9.7.

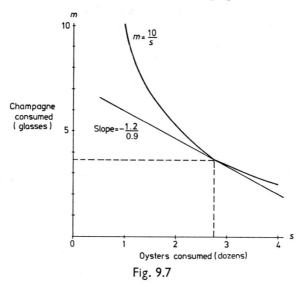

Fig. 9.7

Exercises

1. The firm studied in Exercise 3, Chapter 8, faces a short-run demand curve given by:

$$y = \frac{40 - p}{3}.$$

What level of output will maximise this firm's net profit?

2. An entrepreneur producing shoes uses a single variable input, leather, which he can purchase for $9 per unit. Each pair of shoes sells for $6. There is perfect competition in both product and factor markets. The production function for the process is

$$y = 30x^{\frac{1}{2}}$$

where y = output of shoes in pairs; and
x = input of leather in units.

Derive a function showing this entrepreneur's net revenue as a function of leather input.

3. For Exercise 2 above, determine the level of input which will maximise the entrepreneur's net revenue.

4. A consumer achieves a certain level of satisfaction from consumption of different quantities of apples and bananas according to the following indifference curve:

$$b = \frac{10 + 2a}{a}$$

where a = quantity of apples consumed per day; and
$\quad\quad b$ = quantity of bananas consumed per day.
If the price of apples is 5 cents each, and the price of bananas is $4\frac{1}{2}$ cents each, at what combination of apples and bananas will this consumer achieve his given level of satisfaction at least cost?

5. How would the optimal solution to Exercise 4 above be affected if the prices of both fruits were to double?

6. Solve Exercise 4 above by graphical methods.

7. A small trading nation produces two products, beef (B) and wheat (W) which it sells on export markets at prevailing world prices of $3 per unit for beef and $9 per unit for wheat. The product transformation curve relating the two products is:

$$B = 5 + 2W - \frac{W^2}{2}$$

where B = production of beef per year in units; and
$\quad\quad W$ = production of wheat per year in units.
Answer the following questions graphically:
(a) Over what range of outputs are these two products *complementary*, that is, over what range is an increase in the output of one product associated with an increase in the output of the other?
(b) What combination of products should the country produce in order to maximise its foreign exchange earnings?

8. Solve Exercise 7 above algebraically.

*Part III: Functions of
Several Variables in
Economic Analysis*

Chapter 10

Functions of Several Variables

10.1 Introduction

In Chapter 2, when the notion of functional relationships between variables was first introduced, we considered examples involving just two variables. In each case, the dependent variable was a function of a single independent variable. For instance, we noted that the quantity of potatoes demanded by our particular housewife was a function of the price of potatoes, our farmer's output of wheat was a function of his fertiliser input, and the level of consumption expenditure of our family was a function of the family's income. In subsequent chapters we have gone quite a long way in developing techniques of use in economic analysis in terms of functions of a single variable.

It is apparent, however, that functions of a single variable are of only limited use in describing the complex economic processes encountered in the everyday world. For instance, our housewife, far from being influenced by price alone in purchasing potatoes, is likely to be affected also by a wide variety of other factors such as the income of her family, the prices of substitutes for potatoes (e.g., rice), the tastes of members of her family, and so on. In fact we may expand our general functional statement from Equation (2.1) to accommodate these extra variables, by writing, for example,

$$q = f(p, Y, r, t) \tag{10.1}$$

where q = weekly quantity of potatoes demanded in kg;
    p = price of potatoes in cents per kg;
    Y = family income in $'000 year;
    r = price of rice in cents per kg; and
    t = some variable measuring the tastes of the family.

In other words, Equation (10.1) acknowledges that demand is not a function simply of price but of the several other variables as well. This is an example of a *function of several variables*. It is hypothesised in Equation

(10.1) that, by virtue of the underlying economic relationships, each variable on the RHS in some way influences the variable on the LHS. Using our earlier terminology, q is still regarded as the dependent variable, but there are now altogether four independent variables, p, Y, r and t, whose levels jointly determine q. We may think of q as being the value of the function on the RHS when specific values are inserted for the independent variables.

Similarly, we may expand the production and consumption functions in Equations (2.2) and (2.3) to cope with the suggestion that when they contain only one explanatory variable, they are oversimplifications of reality. For instance, it would probably be nearer the mark to hypothesise that, for the production function,

$$y = f(x, R) \tag{10.2}$$

where y = output of wheat in centals per hectare;
$\quad\quad x$ = input of fertiliser in kg per hectare; and
$\quad\quad R$ = rainfall in millimetres per year;
and, for the consumption function,

$$C = f(Y, n, A) \tag{10.3}$$

where C = family consumption expenditure in $'000 per year;
$\quad\quad Y$ = family income in $'000 per year;
$\quad\quad n$ = number of persons in the family; and
$\quad\quad A$ = average age of the parents.

These are all examples of functions of several variables. The reader will no doubt be able to think of further independent variables which could be added to the RHS of Equations (10.1), (10.2) and (10.3) to make them even more accurate descriptions of the underlying economic realities.

As in the case of functions of a single variable, our next task is to impose a specific mathematical form on the general functional statements of Equations (10.1) to (10.3). Almost all of the various functional forms considered for functions of a single variable in Chapter 5 have counterparts in functions of two or more variables. The most commonly encountered functional forms in economic analysis of functions containing several variables are the various polynomials and power functions. We shall treat these now, beginning with the simplest and most widely used multivariable function, the linear form.

10.2 Linear Relationships Involving Three Variables
10.2.1 AN EXAMPLE

Imagine a butcher who observes over a period of time that the demand for steak is a function not only of its own price, but also of the price of chicken meat. That is, he observes that the demand for steak declines when its own price rises, but increases when the price of chicken rises, since consumers switch from chicken to steak when the price of chicken goes up. In mathematical terms, that is, there is a negative relationship between demand for steak and its own price, and a positive relationship between demand for steak and the price of chicken. The butcher, being an amateur econometrician, has been able to quantify this relationship in the form of the following equation:

$$q = 8 - 0.2p_s + 0.1p_c \qquad (10.4)$$

where q = quantity of steak demanded per customer in kg;
$\quad p_s$ = price of steak in cents per kg; and
$\quad p_c$ = price of chicken in cents per kg.
In Equation (10.4) there are three variables, q, p_s and p_c. The dependent variable q is a function of the two independent variables p_s and p_c.

Let us suppose that both prices are able to range only between 30 and 50 cents per kg. Now suppose we fix p_c at 30 cents. Then Equation (10.4) can be written as

$$q = 8 - 0.2p_s + 0.1(30), \qquad (10.5)$$

that is, as

$$q = 11 - 0.2p_s, \qquad (10.6)$$

which we immediately recognise as a linear equation involving two variables, q and p_s. Similarly, suppose the price of chicken were held constant at a different level, say 40 cents. Equation (10.4) would then reduce to

$$q = 12 - 0.2p_s, \qquad (10.7)$$

which is again a linear equation, with the same slope as (10.6) but with a larger intercept.

Now fix the price of steak, p_s, at, say, 50 cents, allowing p_c to remain variable. Then Equation (10.4) becomes

$$q = 8 - 0.2(50) + 0.1p_c, \qquad (10.8)$$

which reduces to

$$q = -2 + 0.1p_c, \qquad (10.9)$$

which is again a linear expression involving two variables q and p_c. Fixing p_s at any other arbitrary level would again enable Equation (10.4) to be reduced to a linear equation in these two variables.

It is therefore apparent that Equation (10.4) is reducible to a linear equation involving *each* of the independent variables p_s and p_c. Equation (10.4) is thus an example of a *linear function of two variables*. More specifically, this equation shows the demand for steak as a linear function of the two variables p_s and p_c.

By substituting various sets of values for p_s and p_c into Equation (10.4) we can predict the demand for steak at any required combination of steak and chicken prices. Table 10.1 shows the quantity demanded with p_s and p_c both ranging from 30 to 50 cents per kg. Thus, for example, we read that if chicken costs 50 cents per kg and steak costs 30 cents per kg, demand per customer will be 7 kg. The reader should verify the use of Equation (10.4) to calculate the figures in Table 10.1.

TABLE 10.1

Quantity of Steak (q) Demanded as a Function of Steak and Chicken Prices

		Price of Steak (p_s) (cents/kg)		
		30	40	50
Price of Chicken (p_c) (cents/kg)	30	5	3	1
	40	6	4	2
	50	7	5	3

10.2.2 THREE-DIMENSIONAL GRAPHS

In Chapter 3 we discussed the method for drawing graphs showing only two-variable relationships. For example, in Section 3.5 we constructed the graph of a demand schedule in which the quantity demanded was a linear function of a single price (Equation (3.4), Fig. 3.7 (a)). The price was measured on one axis of a Cartesian† diagram, and quantity measured on the other. The demand was calculated for a set of price figures and the relevant points plotted on the diagram. Assuming price and quantity to be continuously variable, these points were linked via an appropriate line to give a graph of the demand schedule. In such a case we used two axes—one for each variable—and obtained a result in the form of a straight line in two-dimensional space.

In the case of Equation (10.4) we have three variables, so to draw a graph of this equation we require three dimensions. In other words, we require a third axis, at right angles to the other two, on which to measure our third variable. The three axes create three-dimensional space, giving

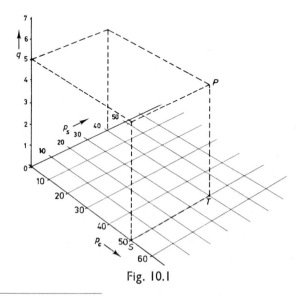

Fig. 10.1

---

† Named after the French philosopher and mathematician, René Descartes (1596–1650).

us a diagram looking rather like the corner of an ordinary room. The origin of the diagram, where each variable equals zero, corresponds to the meeting point of the two walls and the floor. The vertical corner, where the two walls meet, may be thought of as the axis of the dependent variable, and the two horizontal edges of the floor at right angles to each other are the axes of the two independent variables. Thus, in respect of Equation (10.4), p_s may be measured along one edge of the floor, p_c along the other edge, and q is then measured as the height above the floor. The axes are sketched in Fig. 10.1.

Consider how any point in Table 10.1 may be located in our three-dimensional diagram. Take the situation where the price of steak is 40 cents and the price of chicken is 50 cents, yielding a demand of 5 kg. Measuring p_c first, we move 50 units along the p_c axis to the point S. The value of 40 for p_s leads us to T. By moving vertically 5 units of quantity demanded, taking us upwards from T, we establish the required point at P. Of course, it is possible to move from the origin to point P in any sequence. We could equally well have started out measuring p_s or q in the first step. Different sequences of plotting the variables will merely carry us to point P along different edges of the rectangular "block" sketched in on the diagram.

So much for the method of establishing one point from Table 10.1; the table contains nine such points, all of which may be located in a similar manner. What emerges is a distribution of points in three-dimensional space. Since the underlying equation is linear, these points all lie on a *plane*, or flat surface, in three-dimensional space. Supposing p_s and p_c to be continuously variable within the specified range of 30 to 50 cents, we

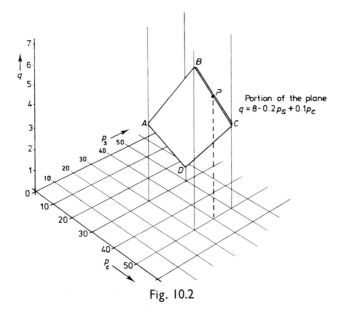

Fig. 10.2

can draw a picture of this plane as in Fig. 10.2.† The plane $ABCD$ in Fig. 10.2 is only a portion of the complete plane corresponding to Equation (10.4). Specifically, it is that portion where $30 \leqslant p_c \leqslant 50$ and $30 \leqslant p_s \leqslant 50$. The "complete plane" would be obtained by allowing the independent variables to vary from minus to plus infinity. Note that the point P from Fig. 10.1 has been drawn in Fig. 10.2.

Of course Fig. 10.2, being only a perspective drawing, is not a very accurate picture of Equation (10.4). It can only give a very rough reading of the value of q for any particular pair of values of p_c and p_s. So it is not uncommon to find three-dimensional pictures such as Fig. 10.2 reduced to a series of two-dimensional graphs. For instance, suppose we fix p_c first at 30 cents, then at 40 cents. This is equivalent to taking two "slices" through the plane in the p_s direction at the levels where $p_c = 30$ and $p_c = 40$. In Fig. 10.3, the planes of these two "slices" are indicated by the vertical panels marked 30 and 40 respectively. Their intersection with the plane $ABCD$ is along the straight lines AD (the point D is obscured in Fig. 10.3) and EF respectively. Transferring the lines AD and EF to a two-dimensional graph where the axes are simply q and p_s, we obtain Fig. 10.4.

In the diagrammatic analysis below we have moved from a relationship in three dimensions (Fig. 10.3) to a series of relationships in two dimensions (Fig. 10.4) simply by holding one variable constant, in this case p_c. It should be clear to the reader that this is the graphical equivalent of our earlier algebraic analysis when we converted an equation involving three variables (Equation (10.4)) into a series of equations involving two variables (Equations (10.6) and (10.7)) by holding one variable (p_c)

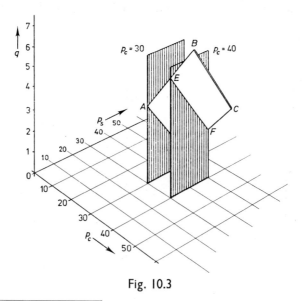

Fig. 10.3

---

† Note that the plane in Fig. 10.2 is drawn as a slab in order to emphasise its position in the three-dimensional space. In fact, of course, a plane has no thickness.

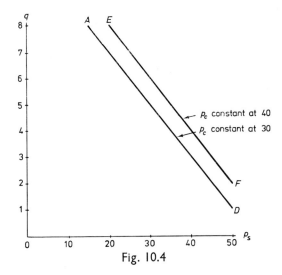

Fig. 10.4

constant at a series of levels. In fact the reader should verify that the lines AD and EF in Fig. 10.4 map Equations (10.6) and (10.7) respectively. In addition he should confirm that these two graphs and equations correspond to the first two lines of Table 10.1.

In a similar fashion we could instead hold the variable p_s constant at several levels within the specified range, and take "slices" through our diagram in the p_c direction. The intersection of these slices with the plane $ABCD$ would give a series of straight lines mapping q as a function of p_c with p_s held constant. These straight lines could be transferred to a two-dimensional diagram with axes q and p_c. These manipulations are left as an exercise for the reader.

10.3 Linear Equations Involving More than Three Variables

The extension of linear functions to embrace any number of independent variables is quite straightforward. For example, a linear form for the housewife's demand function in Equation (10.1) would be

$$q = a + b_1 p + b_2 Y + b_3 r + b_4 t \tag{10.10}$$

where q, p, Y, r and t are as defined above, and a, b_1, b_2, b_3 and b_4 are coefficients. It is of course impossible to graph (10.10) because it would require five dimensions, one for each variable. Nevertheless the terminology from two-variable linear relationships is sometimes applied to Equation (10.10), that is, a is referred to as the *intercept* or *constant term* located when all variables on the RHS are zero, and the various b coefficients are the *slopes* with respect to the associated independent variables. For example, b_2 is the "slope of the function in the Y direction". Conceptually, Equation (10.10) maps a *hyperplane*, that is, the equivalent in more than three dimensions of a plane such as that pictured in Fig. 10.2.

10.4 Implicit and Explicit Functions Involving Several Variables

Functions of several variables are frequently written in implicit form.†
Imagine a farmer, with 12 hectares of land, who is able to produce three
different crops—say wheat, barley and oats. Let output of these commodities be denoted y_1, y_2 and y_3 respectively. Suppose 2 hectares of land
are required to produce 1 unit of y_1, 3 hectares for 1 unit of y_2 and $\frac{1}{2}$
hectare for 1 unit of y_3. We may thus put down an equation describing the
maximum quantities of the three crops the farmer is capable of producing
with his 12 hectares of land,

$$2y_1 + 3y_2 + \tfrac{1}{2}y_3 = 12, \qquad (10.11)$$

where we assume that y_1, y_2 and y_3 cannot be negative. Here we have a
linear function involving three variables. Equation (10.11) can be written
in *implicit* form as

$$2y_1 + 3y_2 + \tfrac{1}{2}y_3 - 12 = 0. \qquad (10.12)$$

The values of y_1, y_2 and y_3 that satisfy the function (10.12) lie on a plane
in three-dimensional space, as shown in Fig. 10.5. Each point on the plane
represents a combination of outputs that may be obtained from 12 hectares.

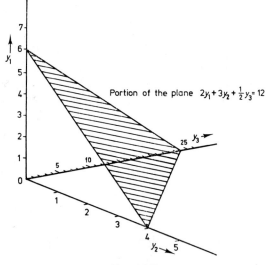

Fig. 10.5

Further properties of the implicit function (10.12) may be explored by
taking each variable as an *explicit* function of the other two. For our
particular example, there are three explicit functions:

$$y_1 = \tfrac{1}{2}(12 - 3y_2 - \tfrac{1}{2}y_3) \qquad (10.13a)$$
$$y_2 = \tfrac{1}{3}(12 - 2y_1 - \tfrac{1}{2}y_3) \qquad (10.13b)$$
$$y_3 = 2(12 - 2y_1 - 3y_2). \qquad (10.13c)$$

Each of these three functions will yield the plane in Fig. 10.5.

---

† To revise the distinction between implicit and explicit functions, see Section 2.7.

In more general cases we may be dealing with any number of variables. A single commodity y, for instance, may require n different inputs $x_1, x_2, \ldots, x_n$ in production. Such a relationship may be written in implicit form as

$$F(y, x_1, x_2, \ldots, x_n) = 0. \qquad (10.14)\dagger$$

Alternatively we may wish to take total output as an explicit function of the n inputs:

$$y = f(x_1, x_2, \ldots, x_n) \qquad (10.15)$$

or, again, we may wish to express (10.14) as an explicit function with one of the inputs on the LHS, say as

$$x_2 = g(y, x_1, x_3, \ldots, x_n), \qquad (10.16)$$

and so on.

10.5 Higher-Degree Polynomial Functions of Several Variables

Polynomials of degrees higher than one are also frequently encountered as functions of several variables. For example, suppose output y of a certain crop is known to be a quadratic function of the inputs of two different fertilisers—nitrogen (N) and phosphorus (P). Then the general form of this quadratic equation would be:

$$y = a_0 + a_1 N + a_2 P + a_3 N^2 + a_4 P^2 + a_5 NP \qquad (10.17)$$

where $a_0, \ldots, a_5$ are coefficients.

If a third, fourth, . . . , fertiliser component were introduced we would simply extend Equation (10.17) appropriately. For instance, if molybdenum (M) were also known to be related to y in addition to P and N, the overall relationship being a quadratic, we would redefine the function as:

$$y = a_0 + a_1 N + a_2 P + a_3 M + a_4 N^2 + a_5 P^2 + a_6 M^2$$
$$+ a_7 NP + a_8 NM + a_9 PM \qquad (10.18)$$

where $a_0, \ldots, a_9$ are coefficients.

Similarly, cubics and higher-degree polynomials may be obtained by expanding the simple two-variable relationships examined in Chapter 5. However, we do not need to consider these questions any further here.

10.6 The Cobb-Douglas Production Function with Two Inputs

10.6.1 AN EXAMPLE

Imagine some commodity—say cloth—which may be produced by capital-intensive methods, by labour-intensive methods, or by techniques some-where between these two extremes. In such production situations, capital may be substituted for labour to produce a given volume of output; and variations in total output may be achieved by changing the input of labour alone, of capital alone or of both labour and capital together.

---

† Compare Equation (10.14) with Equation (2.12).

Consider the following Cobb-Douglas (power) production function which exhibits properties of this kind:

$$y = AL^{\alpha}K^{\beta} \tag{10.19}$$

where y = total output of cloth in '000 metres per year;

    L = labour input in man days per year;

    K = capital input in \$'000 per year; and

    A, α, β are constants.

The variables of the production function are y, L and K. Here we have an example of one variable (y) being an explicit function of *two* variables (L and K). Compare Equation (10.19) with Equation (5.6), which was a Cobb-Douglas production function showing output as a function of only *one* variable input.

As a specific case, let us suppose $\alpha = 0.6$, $\beta = 0.4$ and $A = 5$. Then our Cobb-Douglas function (10.19) becomes

$$y = 5L^{0.6}K^{0.4}. \tag{10.20}$$

By ascribing arbitrary values to L and K in Equation (10.20), a table of production figures can easily be obtained. Table 10.2 has been derived in this way.† Inputs of capital are given along the top row of the table, while labour inputs appear as a column on the left. Total output figures corresponding to each input combination are given in the body of the table. Thus, with 6 units of capital and 8 of labour, 36 units of cloth can be produced; with 10 of capital and 2 of labour, total output is 19, and so forth.

TABLE 10.2

Total Output of Cloth (y) as a Function of Labour and Capital Inputs ‡

		Capital (K)				
		2	4	6	8	10
	2	10	13	16	17	19
	4	15	20	24	26	29
Labour (L)	6	19	26	30	34	37
	8	23	30	36	40	44
	10	26	35	41	46	50

‡ Numbers in this table are rounded to the nearest integer.

Several characteristics of the production function (10.20) are of special interest. First, it is evident that at least something of both factors must be used to obtain a positive output. If either L or K is zero in Equation (10.20), y itself will equal zero. From an economic viewpoint this is quite a sensible proposition: no matter how much capital is on hand (K could approach infinity), if there is no labour to operate the capital, output of

---

† Actual calculations are simplified by taking logs of Equation (10.20). In log form the function becomes log y = log 5 + 0.6 log L + 0.4 log K (compare Equation (5.8)). After carrying out the calculations in log form, total output may be found by taking antilogs.

cloth will simply not be forthcoming. Likewise, a large labour force will be totally unproductive unless it has some capital to use.

Second, total output may be increased by holding one input constant and raising the level of the other. Labour, for example, may be held at 4 units. As capital inputs increase from 2 through to 10, we can read from Table 10.2 that total output will rise from 15 to 29 units. Similarly, if capital is fixed at 6 units, an increasing usage of labour from 2 to 10 units will raise total output from 16 through to 41 units. Total output can also be increased if extra units of both inputs are employed. Reading the table along any downward left-to-right diagonal immediately confirms this proposition.

Third, input substitution is reflected in the fact that the same level of output may be produced using different combinations of labour and capital. For example, 30 units of output may be produced with a combination of 4 capital and 8 labour, or with 6 capital and 6 labour. In other words, the table reveals two points which are obviously on the same isoquant—but this will be discussed more fully later.

10.6.2 GRAPHING THE PRODUCTION FUNCTION

We may use the same techniques to draw a graph of Equation (10.20) as used in Section 10.2.2. That is, we construct the axes in three dimensions, with inputs of labour and capital measured at right angles to each other in the horizontal plane ("on the floor") and with output of cloth measured vertically. Thus any point from Table 10.2 may be located in three-dimensional space by counting the appropriate number of units of labour and of capital to locate the required input combination on the floor of the diagram, and then erecting a perpendicular at that point of a height equal to the appropriate output level shown in the table. Repeating this for all twenty-five points in Table 10.2 leads to a distribution of points in three-dimensional space. But this time we are not dealing with a linear function, and hence these points will not lie on a plane in three-dimensional space. Rather, they will lie on a curved surface.

The reader may prefer to think of the construction of this diagram in terms of the techniques used by geographers to build three-dimensional models of landforms such as mountain ranges. The labour and capital inputs on the floor of our diagram form a latitude-longitude grid pattern. On each intersection on the grid a stick can be erected, the length of which reflects the total output level (the height of the mountain) corresponding to that particular capital-labour input combination. The ends of all the sticks will then suggest a three-dimensional surface, in the same way as the points of a two-dimensional graph suggest a curve. Indeed, assuming that capital input, labour input and total output are continuously variable, we can in theory obtain the complete surface, which is called a *production surface*, by taking all possible values of y, L and K that satisfy the function, thereby filling the interstices of the points already plotted—or, if one prefers the model-building analogy, by plastering the

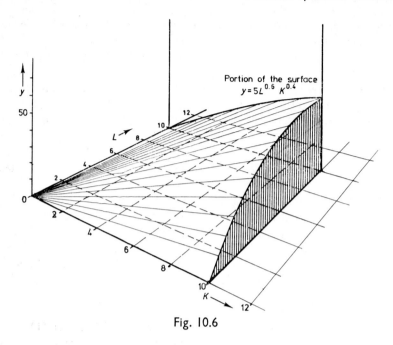

Fig. 10.6

ends of the sticks with papier maché and smoothing the whole thing over.

A portion of the smooth continuous production surface corresponding to Table 10.2 and Equation (10.20) is depicted in Fig. 10.6 (specifically, that portion where $0 \leqslant L, K \leqslant 10$). Note that the surface commences at the origin, where y, L and K are zero. It also runs along the labour and capital axes, indicating graphically the property of the function we discussed earlier, i.e., when one input is zero, total output will be zero even if an infinite quantity of the other input is employed. The reader may, as an exercise, locate some of the points contained in Table 10.2 on the diagram of the surface in Fig. 10.6.

10.6.3 THE LAW OF DIMINISHING MARGINAL RETURNS

The *shape* of the production surface has important implications for economic analysis. Accordingly we shall now discuss various ways in which the surface may be examined. Suppose we make a series of vertical "slices" through the surface in the same way as we did earlier with our linear function. To begin with, let us take the slices parallel to the K "wall" at given intervals along the labour axis—say where L equals 2 and 6. This is illustrated in Fig. 10.7 (a). The slices give rise to a series of cross-section two-dimensional curves in the plane y, K. Specifically, each slice on Fig. 10.7 (a) represents the total output of cloth that may be obtained by increasing the input of capital while holding the input of labour constant. These curves are shown in Fig. 10.7 (b). When labour inputs are held constant at 6 units, for example, raising capital inputs from 2 through to 10 will lead to an expansion of total output from 19 to

37 units. Indeed, the relevant curve can be graphed merely by turning to $L = 6$ in Table 10.2 and plotting the total output figures for $K = 2, 4, 6, 8$ and 10. Thus, each slice in Fig. 10.7 (a), with its counterpart in Fig. 10.7 (b), represents a particular *row* from Table 10.2, corresponding to $L = 2$ and 6.

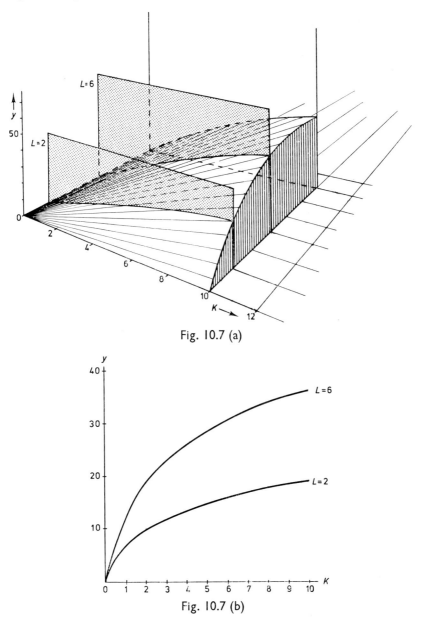

Fig. 10.7 (a)

Fig. 10.7 (b)

Observe the shape of one of the curves in Fig. 10.7 (b), when labour is held constant at, say, 6 units. Total output of cloth can always be increased by adding further capital to production; the curve always has a positive

slope and does not turn downwards. However, the *marginal* contribution
of capital to production clearly declines as higher capital input levels are
reached. For instance, raising capital input by 2 units from 4 to 6 leads to
an increase in output from 26 to 30 units, an additional 4 units. But at
higher capital input levels, say where K rises from 8 to 10 units (still
maintaining $L = 6$) the resultant increase in total output is only 3 units
(a rise from 34 to 37). In other words, the marginal product of capital
declines as K is increased with L held constant. Hence, the production
function obviously satisfies the *law of diminishing marginal returns*, which
states that, *all other inputs held constant*, the extra total output obtainable

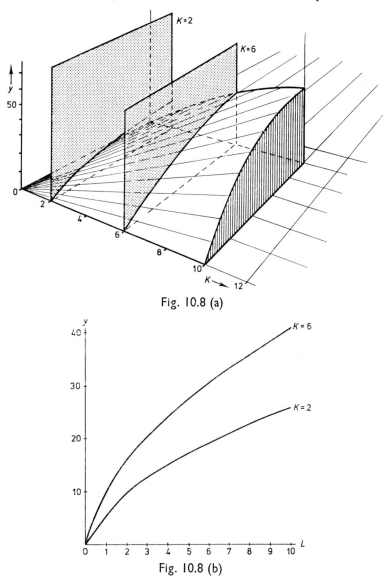

Fig. 10.8 (a)

Fig. 10.8 (b)

from successive increments of a variable input will eventually decline. Thus we observe that each curve in Fig. 10.7 (b) becomes flatter at higher output levels. Compare this with the single factor case studied in Fig. 5.2.

A similar picture emerges when we take a series of vertical slices parallel to the *L* "wall" at given intervals along the capital axis, as in Fig. 10.8 (a). The cross-sections are described in two dimensions by Fig. 10.8 (b). Each curve is merely a graph of a particular *column* of Table 10.2; the levels chosen for illustration are $K = 2$ and $K = 6$. Thus capital input is held constant and total output increased solely by using greater quantities of labour. Again, the law of diminishing marginal returns can be seen to operate. Given a constant level of capital input, the marginal product of labour declines as more is applied to production.

Algebraically, diminishing marginal returns to a factor (with the other factor held constant) will be reflected in the numerical value of its exponent (α or β). If the exponent of a factor is less than unity (as in the case of both *L* and *K* in our example), diminishing returns with respect to the factor are indicated. This will become clearer in Chapter 11, when we shall consider problems of *measuring* marginal products.

10.6.4 ISOQUANTS AND FACTOR SUBSTITUTION

The production surface can also be studied by taking a series of *horizontal* slices as shown in Fig. 10.9 (a). Each such slice, with its associated cross-section, denotes a constant level of total output. In two dimensions, the horizontal cross-sections of the production surface take the form of an *isoquant map*,† shown in Fig. 10.9 (b). Recalling our earlier analogy with models of mountains, you can, if you like, imagine Fig. 10.9 (b) as

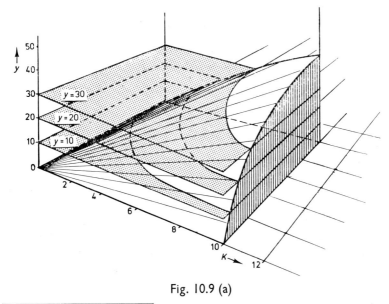

Fig. 10.9 (a)

---

† For earlier reference to isoquants see Section 7.2.4.

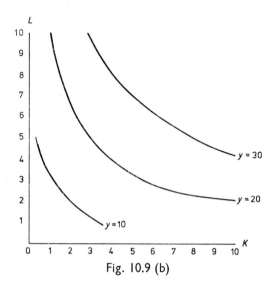

Fig. 10.9 (b)

a *contour map*, where each contour (isoquant) represents a given altitude of the mountain (production surface) above the floor of the diagram.

Unfortunately, there is insufficient information in Table 10.2 to construct an accurate isoquant map. The production function in Equation (10.20) shows y as a function of K and L; to derive Fig. 10.9 (b) one must rearrange the production function to obtain an expression showing either L as a function of y and K, or K as a function of y and L. The following manipulations lead to an equation describing the isoquant map for our Cobb-Douglas production function in the form $K = f(y, L)$. Starting with the function in its original general form (10.19) we get, by simple rearrangement,

$$K^\beta = \left(\frac{y}{A}\right) L^{-\alpha}. \qquad (10.21)$$

Taking the βth root of Equation (10.21) yields our required equation:

$$K = \left(\frac{y}{A}\right)^{\frac{1}{\beta}} L^{-\frac{\alpha}{\beta}}. \qquad (10.22)$$

Now when $A = 5$, $\alpha = 0.6$ and $\beta = 0.4$, as in our example production function (10.20), Equation (10.22) becomes:

$$K = \left(\frac{y}{5}\right)^{\frac{5}{2}} L^{-\frac{3}{2}}. \qquad (10.23)$$

As we know, an isoquant refers to a given fixed level of output. Thus, to obtain a *particular* isoquant from Equation (10.23), y must be held constant. Arbitrary values can then be ascribed to L, and the corresponding values of K calculated. The results of such an exercise are contained in Table 10.3. For the first set of figures total output has been held constant at 30 units. That is, setting $y = 30$ in (10.23), we use the resulting equation to calculate the values of K corresponding to

$L = 2, \ldots, 10$. Then, repeating the process for $y = 20$ and $y = 10$ units, we calculate the corresponding capital levels, as shown in the table. It is this information which has been employed to construct the isoquant map of Fig. 10.9 (b).

TABLE 10.3

Isoquant Data: Total Output (y) as a Function of Labour (L) and Capital (K) Inputs

y = 30		y = 20		y = 10	
L	K	L	K	L	K
2	31.2	2	11.3	2	2.0
4	11.0	4	4.0	4	0.7
6	6.0	6	2.2	6	0.4
8	3.9	8	1.4	8	0.3
10	2.8	10	1.0	10	0.2

It is apparent from Table 10.3 that decreasing amounts of labour must be offset by higher capital usage to maintain the same rate of output. This negative relationship between labour and capital, reflecting a downward-sloping isoquant, can be deduced at once by setting y in Equation (10.22) equal to some constant level y^*, and differentiating the function with respect to L:†

$$\frac{dK}{dL} = -\frac{\alpha}{\beta} \left(\frac{y^*}{A}\right)^{\frac{1}{\beta}} L^{-\left(\frac{\alpha}{\beta}+1\right)}. \qquad (10.24)$$

Since in this model A, L, y^*, α and β are always positive, the RHS of (10.24) will always be negative, showing that (10.22) must exhibit a downward slope. The reader may also like to prove for himself that each isoquant is convex to the origin, by ascertaining that Equation (10.22) has a positive second derivative.

10.6.5 RETURNS TO SCALE

A final way of studying our production function is to consider what the effect will be on total output when both inputs are *simultaneously* increased by a given percentage. There are three possible outcomes, each indicating a certain type of returns to scale in production. First, there may be an equal percentage rise in total output, reflecting *constant returns to scale*; second, the percentage rise in output may be less than the percentage

---

† If you do not immediately understand the mechanics of this differentiation, look back to Section 6.3.4. In terms of the rule for finding the derivative of the general function $y = ax^n$, we may interpret (10.22) as $K = aL^b$ where $a = \left(\frac{y^*}{A}\right)^{\frac{1}{\beta}}$ and $b = -\frac{\alpha}{\beta}$. Application of the usual derivation rules to the equation $K = aL^b$ yields the result $dK/dL = baL^{b-1}$. Then substitution of the full values for a and b into this result yields the required answer.

factor increase, in which case *diminishing returns to scale* are said to prevail; and third, there may be a greater percentage rise in total output, signifying *increasing returns to scale*. This terminology arises quite naturally from the idea of investigating what occurs when a given level of operations is "scaled up" by a constant multiple.

Let us examine the scale properties of the production function (10.20) by turning to Table 10.2. Consider an output position where 4 units of labour and 4 of capital are employed, giving a total output of 20 units of cloth. Now raise both inputs by 50 per cent, such that 6 of labour and 6 of capital are used in the new situation. We can see from the table that total output rises to 30 units—an increase of 50 per cent. Thus, with an equal percentage increase in inputs and output, constant returns to scale are indicated for this function. Indeed, this property holds at *all* output levels for the function (10.20).

Algebraic verification of constant returns to scale is quite straight-forward. The function (10.20) is an example of a Cobb-Douglas function in which the factor exponents sum to unity; that is,

$$\alpha + \beta = 1. \tag{10.25}$$

Thus

$$\beta = 1 - \alpha,$$

and (10.20) can be written as

$$y = AL^\alpha K^{1-\alpha}. \tag{10.26}$$

Suppose in an initial situation labour input is L_0, capital input is K_0, and total output is y_0. We thus have:

$$y_0 = AL_0^\alpha K_0^{1-\alpha}. \tag{10.27}$$

Now suppose that inputs of both labour and capital change by the same multiple, λ, to λL_0 and λK_0 respectively, where $\lambda > 0$.† Substituting these new values into Equation (10.27) we get the following expression for the new level of total output, which we shall denote by y_1:

$$y_1 = A(\lambda L_0)^\alpha (\lambda K_0)^{1-\alpha}, \tag{10.28}$$

from which we obtain:

$$y_1 = A\lambda^\alpha L_0^\alpha \lambda^{1-\alpha} K_0^{1-\alpha}$$
$$= \lambda AL_0^\alpha K_0^{1-\alpha},$$

that is, using Equation (10.27),

$$y_1 = \lambda y_0. \tag{10.29}$$

Equation (10.29) shows that output has changed by the same multiple (λ) as the inputs were changed, proving constant returns to scale.

Diagrammatically, returns to scale will be reflected in the cross-sections of vertical slices passing through the origin, as in Figs 10.10 (a), (b) and (c). In the case of constant returns to scale any such cross-section through the

† Throughout, we can allow for either an increase or a decrease in the variables, by assuming a constant multiplier $\lambda > 0$. Thus if we multiply a variable by λ when $0 < \lambda < 1$, the variable's value is diminished; if $\lambda > 1$, its value is increased.

surface is linear, as shown in Fig. 10.10 (a). Remember that, as we have seen, this is the case for a two-input Cobb-Douglas function when $\alpha + \beta = 1$.

Figure 10.10 (b) illustrates a case of increasing returns to scale. A cross-section through the surface radiating out from the origin curves

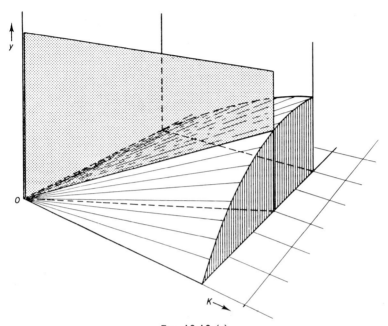

Fig. 10.10 (a)

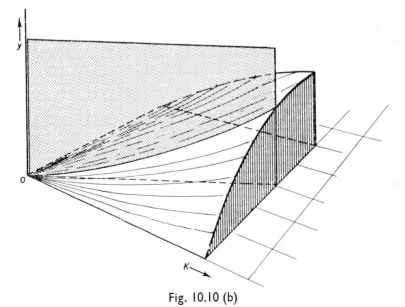

Fig. 10.10 (b)

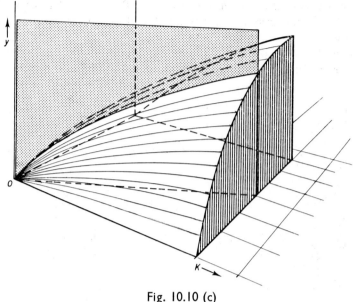

Fig. 10.10 (c)

upwards. For a Cobb-Douglas function, increasing returns to scale will prevail when $\alpha + \beta > 1$. Finally, in Fig. 10.10 (c), we have an example of decreasing returns to scale; the cross-section has a decreasing positive slope. Again using a Cobb-Douglas function, such a case arises when $\alpha + \beta < 1$. As an exercise, the reader may like to verify these last two assertions by repeating the above analysis, beginning at Equation (10.25), for Cobb-Douglas functions where $\alpha + \beta$ equals, say, 2, and $\frac{1}{2}$.

Finally, it should be carefully noted that various types of returns to scale are compatible with the existence of diminishing returns to inputs in the underlying production function. For example, suppose in a particular Cobb-Douglas function $\alpha = 0.8$ and $\beta = 0.7$ (notation again from Equation (10.19)). Here the individual exponents are less than one, indicating diminishing marginal returns with respect to each input. But $\alpha + \beta = 1.5$, which is greater than unity, indicating increasing returns to scale.

This situation may be studied with the aid of an isoquant diagram such as in Fig. 10.11. Parts (a), (b) and (c) of the figure show constant, increasing and decreasing returns to scale respectively. The isoquants in each figure represent contour maps of Figs 10.10 (a), (b) and (c) respectively, where the contours are taken at altitudes equidistant from one another. In other words, successive isoquants represent constant increases in output.

The *scale* properties of each figure are seen by looking at the distances between the isoquants along any ray radiating from the origin. Any such ray indicates expansion of both inputs in fixed proportions. In each figure, OA is an example of such a ray. In Fig. 10.11 (a), where constant returns prevail, the distances BC, CD, $DE, \ldots$, are equal, showing

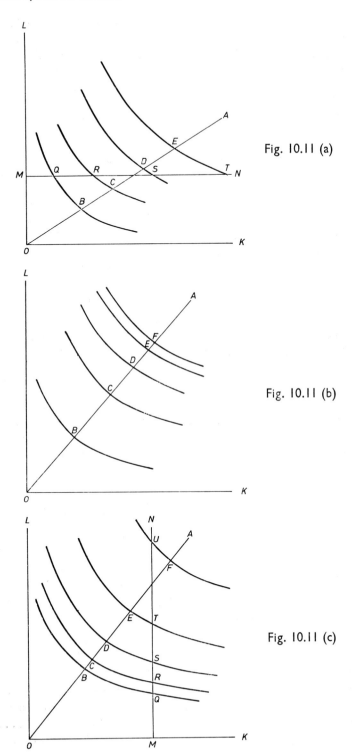

Fig. 10.11 (a)

Fig. 10.11 (b)

Fig. 10.11 (c)

that to achieve constant increases in output, constant increases in the levels of both inputs are needed. In Fig. 10.11 (b), which illustrates increasing returns, the distances *BC, CD, DE,* . . . , become smaller, showing that smaller and smaller increments of the factors in fixed proportions are required to achieve constant increases in output. Finally, the distances *BC, CD, DE,* . . . , in Fig. 10.11 (c) become larger, indicating that when diminishing returns to scale operate, larger and larger increments in factor inputs are required to maintain constant increments in output.

On the other hand, the existence of diminishing, constant, or increasing *marginal returns* to any one factor when the other factor is held constant, may be examined by erecting a horizontal or perpendicular from one of the axes. For instance, in Fig. 10.11 (a), the marginal contribution of capital to production is investigated by holding labour constant at the point *M*, and drawing a horizontal line *MN*. We observe that the distances *QR, RS, ST,* . . . , along *MN increase*, showing that greater and greater increments of capital input are necessary to achieve constant increments in output, while labour is held constant. In other words, in this case the law of diminishing marginal returns operates for capital.

As another illustration, the line *MN* in Fig. 10.11 (c) shows the nature of the marginal contribution of labour to production when capital is held constant at the level *M*. Again we see the distances *QR, RS, ST,* . . . , increasing, showing, in this example, the operation of the law of diminishing returns with respect to labour.

Notice that, in expanding one factor while holding the other constant, we *vary* the proportion in which the inputs are used (compare with the expansion of factor use in *fixed* proportions in the returns-to-scale case). For this reason, the law of diminishing returns is sometimes also referred to as the *law of variable proportions*.

10.7 Production Functions with More than Two Inputs

In some circumstances we may wish to describe the relationship between output and *more than two* inputs for a firm or an industry. For example, denote output by y and a total of n inputs by $x_1, x_2, \ldots, x_n$. Then the Cobb-Douglas function describing this relationship is of the form

$$y = A x_1^{\alpha_1} x_2^{\alpha_2} \ldots x_n^{\alpha_n} \tag{10.30}$$

where $A, \alpha_1, \ldots, \alpha_n$ are constants. We can see that Equation (10.30) is simply an extension to n inputs of the simple one-input Cobb-Douglas function (Equations (5.6) and (5.7)), and of the two-input functions studied in the previous section (Equations (10.19) and (10.20)).

We can extend our earlier analysis of the properties of Cobb-Douglas functions to cover the n-input case. In particular, if a specific factor exponent is less than unity (that is, if $0 < \alpha_i < 1$ for any $i = 1, \ldots, n$), diminishing marginal returns are indicated with respect to variation in that factor when all other factors are held constant. Likewise, the sum of all the exponents α_i indicates the degree of returns to scale, as follows:

- if $\alpha_1 + \alpha_2 + \ldots + \alpha_n < 1$, the production function exhibits decreasing returns to scale;

- if $\alpha_1 + \alpha_2 + \ldots + \alpha_n = 1$, the production function exhibits constant returns to scale;

- if $\alpha_1 + \alpha_2 + \ldots + \alpha_n > 1$, the production function exhibits increasing returns to scale.

As we have seen, we cannot graph Equation (10.30) for more than two inputs, since we do not have enough dimensions. Similarly, we cannot draw diagrams of isoquants for more than two variable factors. However, if we have a specific example of an *n*-variable input production function $(n > 2)$, we can draw production surfaces and isoquants corresponding to any *pair* of inputs by holding all other inputs constant at some given level.

10.8 Utility Functions

An individual's total utility can be taken as a function of the quantities of various commodities he consumes. If we are prepared to accept the propositions of the theory of *cardinal utility*, which assumes that total utility can be numerically measured, it is easy to contrive examples of total utility functions which may be handled along similar lines to the Cobb-Douglas production functions studied above. For instance, we may write the following explicit function:

$$U = y^{\frac{1}{2}} z^{\frac{1}{2}} \tag{10.31}$$

where y and z = quantities of two commodities consumed per time period; and

U = total utility derived from the consumption of these two commodities.

Equation (10.31) contains three variables. By ascribing arbitrary values to y and z, we may construct a table similar to Table 10.2 and proceed to represent the function (10.31) diagrammatically as a surface in three-dimensional space. The diagram of this surface, called a *utility surface*, would resemble Fig. 10.6, but with y and z plotted on the floor of the diagram and total utility measured on the vertical axis. Any horizontal cross-section of this surface will represent a constant level of utility, reflecting all combinations of y and z between which the consumer is indifferent. If we were to take a series of such horizontal cross-sections at different levels of total utility, we could transfer the resulting contours to a diagram in two-dimensional space with axes representing the two goods y and z. The diagram so obtained would be the individual's indifference map. In other words, with a total utility surface shaped like the surface in Fig. 10.9 (a), the individual's indifference map may be derived in exactly the same fashion as the isoquant map of Fig. 10.9 (b).

Algebraically, Equation (10.31) can be squared and rearranged to give

$$y = \frac{U^2}{z}. \tag{10.32}$$

If U is set at any arbitrary constant level of utility, Equation (10.32) describes the relevant indifference curve taking y as an explicit function of z. Then, setting U at other levels, we may build up a picture of the complete indifference map.

Under the theory of *ordinal utility*, on the other hand, total utility is deemed nonmeasurable. In this theory, a consumer's preferences for various goods can be expressed only in terms of rankings, that is, the individual can say that he *prefers* a certain level of good y (say 3 bananas) to a certain level of good z (say 5 apples), but he cannot say *by how much* this preference is felt. If we studied the effects of changes in commodity prices and in the consumer's income on his pattern of consumption (that is, his *revealed preferences*) we could in fact derive the individual's indifference map for the two consumption goods y and z. But we could *not* specify the absolute level of total utility corresponding to any single indifference curve. All we can say is that associated with any given indifference map there must be a total utility surface; a single indifference curve will represent a contour of this surface, reflecting a constant level of total utility, and movement from one indifference curve to a higher one will indicate an increase in total utility. But because total utility itself is not measurable, we do not know how "high above the floor" the total utility surface is located, or by how much total utility will change when the individual moves from one indifference curve to some other. We can, therefore, only assume that any curve from the individual's indifference map measures a constant value of some variable (u) which serves as an *indicator* of total utility. In the case of two commodities y and z, we may thus write the equation of a given indifference curve as

$$f(y, z) = \text{constant}. \tag{10.33}$$

Introducing our indicator variable u as the constant, we have

$$u = f(y, z). \tag{10.34}$$

If a specific functional form is known for the function f in Equation (10.34), we may, by setting the indicator variable u at various arbitrary levels, build up a picture of the consumer's indifference map for the commodities y and z. We would be implicitly assuming that a relationship exists between U, total utility, and u, the indicator variable. But all we know about this relationship is that higher levels of u indicate higher levels of U. In mathematical language we can state this assumption as follows. We assume

$$U = g(u) \tag{10.35}$$

where we know only that g is an *increasing* function. In the case of n commodities, the utility function generalises to

$$u = f(z_1, z_2, \ldots, z_n) \tag{10.36}$$

where u is again a utility indicator and $z_1, z_2, \ldots, z_n$ are commodities consumed.

Exercises

1. A relationship is hypothesised between the demand for money (D) and two explanatory variables, gross national product (GNP) and the rate of interest on fixed deposits (i), as follows:
$$D = \phi(GNP, i).$$
Defining coefficients $\beta_1, \beta_2, \ldots$, write down the general form of this relationship if ϕ is:
(a) a linear function;
(b) a power function;
(c) a quadratic function.

2. The isorevenue equation for a firm producing three products x, y and z is given by the following relationship:
$$2x + 3y + z = R$$
where R = revenue. Draw a sketch of this equation for the case where $R = 10$.

3. Write the function in Exercise 2 above as an implicit function and as three explicit functions for the case where again $R = 10$.

4. For the problem in Exercises 2 and 3 above demonstrate both graphically and algebraically the effect of holding y constant at 2 units, given again $R = 10$.

5. Comment on returns to scale in the following production functions, where y = output, and L and K = labour and capital inputs respectively.
(a) $y = 2L^{0.7}K^{0.3}$,
(b) $y = 3L^{0.8}K^{0.4}$,
(c) $y = 2L^{0.4}K^{0.2}$,
(d) $y = 5L^{0.1}K^{1.3}$.

6. Consider the production function
$$y = 5L^{\frac{1}{3}}K^{\frac{1}{3}}.$$
Using arbitrary values for L and K, derive a table of total output figures and sketch the associated production surface.

7. Comment on the properties of the isoquant map for the production function in Exercise 6 above.

8. Assuming L remains constant at 2 units, draw a total product curve reflecting capital usage. What do you deduce about the marginal product of capital?

Chapter 11

Partial Derivatives

11.1 Marginal Products in the Two-Input Cobb-Douglas Production Function

11.1.1 AN EXAMPLE

In Section 10.6.3 we observed that taking a series of "slices" through a production surface in the vertical plane of one of the input axes yields a series of two-dimensional graphs showing the variation of output with respect to variation in that input, holding the other input constant at different fixed levels. In the case of our illustrative Cobb-Douglas production function

$$y = 5L^{0.6}K^{0.4}, \tag{11.1}$$

Fig. 10.7 (b) shows the results of taking slices in the capital (K) direction at two fixed levels of labour, namely, $L = 2$ and 6. Similarly, Fig. 10.8 (b) shows the variation of output (y) with respect to L, where K is held constant at levels of 2 units and 6 units. We observed in Chapter 10 that the production function in Equation (11.1) exhibits diminishing marginal returns to each factor; hence the curves in both Figs 10.7 (b) and 10.8 (b) are concave.

As we have seen, the *slopes* of the curves in Figs 10.7 (b) and 10.8 (b) measure the extra output which can be obtained per extra unit of input, that is, the *marginal products* of the factors. In this chapter we turn our attention to *measuring* the slopes of functions of several variables. We shall begin by using the Cobb-Douglas function from Equation (11.1) as an example.

Suppose we wish to measure the marginal product of the factor labour in Equation (11.1). Consider first the situation where capital is held constant at, say, 6 units. Setting $K = 6$ in Equation (11.1) yields

$$y = 5L^{0.6}6^{0.4}. \tag{11.2}$$

Using log tables, we evaluate $6^{0.4} = 2.047$, thus enabling us to simplify Equation (11.2) to

$$y = 10.235L^{0.6}. \tag{11.3}$$

Now, from our analysis in Chapter 7 we know that the marginal product of a factor in a given production function is the first derivative of that production function. Thus for our example we find the *MP* of labour (MP_L), with capital held constant at 6 units, by differentiating Equation (11.3). We obtain

$$MP_L \underset{(K=6)}{} = \frac{dy}{dL} = 0.6 \times 10.235L^{0.6-1}$$

$$= \frac{6.141}{L^{0.4}}. \qquad (11.4)$$

So, for example, we calculate MP_L at a labour input of, say, 4 units by substitution of 4 for L in Equation (11.4), giving a result of 3.528.

Next, consider the situation where capital input is held constant at a different level, say 2 units. Setting $K = 2$ in Equation (11.1) and simplifying, gives

$$y = 6.595L^{0.6}. \qquad (11.5)$$

To obtain MP_L for this function, we again find its first derivative:

$$MP_L \underset{(K=2)}{} = \frac{dy}{dL} = \frac{3.957}{L^{0.4}}. \qquad (11.6)$$

Comparison of Equation (11.6) with (11.4) reveals immediately that MP_L is different when capital is held constant at different levels. For instance, we calculated above that MP_L for $L = 4$ is 3.528 when K is held constant at 6. From Equation (11.6) we calculate that MP_L is 2.273 at the same level of labour but when K is held constant at 2 units. In other words, a given labour force is more productive when it is supplied with larger quantities of capital.

In general, therefore, the *MP* of labour will vary not only with the level of labour input itself, but also with the quantity of capital used. Thus we may obtain a *general* expression for the *MP* of labour in Equation (11.1) by differentiating this function with respect to L, but only on the understanding that *K is held constant at some given level*. Hence, on the RHS of (11.1) we may regard both the 5 and the expression $K^{0.4}$ as *constant* components, and the expression $L^{0.6}$ as a *variable* component. Then applying our usual differentiation rules to (11.1) we obtain

$$\frac{dy}{dL} = 0.6 \times 5K^{0.4} \times L^{0.6-1}$$

$$= \frac{3K^{0.4}}{L^{0.4}}. \qquad (11.7)$$

The process of obtaining Equation (11.7) does not represent a complete differentiation of our production function because we have differentiated with respect to only one of the factors, labour, while holding the other factor, capital, constant at a level of K units. Thus this differentiation is only *partial* and we refer to the derivative in Equation (11.7) as a *partial derivative*. In order to distinguish it symbolically as a partial derivative, we replace the notation dy/dL with the symbols $\partial y/\partial L$. Hence we write the partial derivative of (11.1) with respect to labour in the form

$$\frac{\partial y}{\partial L} = \frac{3K^{0.4}}{L^{0.4}}.$$ (11.8)

Since we have performed only one differentiation to arrive at Equation (11.8), $\partial y/\partial L$ is called a *first-order* partial derivative.

An alternative notation is sometimes used. The first-order partial derivative with respect to L of the function $y = f(L,K)$ is sometimes written $f_L(L,K)$ or simply f_L.

A similar line of reasoning may be followed in the examination of capital productivity. The *MP* of capital (MP_K) may be found by partially differentiating the function (11.1) with respect to K, on the understanding that L is held constant at a given level. Thus, in performing this differentiation, we must regard the expression $5L^{0.6}$ on the RHS of (11.1) as being *constant*. Hence we obtain:

$$MP_K = \frac{\partial y}{\partial K} = 0.4 \times 5L^{0.6} \times K^{0.4-1}$$

$$= \frac{2L^{0.6}}{K^{0.6}}.$$ (11.9)

We see that the *MP* of capital varies not only with the level of capital itself, but also with the level of labour employed.

Again, taking the function $y = f(L,K)$, we can express the *MP* of capital as $f_K(L,K)$ or simply f_K.

11.1.2 GRAPHICAL SIGNIFICANCE OF PARTIAL DERIVATIVES

In graphical terms, the partial derivative of Equation (11.1) with respect to K represents the slope of the production surface in the K direction, with L held constant. Likewise the partial derivative of (11.1) with respect to L represents the slope of the surface in the L direction, with K held constant. To illustrate, Fig. 11.1 shows the production surface with two vertical slices in the L direction taken where $K = 2$ and 6 respectively. It should be apparent that "the slope of the production surface in the L direction" (i.e., $\partial y/\partial L$) is simply the slope of the curves generated by these cross-sections. For example, suppose we wish to measure $\partial y/\partial L$ where $L = 4$ for the two capital levels $K = 2$ and $K = 6$. These slopes may be found graphically by drawing tangents to the surface in the $K = 2$ and $K = 6$ planes at the point where $L = 4$. The tangents are shown on Fig. 11.1, and the points of tangency are A (for $K = 6$) and B (for $K = 2$).

These two cross-sections through the production surface generate the curves shown in two dimensions in Fig. 11.2 (a) (compare with Fig. 10.8 (b)). Hence "the slope of the production surface in the L direction where $K = 6$" may be equivalently measured as the slope of the upper graph in Fig. 11.2 (a). This slope, which is $\partial y/\partial L$, or MP_L for $K = 6$, is graphed

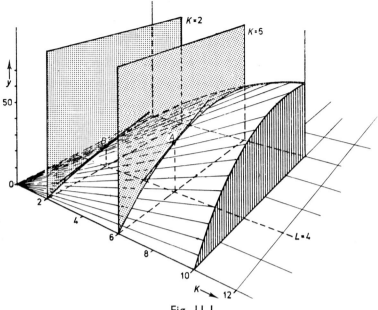

Fig. 11.1

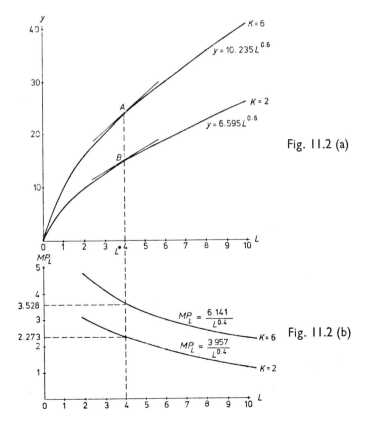

Fig. 11.2 (a)

Fig. 11.2 (b)

in Fig. 11.2 (b). Similarly, $\partial y/\partial L$, or MP_L for $K = 2$, may be obtained as the slope of the lower curve in Fig. 11.2 (a). It too is shown on Fig. 11.2 (b). The two graphs in Fig. 11.2 (b) in fact depict Equations (11.4) and (11.6) respectively.

Because the curves in Fig. 11.2 (a) have a positive decreasing slope, the *MP* curves in Fig. 11.2 (b) are downward sloping. Notice that the slopes of the two curves in Fig. 11.2 (a) at the point where $L = 4$ (L^* on the diagram) have been indicated by the appropriate tangents. These tangents are identical with those shown on Fig. 11.1, and the points of tangency are marked A and B in Fig. 11.2 (a) to correspond with Fig. 11.1. The numerical values of the slopes at this level of L can be read from Fig. 11.2 (b), confirming our earlier calculations.

11.1.3 GENERAL FORM OF PARTIAL DERIVATIVES

The general form of the marginal products for the two-input Cobb-Douglas production function may be seen by partial differentiation of the general form of this function, which was stated in Equation (10.19) as
$$y = AL^\alpha K^\beta. \tag{11.10}$$
The partial derivative of Equation (11.10) with respect to L is obtained by regarding AK^β as a constant, and that with respect to K by treating AL^α as a constant. Thus we obtain:

$$MP_L = \frac{\partial y}{\partial L} = \alpha AK^\beta L^{\alpha-1} \tag{11.11a}$$

$$MP_K = \frac{\partial y}{\partial K} = \beta AL^\alpha K^{\beta-1}. \tag{11.11b}$$

As an exercise, the reader may compose some numerical examples of functions of this general form, and determine the *MP* of the inputs using the above methods.

Two further points should be noted about the properties of this general Cobb-Douglas production function.

First, let us consider the *elasticity of production* (or output) of the function in (11.10). Following Section 7.1, we can define elasticity of production with respect to one of the inputs as the percentage change in output per unit percentage change in the level of that input. In other words,

$$E_L = \frac{\partial y}{\partial L} \times \frac{L}{y} \tag{11.12a}$$

and

$$E_K = \frac{\partial y}{\partial K} \times \frac{K}{y} \tag{11.12b}$$

where E_L and E_K = elasticity of production with respect to labour and capital respectively. (Since the derivatives contained in these expressions are partials, these elasticities are referred to as *partial* elasticities.)

Evaluating (11.12a) gives

$$E_L = \alpha AK^\beta L^{\alpha-1} \times \frac{L}{y} \tag{11.13}$$

and since $L^{\alpha-1} \times L = L^{\alpha}$ and $y = AL^{\alpha} K^{\beta}$, we may write Equation (11.13) as

$$E_L = \frac{\alpha AK^{\beta} L^{\alpha}}{AL^{\alpha} K^{\beta}} = \alpha.$$

We may show by a similar method that $E_K = \beta$. In other words, the elasticity of production with respect to each factor in the Cobb-Douglas function is simply the exponent of that factor.

Secondly, we should note that the marginal products (MP) in the Cobb-Douglas function are proportional to the average products (AP). Taking labour as an illustration, we define its MP as in Equation (11.11a). Now the term $L^{\alpha-1}$ may be written $L^{\alpha} \times L^{-1} \equiv L^{\alpha}/L$. Substituting the latter expression for $L^{\alpha-1}$ in (11.11a), we obtain

$$MP_L = \frac{\alpha AK^{\beta} L^{\alpha}}{L} = \frac{\alpha y}{L}, \tag{11.14}$$

and since $y/L = AP$ of labour, we may write Equation (11.14) as

$$MP_L = \alpha AP_L. \tag{11.15}$$

Similarly, we may show that

$$MP_K = \beta AP_K. \tag{11.16}$$

Thus, in the Cobb-Douglas function the MP of the factors are proportional to their AP, the coefficients of proportionality being the exponents α and β respectively.

11.2 Partial Derivatives of Cobb-Douglas Functions with More than Two Inputs

Suppose the output (y) of an agricultural industry can be expressed as a Cobb-Douglas function of the inputs of capital (K), labour (L) and land (M) in the form:

$$y = 160 K^{0.3} L^{0.5} M^{0.1}. \tag{11.17}$$

We may investigate the MP of each of these factors in turn while holding the other two factors constant. The MP of labour in Equation (11.17) may be found by partially differentiating (11.17) with respect to L, holding *both* K and M constant. In other words, in performing such a differentiation, we would regard the expression $160 K^{0.3} M^{0.1}$ on the RHS of Equation (11.17) as a constant. In this way we obtain

$$\frac{\partial y}{\partial L} = 0.5 \times 160 K^{0.3} M^{0.1} \times L^{0.5-1}. \tag{11.18}$$

In a similar fashion we could obtain the other two MP, giving the full set as follows:

$$MP_K = \frac{\partial y}{\partial K} = \frac{48 L^{0.5} M^{0.1}}{K^{0.7}} \tag{11.19a}$$

$$MP_L = \frac{\partial y}{\partial L} = \frac{80 K^{0.3} M^{0.1}}{L^{0.5}} \tag{11.19b}$$

$$MP_M = \frac{\partial y}{\partial M} = \frac{16 K^{0.3} L^{0.5}}{M^{0.9}}. \tag{11.19c}$$

More generally, if we have a Cobb-Douglas production function in which n inputs $x_1, x_2, \ldots, x_n$ are used to produce a commodity y, as in Equation (10.30), the appropriate partial derivatives $\partial y/\partial x_1$, $\partial y/\partial x_2$, $\ldots, \partial y/\partial x_n$ may be calculated using a logical extension of the above reasoning.

11.3 Some Further Examples of Partial Derivation
11.3.1 LINEAR FUNCTIONS

The partial derivatives of linear functions of several variables may be easily found by applying similar logic to that used in the previous sections. For example, consider the function (10.4), which related the demand for steak (q) to its own price (p_s) and the price of chicken (p_c):

$$q = 8 - 0.2p_s + 0.1p_c. \qquad (11.20)$$

If we wish to determine the slope of this function in the p_s direction we must hold p_c constant. In other words, in partially differentiating Equation (11.20) with respect to p_s in order to find its slope, we must regard *both* of the terms 8 and $0.1p_c$ on the RHS of (11.20) as *constant*.

Now, we have already seen in Section 6.4 that in differentiating a polynomial, constant terms disappear. Thus in differentiating (11.20) with respect to p_s, the terms 8 and $0.1p_c$ disappear. We are therefore left with

$$\frac{\partial q}{\partial p_s} = -0.2. \qquad (11.21)$$

It is important to notice that Equation (11.21) shows the slope of the function in the p_s direction to be -0.2, *regardless of the level of p_c*. To understand why this is so, refer back to Figs 10.3 and 10.4. In Fig. 10.3, the slope of the plane $ABCD$ in the p_s direction is investigated by taking two vertical slices at $p_c = 30$ and $p_c = 40$. The slope of the plane at these two levels of p_c is indicated by the lines EF and AD, which are transferred from Fig. 10.3 to Fig. 10.4. It is apparent that the slopes of these two lines are the same; in fact we have calculated their slope in Equation (11.21) as -0.2. It should also be apparent that since the surface mapped by Equation (11.20) is completely flat (as (11.20) is a linear equation), we could take the slices through the plane in the p_s direction at *any* level of p_c, and the slope of the cross-section would always be -0.2.

Similarly, if we wish to measure the slope of the same function in the p_c direction, we could take a series of vertical slices at various constant levels of p_s. It is clear from Fig. 10.3 that the resulting cross-sections would again all be straight lines with equal slope. To calculate this slope algebraically, we may partially differentiate Equation (11.20) with respect to p_c. In so doing, we regard the terms 8 and $-0.2p_c$ as constant, so they disappear in the process of differentiation. Therefore we obtain

$$\frac{\partial q}{\partial p_c} = 0.1. \qquad (11.22)$$

Thus, whereas the plane slopes *downwards* in the p_s direction (confirm this with the negative slope in Equation (11.21)), it slopes upwards in the p_c direction, as evidenced by the positive partial derivative in Equation (11.22).

The latter property of the demand function may be stated in terms of (partial) elasticities, as follows: the *elasticity* of steak demand with respect to its own price, $\dfrac{\partial q}{\partial p_s} \times \dfrac{p_s}{q}$, is negative; the *cross elasticity* of steak demand with respect to the price of chicken, $\dfrac{\partial q}{\partial p_c} \times \dfrac{p_c}{q}$, is positive. Once again we observe that the elasticity of a linear function varies as we move along it, provided the intercept term is nonzero (compare Table 7.2).

11.3.2 HIGHER-DEGREE POLYNOMIALS

The same reasoning may be extended if we wish to find partial derivatives of polynomials of degree greater than one. For example, consider the quadratic production function from Equation (10.17), which has the form

$$y = a_0 + a_1 N + a_2 P + a_3 N^2 + a_4 P^2 + a_5 NP. \tag{11.23}$$

The *MP* of nitrogen (N) may be determined by performing the differentiation of Equation (11.23) with respect to N, regarding phosphorus (P) throughout as a constant. Thus, the terms a_0, $a_2 P$ and $a_4 P^2$ will disappear, and the expression $a_5 P$ in the last term in Equation (11.23) will be treated as a constant. Hence we obtain

$$MP_N = \frac{\partial y}{\partial N} = a_1 + 2a_3 N + a_5 P. \tag{11.24}$$

By the same token, the *MP* of P is obtained by regarding N throughout Equation (11.23) as a constant. Then we have

$$MP_P = \frac{\partial y}{\partial P} = a_2 + 2a_4 P + a_5 N. \tag{11.25}$$

Similar procedures apply in the search for partial derivatives of higher-degree polynomials and to equations containing further variables. As an exercise, the reader may find all the first-order partial derivatives of Equation (10.18).

11.4 Second-Order Partial Derivatives

Just as a function of a single variable may be differentiated once to give the first derivative of the function, then this result differentiated again to find the function's second derivative (see Section 8.4), so may a function of several variables be partially differentiated twice to obtain the *second-order partial derivatives* of the function. We shall not dwell on this topic, but merely offer some food for thought to readers who wish to understand a little of what is involved.

Consider a cardinal utility function which happens to take the form

$$U = 2yz - y^2 - 2z^2 + 4y \tag{11.26}$$

where y and $z =$ quantities of two commodities consumed per time period; and

$\quad\quad U =$ total utility derived from the consumption of these two commodities.

The marginal utilities derived from the consumption of the goods y and z are the first-order partial derivatives of Equation (11.26) with respect to y and z respectively. Thus we can write:

$$MU_y = \frac{\partial U}{\partial y} = 2z - 2y + 4 \tag{11.27a}$$

$$MU_z = \frac{\partial U}{\partial z} = 2y - 4z. \tag{11.27b}$$

The second-order partial derivatives of the function (11.26) are obtained by differentiating Equations (11.27a) and (11.27b) with respect to y and z respectively, to give

$$\frac{\partial}{\partial y}\left(\frac{\partial U}{\partial y}\right) = \frac{\partial^2 U}{\partial y^2} = -2 \tag{11.28a}$$

$$\frac{\partial}{\partial z}\left(\frac{\partial U}{\partial z}\right) = \frac{\partial^2 U}{\partial z^2} = -4. \tag{11.28b}$$

Note that the process is like that involved in finding second derivatives of functions of a single variable. The notation is also similar, except that in the case of partials we continue to use the symbol "∂" in place of the simple "d".

The two second derivatives in (11.28) are negative, showing that the *MU* curve for each consumption good slopes downwards, given that consumption of the other good is held constant. In other words the function (11.26) obeys the law of diminishing marginal utility with respect to both goods.

To obtain the second-order partials above, we differentiated $\partial U/\partial y$ with respect to y, and $\partial U/\partial z$ with respect to z. But it is also possible to differentiate $\partial U/\partial y$ with respect to z, and $\partial U/\partial z$ with respect to y. If we do so, we obtain the so-called *mixed* or *cross second-order partial derivatives* of the function. They are identical, as we can see from the following operations performed on Equations (11.27a and b) respectively.

$$\frac{\partial}{\partial z}\left(\frac{\partial U}{\partial y}\right) = \frac{\partial^2 U}{\partial z\,\partial y} = 2 \tag{11.29a}$$

$$\frac{\partial}{\partial y}\left(\frac{\partial U}{\partial z}\right) = \frac{\partial^2 U}{\partial y\,\partial z} = 2. \tag{11.29b}$$

The second-order partial derivatives of our utility function provide us with valuable insight into the characteristics of the underlying utility surface. More generally, second-order partial derivatives yield information about the nature of functions, and are of particular significance in the search for maxima and minima. Further reference to second-order partials will be made in Chapter 13. Appendix B, Section 1, also contains additional information on this topic.

Exercises

1. Partially differentiate the following production function with respect to L and K to obtain the marginal products of labour and capital respectively:
$$y = 5L^{0.7}K^{0.3}.$$

2. Prove that constant returns to scale prevail for the production function in Exercise 1 above.

3. Draw a sketch of the production surface from Exercise 1 above for the range $0 \leqslant L, K \leqslant 5$.

4. Use a graph to determine the marginal product of capital when $K = 2$ and $L = 3$ for the function in Exercise 1 above. Check your answer algebraically.

5. Obtain the partial derivatives of the following production function, where the variables y, L, K are as defined above:
$$y = 3LK + 3L - K^2 - 3L^2 + 25.$$

6. What can we say about the properties of the marginal product functions obtained in Exercise 5?

7. Derive expressions for the partial elasticity of production with respect to both labour and capital for:
   (a) the production function in Exercise 1 above;
   (b) the production function in Exercise 5 above.

8. Find all the first-order partial derivatives of the following functions:
   (a) the function in Exercise 5 (b), Chapter 10;
   (b) the function in Exercise 5 (d), Chapter 10;
   (c) the function in Exercise 1 (a), Chapter 10.

9. A firm produces three products—leather, cardboard and string—denoted y_1, y_2 and y_3 respectively. Its total revenue function is of the form
$$TR = 5 + 75y_1 - 2y_1^2 + 8y_2 - \tfrac{1}{2}y_1 y_2 + 4y_3^2.$$
At what combination of outputs will the marginal revenues of all three products simultaneously equal zero?

Chapter 12

Homogeneous Functions and Euler's Theorem

12.1 Homogeneous and Nonhomogeneous Functions

12.1.1 SOME EXAMPLES OF HOMOGENEOUS FUNCTIONS

In Section 10.6.5 we examined what happened to a particular two-input Cobb-Douglas production function when the levels of both inputs were changed simultaneously by a multiple λ. Let us now consider this question more deeply, with the aid of some further examples.

Example A

In considering the relationship between gross national product per head of population (Y), aggregate GNP (X), and population (P), we might write the following *identity* or definitional equation:

$$Y = \frac{X}{P}. \qquad (12.1)$$

Now, what happens if we increase or decrease *both* variables on the RHS of Equation (12.1) by a constant multiple λ? The new level of GNP is λX, the new level of population is λP, and we shall denote the new level of GNP per head as Y_1. Since the RHS of Equation (12.1) now equals $\lambda X / \lambda P = X/P$, it is clear that $Y_1 = Y$. In other words, multiplying both variables on the RHS of (12.1) by the same constant leaves the value of the function unchanged.

Example B

Consider again our illustrative Cobb-Douglas production function from Equation (10.20):

$$y = 5L^{0.6}K^{0.4}. \qquad (12.2)$$

In this function the exponents sum to unity, so it is an example of the function depicted in Equation (10.26). Thus, if we multiply both L and K in Equation (12.2) by λ, the new level of y will be λ times the old level, as demonstrated in Equation (10.29).

Example C

Suppose that for a group of individuals with incomes of less than $1 thousand per year, a savings function is found to exist of the form:

$$S = 0.3Y^2 + 85i^2 \tag{12.3}$$

where S = level of savings in $'000;

Y = level of disposable income in $'000; and

i = rate of interest.

Suppose both variables on the RHS of Equation (12.3) happen to change by the same multiple, λ. The new income level is λY and the new interest rate λi. Call the new level of savings S_1. Then we may calculate:

$$\begin{aligned} S_1 &= 0.3(\lambda Y)^2 + 85(\lambda i)^2 \\ &= \lambda^2(0.3Y^2 + 85i^2) \\ &= \lambda^2 S. \end{aligned}$$

In other words, multiplying the two variables on the RHS of (12.3) by λ increases the value of the function by λ^2.

Let us collect together the results from these three illustrations. Multiplying *both* variables on the various RHS by λ causes the value of the respective functions to be multiplied by:

$$1(= \lambda^0) \text{ in the case of Example A;}$$
$$\lambda(= \lambda^1) \text{ in the case of Example B;}$$
$$\lambda^2 \text{ in the case of Example C.}$$

In each case we see that the value of the function is multiplied by a constant. A function whose value is multiplied by a *constant* amount when a given constant multiplier is applied to the levels of all variables on the RHS is called a *homogeneous function*. If the independent variables in a homogeneous function are all multiplied by a constant λ, and the value of the function consequently changes by a multiple λ^k, the function is called *homogeneous of degree k*. Thus, Example A above is called homogeneous of degree zero, Example B is homogeneous of degree one, and Example C is homogeneous of degree two.

As we shall see directly, it is those functions that are homogeneous of degree one, or homogeneous of the first degree, which are of particular interest to economists. These functions are often called *linearly homogeneous*, or simply *linear homogeneous*. But this does not indicate that the function itself is necessarily linear. A glance at Equation (12.2) should confirm this.

12.1.2 GENERAL DEFINITION OF HOMOGENEITY

The definition of a homogeneous function given in the previous section may now be extended to a general statement applicable to any function of several variables. Suppose in the function

$$y = f(x_1, x_2, \ldots, x_n) \tag{12.4}$$

the levels of all the variables $x_1, x_2, \ldots, x_n$ are multiplied by λ, giving a new level of y, say y_1, where

$$y_1 = f(\lambda x_1, \lambda x_2, \ldots, \lambda x_n). \tag{12.5}$$

Then the function in Equation (12.4) is *homogeneous of degree k* if
$$y_1 = \lambda^k y. \tag{12.6}$$
It should be noted that the first, second . . . derivatives of a homogeneous function of degree k are homogeneous of degree $k - 1$, $k - 2$, . . . respectively. As an exercise, confirm this proposition in terms of the above examples.

12.1.3 NONHOMOGENEOUS FUNCTIONS

The opposite of a homogeneous function is, naturally enough, a *nonhomogeneous function*, defined as one whose value changes by a *nonconstant* amount when the levels of its independent variables are altered by a given constant multiple.

To emphasise the difference between homogeneous and nonhomogeneous functions, Table 12.1 shows the effects of twice doubling the levels of the independent variables in a homogeneous and a nonhomogeneous function, beginning from an arbitrary initial position. The homogeneous function used is Equation (12.3), and the example of a nonhomogeneous function is the linear demand function from Equation (10.4). Observe that, since (12.3) is homogeneous of degree two, a doubling of both independent variables ($\lambda = 2$) always leads to a scaling up of S by a constant $\lambda^2 = 2^2 = 4$. The same treatment applied to the nonhomogeneous function, however, causes the value of the function to be multiplied by a nonconstant multiple; from the particular starting position chosen in Table 12.1, the multipliers turn out to be 0.867 for the first doubling and 0.75 for the second, as shown in the table.

TABLE 12.1

Comparison of a Homogeneous and a Nonhomogeneous Function

Homogeneous Function: $S = 0.3Y^2 + 85i^2$

Y	i	S	Multiplier Applied to: Y and i (λ)	S
0.2	0.01	0.0205		
			2	4
0.4	0.02	0.0820		
			2	4
0.8	0.04	0.3280		

Nonhomogeneous Function: $q = 8 - 0.2p_s + 0.1p_c$

p_s	p_c	q	Multiplier Applied to: p_s and p_c (λ)	q
10	12	7.2		
			2	0.867
20	24	6.4		
			2	0.750
40	48	4.8		

12.2 Homogeneous Production Functions

12.2.1 GENERAL

It is easy to show that the general two-input Cobb-Douglas production function

$$y = AL^{\alpha}K^{\beta} \tag{12.7}$$

is homogeneous of degree $\alpha + \beta$. Let the levels of L and K be multiplied by λ, and let the new output level be y_1. Then we have

$$\begin{aligned} y_1 &= A(\lambda L)^{\alpha}(\lambda K)^{\beta} \\ &= \lambda^{\alpha+\beta} AL^{\alpha}K^{\beta}. \end{aligned}$$

That is,

$$y_1 = \lambda^{\alpha+\beta}y, \tag{12.8}$$

and we can compare Equation (12.8) with (12.6) to see that Equation (12.7) is homogeneous of degree $\alpha + \beta$.

It is left as a simple exercise for the reader to prove that the degree of homogeneity of the n-input Cobb-Douglas production function (see Equation (10.30)) is given by the sum of the exponents $\alpha_1, \alpha_2, \ldots, \alpha_n$.

12.2.2 LINEAR HOMOGENEOUS PRODUCTION FUNCTIONS

Production functions which are linear homogeneous play a significant role in economic analysis. They exhibit the property of constant returns to scale, they generally satisfy the law of diminishing marginal returns, and they are compatible with the theory of perfect competition, as we shall see in Section 12.3. Furthermore, a good deal of empirical evidence has been compiled which suggests that, in reality, a number of industries do possess production functions of this type.

Some significant theoretical conclusions about linear homogeneous production functions can be drawn from a further consideration of the two-input Cobb-Douglas case from Equation (10.26), namely,

$$y = AL^{\alpha}K^{1-\alpha}. \tag{12.9}$$

Suppose we multiply each input in Equation (12.9) by a constant $1/L$. Since this function is linear homogeneous, output will also be multiplied by the same constant. That is, we will have

$$\frac{1}{L}y = A\left(\frac{1}{L}\times L\right)^{\alpha}\left(\frac{1}{L}\times K\right)^{1-\alpha}. \tag{12.10}$$

Now

$$\left(\frac{1}{L}\times L\right)^{\alpha} = 1^{\alpha} = 1,$$

and

$$\left(\frac{1}{L}\times K\right)^{1-\alpha} = \left(\frac{K}{L}\right)^{1-\alpha}.$$

Hence Equation (12.10) simplifies to

$$\frac{1}{L}y = A\left(\frac{K}{L}\right)^{1-\alpha},$$

that is,

$$y = L \times A \left(\frac{K}{L}\right)^{1-\alpha}. \tag{12.11}$$

Equation (12.11) shows that output may be written not only as the original function (12.9), but also as a function of the capital–labour ratio (K/L) and the level of labour input (L) within the industry.

In fact, it is a general proposition (which will not be proved here) that if *any* production function, Cobb-Douglas or otherwise, of the form

$$y = f(L, K) \tag{12.12}$$

is linear homogeneous, it may also be expressed as:

$$y = L \times g\left(\frac{K}{L}\right) \tag{12.13}$$

where g is some function.

These findings have widespread application in microeconomic theory, as well as in the pure theory of foreign trade where international differences in "factor intensities" (another name for input ratios) have been shown to provide quite a plausible explanation of why countries will enter into trade.

12.3 Euler's Theorem and Income Distribution
12.3.1 GENERAL

Suppose we have an industry operating under perfect competition and employing only two factors of production, labour (L) and capital (K). Suppose this industry has a linear homogeneous production function of the form of Equation (12.12) above. Let

    w = wage rate;
    r = rate of return on capital; and
    p = selling price of final output.

From the theory of perfect competition we know that, in equilibrium, inputs will be employed up to that point at which their rates of return equal the value of their marginal products. The marginal product of labour is the partial derivative of Equation (12.12) with respect to L, and the value of labour's marginal product is this partial derivative *times p*. Likewise for capital. Thus we may write for both labour and capital:

$$w = \frac{\partial y}{\partial L} \times p \quad \text{and} \quad r = \frac{\partial y}{\partial K} \times p,$$

or,

$$\frac{w}{p} = \frac{\partial y}{\partial L} \quad \text{and} \quad \frac{r}{p} = \frac{\partial y}{\partial K}. \tag{12.14}$$

Now, it is asserted without proof that any linear homogeneous production function of the form of Equation (12.12) may be expressed in the form:

$$y = \frac{\partial y}{\partial L} \times L + \frac{\partial y}{\partial K} \times K. \tag{12.15}$$

This is an application of *Euler's Theorem.*† Let us substitute the results from (12.14) into (12.15). We obtain

$$y = \frac{w}{p} \times L + \frac{r}{p} \times K \qquad (12.16)$$

and multiplying Equation (12.16) through by p gives:

$$py = wL + rK. \qquad (12.17)$$

Now it is clear that since y is total output, and p is the price per unit of output, the LHS of Equation (12.17) is the total revenue of the industry. Further, L and K are the quantities of labour and capital employed by the industry at a cost per unit of w and r respectively. Thus, wL is the industry's total wage costs and rK is the total cost of capital. Since by assumption these are the only factors of production, the RHS of Equation (12.17) measures the industry's total costs of production. Thus, Equation (12.17) shows that total revenue to the industry just covers total costs of production, that is, the costs just "exhaust" the returns.

Let us turn our attention to the factor shares, that is, the *proportions* of the total proceeds of the industry, which are distributed to labour and capital respectively. The proportion going to labour is given by the fraction:

$$\frac{\text{total labour cost}}{\text{total revenue}} = \frac{wL}{py}, \qquad (12.18)$$

and likewise the proportion going to the other factor, capital, is rK/py. Dividing both sides of Equation (12.17) by py we obtain

$$1 = \frac{wL}{py} + \frac{rK}{py}. \qquad (12.19)$$

Thus, the fractional shares of total proceeds accruing to labour and capital add up to one. In other words, in an industry characterised by perfect competition and a linear homogeneous production function, there will be no "surplus earnings" at equilibrium, and total revenue will accrue solely to the factors that have contributed to production.

The latter statement has been demonstrated above in the context of an industry using only two inputs. However, the result can be generalised (maintaining the assumptions of perfect competition and a linear homogeneous production function) to industries using any number of factors of production.

---

† Named after Leonard Euler (1707–83), a Swiss mathematician. In general, given $y = f(x_1, x_2, \ldots, x_n)$, where the function on the RHS is homogeneous of degree k, Euler's Theorem states that

$$ky = \frac{\partial y}{\partial x_1} x_1 + \frac{\partial y}{\partial x_2} x_2 + \ldots + \frac{\partial y}{\partial x_n} x_n.$$

For our example above, we have $y = f(L, K)$, so that

$$ky = \frac{\partial y}{\partial L} L + \frac{\partial y}{\partial K} K.$$

Since this function is assumed to be linear homogeneous, $k = 1$, yielding Equation (12.15).

12.3.2 FACTOR SHARES FOR THE COBB-DOUGLAS FUNCTION

Suppose the industry considered in the previous section has a Cobb-Douglas production function of the form of Equation (12.9). Then we can write down explicit expressions for the marginal products of the two factors, as follows:

$$\frac{\partial y}{\partial L} = \alpha A L^{\alpha-1} K^{1-\alpha} \tag{12.20a}$$

$$\frac{\partial y}{\partial K} = (1-\alpha)AL^{\alpha} K^{-\alpha}. \tag{12.20b}$$

Earlier we noted that the first derivatives of a homogeneous function of degree k are homogeneous of degree $k-1$; the reader should confirm that the *MP* equations in (12.20) are therefore homogeneous of degree zero. Now, to derive an expression for the relative share of labour in this model (i.e., wL/py) let us multiply both sides of the left-hand equation in (12.14) by L/y. We obtain

$$\frac{wL}{py} = \frac{\partial y}{\partial L}\left(\frac{L}{y}\right). \tag{12.21}$$

Now substitute Equation (12.20a) for $\partial y/\partial L$ on the RHS of Equation (12.21):

$$\frac{wL}{py} = \frac{\alpha A L^{\alpha-1} K^{1-\alpha} L}{y}$$

$$= \frac{\alpha A L^{\alpha} K^{1-\alpha}}{y} = \frac{\alpha y}{y}.$$

That is,

$$\frac{wL}{py} = \alpha. \tag{12.22}$$

Likewise, for capital, the relative share may be written

$$\frac{rK}{py} = \frac{\partial y}{\partial K}\left(\frac{K}{y}\right) \tag{12.23}$$

$$= \frac{(1-\alpha)AL^{\alpha}K^{-\alpha}K}{y}$$

which reduces, by a similar process to the above, to the result

$$\frac{rK}{py} = (1-\alpha). \tag{12.24}$$

The results in Equations (12.22) and (12.24) show that in the linear homogeneous Cobb-Douglas production function with two inputs, the exponents measure the respective shares of the inputs in total revenue. This result generalises to the linear homogeneous Cobb-Douglas function containing more than two inputs. In Equation (10.30), for example, when constant returns to scale prevail, the reward which is distributed in equilibrium to the ith factor x_i is simply the fraction α_i of the industry's total revenue.

Exercises

1. Are the following functions homogeneous or nonhomogeneous? If any function is homogeneous, state its degree.

   (a) $q = 11 - 3p$,

   (b) $w = 3v^2$,

   (c) $z = \dfrac{2x_1 + x_2}{5x_3}$,

   (d) $y = 13.5x_1^{0.3} x_2^{0.4} x_3^{0.6}$,

   (e) $y = 9K - 3L + \dfrac{L^2}{2K}$.

2. Show that the production function
$$y = 3L^{\frac{1}{2}}K^{\frac{1}{2}}$$
   may also be written as
$$y = 3L\sqrt{\frac{K}{L}}.$$

3. What are the percentage shares of proceeds accruing to labour and capital in the production function in Exercise 1, Chapter 11?

4. Suppose the function
$$y = 18x_1^{0.2} x_2^{0.1} x_3^{0.7}$$
   is a three-input Cobb-Douglas production function for the United States wheat industry where $y =$ wheat output, $x_1 =$ land input, $x_2 =$ labour input, and $x_3 =$ capital input, all variables measured in billions of dollars per year. Consider an industry equilibrium where total revenue was $9 billion. What will be the share of each factor in total industry revenue?

5. The following industry production function is homogeneous of degree 0.8, the variables being measured in millions of dollars:
$$y = 6L^{0.2} K^{0.6}.$$
   Assuming perfect competition in the product and factor markets, if the wage rate is $8 per unit, the price of capital $10 per unit, and the output price is $2 per unit, find the equilibrium factor usages in this industry.

6. Suppose a firm possesses the production function shown in Exercise 1 (e) above. Taking the price of output as p, the wage rate as w and the cost of capital as r, demonstrate that the profit-maximising level of output of this firm is indeterminate.

Chapter 13

Optimisation of Functions of Several Variables

13.1 Introduction

The use of the differential calculus to find extreme values of functions of a single variable was discussed in Chapter 8. We saw there that the maximum and/or minimum of a smooth continuous differentiable function can be found, if it exists, by equating the first derivative of the function to zero, and solving the resulting equation. The calculation of second derivatives then provides a means of telling whether a particular extreme point is a maximum or a minimum. Then, in Chapter 9, still in the context of functions of a single variable, we noted the distinction between un-constrained and constrained optimisation problems in mathematics and economics. The former group of problems involves the search for maximum or minimum values of functions that have no limitations placed on the values taken by the variables they contain. On the other hand, constrained optimisation problems entail the extremisation of an objective function subject to one or more explicit constraints, or side-conditions, which specify the range of the variables concerned.

These concepts may be extended from the case of functions of a single variable to the wider field of functions of several variables, which we have been considering in the last few chapters. It is the purpose of the present chapter to show how the calculus may be applied to the problem of extremising functions of several variables, and to look more closely at problems of constrained optimisation when the functions involved are more complicated than those which contain only a single independent variable. We shall begin by looking at the unconstrained extremisation of typical functions in which the dependent variable is a function of two independent variables.

13.2 Unconstrained Optimisation
13.2.1 A MAXIMISATION EXAMPLE

Imagine a farmer who has a given amount of land and is free to vary the
input of his own labour and capital equipment in the production of a
single crop—say beans. The market price of beans is fixed and we assume
the opportunity costs of his factors of production to be zero; therefore,
the farmer may consider his economic optimum to be the maximisation
of sales proceeds. From a production viewpoint, this means getting the
greatest possible total output from the resources at his disposal. As a
result of the fixed properties of his land, however, his inputs of labour and
capital are assumed to be subject to severely diminishing returns. His
production function for beans takes the form

$$y = 3LK + 3L - K^2 - 3L^2 + 25 \qquad (13.1)$$

where y = the quantity of beans produced per season;
L = labour input; and
K = capital input.

It is obviously a simple matter to work out a production schedule for
beans, using a range of values for L and K. Such a procedure leads to
Table 13.1, which suggests that the farmer's maximum output will be
28 units of beans, achievable with an input of 2 units of labour and 3 of
capital.

TABLE 13.1
Total Output of Beans (y) as a Function of Labour and Capital Inputs

		Labour (L)			
		0	1	2	3
	0	25	25	19	7
	1	24	27	24	15
Capital (K)	2	21	27	27	21
	3	16	25	28	25
	4	9	21	27	27

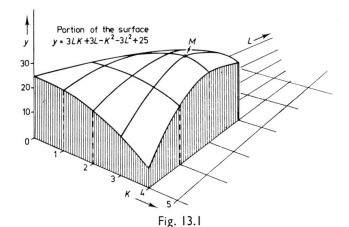

Fig. 13.1

Alternatively, we could study this production function diagrammatically, as in Fig. 13.1, which shows a portion of the production surface described by Equation (13.1). Specifically, Fig. 13.1 shows the part of the surface for $0 \leqslant L \leqslant 3$ and $0 \leqslant K \leqslant 4$. The top of the hill is shown at point M.

The question now arises: how could we find the maximum of this function using the calculus? In Chapter 11 we learned that the partial derivative of Equation (13.1) with respect to, say, L, measures the slope of the surface "in the L direction" with K held constant. Thus, if we just concentrate on the variation of y with respect to L alone, we can apply our simple calculus maximisation rules to find the maximum point on the surface with respect to L, for a given constant level of K.

To illustrate, suppose $K = 1$. The second row of Table 13.1 suggests that if capital is held constant at 1 unit, the maximum of the function will be achieved where $L = 1$; the highest value in the second row is 27. Algebraically this point could be determined by looking at the derivative of Equation (13.1) with respect to L. We have

$$\frac{\partial y}{\partial L} = 3K + 3 - 6L, \qquad (13.2)$$

and setting $K = 1$, and equating the derivative to zero to find a maximum point, we obtain

$$3(1) + 3 - 6L = 0 \qquad (13.3)$$

or $L = 1$. In other words, we have confirmed that the highest point on the surface in the L direction with K held constant at one unit, is achieved when $L = 1$. Diagrammatically we may study the same problem by taking a slice through the function in the L direction at the point $K = 1$, using the methods studied in Chapters 10 and 11. The resulting cross-section through the surface appears as in Fig. 13.2 and again we verify that the maximum point occurs where $L = 1$.

More generally, for *any* constant level of K, the highest point on the surface in the L direction can be found by equating to zero the partial

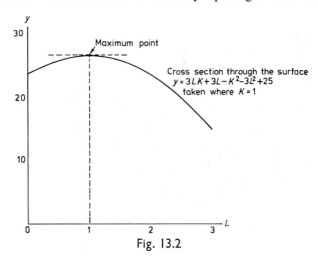

Fig. 13.2

derivative of Equation (13.1) with respect to L. That is, the maximum of the function with respect to L, with K held constant, is given where

$$\frac{\partial y}{\partial L} = 3K + 3 - 6L = 0. \tag{13.4}$$

Similar reasoning may be employed to find the maximum point on the surface "in the K direction" when L is held constant at a given level. In terms of Table 13.1 this entails searching down a column of the table (corresponding to the given L level) to find the largest value. Diagrammatically this process is equivalent to finding the highest point on a slice through the surface in Fig. 13.1 taken in the K direction at a given level of L. Algebraically we find the point where the surface has zero slope in the K direction, i.e., attains a maximum with respect to K for a given level of L, by equating $\partial y / \partial K$ taken from Equation (13.1) to zero. That is, the maximum of (13.1) with respect to K is given where

$$\frac{\partial y}{\partial K} = 3L - 2K = 0. \tag{13.5}$$

It can be seen that the maxima expressed in Equations (13.4) and (13.5), when taken separately, comprise only *partial* statements of the maximisation of Equation (13.1)—that is, each finds a maximum of (13.1) with respect to one variable while holding the other variable constant. But the farmer's problem as originally expressed is one of maximisation of Equation (13.1) with respect to *both* labour *and* capital. To obtain this overall maximum we must specify that *both* Equation (13.4) *and* Equation (13.5) hold simultaneously. In so doing we obtain from (13.4) and (13.5) the two simultaneous equations:

$$3K + 3 - 6L = 0 \tag{13.6a}$$
$$3L - 2K = 0. \tag{13.6b}$$

Equations (13.6a and b) may now be solved for L and K. Multiplying (13.6b) by 2 and adding the result to (13.6a) we obtain

$$3K + 3 - 4K = 0 \tag{13.7}$$

whence $K = 3$. Substituting 3 for K in (13.6b) we get

$$3L - 6 = 0 \tag{13.8}$$

giving $L = 2$. Total output of beans for inputs of 3 units of capital and 2 units of labour may be found by substituting these values into Equation (13.1). Thus the maximum level of y is:

$$y = 3(2)(3) + 3(2) - (3)^2 - 3(2)^2 + 25 = 28.$$

These results confirm those found earlier from inspection of Table 13.1 and Fig. 13.1.

Equating both partial derivatives of an equation such as (13.1) to zero in order to find an extreme value of the function constitutes the necessary *first-order conditions* for the existence of a maximum. As in the case of functions of a single variable, an identical set of first-order conditions also applies to the determination of a minimum. Again as before, the distinction between a maximum and a minimum must be made by way of *second-order conditions*, which are specified in terms of the second derivatives of the function being studied. As we saw in Section 11.4, the second derivatives of functions of several variables become quite complicated and hence, as might be expected, so does the statement of second-order conditions for the existence of extreme points in such functions. The reader who wishes to pursue such questions should consult Appendix B, then move on to more advanced texts. For our purposes, we shall henceforth take the second-order conditions for granted. In further justification of this, we may note that frequently the well-behaved nature of economic functions makes it obvious that a particular extreme point is a maximum or a minimum. For example, if we deal with a hill-shaped production function, we can be confident that setting its first derivatives to zero will yield a maximum point without our needing to consider the second-order conditions.

13.2.2 A MINIMISATION EXAMPLE

To illustrate the application of first-order conditions to the determination of the unconstrained *minimum* of a function of several variables, consider the following example. A flour miller has available to him three separate processes for milling flour. Let

$$y = y_1 + y_2 + y_3 \qquad (13.9)$$

where y = total output of flour in thousands of kg; and
   y_1, y_2, y_3 = output of flour using process 1, 2, 3 respectively, also in thousands of kg.

We may define average costs (AC) in the usual way as cost (in dollars) per unit of total output y. Suppose this miller's average costs are given as a function of the outputs of flour from the three processes, according to the following equation:

$$AC = 45 - 8y_1 - 3y_2 + y_1^2 + \tfrac{1}{2}y_2^2 + 4y_3^2. \qquad (13.10)$$

Let us consider the problem of determining what levels of output y_1, y_2 and y_3 will minimise average costs. Mathematically, this problem is one of finding the unconstrained minimum of function (13.10).

To find the minimum of (13.10) with respect to the three arguments y_1, y_2, y_3,† we find the three partial derivatives and equate them to zero. This will give us three simultaneous equations which can be solved for the three unknowns y_1, y_2 and y_3.

The procedure is as follows:

$$\frac{\partial AC}{\partial y_1} = -8 + 2y_1 = 0 \qquad (13.11a)$$

$$\frac{\partial AC}{\partial y_2} = -3 + y_2 = 0 \qquad (13.11b)$$

$$\frac{\partial AC}{\partial y_3} = 8y_3 = 0. \qquad (13.11c)$$

---

† In any function $y = f(x_1, x_2, \ldots, x_n)$ the quantities $x_1, x_2, \ldots, x_n$ are called the *arguments* of the function.

The solutions to the three Equations (13.11) fall out very simply as:

$$y_1 = 4,$$
$$y_2 = 3,$$
$$y_3 = 0.$$

Substituting these values back into Equation (13.10) indicates that the minimum level of AC is $24\frac{1}{2}$.

We cannot easily verify this result graphically because Equation (13.10) contains four variables, AC, y_1, y_2 and y_3, and therefore cannot be represented in full in a three-dimensional diagram. However, noting that our optimum solution contains one variable, y_3, at zero level, we may eliminate this variable from (13.10) and study the effects of y_1 and y_2 alone on AC. In other words, setting $y_3 = 0$ in (13.10) we obtain

$$AC = 45 - 8y_1 - 3y_2 + y_1^2 + \tfrac{1}{2}y_2^2 \tag{13.12}$$

TABLE 13.2

Average Costs of Flour Produced by Two Processes
($/'000 kg)

		Output Using Process I (y_1)					
		0	1	2	3	4	5
	0	45	38	33	30	29	30
	1	$42\frac{1}{2}$	$35\frac{1}{2}$	$30\frac{1}{2}$	$27\frac{1}{2}$	$26\frac{1}{2}$	$27\frac{1}{2}$
Output Using	2	41	34	29	26	25	26
Process 2 (y_2)	3	$40\frac{1}{2}$	$33\frac{1}{2}$	$28\frac{1}{2}$	$25\frac{1}{2}$	$24\frac{1}{2}$	$25\frac{1}{2}$
	4	41	34	29	26	25	26
	5	$42\frac{1}{2}$	$35\frac{1}{2}$	$30\frac{1}{2}$	$27\frac{1}{2}$	$26\frac{1}{2}$	$27\frac{1}{2}$

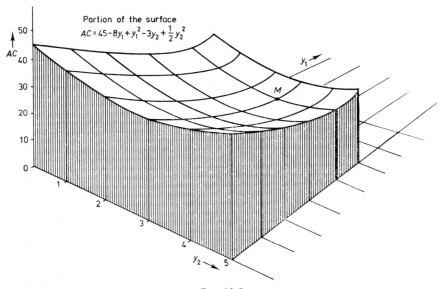

Fig. 13.3

and we may draw a three-dimensional picture of this equation. First we calculate a series of coordinates for a range of values of the independent variables, as shown in Table 13.2. Then a diagram of Equation (13.12) may be constructed as shown in Fig. 13.3. The figure shows only a portion of the surface corresponding to Equation (13.12), specifically that part where $0 \leqslant y_1, y_2 \leqslant 5$. The surface is clearly convex from below, and its lowest point is seen at M, where $y_1 = 4$ and $y_2 = 3$. Inspect Table 13.2 and confirm the values of AC, y_1 and y_2 at the unconstrained minimum point of this function.

13.3 Constrained Optimisation and Lagrange Multipliers

13.3.1 A CONSTRAINED MAXIMISATION EXAMPLE: FOREIGN TRADE EQUILIBRIUM

As we have already noted, the majority of optimisation problems occurring in economic analysis are of the constrained variety. Let us consider these problems in the context of functions of several variables by means of an example. At the same time we shall introduce a powerful technique for solving constrained optimisation problems.

Consider a group of village craftsmen who earn their entire living by producing violins and harpsichords. Their handiwork is exported to America, where the violins command a price of $600 apiece, and the harpsichords a price of $800. The villagers' objective function, assuming their motives to be entirely pecuniary, can be summarised as follows: Maximise

$$Y = 600v + 800z \tag{13.13}$$

where $Y =$ total income of the villagers in dollars per year;
         $v =$ number of violins produced per year; and
         $z =$ number of harpsichords produced per year.

Let us suppose, however, that annual production possibilities are limited by the transformation function

$$18v = 84 - 3z^2. \tag{13.14}$$

The villagers' economic problem therefore emerges as: Maximise

$$Y = 600v + 800z \tag{13.15a}$$

subject to

$$18v = 84 - 3z^2. \tag{13.15b}$$

A diagrammatic exposition is provided by Fig. 13.4. The objective function appears as a set of iso-income lines, YY. The production possibilities frontier has the usual concave shape. An economic optimum clearly arises at the tangency solution at point P, where 2 violins and 4 harpsichords are produced and sold on overseas markets. This point, in fact, reflects a trading equilibrium which yields a total income of $600(2) + $800(4) = $4,400.

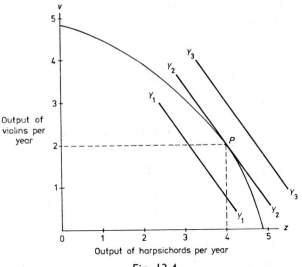

Fig. 13.4

Algebraically the problem posed in (13.15) can most easily be solved using a method known as *Lagrange multipliers*.† Let us first see how this method is applied, and then discuss some of the principles on which it is based. We can distinguish five steps, as follows:

(a) Write the constraint as an implicit function. The transformation function (13.14) thus becomes

$$18v + 3z^2 - 84 = 0. \tag{13.16}$$

(b) Multiply Equation (13.16) by a new variable (λ) whose value remains, for the moment, undetermined. This gives us

$$\lambda(18v + 3z^2 - 84) = 0. \tag{13.17}$$

(c) Add the last result (Equation (13.17)) to the objective function to get the so-called Lagrangean expression

$$L = 600v + 800z + \lambda(18v + 3z^2 - 84). \tag{13.18}$$

(d) Observing that the Lagrangean expression contains three variables (v, z and λ) whose values are unknown, obtain the three first-order derivatives of the function ($\partial L / \partial v$, $\partial L / \partial z$ and $\partial L / \partial \lambda$) and set these equal to zero.

We thus obtain the three simultaneous equations:

$$\frac{\partial L}{\partial v} = 600 + 18\lambda = 0 \tag{13.19a}$$

$$\frac{\partial L}{\partial z} = 800 + 6\lambda z = 0 \tag{13.19b}$$

$$\frac{\partial L}{\partial \lambda} = 18v + 3z^2 - 84 = 0. \tag{13.19c}$$

† After the French mathematician and astronomer, Count Joseph L. Lagrange (1736–1813).

(e) Solve the set of three equations for the three unknowns. From Equation (13.19a) we obtain

$$\lambda = -\frac{600}{18},\tag{13.20}$$

and from Equation (13.19b) we get

$$\lambda = -\frac{800}{6z}.\tag{13.21}$$

Equating (13.20) and (13.21) and simplifying yields

$$z = 4.$$

Substituting for z in (13.19c) yields

$$18v + 48 - 84 = 0,$$
$$v = 2.$$

We observe that the solution $v = 2$, $z = 4$ is in fact the constrained optimum solution found earlier by graphical methods.

How does this Lagrange multiplier technique work? It is first apparent that because the production restriction has been written as an implicit function, any multiple of it must equal zero. Specifically, if, as in Equation (13.16),

$$18v + 3z^2 - 84 = 0,$$

then

$$\lambda(18v + 3z^2 - 84) = 0.\tag{13.22}$$

Thus, when the LHS of Equation (13.22) is added to the objective function it will not affect the value of the objective function whatever the value of λ. In the course of setting up the Lagrangean expression, the value of λ is left undetermined, as noted in Equations (13.17) and (13.18). By maximising the Lagrangean function we simultaneously maximise the objective function itself (Equation (13.15a)) and satisfy the constraint (Equation (13.15b)). As we have seen, this maximisation is achieved as usual by taking partial derivatives of the Lagrangean function and setting them equal to zero. In the solution a specific value for λ emerges, as in Equation (13.20).

A closer scrutiny of the equations in (13.19) yielded by the Lagrange multiplier technique reveals certain features of considerable economic interest. In particular, take the first two Equations (13.19a) and (13.19b). These tell us immediately that

$$\frac{1}{3}z = \frac{800}{600}\tag{13.23}$$

which may be obtained by equating the RHS of Equations (13.20) and (13.21) and rearranging.

Let us leave this result aside for the moment, and turn to a well-known axiom of economic theory which states that an optimal trading position will be attained when the marginal rate of transformation for any two commodities equals the negative of their foreign price ratio. For two commodities v and z this equilibrium condition may be stated:

$$MRT = \frac{dv}{dz} = -\frac{p_z}{p_v} \qquad (13.24)$$

where p_z and p_v are the prices of z and v respectively, and the MRT of v into z is given (as we saw in Section 7.2.5) by the derivative dv/dz of the production possibilities curve $v = f(z)$.

So, we can also solve our villagers' problem by application of this conventional theoretical result. The price ratio on the RHS of Equation (13.24) is given as $-800/600$ and it only remains to find the MRT or the slope of the production possibilities frontier. From Equation (13.14) we obtain

$$v = \frac{84}{18} - \frac{3}{18} z^2, \qquad (13.25)$$

and differentiating and simplifying, we get

$$\frac{dv}{dz} = -\frac{1}{3} z. \qquad (13.26)$$

Inserting these results in Equation (13.24) we find that the villagers' optimum position is reached where

$$-\frac{1}{3} z = -\frac{800}{600}$$

or

$$\frac{1}{3} z = \frac{800}{600}. \qquad (13.27)$$

Equation (13.27) is identical with Equation (13.23). Thus the Lagrange multiplier technique yields precisely the same results as does the application of traditional marginal theory. Indeed, the Lagrange technique is superior to the traditional approach as a means of theoretical analysis. In our example it was possible for us to employ the "tangency solution" method (namely, Equation (13.24)) only because we knew beforehand that an economic optimum would result. With the Lagrange multiplier approach, however, the mathematical conditions of optimality are automatically provided with application of the method. Equation (13.23), derived from the Lagrange analysis, is in fact a statement of the general economic principle (Equation (13.24)) for the particular example we have studied.

The reader may still ask: why bother with the apparently cumbersome Lagrange multiplier technique, when a solution to our simple problem was obtainable using elementary methods as in Equations (13.24) to (13.27)? The answer to this question lies in the word "simple". Our problem was soluble by traditional means because the product transformation function (13.25) was simple enough to be differentiated easily. In many problems, however, the constraint may appear in a form which is not amenable to simple differentiation.

For example, consider the difficulties of tackling the violins and harpsichords problem via elementary optimisation techniques if the product transformation curve had comprised a circular function such as:

$$v^2 + z^2 = 25. \tag{13.28}$$

To apply Equation (13.24) we must first obtain $v = f(z)$. We find

$$v = \sqrt{25 - z^2}. \tag{13.29}$$

But our simple techniques of differentiation are incapable of finding dv/dz from this function, and so we can proceed no further along this avenue.

However, let us apply the method of Lagrange multipliers. Taking the previous objective function (13.13) and the new constraint (13.28), we may write the villagers' new problem as follows:
Maximise

$$Y = 600v + 800z \tag{13.30a}$$

subject to

$$v^2 + z^2 = 25. \tag{13.30b}$$

Converting the constraint to an implicit function, introducing an undetermined multiplier (λ) and adding the result to the objective function, we form the Lagrangean expression

$$L = 600v + 800z + \lambda(v^2 + z^2 - 25). \tag{13.31}$$

Maximising L by taking partial derivatives and setting these equal to zero we have:

$$\frac{\partial L}{\partial v} = 600 + 2\lambda v = 0 \tag{13.32a}$$

$$\frac{\partial L}{\partial z} = 800 + 2\lambda z = 0 \tag{13.32b}$$

$$\frac{\partial L}{\partial \lambda} = v^2 + z^2 - 25 = 0. \tag{13.32c}$$

We now solve the set of three equations. From the first two equations we get:

$$\lambda = -\frac{600}{2v} \tag{13.33a}$$

$$\lambda = -\frac{800}{2z}. \tag{13.33b}$$

Equating the RHS of Equations (13.33) gives:

$$v = \frac{3}{4}z. \tag{13.34}$$

Substitution for v in Equation (13.32c) yields

$$\left(\frac{3}{4}z\right)^2 + z^2 - 25 = 0,$$

$$\left(\frac{25}{16}\right)z^2 = 25,$$

whence we obtain:

$$z = \sqrt{\frac{25 \times 16}{25}} = 4.$$

Substitute 4 for z in Equation (13.34) to obtain v:

$$v = \frac{3}{4}(4) = 3.$$

Substitution of 3 for v and 4 for z in Equation (13.30a) enables Y to be calculated as $600(3) + 800(4) = \$5,000$.

The optimal trading position would thus necessitate the output of 3 violins and 4 harpsichords, yielding a total income of $5,000.

So, for practical as well as theoretical reasons, the Lagrange technique is a valuable optimisation device.

Lagrange multiplier theory also extends to cases involving more than two variables and more than one constraint. The basic principles are the same; a fuller treatment of this subject is contained in Appendix B, Section 2.

13.3.2 ANOTHER CONSTRAINED MAXIMISATION EXAMPLE: CONSUMER EQUILIBRIUM

The theory of consumer behaviour is another fruitful area for the use of Lagrange multipliers. The individual consumer's economic problem may be stated as the maximisation of his total utility subject to a budget constraint. Suppose an individual consumes two commodities, x and y, at prices p_x and p_y respectively. With a fixed sum of money M to spend on consumption, his purchases of x and y will be constrained by the budget equation

$$p_x x + p_y y = M. \tag{13.35}$$

Now the form of the utility function to be maximised depends on which theory of utility is applied. If the cardinal utility approach is adopted, the individual's objective entails the maximisation of

$$U = TU_x + TU_y \tag{13.36}$$

where total utility (U) is a measurable variable, and comprises the sum of the total utilities $(TU_x$ and $TU_y)$ separately derived from the consumption of commodities x and y respectively. The total utility yielded by each commodity is a function of the quantity consumed; thus we may write:

$$TU_x = f(x) \tag{13.37a}$$
$$TU_y = g(y). \tag{13.37b}$$

Differentiating functions (13.37a and b) we get

$$\frac{d}{dx} TU_x = f'(x) = MU_x \tag{13.38a}$$

$$\frac{d}{dy} TU_y = g'(y) = MU_y \tag{13.38b}$$

which represent the individual's marginal utility functions for the two

---

commodities. Typically, the total utility functions in Equations (13.37) will be concave, such that the marginal utility functions in Equations (13.38) will be positive and decreasing. An illustration is given in Fig. 13.5.

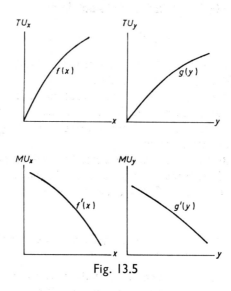

Fig. 13.5

Substituting the functions (13.37) in Equation (13.36) and adding the budget constraint, the individual consumer's economic problem becomes: Maximise

$$U = f(x) + g(y) \tag{13.39a}$$

subject to

$$p_x x + p_y y = M. \tag{13.39b}$$

To solve this constrained maximisation problem we may apply Lagrange multiplier theory. Writing Equation (13.39b) in implicit form we get:

$$p_x x + p_y y - M = 0. \tag{13.40}$$

A Lagrange multiplier is introduced to obtain

$$\lambda(p_x x + p_y y - M) = 0, \tag{13.41}$$

which is added to our objective function, yielding the following Lagrangean expression:

$$L = f(x) + g(y) + \lambda(p_x x + p_y y - M). \tag{13.42}$$

Maximising L, we take partial derivatives of the Lagrangean expression (13.42) and set them equal to zero:

$$\frac{\partial L}{\partial x} = f'(x) + \lambda p_x = 0 \tag{13.43a}$$

$$\frac{\partial L}{\partial y} = g'(y) + \lambda p_y = 0 \tag{13.43b}$$

$$\frac{\partial L}{\partial \lambda} = p_x x + p_y y - M = 0. \tag{13.43c}$$

The properties of economic interest are apparent in Equations (13.43a and b). Rearranging these we get:

$$\lambda = -\frac{f'(x)}{p_x} \qquad (13.44a)$$

$$\lambda = -\frac{g'(y)}{p_y}. \qquad (13.44b)$$

Equating the RHS of Equations (13.44) we see that

$$\frac{f'(x)}{g'(y)} = \frac{p_x}{p_y} \qquad (13.45)$$

or, using the expressions from Equations (13.38),

$$\frac{MU_x}{MU_y} = \frac{p_x}{p_y}, \qquad (13.46)$$

which is the same as

$$\frac{MU_x}{p_x} = \frac{MU_y}{p_y}. \qquad (13.47)$$

What we have proved, in other words, is the well-known principle that a consumer will maximise his total utility when his marginal utilities are proportional to commodity prices, as shown by Equation (13.46), or equivalently, when his marginal utilities per dollar are equal between commodities (Equation (13.47)).†

Suppose that instead of cardinal utility theory, we adopt the ordinal approach involving indifference analysis (see Section 10.8). Using the

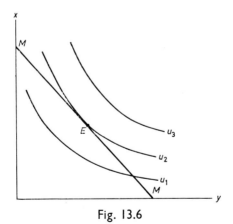

Fig. 13.6

---

† Note that it follows from Equation (13.44) that Equation (13.47) may be extended to the following:

$$\frac{MU_x}{p_x} = \frac{MU_y}{p_y} = \lambda.$$

It can be shown that in this model $\lambda = \frac{dU}{dM}$, the consumer's marginal utility per dollar of his "income" or budget, M.

ordinal assumptions, we must maximise an indicator variable (u) which acts as a proxy for total utility itself. Accordingly, we have:
Maximise

$$u = h(x,y) \tag{13.48a}$$

subject to

$$p_x x + p_y y = M \tag{13.48b}$$

where u is a function of x and y and describes the individual's indifference map. The problem appears in diagrammatic form in Fig. 13.6. The curves marked u_1, u_2 and u_3 are indifference curves, the budget line is MM, and the constrained optimum solution is given at the tangency point E.

Now let us solve the problem algebraically. Expressing the budget constraint (13.48b) as an implicit function, introducing a Lagrange multiplier and converting the objective function to a Lagrangean expression, we obtain the function to be maximised as

$$L = h(x,y) + \lambda(p_x x + p_y y - M). \tag{13.49}$$

Taking partial derivatives, we get

$$\frac{\partial L}{\partial x} = h_x(x,y) + \lambda p_x = 0 \tag{13.50a}$$

$$\frac{\partial L}{\partial y} = h_y(x,y) + \lambda p_y = 0 \tag{13.50b}$$

$$\frac{\partial L}{\partial \lambda} = p_x x + p_y y - M = 0. \tag{13.50c}$$

Rearranging Equations (13.50a and b) we have:

$$\lambda = -\frac{h_x(x,y)}{p_x} \tag{13.51a}$$

$$\lambda = -\frac{h_y(x,y)}{p_y}, \tag{13.51b}$$

so that

$$\frac{h_x(x,y)}{h_y(x,y)} = \frac{p_x}{p_y}. \tag{13.52}$$

Now the left-hand side of Equation (13.52) represents the ratio of small changes in utility yielded by small changes in the quantities consumed of x and y, and in fact denotes the marginal rate of substitution of one commodity for the other in consumption. Hence Equation (13.52) at once proves the familiar theorem that, in order for a consumer to maximise utility, his marginal rate of substitution must equal the ratio of commodity prices.

13.3.3 A CONSTRAINED MINIMISATION EXAMPLE

To illustrate the application of the Lagrange method of undetermined multipliers to a problem of constrained *minimisation*, reconsider the problem posed in Section 9.3.1. The problem concerned a newspaper publisher who uses capital (K) and labour (L) in the production of a given number of newspapers per day. The isoquant equation for this entrepreneur is of the form

$$K = \frac{100}{L^2} + 30. \tag{13.53}$$

With prices per unit for labour and capital of $6 and $3 respectively, the publisher aims to produce his given output volume so as to minimise the total costs of purchasing the two factors, given by the equation

$$TC = 6L + 3K. \tag{13.54}$$

As we saw in Section 9.3.1 this is a problem of constrained minimisation; that is, the entrepreneur should attempt to:
Minimise

$$TC = 6L + 3K \tag{13.55a}$$

subject to

$$K = \frac{100}{L^2} + 30. \tag{13.55b}$$

In Section 9.3.1 we solved this problem by application of traditional marginal theory. Let us now illustrate how Lagrange multipliers may also be used to give an alternative means of solution.

Converting the constraint in Equation (13.55b) to an implicit function and introducing a multiplier λ, we may combine Equations (13.55a and b) to yield the following Lagrangean function. We shall designate the function ϕ on this occasion, since our former symbol L is currently in use for another purpose. We have

$$\phi = 6L + 3K + \lambda \left(\frac{100}{L^2} + 30 - K \right). \tag{13.56}$$

The partial derivatives of Equation (13.56) are equated to zero:

$$\frac{\partial \phi}{\partial L} = 6 - \frac{200\lambda}{L^3} = 0 \tag{13.57a}$$

$$\frac{\partial \phi}{\partial K} = 3 - \lambda = 0 \tag{13.57b}$$

$$\frac{\partial \phi}{\partial \lambda} = \frac{100}{L^2} + 30 - K = 0. \tag{13.57c}$$

From Equation (13.57b) we obtain directly $\lambda = 3$. Substituting this value for λ into (13.57a) yields

$$6 - \frac{600}{L^3} = 0,$$

whence

$$L^3 = 100 \text{ and } L = 4.642,$$

and finally substitution in (13.57c) gives the result $K = 34.642$. These results confirm those found in Section 9.3.1.

As an exercise, the reader may derive the above result for the general case where the isoquant equation is expressed simply as

$$K = f(L) \tag{13.58a}$$

and the total cost equation is

$$TC = wL + rK. \tag{13.58b}$$

That is, minimise Equation (13.58b) subject to (13.58a) using Lagrange multipliers, and show that an equilibrium condition of the familiar form

$$RTS = \frac{dK}{dL} = -\frac{w}{r} \tag{13.59}$$

may be obtained.

Exercises

1. Consider the utility surface for two consumption goods A and B:
$$U = AB - 2A^2 - B^2 + 14B.$$
   What is the maximum utility level which may be achieved?

2. Take a country producing only two goods, with a product transformation function of the form

$$y_1^2 + 4y_2^2 - 52 = 0,$$

   where y_1 and y_2 are outputs of the two commodities. Suppose the international prices of y_1 and y_2 are $5 and $15 per unit respectively. Use Lagrange multipliers to find the output combination which should be produced to maximise the country's national income. What is the resultant income?

3. Consider a firm which has $2,400 to spend on inputs of labour and capital. The costs of labour and capital are $4 and $3 per unit respectively. Suppose the firm's production function takes the form
$$y = 2L^{\frac{1}{4}}K^{\frac{1}{4}}.$$
   What quantities of labour and capital should the firm buy so as to maximise output from the funds available? Note that the problem can be written as:
   Maximise
$$y = 2L^{\frac{1}{4}}K^{\frac{1}{4}}$$
   subject to
$$4L + 3K = 2,400.$$

4. Suppose a firm wishes to produce a given volume of output (y_0), and purchases inputs of labour and capital at prices of w and r respectively. The production function of the firm is
$$y = AL^aK^b.$$
   Now if the firm wishes to produce y_0 at minimum total cost, it must find the solution to the following problem:
   Minimise
$$wL + rC$$
   subject to
$$y_0 = AL^aK^b.$$

Using Lagrange multiplier theory, show that the condition of optimality is:

$$\frac{w}{r} = \frac{\partial y/\partial L}{\partial y/\partial K}.$$

5. Consider the firm studied in Exercise 9, Chapter 11. Suppose its total cost function is of the form:

$$TC = 5y_1 + y_2 + 3y_3 + 3.$$

Defining profit as net revenue $(NR) = TR - TC$, calculate the levels of output of leather, cardboard and string which will maximise profit for the firm.

6. Consider the case of a monopsonist (a producer who is the sole buyer of the inputs he uses) whose production function is of the form

$$y = 7L - L^2 + 13K - \tfrac{3}{2}K^2.$$

Suppose his output sells for a fixed price of \$1 per unit. The supply price of capital is given by the function

$$r = 1 + \tfrac{1}{2}K$$

and the supply price (wage rate) of labour is

$$w = 1 + \tfrac{1}{2}L.$$

Calculate the quantities of labour and capital he should purchase so as to maximise profit.

Part IV: Linear Economic Models and Matrix Algebra

Chapter 14

Linear Models in Matrix Form

14.1 The Role of Linear Algebra in Economics

In Chapter 4 we saw some simple examples of linear models—a model of supply and demand, and an elementary Keynesian income determination system. As we have already observed, linear functions have many applications in theoretical and empirical economics. Indeed, there is a strong case for casting economic relationships in linear form wherever common sense permits. For ease of theoretical manipulation, linear functions have much in their favour. In macroeconomics, for example, analysis of various multipliers—such as the Keynesian investment multiplier, the foreign trade multiplier and the government expenditure multiplier—can be conducted without great difficulty in systems based on linear functions.

Linear functions are important also because econometricians, when studying statistical data to investigate possible patterns of behaviour, very frequently test their ideas in linear form. As an hypothetical example, imagine we have been able to collect a series of statistics describing consumption expenditure by families in different income groups within the community. The data are presented in Table 14.1.

TABLE 14.1

Consumption Expenditure at Various Median Family Incomes

Income (Y) ($)	Consumption (C) ($)
1000	1800
2000	3600
3000	3100
4000	4000
5000	4400
6000	5400
7000	6000
8000	6100

A graph of the data reveals a scatter of observed points, as in Fig. 14.1. The relationship between consumption (C) and income (Y) may accordingly be found by superimposing the line of best fit on the scatter of points. Alternatively, more refined statistical methods (some of which will be studied in Chapter 20) may be applied to the data. We may then "fit" the equation:

$$C = a + cY, \tag{14.1}$$

and obtain an appropriate value for autonomous consumption expenditure (a) and the marginal propensity to consume (c).

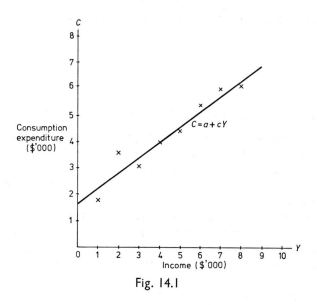

Fig. 14.1

However, although the use of linear functions may be desirable on the grounds of simplicity or convenience, this does not mean that all economic interrelations ought to be cast in this form. Consider an aggregate labour-supply function, where the volume of labour on offer may be presumed to increase as the real wage rate is raised. Over certain ranges of the function, a linear function may be appropriate. We might write

$$N = m + nW \tag{14.2}$$

to represent the supply function, where N is the number of man-hours on offer, m is a constant, W is the real wage rate and n is a positive coefficient. Such an equation interpreted literally, however, implies no limit to the volume of labour supplied. Given a sufficiently high real wage, N may approach infinity. But in reality there are upper constraints on the supply of labour. The economy clearly cannot proceed beyond the full-employment point, and for this reason a nonlinear function would undoubtedly be a wiser choice to describe the complete function. The difference between a nonlinear and linear supply schedule is at once apparent in Fig. 14.2.

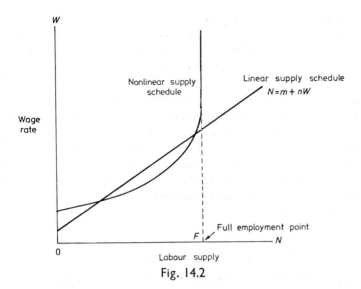

W

Nonlinear supply schedule

Linear supply schedule
$N = m + nW$

Wage rate

Full employment point
N

F

0

Labour supply

Fig. 14.2

(Notice that since Fig. 14.2 depicts a supply schedule, the dependent variable N is shown on the horizontal axis.) In this situation we may in fact have a choice between using a nonlinear function to describe the *complete* relationship between N and W, or a linear function to approximate a *part* of this relationship, i.e., in the range of W below the point F on Fig. 14.2.

The typical linear static economic model (the only type we shall consider) takes the form of a set of linear simultaneous equations. An appropriate linear equation describes some part of the model, and the collection of equations taken together represents the model in its entirety. Economics textbooks abound in simple two-variable, two-equation static linear systems. In microeconomic theory, the classic example is the linear supply and demand model such as that studied in Section 4.2. Within macroeconomics, the best-known two-by-two linear system is the Keynesian "$C + I$" income-determination model utilising a linear consumption function and an autonomous level of investment expenditure, as seen in Section 4.4.

No economist would argue—especially at the macroeconomic level— that such primitive models realistically explain the complex workings of a modern economy. At best, they convey a method of analysis through which intricate problems involving many variables and interrelations might be studied. The naive examples with which the beginning student of economics may find himself so preoccupied can be conceived only as prototypes, pointing the way to more realistic and, of necessity, more complicated mathematical systems.

The simple linear systems studied in Chapter 4 were so small that they could be manipulated using no more than elementary school-level algebra. Larger systems, however, require more powerful tools of analysis. The branch of mathematics which we bring to bear on the study of linear equation systems is called *linear* or *matrix algebra*. In this and the ensuing chapters we shall be studying some basic concepts of matrix algebra. The techniques will be developed in the context of some simple macroeconomic models, which are essentially of a theoretical nature and only go part of the way in explaining how workable macromodels can be constructed and used for forecasting and economic control. The full flowering of the development of large-scale systems is seen in the big econometric macro-models of the economy, which may incorporate several hundred variables and equations. Such models may contain many features, such as time-lags and nonlinearities, which the student will properly understand only after a fuller study of mathematical economics and econometrics. Nevertheless, as mentioned above, a prerequisite to the understanding of all linear systems, whether simple or more complicated, is a knowledge of the basic tools of linear algebra.

14.2 Elementary Matrix Notation

Let us return to the simple Keynesian macroeconomic model first studied in Section 4.4:

$$Y = C + I^*   \tag{14.3a}$$

$$C = a + cY,   \tag{14.3b}$$

where Y = aggregate demand;
C = aggregate planned consumption expenditure;
I^* = investment expenditure, determined exogenously;
a = autonomous consumption expenditure; and
c = marginal propensity to consume.

Each endogenous variable in the system (i.e., Y and C) has associated fixed coefficients in the set of equations. The above equations can be rearranged to give the equivalent system:

$$1Y - 1C = I^*   \tag{14.4a}$$

$$-cY + 1C = a.   \tag{14.4b}$$

We have written these equations so that the unknowns of the system (Y and C) have been arranged with their associated coefficients in columns on the LHS of the two equations, and the intercept terms representing the model's exogenous elements have been placed on the RHS. Y from Equation (14.3a) has been rewritten in Equation (14.4a) as $1 \times Y$. The fixed coefficient attached to Y in (14.4a) is, accordingly, 1. Similarly, in Equation (14.4b), C has a coefficient of 1. This is not mathematical pedantry, but an important concept required in drafting linear systems in matrix form. In every equation, each endogenous variable must have an associated coefficient. Indeed, it is worth remembering that in certain cases the relevant coefficient may be zero. For example, an expression such as

$$x = 8   \tag{14.5}$$

can quite legitimately be conceived as a linear equation *in the variables x and y* of the form

$$1x + 0y = 8. \tag{14.6}$$

Here, we have attached a coefficient of 1 to x and 0 to y, thereby establishing the equivalence of Equations (14.5) and (14.6).

In the linear macromodel described by Equations (14.4a and b), there are three sets of elements: a set of two unknowns (Y and C); a set of four coefficients attached to these unknowns; and a set of two intercept terms (I^* and a) that describe the model's exogenous components. Our ability to analyse the various quantitative properties of economic equilibrium will obviously be greatly extended if we can find some way of writing down the equations in such a form that these three sets of elements are kept in separate categories.

Consider what Equations (14.4a) and (14.4b) actually describe. The four coefficients on the LHS multiply the two unknowns to give the two intercept terms on the right. The three sets of elements in the equation interact simultaneously. Let us write down the three sets of elements as if they were a *single* equation of the form:

$$\begin{bmatrix} \text{Set of} \\ \text{coefficients} \end{bmatrix} \times \begin{bmatrix} \text{Set of} \\ \text{unknowns} \end{bmatrix} = \begin{bmatrix} \text{Set of} \\ \text{intercept terms} \end{bmatrix}. \tag{14.7}$$

For our example this might be written as:

$$\begin{bmatrix} 1 & -1 \\ -c & 1 \end{bmatrix} \begin{bmatrix} Y \\ C \end{bmatrix} = \begin{bmatrix} I^* \\ a \end{bmatrix}. \tag{14.8}$$

Equation (14.8) is in fact an expression in *matrix* terms of Equations (14.4). Each of the bracketed expressions in (14.8) is a *matrix*. A matrix is defined quite simply as an ordered array of elements.

The first matrix on the LHS of Equation (14.8) is a rectangular array of the coefficients which in (14.4) were attached to the unknowns. Notice that inside the matrix the coefficients are arranged in exactly the same way as they appear in the pair of Equations (14.4). In effect, this matrix is obtained merely by blotting out the unknowns from the LHS of the system of equations.

The unknowns are introduced in the form of a column, giving us the second matrix in Equation (14.8). In the original set of Equations (14.4), Y was listed first in each equation, hence Y becomes the leading element in the column. Similarly, C was the second variable in each equation, and so becomes the second element in the column when the equation is written in matrix form.

The final matrix is a column describing the intercept terms. The intercept term (I^*) from the first equation heads the column. The second space in the column is filled by the second equation's intercept term (a).

14.3 Further Linear Macromodels

14.3.1 ANOTHER TWO-EQUATION MODEL

Take another simple macromodel in which aggregate demand comprises autonomous consumption expenditure (C^*), exogenously determined export demand (X^*), and import demand (M), which is linearly dependent upon income. Such a system may be written as:

$$Y = C^* + X^* - M \qquad (14.9a)$$

$$M = s + pY. \qquad (14.9b)$$

Equation (14.9a) is a national accounting identity which ensures that equilibrium will be attained. For the import-demand function (14.9b), s represents autonomous import expenditure, and the coefficient p is the marginal propensity to import. A diagrammatic interpretation is provided in Fig. 14.3. Consumption expenditure and export demand are, by assumption, exogenous and yield a horizontal expenditure line. The import-demand schedule is upward-sloping. Aggregate demand for domestic output $(C + X - M)$ is thus represented by a downward-sloping line. Equilibrium income is determined by the intersection of the aggregate demand and supply lines at point E. The level of income at equilibrium is OA. Note, however, that total import expenditure M is also an endogenous variable in the model, and for a full analysis of the properties of equilibrium, the system should be solved for this variable as well. Graphically, the equilibrium level of imports is represented by the distance OB in Fig. 14.3.

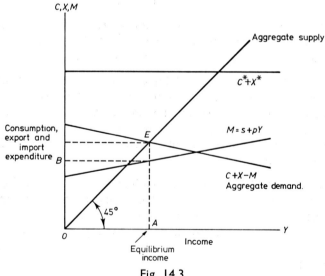

Fig. 14.3

To represent Equations (14.9) in matrix notation, we first rearrange the system, as before, by transferring the endogenous variables with associated coefficients to columns on the LHS of each equation, leaving the exogenous elements on the RHS. We thus obtain:

$$1Y + 1M = C^* + X^* \tag{14.10a}$$
$$-pY + 1M = s. \tag{14.10b}$$

Following our earlier procedure, we may now write the set of Equations (14.10) as the matrix equation

$$\begin{bmatrix} 1 & 1 \\ -p & 1 \end{bmatrix} \begin{bmatrix} Y \\ M \end{bmatrix} = \begin{bmatrix} C^* + X^* \\ s \end{bmatrix}. \tag{14.11}$$

14.3.2 A THREE-EQUATION MODEL

The same rules may be applied to larger models. Consider a slightly more complicated system in which aggregate investment is partly autonomous but is also influenced by national income. The higher the level of income and aggregate demand, the greater will be the inducement to invest. An appropriate linear investment function is:

$$I = m + vY \tag{14.12}$$

where m is autonomous investment expenditure and v is a proportionality factor. Including this equation in a system containing a linear consumption function and the income-expenditure identity, we derive the following model:

$$Y = C + I \tag{14.13a}$$
$$C = a + cY \tag{14.13b}$$
$$I = m + vY. \tag{14.13c}$$

This model is the same as that represented by Equations (14.3) except that we have replaced I^* with our new investment function (14.12).

Rearranging the set of Equations (14.13) we obtain:

$$1Y - 1C - 1I = 0 \tag{14.14a}$$
$$-cY + 1C + 0I = a \tag{14.14b}$$
$$-vY + 0C + 1I = m. \tag{14.14c}$$

In matrix form the above equations emerge as follows:

$$\begin{bmatrix} 1 & -1 & -1 \\ -c & 1 & 0 \\ -v & 0 & 1 \end{bmatrix} \begin{bmatrix} Y \\ C \\ I \end{bmatrix} = \begin{bmatrix} 0 \\ a \\ m \end{bmatrix}. \tag{14.15}$$

14.3.3 A FOUR-EQUATION MODEL

Again, we may construct a still larger model by adding, say, a fixed level of autonomous government expenditure G^*, constant export demand X^* and a linear import function. The model now becomes:

$$Y = C + I + G^* + X^* - M \tag{14.16a}$$
$$C = a + cY \tag{14.16b}$$
$$I = m + vY \tag{14.16c}$$
$$M = s + pY. \tag{14.16d}$$

Rearranging we get:

$$1Y - 1C - 1I + 1M = G^* + X^* \tag{14.17a}$$
$$-cY + 1C + 0I + 0M = a \tag{14.17b}$$
$$-vY + 0C + 0I + 0M = m \tag{14.17c}$$
$$-pY + 0C + 0I + 1M = s. \tag{14.17d}$$

which can be expressed in matrix form as:

$$\begin{bmatrix} 1 & -1 & -1 & 1 \\ -c & 1 & 0 & 0 \\ -v & 0 & 0 & 0 \\ -p & 0 & 0 & 1 \end{bmatrix} \begin{bmatrix} Y \\ C \\ I \\ M \end{bmatrix} = \begin{bmatrix} G^*+X^* \\ a \\ m \\ s \end{bmatrix}. \tag{14.18}$$

14.3.4 LARGER MACROMODELS

It should be clear from the above that larger models may be built by simply extending the range of variables brought into the system as endogenously determined. For instance further equations could be added to (14.18) to "explain" the variables G and X, that is, to make them endogenous in the system. Additional equations might be introduced to separate out the demands for various components of C, I and M, that is, for a variety of consumption, investment and imported goods.

14.4 The Linear Supply and Demand Model in Matrix Terms

In a similar fashion, we may express the simple linear model of supply and demand in matrix terms. Take, for example, the potato market example from Section 4.2.3, which consisted of a linear demand equation and a linear supply equation of the forms, respectively:

$$q = 20 - 3p \tag{14.19a}$$
$$q = \tfrac{5}{2}p. \tag{14.19b}$$

Rearranging these equations as we did in the previous section gives

$$q + 3p = 20 \tag{14.20a}$$
$$q - \tfrac{5}{2}p = 0, \tag{14.20b}$$

and we may now separate out the coefficients of the endogenous variables p and q to give us the matrix equation

$$\begin{bmatrix} 1 & 3 \\ 1 & -\tfrac{5}{2} \end{bmatrix} \begin{bmatrix} q \\ p \end{bmatrix} = \begin{bmatrix} 20 \\ 0 \end{bmatrix}. \tag{14.21}$$

14.5 Some Properties of Matrices

Matrices always consist of *rows* and *columns*. The number of rows and columns in any matrix is said to determine the dimensions or *order* of the matrix. In stating the order of a matrix we always mention the number of rows first, then the number of columns. The matrix from Equation (14.8), which is of the form

$$\begin{bmatrix} 1 & -1 \\ -c & 1 \end{bmatrix},$$

has two rows and two columns and is therefore of order 2×2. A matrix such as

$$\begin{bmatrix} 2 & 2 & 9 \\ 3 & 5 & 7 \end{bmatrix}$$

is of order 2×3.

When a matrix has an equal number of rows and columns it is said to be *square*. Hence the 2×2 matrix on the LHS of Equation (14.8) is square. The first matrix on the LHS of Equation (14.15) is a square matrix of order 3×3, while in the matrix Equation (14.18) we clearly have a 4×4 square matrix. An $n \times n$ matrix is sometimes called an *nth-order* matrix.

Consider the matrix

$$\begin{bmatrix} Y \\ C \end{bmatrix}.$$

This matrix has 2 rows (each row containing only a single element) and 1 column and is thus of order 2×1.

The matrix

$$\begin{bmatrix} I^* \\ a \end{bmatrix}$$

is also of order 2×1. On the other hand, the matrix $\begin{bmatrix} 2 & 2 & 5 \end{bmatrix}$ is of order 1×3, since it contains 1 row and 3 columns (each column containing only a single element).

There is a special name for any matrix which consists only of a single column or a single row of elements. Any such matrix is called a *vector*. The single column of endogenous variables $\begin{bmatrix} Y \\ C \end{bmatrix}$ from (14.8) is a *column vector*. So also is the column of intercept terms on the RHS of the same equation. The 1×3 matrix $\begin{bmatrix} 2 & 2 & 5 \end{bmatrix}$ which we examined above is an example of a *row vector*.

Finally, it is worth remembering that any matrix can be envisaged as a collection of vectors. For example, the matrix

$$\begin{bmatrix} 1 & -1 \\ -c & 1 \end{bmatrix}$$

consists of the two column vectors:

$$\begin{bmatrix} 1 \\ -c \end{bmatrix} \text{ and } \begin{bmatrix} -1 \\ 1 \end{bmatrix}.$$

Alternatively, the same matrix may be seen to consist of the two row vectors

$$\begin{bmatrix} 1 & -1 \end{bmatrix} \text{ and } \begin{bmatrix} -c & 1 \end{bmatrix}.$$

Similarly, the 2 × 3 matrix $\begin{bmatrix} 2 & 2 & 9 \\ 3 & 5 & 7 \end{bmatrix}$ can be conceived as the set of column vectors

$$\begin{bmatrix} 2 \\ 3 \end{bmatrix} \begin{bmatrix} 2 \\ 5 \end{bmatrix} \text{ and } \begin{bmatrix} 9 \\ 7 \end{bmatrix},$$

or as the two row vectors

$$[\,2 \ 2 \ 9\,] \text{ and } [\,3 \ 5 \ 7\,].$$

14.6 Subscript Notation

When dealing with larger models, the need soon arises to develop more compact notation. We may illustrate such a system of notation by putting forward a general way of writing down a system of simultaneous linear equations such as that shown in Equation (14.17). Suppose we replace the endogenous variables in (14.17) by a set of x, with subscripts 1 to 4 attached to distinguish each of the four variables involved. In other words, let

$$x_1 \equiv Y, \quad x_2 \equiv C, \quad x_3 \equiv I, \quad x_4 \equiv M.$$

Similarly, let us relabel the intercept terms on the RHS of Equation (14.17) as a set of b, again with distinguishing subscripts attached, such that we can define:

$$b_1 \equiv G^* + X^*, \quad b_2 \equiv a, \quad b_3 \equiv m, \quad b_4 \equiv s.$$

Now consider the set of fixed coefficients. A set of a may be employed to describe these, but because we are dealing with a rectangular array of elements a double subscript becomes necessary. Let the first subscript refer to the row (or equation) in which the coefficient is situated in Equation (14.17), and let the second subscript refer to the column. Hence the coefficient a_{21} will be found in the second row, first column, and corresponds to $-c$ in the original Equation (14.17).

So, using these new symbols, we may write the set of Equations (14.17) in more orderly fashion as follows:

$$a_{11} x_1 + a_{12} x_2 + a_{13} x_3 + a_{14} x_4 = b_1 \qquad (14.22a)$$
$$a_{21} x_1 + a_{22} x_2 + a_{23} x_3 + a_{24} x_4 = b_2 \qquad (14.22b)$$
$$a_{31} x_1 + a_{32} x_2 + a_{33} x_3 + a_{34} x_4 = b_3 \qquad (14.22c)$$
$$a_{41} x_1 + a_{42} x_2 + a_{43} x_3 + a_{44} x_4 = b_4. \qquad (14.22d)$$

Just as the set of Equations (14.17) could be written as the matrix Equation (14.18), so also may the system (14.22) be expressed in matrix terms. Detaching the coefficients as before, we obtain

$$\begin{bmatrix} a_{11} & a_{12} & a_{13} & a_{14} \\ a_{21} & a_{22} & a_{23} & a_{24} \\ a_{31} & a_{32} & a_{33} & a_{34} \\ a_{41} & a_{42} & a_{43} & a_{44} \end{bmatrix} \begin{bmatrix} x_1 \\ x_2 \\ x_3 \\ x_4 \end{bmatrix} = \begin{bmatrix} b_1 \\ b_2 \\ b_3 \\ b_4 \end{bmatrix}. \qquad (14.23)$$

The a clearly form a square matrix of coefficients. The unknowns of the system, represented by the x, come together as a column vector. The intercept terms, the set of b, also give rise to a column vector.

In the interests of even greater notational efficiency, the matrix of coefficients in Equation (14.23) may be replaced by the single letter **A**, the vector of unknowns by **x** and the vector of intercept terms by **b**. The bold typeface indicates that **A**, **x** and **b** are matrices and vectors and not single variables or coefficients. The set of Equations (14.22) accordingly reaches the ultimate compact form:

$$\mathbf{A}\mathbf{x} = \mathbf{b}. \tag{14.24}$$

The matrix Equation (14.24) tells us that a matrix of coefficients **A** multiplies a vector **x** to give a vector **b**.† In fact, this equation typifies static linear economic models. To set up any such model, regardless of size, we may proceed directly to the formulation expressed in Equation (14.24). The only task required in fully describing the system is to provide the details of the coefficients in the matrix **A** and the elements of the vectors **x** and **b**.

To illustrate the point, the economic model represented by the equation system (14.8) can be equally well described by Equation (14.24) on the understanding that:

$$\mathbf{A} \equiv \begin{bmatrix} a_{11} & a_{12} \\ a_{21} & a_{22} \end{bmatrix} \equiv \begin{bmatrix} 1 & -1 \\ -c & 1 \end{bmatrix},$$

$$\mathbf{x} \equiv \begin{bmatrix} x_1 \\ x_2 \end{bmatrix} \equiv \begin{bmatrix} Y \\ C \end{bmatrix},$$

$$\mathbf{b} \equiv \begin{bmatrix} b_1 \\ b_2 \end{bmatrix} \equiv \begin{bmatrix} I^* \\ a \end{bmatrix}.$$

Again, Equation (14.24) can depict the model (14.15) where:

$$\mathbf{A} \equiv \begin{bmatrix} a_{11} & a_{12} & a_{13} \\ a_{21} & a_{22} & a_{23} \\ a_{31} & a_{32} & a_{33} \end{bmatrix} \equiv \begin{bmatrix} 1 & -1 & -1 \\ -c & 1 & 0 \\ -v & 0 & 1 \end{bmatrix},$$

$$\mathbf{x} \equiv \begin{bmatrix} x_1 \\ x_2 \\ x_3 \end{bmatrix} \equiv \begin{bmatrix} Y \\ C \\ I \end{bmatrix},$$

$$\mathbf{b} \equiv \begin{bmatrix} b_1 \\ b_2 \\ b_3 \end{bmatrix} \equiv \begin{bmatrix} 0 \\ a \\ m \end{bmatrix}.$$

The subscripts appearing in systems of equations such as (14.22) can be expressed in *general* terms by introducing the subscript i to indicate the row or equation in which any element may be found, and subscript j to distinguish columns. Specific numeration of i and j gives a complete coverage of the model. Thus, the a coefficients of the equation system (14.22) can be described as the set of a_{ij} where $i = 1, 2, 3, 4$ and $j = 1, 2, 3, 4$. Likewise, the intercept terms are the collection of b_i where $i = 1, 2, 3, 4$. As another illustration, a matrix **Z** which is of order 2×6 can be represented by a set of z_{ij} where $i = 1, 2$ and $j = 1, 2, \ldots, 6$.

---

† The order in which **A** and **x** are written is important; as we shall see in the next chapter, we must write **Ax** in this equation, not **xA**.

14.7 Sigma Notation

Consider the simple equation

$$x_1 + x_2 = b.$$

With only two terms being added on the LHS it is no great inconvenience to write this equation in full. This is hardly the case, however, when we have, say,

$$x_1 + x_2 + x_3 + x_4 + x_5 + x_6 = b. \tag{14.25}$$

To avoid having to write out the full series of subscripted variables in Equation (14.25), we may use the symbol $\sum$, a Greek capital sigma, which is taken to indicate "the sum of". Any subscript may be used as an index for the summation. Suppose we use the subscript k to distinguish the various x in (14.25), i.e., we define the variables in (14.25) as x_k where $k = 1, 2, \ldots, 6$. Then using the $\sum$ notation we may write (14.25) as

$$\sum x_k = b. \tag{14.26}$$

The LHS of Equation (14.26) reads "the sum of x_k". To be more specific about the x which are included in the sum, we may indicate the range of k below and above the $\sum$ sign. Thus, to denote "the sum of x_k for k ranging from 1 to 6" we write simply

$$\sum_{k=1}^{6} x_k.$$

Similarly, the expression $\sum_{k=3}^{n} x_k$ indicates "the sum of x_k for k ranging from 3 to n", that is, simply $x_3 + x_4 + \ldots + x_n$.

In cases where a double subscript is being used, the notation may still be employed. So, for example,

$$\sum_{j=i}^{5} x_{ij}$$

indicates "the sum of x_{ij} for values of j ranging from 1 to 5", that is,

$$x_{i1} + x_{i2} + x_{i3} + x_{i4} + x_{i5}.$$

In an equation such as

$$a_1 x_1 + a_2 x_2 + a_3 x_3 + a_4 x_4 = b \tag{14.27}$$

the product of two terms is being summed. Thus, denoting each term on the LHS as, say, $a_j x_j$, we may write Equation (14.27) compactly as

$$\sum_{j=1}^{4} a_j x_j = b. \tag{14.28}$$

Carefully compare Equations (14.28) and (14.27) to ensure that you understand this notation.

A set of linear simultaneous equations can also be compactly represented by the $\sum$ notation. Take, for example, the set of four equations in four unknowns shown in (14.22). The subscript j denotes elements by columns within a system; hence the LHS of each equation represents the sum of terms $a_{ij}x_j$ for j ranging from 1 to 4. The *first* equation may thus be written as

$$\sum_{j=1}^{4} a_{1j}x_j = b_1 \tag{14.29}$$

and since the subscript i is used to denote rows in a system, the full set of equations (14.22) may be written:

$$\sum_{j=1}^{4} a_{ij}x_j = b_i \quad i = 1,\ldots,4. \tag{14.30}$$

The student should note carefully that Equation (14.30) is simply an alternative way of writing down the sets of Equations (14.22), (14.23) and (14.24). More generally, in the case of a system with n equations and m unknowns the set of equations can be described as

$$\sum_{j=1}^{m} a_{ij}x_j = b_i \quad i = 1,2,\ldots,n, \tag{14.31}$$

and again the equivalence between (14.31) and the matrix form of this set of equations given in (14.24) should be noted.

The sigma notation discussed in this section has very wide usage in statistics, mathematics and quantitative economics. In the specific area of linear algebra it provides us with an alternative way of writing down matrix equations that we may prefer to use in some circumstances.

Exercises

1. Consider the following macromodel:

$$Y = C + I^*$$
$$C = a + cY$$

where $I^* = \$200$ million, $a = \$440$ million, and $c = 0.6$.
Determine the equilibrium levels of income and consumption expenditure.

2. Suppose, in the above model, I^* rises to $250 million.
   (a) What is the effect on equilibrium income?
   (b) What is the relationship between the change in investment and the resultant change in income?

3. Which of the following expenditure components are exogenous? Give reasons.

export demand,	import demand,
government expenditure,	tax revenue,
investment expenditure,	corporate profits.

4. (a) Write the following set of equations in full:

$$\sum_{j=1}^{2} a_{ij}x_j = b_i \quad i = 1,\ldots,3.$$

   (b) What is the order of the coefficient matrix of this system?

5. In the following model, x,y and z are endogenous variables and b,c and d are exogenous elements. Rearrange the set of equations so that the endogenous variables and associated coefficients are written as columns on the LHS and the exogenous elements are placed on the RHS. Ensure that each endogenous variable appears in every equation:

$$4x + b - 3y = c + 5z,$$
$$z = 2x + 4y,$$
$$2y + d = 4x.$$

6. Write the result of Exercise 5 above in matrix form, describing in full the coefficient matrix of the system, the vector of unknowns and the vector of intercept terms.

7. Consider the following set of equations where (a) represents a market demand function and (b) a market supply function. The variables of the system are quantity q and market price p.

$$q = 15 - 2p \qquad\qquad (a)$$
$$q = 10 + 3p. \qquad\qquad (b)$$

Cast this model in the form $\mathbf{A}x = \mathbf{b}$, explaining fully the nature of the matrix $\mathbf{A}$ and the vectors $\mathbf{x}$ and $\mathbf{b}$.

8. Solve the equations in Exercise 7 above to determine equilibrium price and quantity exchanged.

9. Determine the order of the following matrices:

(a) $\begin{bmatrix} 3 & 0 \\ 0 & 4 \end{bmatrix}$, (b) $\begin{bmatrix} 1 \\ 6 \\ 0 \\ 0 \\ 4 \end{bmatrix}$, (c) $[8 \ 3]$, (d) $[2]$.

Chapter 15

Matrix Multiplication

15.1 Multiplying a Matrix by a Vector
15.1.1 THE BASIC KEYNESIAN SYSTEM EXAMPLE

Let us reconsider the matrix equation

$$\begin{bmatrix} 1 & -1 \\ -c & 1 \end{bmatrix} \begin{bmatrix} Y \\ C \end{bmatrix} = \begin{bmatrix} I^* \\ a \end{bmatrix}. \tag{15.1}$$

The coefficients of the square matrix multiply the vector of unknowns to give the intercept terms representing the model's exogenous expenditure components. In Chapter 14 we saw that Equation (15.1) is equivalent to the set of equations

$$1Y + (-1)C = I^* \tag{15.2a}$$
$$-cY + 1C = a. \tag{15.2b}$$

Let us consider in more detail how Equations (15.2) are derived from Equation (15.1). This will introduce us to the notion of *matrix multiplication*.

To obtain (15.2a) from (15.1) we take the first row in the matrix of coefficients and take the column of unknowns. The first element of this matrix row multiplies the first element of the vector of unknowns. The second element of the matrix row multiplies the second element of the unknowns column, and this product is added to the former product. The resultant sum gives us the LHS of (15.2a); this is then equated to the first element of the intercept-term column of (15.1), yielding the Equation (15.2a).

Let us reiterate this process in diagrammatic form:
Add the product of these two elements $(1 \times Y)$

$$\begin{bmatrix} 1 & -1 \\ -c & 1 \end{bmatrix} \begin{bmatrix} Y \\ C \end{bmatrix} = \begin{bmatrix} I^* \\ a \end{bmatrix}$$

to the product of the following elements $(-1 \times C)$

$$\begin{bmatrix} 1 & -1 \\ -c & 1 \end{bmatrix} \begin{bmatrix} Y \\ C \end{bmatrix} = \begin{bmatrix} I^* \\ a \end{bmatrix}$$

and set this equal to I^*. We obtain:

$$1Y + (-1)C = I^*$$

which is the first Equation (15.2a) of the system.

To derive the second Equation (15.2b) from (15.1), we take the second row of the matrix of coefficients in (15.1). Multiply the first element of this row by the first element in the vector of unknowns (giving $-c \times Y$) and add this to the product of the second element of the matrix row *times* the second element in the column of unknowns (this product is $1 \times C$). Equating this sum to the second element in the vector of intercept terms on the RHS of (15.1) gives

$$-cY + 1C = a$$

which is the second equation in (15.2).

Again repeating this process diagrammatically, we have:
Add this product

$$\begin{bmatrix} 1 & -1 \\ -c & 1 \end{bmatrix} \begin{bmatrix} Y \\ C \end{bmatrix} = \begin{bmatrix} I^* \\ a \end{bmatrix}$$

to the following product

$$\begin{bmatrix} 1 & -1 \\ -c & 1 \end{bmatrix} \begin{bmatrix} Y \\ C \end{bmatrix} = \begin{bmatrix} I^* \\ a \end{bmatrix}$$

and set the resultant expression equal to a to obtain the second Equation (15.2b).

15.1.2 THE LINEAR SUPPLY AND DEMAND SYSTEM

As a further demonstration of the simple multiplication of matrices, consider the supply and demand model we studied in Sections 4.2.3 and 14.4. Equation (14.21) showed this model in matrix terms as:

$$\begin{bmatrix} 1 & 3 \\ 1 & -\frac{5}{2} \end{bmatrix} \begin{bmatrix} q \\ p \end{bmatrix} = \begin{bmatrix} 20 \\ 0 \end{bmatrix}. \tag{15.3}$$

Let us perform on this system the multiplication procedures outlined in the previous section. First we take the first row of the square matrix and multiply each element in it by the corresponding element in the column vector of unknowns (first element *times* first element, second element *times* second element). The sum of these products equals the first element in the vector on the RHS.

Diagrammatically we have

$$\left[\begin{array}{cc} 1 & 3 \\ 1 & -\tfrac{5}{2} \end{array}\right] \left[\begin{array}{c} q \\ p \end{array}\right] = \left[\begin{array}{c} 20 \\ 0 \end{array}\right]$$

yielding $\qquad\qquad 1q + 3p = 20.$ (15.4)

We see that Equation (15.4) is the demand equation of our model (see Equation (14.20a)).

Secondly we take the second row of the square matrix in (15.3) and multiply each element in it by the corresponding element in the vector of unknowns (again first element *times* first element, second element *times* second element). The sum of these products is equated to the second element in the RHS vector. Thus we have

$$\left[\begin{array}{cc} 1 & 3 \\ 1 & -\tfrac{5}{2} \end{array}\right] \left[\begin{array}{c} q \\ p \end{array}\right] = \left[\begin{array}{c} 20 \\ 0 \end{array}\right]$$

giving $\qquad\qquad 1q - \tfrac{5}{2}p = 0,$ (15.5)

which is the supply equation of our model (see Equation (14.20b)).

Again we have demonstrated the process of matrix multiplication by multiplying a 2×2 matrix by a 2×1 vector. The product, as we have seen, is a 2×1 vector.

15.1.3 A LARGER EXAMPLE

In the two previous sections we have developed some simple rules for multiplying a 2×2 matrix by a 2×1 vector. These examples may be seen as special cases of our more general matrix equation

$$\mathbf{Ax} = \mathbf{b} \qquad (15.6)$$

where $\mathbf{A}$ is of order, say, $m \times n$, and $\mathbf{x}$ and $\mathbf{b}$ are of order $n \times 1$. As we observed in connection with Equation (14.24), this equation may be taken as the basic representation of general linear economic systems.

Suppose $\mathbf{A}$ is larger than 2×2 and $\mathbf{x}$ and $\mathbf{b}$ are larger than 2×1. We may show that the basic rules for multiplying a matrix by a vector developed in Sections 15.1.1 and 15.1.2 above may be easily extended to cope with larger problems.

For example, suppose the multiplication operation on the LHS of Equation (15.6) is to be performed, where

$$\mathbf{A} = \left[\begin{array}{ccc} 1 & 3 & 4 \\ 2 & 7 & 8 \end{array}\right] \text{ and } \mathbf{x} = \left[\begin{array}{c} 6 \\ 5 \\ 9 \end{array}\right].$$

Again we begin with the first row of the matrix $\mathbf{A}$ and multiply each of its elements in turn by each of the elements of $\mathbf{x}$. The sum of these products will be the first element of the RHS vector $\mathbf{b}$.

Diagrammatically we have

$$\begin{bmatrix} 1 & 3 & 4 \\ 2 & 7 & 8 \end{bmatrix} \begin{bmatrix} 6 \\ 5 \\ 9 \end{bmatrix} = \begin{bmatrix} b_1 \\ b_2 \end{bmatrix}.$$

That is,

$$(1 \times 6) + (3 \times 5) + (4 \times 9) = 57 = b_1.$$

Next, we take the second row of **A** and multiply each element in turn by the corresponding element of **x**, and sum the resulting products:

$$\begin{bmatrix} 1 & 3 & 4 \\ 2 & 7 & 8 \end{bmatrix} \begin{bmatrix} 6 \\ 5 \\ 9 \end{bmatrix} = \begin{bmatrix} b_1 \\ b_2 \end{bmatrix}.$$

That is,

$$(2 \times 6) + (7 \times 5) + (8 \times 9) = 119 = b_2.$$

Thus for this example we may write Equation (15.6) out in full as:

$$\begin{bmatrix} 1 & 3 & 4 \\ 2 & 7 & 8 \end{bmatrix} \begin{bmatrix} 6 \\ 5 \\ 9 \end{bmatrix} = \begin{bmatrix} 57 \\ 119 \end{bmatrix}. \tag{15.7}$$

Before proceeding further, the reader should fix in his mind these simple rules by verifying the following illustrative multiplications:

$$\begin{bmatrix} -1 & -4 \\ 2 & 1 \\ 0 & \frac{1}{2} \end{bmatrix} \begin{bmatrix} 5 \\ 3 \end{bmatrix} = \begin{bmatrix} (-1 \times 5) + (-4 \times 3) \\ (2 \times 5) \quad + (1 \times 3) \\ (0 \times 5) \quad + (\frac{1}{2} \times 3) \end{bmatrix} = \begin{bmatrix} -17 \\ 13 \\ 1\frac{1}{2} \end{bmatrix}, \tag{15.8}$$

$$\begin{bmatrix} 8 & 0 & -1 \\ 2 & 1 & 11 \\ 5 & 0 & 7 \\ 3 & 0 & 9 \end{bmatrix} \begin{bmatrix} 4 \\ 6 \\ 8 \end{bmatrix} = \begin{bmatrix} (8 \times 4) + (0 \times 6) + (-1 \times 8) \\ (2 \times 4) + (1 \times 6) + (11 \times 8) \\ (5 \times 4) + (0 \times 6) + (7 \times 8) \\ (3 \times 4) + (0 \times 6) + (9 \times 8) \end{bmatrix} \tag{15.9}$$

$$= \begin{bmatrix} 24 \\ 102 \\ 76 \\ 84 \end{bmatrix}.$$

The alert student will have noticed that in all of these examples showing the product of matrix *times* vector, the number of columns in the matrix always equals the number of rows in the vector. Thus when we say for any particular row of the matrix **A**, "multiply each element in the row by the corresponding element in the vector **x**" (that is, first element *times* first element, second element *times* second element, . . .), there is always an equal total number of "corresponding elements". For example, in Equation (15.7) there are 3 columns in **A** and 3 rows in **x**, in Equation (15.8) there are 2 columns in **A** and 2 rows in **x**, and so on. If the number of columns in **A** does *not* equal the number of rows in **x**, the required multiplication *cannot be performed*. We shall return to this question later in this chapter.

15.2 Multiplying a Matrix by a Matrix

15.2.1 A LINEAR IMPORT-DEMAND MODEL

In the previous sections, the second matrix in the multiplication operation consisted only of a single column—that is, a vector. It is often necessary, however, to multiply together two matrices which both have several rows and columns. To see how useful such a technique can be, let us construct an elementary linear import-demand model. Imagine an economy that produces only two commodities, cars and boats, outputs of which may be denoted x_1 and x_2 respectively. The domestic final demands for cars and boats are assumed to be functions of national income (y_1) and the population size (y_2). That is, we can write:

$$x_1 = f_1(y_1, y_2) \qquad (15.10a)$$
$$x_2 = f_2(y_1, y_2). \qquad (15.10b)$$

Suppose that in fact Equations (15.10) comprise a linear model in which the relative strengths of the influences of income and population on final demands can be described by a set of coefficients b_{ij}† where $i = 1,2$ and $j = 1,2$. In other words, we may write Equations (15.10) as the following system of linear equations:

$$x_1 = b_{11}y_1 + b_{12}y_2 \qquad (15.11a)$$
$$x_2 = b_{21}y_1 + b_{22}y_2. \qquad (15.11b)$$

Let us now assume that to produce cars and boats the economy must import steel and wood, the quantities of which may be denoted m_1 and m_2 respectively. A set of coefficients a_{ij} $(i = 1,2; j = 1,2)$ indicates the quantities of steel and wood needed to produce each car and boat demanded. The community's import demands thus take the form of a set of linear simultaneous equations:

$$m_1 = a_{11}x_1 + a_{12}x_2 \qquad (15.12a)$$
$$m_2 = a_{21}x_1 + a_{22}x_2. \qquad (15.12b)$$

Check carefully that you understand the meanings of Equations (15.11) and (15.12).

It is apparent that, by taking the expressions for x_1 and x_2 from Equations (15.11a and b), the derived demands for imported steel and wood can be obtained as linear functions of income and population. That is, substituting (15.11a) for x_1 and (15.11b) for x_2 in (15.12) we obtain

$$m_1 = a_{11}(b_{11}y_1 + b_{12}y_2) + a_{12}(b_{21}y_1 + b_{22}y_2) \qquad (15.13a)$$
$$m_2 = a_{21}(b_{11}y_1 + b_{12}y_2) + a_{22}(b_{21}y_1 + b_{22}y_2). \qquad (15.13b)$$

The equation system (15.13) can, however, be rearranged to give

$$m_1 = (a_{11}b_{11} + a_{12}b_{21})y_1 + (a_{11}b_{12} + a_{12}b_{22})y_2 \qquad (15.14a)$$
$$m_2 = (a_{21}b_{11} + a_{22}b_{21})y_1 + (a_{21}b_{12} + a_{22}b_{22})y_2. \qquad (15.14b)$$

---

† These coefficients b_{ij} are quite different from the b coefficients defined in previous sections.

Using the methods studied in Chapter 14, Equations (15.14) may in turn
be written in matrix notation as

$$\begin{bmatrix} m_1 \\ m_2 \end{bmatrix} = \begin{bmatrix} a_{11}b_{11} + a_{12}b_{21} & a_{11}b_{12} + a_{12}b_{22} \\ a_{21}b_{11} + a_{22}b_{21} & a_{21}b_{12} + a_{22}b_{22} \end{bmatrix} \begin{bmatrix} y_1 \\ y_2 \end{bmatrix} \tag{15.15}$$

or, more compactly, as

$$\mathbf{m} = \mathbf{Cy} \tag{15.16}$$

where $\mathbf{m}$ is a 2×1 vector, $\mathbf{C}$ is the 2×2 matrix from the RHS of Equation
(15.15), and $\mathbf{y}$ is a 2×1 vector. Notice that $\mathbf{C}$ is composed of elements of
the equation systems (15.11) and (15.12).

The operation of obtaining Equation (15.16) from Equations (15.11)
and (15.12) was accomplished above by rather cumbersome means.
How much more efficient and elegant to achieve the same end using
matrix algebra! Let us examine the steps. First, the final-demand functions
(15.11) can readily be expressed as

$$\begin{bmatrix} x_1 \\ x_2 \end{bmatrix} = \begin{bmatrix} b_{11} & b_{12} \\ b_{21} & b_{22} \end{bmatrix} \begin{bmatrix} y_1 \\ y_2 \end{bmatrix} \tag{15.17}$$

or

$$\mathbf{x} = \mathbf{By}. \tag{15.18}$$

Similarly, the import-demand Equations (15.12) can be written

$$\begin{bmatrix} m_1 \\ m_2 \end{bmatrix} = \begin{bmatrix} a_{11} & a_{12} \\ a_{21} & a_{22} \end{bmatrix} \begin{bmatrix} x_1 \\ x_2 \end{bmatrix} \tag{15.19}$$

or

$$\mathbf{m} = \mathbf{Ax}. \tag{15.20}$$

We now take the expression (15.18) for $\mathbf{x}$ and substitute in (15.20).
Thus

$$\mathbf{m} = \mathbf{ABy}. \tag{15.21}$$

It is clear that the matrix product $\mathbf{A} \times \mathbf{B}$ in Equation (15.21) is simply
the matrix $\mathbf{C}$ from Equation (15.16).
That is,

$$\mathbf{AB} = \mathbf{C}. \tag{15.22}$$

In this equation we see two matrices, $\mathbf{A}$ and $\mathbf{B}$, multiplied together to
yield a third matrix $\mathbf{C}$. Now, in deriving the matrix $\mathbf{C}$ in Equation (15.16)
we saw explicitly how it is obtained from the elements of the matrices $\mathbf{A}$
and $\mathbf{B}$ (see Equation (15.15)). We may now show how this same result
may be achieved by simply extending the rules for multiplication that we
have already discussed in the previous sections.

The key to the matrix multiplication in Equation (15.22) is the fact that
the second matrix $\mathbf{B}$ can be envisaged as the two separate column vectors

$$\begin{bmatrix} b_{11} \\ b_{21} \end{bmatrix} \text{ and } \begin{bmatrix} b_{12} \\ b_{22} \end{bmatrix}.$$

We have already learned in Section 15.1 how to multiply a matrix and a column vector. This process may now be applied to the matrix **A**, taking in turn the two vectors of **B**.

Taking **A** and the first column vector from **B**, we have:

$$\begin{bmatrix} a_{11} & a_{12} \\ a_{21} & a_{22} \end{bmatrix} \begin{bmatrix} b_{11} \\ b_{21} \end{bmatrix} \text{ gives } \begin{bmatrix} a_{11}b_{11} + a_{12}b_{21} \\ a_{21}b_{11} + a_{22}b_{21} \end{bmatrix}$$

and the procedure is then repeated using **A** and the second column of **B**:

$$\begin{bmatrix} a_{11} & a_{12} \\ a_{21} & a_{22} \end{bmatrix} \begin{bmatrix} b_{12} \\ b_{22} \end{bmatrix} \text{ gives } \begin{bmatrix} a_{11}b_{12} + a_{12}b_{22} \\ a_{21}b_{12} + a_{22}b_{22} \end{bmatrix}.$$

These results combine to give the matrix **C**.

$$\mathbf{C} = \begin{bmatrix} c_{11} & c_{12} \\ c_{21} & c_{22} \end{bmatrix} = \begin{bmatrix} a_{11}b_{11} + a_{12}b_{21} & a_{11}b_{12} + a_{12}b_{22} \\ a_{21}b_{11} + a_{22}b_{21} & a_{21}b_{12} + a_{22}b_{22} \end{bmatrix}. \quad (15.23)$$

The RHS of Equation (15.23) is indeed the matrix **C** from Equation (15.15).

Stated more generally, the rules which we have applied to obtain the matrix product **AB** = **C** above are as follows.

The sum of the products of corresponding elements in:

1st row of **A** and 1st column of **B** gives element in 1st row and 1st column of **C**;
2nd row of **A** and 1st column of **B** gives element in 2nd row and 1st column of **C**;
1st row of **A** and 2nd column of **B** gives element in 1st row and 2nd column of **C**;
2nd row of **A** and 2nd column of **B** gives element in 2nd row and 2nd column of **C**.

We can show this diagrammatically for a simple 2×2 numerical example. Suppose

$$\mathbf{A} = \begin{bmatrix} 1 & 3 \\ 2 & 4 \end{bmatrix} \qquad \mathbf{B} = \begin{bmatrix} 5 & 8 \\ 7 & 6 \end{bmatrix}.$$

Then the elements of the matrix **C** formed from the multiplication **A** × **B** are found as follows:

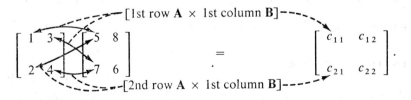

Thus we obtain

$$c_{11} = (1 \times 5) + (3 \times 7) = 26$$
$$c_{21} = (2 \times 5) + (4 \times 7) = 38.$$

To obtain the second column of **C**, we have

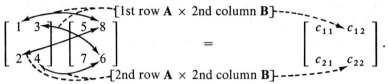

That is,

$$c_{21} = (1 \times 8) + (3 \times 6) = 26$$
$$c_{22} = (2 \times 8) + (4 \times 6) = 40.$$

In all, we have the result

$$\begin{bmatrix} 1 & 3 \\ 2 & 4 \end{bmatrix} \begin{bmatrix} 5 & 8 \\ 7 & 6 \end{bmatrix} = \begin{bmatrix} 26 & 26 \\ 38 & 40 \end{bmatrix}.$$

15.2.2 A MORE GENERAL STATEMENT OF MATRIX MULTIPLICATION

Suppose that the model in the previous section is extended to an economy producing more than just cars and boats, and importing more than just steel and wood, with final demands being influenced by more variables than just population and income. Suppose, in fact, that the model contains l imports, k products and n separate variables influencing final demands. The order of the matrix **A** will therefore be $l \times k$, and that of the matrix **B** will be $k \times n$. Thus in forming the matrix product **AB** to obtain the matrix **C**, we may extend the above statement of the matrix multiplication rule in the following way.

The sum of the products of corresponding elements in:

1st row of **A** and 1st column of **B** gives element in 1st row and 1st column of **C**;
2nd row of **A** and 1st column of **B** gives element in 2nd row and 1st column of **C**;
⋮   ⋮
lth row of **A** and 1st column of **B** gives element in lth row and 1st column of **C**;

1st row of **A** and 2nd column of **B** gives element in 1st row and 2nd column of **C**;
2nd row of **A** and 2nd column of **B** gives element in 2nd row and 2nd column of **C**;
⋮   ⋮
lth row of **A** and 2nd column of **B** gives element in lth row and 2nd column of **C**;

1st row of **A** and nth column of **B** gives element in 1st row and nth column of **C**;
2nd row of **A** and nth column of **B** gives element in 2nd row and nth column of **C**;
⋮   ⋮
lth row of **A** and nth column of **B** gives element in lth row and nth column of **C**.

As can be seen, the application of this general rule successively builds up the columns of the product matrix **C**.

Before proceeding further, the reader should check that he understands the process of multiplying matrices by verifying the following examples:

$$\begin{bmatrix} 1 & 5 & 2 \\ 6 & 3 & 0 \end{bmatrix} \begin{bmatrix} 9 & 10 \\ 7 & 12 \\ 4 & 8 \end{bmatrix}$$

$$= \begin{bmatrix} (1 \times 9) + (5 \times 7) + (2 \times 4) & (1 \times 10) + (5 \times 12) + (2 \times 8) \\ (6 \times 9) + (3 \times 7) + (0 \times 4) & (6 \times 10) + (3 \times 12) + (0 \times 8) \end{bmatrix}$$

$$= \begin{bmatrix} 52 & 86 \\ 75 & 96 \end{bmatrix}. \tag{15.24}$$

Another illustration is the following:

$$\begin{bmatrix} 6 & 2 \\ 0 & \frac{1}{2} \\ -1 & 1 \\ 10 & 3 \end{bmatrix} \begin{bmatrix} -3 & 5 & 7 \\ 12 & -10 & 8 \end{bmatrix} =$$

$$\begin{bmatrix} (6 \times -3) + (2 \times 12) & (6 \times 5) + (2 \times -10) & (6 \times 7) + (2 \times 8) \\ (0 \times -3) + (\frac{1}{2} \times 12) & (0 \times 5) + (\frac{1}{2} \times -10) & (0 \times 7) + (\frac{1}{2} \times 8) \\ (-1 \times -3) + (1 \times 12) & (-1 \times 5) + (1 \times -10) & (-1 \times 7) + (1 \times 8) \\ (10 \times -3) + (3 \times 12) & (10 \times 5) + (3 \times -10) & (10 \times 7) + (3 \times 8) \end{bmatrix}$$

$$= \begin{bmatrix} 6 & 10 & 58 \\ 6 & -5 & 4 \\ 21 & -15 & 1 \\ 6 & 20 & 94 \end{bmatrix}. \tag{15.25}$$

15.3 Aspects of Matrix Multiplication
15.3.1 CONFORMABILITY

Earlier we observed that in multiplying a matrix by a column vector, the number of columns in the matrix had of necessity to equal the number of rows in the vector. Now, more generally, we can see that in any multiplication operation **AB**, the matrix **A** must have the same number of columns as **B** has rows. If this condition is not satisfied the procedure cannot be carried out. For the equation systems (15.1) and (15.3), multiplication was possible because the first matrix in each case had 2 columns and the second matrix (a column vector) had 2 rows. Equation (15.24) similarly complied with this rule, since **A** had 3 columns and **B** had 3 rows. Again, in Equation (15.25) we had a matrix with 2 columns being multiplied by a matrix with 2 rows. So we see at once that, for example, the product

$$\begin{bmatrix} 2 & 1 \\ 3 & 4 \\ 5 & 8 \end{bmatrix} \begin{bmatrix} 2 & 8 \\ 4 & 6 \\ 9 & 0 \end{bmatrix}$$

is a meaningless operation. The first matrix has 2 columns whereas the second has 3 rows.

Two matrices in which the number of columns in the first equals the number of rows in the second are said to be *conformable* for multiplication. Such being the case, the matrix obtained by multiplying the two matrices together will have the same number of rows as the first matrix and the same number of columns as the second. Shown diagrammatically:

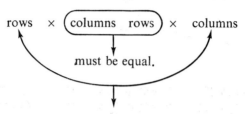

Thus, for example, a 7 × 4 matrix **A** and a 4 × 15 matrix **B** are conformable, and the product **AB** will be a matrix, say **C**, of order 7 × 15. For further illustrations look back to some earlier matrix multiplications in this chapter. Equation (15.3), for instance, shows the multiplication of a 2 × 2 and a 2 × 1 matrix; the result is a 2 × 1 matrix. Similarly, Equation (15.25) shows a 4 × 2 matrix multiplied by a 2 × 3 matrix, giving a 4 × 3 matrix as a result.

15.3.2 PREMULTIPLICATION AND POSTMULTIPLICATION

The sequence in which any two matrices are multiplied together must be carefully observed. In ordinary arithmetic we may write 3 × 2 = 6, or identically 2 × 3 = 6. The order in which the numbers to be multiplied are written is immaterial. But the product of the following matrix multiplication,

$$\begin{bmatrix} 1 & 2 \\ 1 & -3 \end{bmatrix} \begin{bmatrix} 6 & 4 \\ 5 & 1 \end{bmatrix} = \begin{bmatrix} 16 & 6 \\ -9 & 1 \end{bmatrix}, \qquad (15.26)$$

is clearly not the same as that of the following, in which the positions of the matrices on the LHS have been reversed:

$$\begin{bmatrix} 6 & 4 \\ 5 & 1 \end{bmatrix} \begin{bmatrix} 1 & 2 \\ 1 & -3 \end{bmatrix} = \begin{bmatrix} 10 & 0 \\ 6 & 7 \end{bmatrix}. \qquad (15.27)$$

In fact it is true to say that, except in rare circumstances,

$$\mathbf{AB} \neq \mathbf{BA}. \qquad (15.28)$$

In many instances (15.28) holds true simply because the matrices **A** and **B** are conformable while **B** and **A** are not. For example, suppose **A** is of order 5 × 2, and **B** is of order 2 × 8. The product **AB** can be defined as a matrix **C** of order 5 × 8. However, the product **BA** does not exist, since the number of columns in **B** (= 8) does not equal the number of rows in **A** (= 5).

Thus in describing matrix multiplication it is most important to specify exactly the order in which the matrices appear. The prefixes "*pre-*" and "*post-*" are used to describe whether a particular matrix comes before or after another. Thus the operation **AB** may be described as **B** *premultiplied* by **A**, or equivalently, **A** *postmultiplied* by **B**.

The same remarks apply when obtaining the product of three or more matrices. For instance, in deriving the product of **ABC** we may premultiply **B** by **A**, then postmultiply the resultant matrix by **C**. Alternatively, we may premultiply **C** by **B**, then premultiply this product by **A**. Putting this in symbols:

$$\mathbf{ABC} = (\mathbf{AB})\mathbf{C} = \mathbf{A}(\mathbf{BC}). \tag{15.29}$$

Each of the matrices resulting from the three multiplications in Equation (15.29) is equal. Two matrices are defined as *equal* only if they are of the same order and if their corresponding elements are identical.

15.3.3 SCALAR MULTIPLICATION

If any matrix is multiplied by a given number, every element in the matrix should be multiplied by that number. This is referred to as multiplication of the matrix by a scalar, or *scalar multiplication*. Taking a numerical example:

$$4\begin{bmatrix} 2 & 3 \\ 1 & 5 \end{bmatrix} = \begin{bmatrix} 4 \times 2 & 4 \times 3 \\ 4 \times 1 & 4 \times 5 \end{bmatrix} = \begin{bmatrix} 8 & 12 \\ 4 & 20 \end{bmatrix}. \tag{15.30}$$

15.4 Some Important Special Matrices
15.4.1 THE IDENTITY MATRIX

A square matrix with ones on the main diagonal† and zeros elsewhere is called an *identity matrix*. For instance,

$$\begin{bmatrix} 1 & 0 & 0 & 0 \\ 0 & 1 & 0 & 0 \\ 0 & 0 & 1 & 0 \\ 0 & 0 & 0 & 1 \end{bmatrix} \text{ and } \begin{bmatrix} 1 & 0 \\ 0 & 1 \end{bmatrix}$$

are identity matrices of order 4 × 4 and 2 × 2 respectively. An identity matrix is denoted by the symbol **I**. In linear algebra the matrix **I** is the counterpart of the number "1" in ordinary algebra, as we shall see further in later chapters.

---

† Also called the "principal diagonal" or the "leading diagonal".

15.4.2 TRANSPOSITION

If any matrix is "turned on its side" so that rows become columns and columns become rows, it is said to have been *transposed*. For example, if

$$\mathbf{A} = \begin{bmatrix} 3 & \frac{1}{2} & 0 \\ 1 & 2 & 4 \end{bmatrix}$$

the *transpose of* $\mathbf{A}$, denoted $\mathbf{A}'$ or sometimes $\mathbf{A}^t$ or $\mathbf{A}^T$ is given by:

$$\mathbf{A}' = \begin{bmatrix} 3 & 1 \\ \frac{1}{2} & 2 \\ 0 & 4 \end{bmatrix}.$$

Here we see that the first row of $\mathbf{A}$ becomes the first column of $\mathbf{A}'$ and the second row of $\mathbf{A}$ becomes the second column of $\mathbf{A}'$. Equivalently the first, second and third columns of $\mathbf{A}$ become respectively the first, second and third rows of $\mathbf{A}'$.

More generally, if, as before, we denote the element in the ith row and jth column of $\mathbf{A}$ by a_{ij}, we can see that the element a_{ij} in $\mathbf{A}$ becomes the element a_{ji} in $\mathbf{A}'$. Some further types of matrices of use in quantitative economics are considered in Appendix C, Section 1.

Exercises

1. In the following matrix multiplications, write down the order of the two matrices to be multiplied, and the order of the product matrix:

(a) $\begin{bmatrix} 3 & 1 \\ 2 & 5 \end{bmatrix} \begin{bmatrix} 6 \\ 5 \end{bmatrix}$,

(b) $\begin{bmatrix} 2 & 1 \\ 3 & -4 \end{bmatrix} \begin{bmatrix} 5 & -1 \\ 2 & 3 \end{bmatrix}$,

(c) $\begin{bmatrix} 2 & 3 & 1 \\ 4 & 2 & 6 \end{bmatrix} \begin{bmatrix} 5 & 2 \\ 0 & 1 \\ 2 & 3 \end{bmatrix}$,

(d) $\begin{bmatrix} 2 & 3 \end{bmatrix} \begin{bmatrix} 1 \\ 0 \end{bmatrix}$.

2. Perform the multiplications (a) to (d) in Exercise 1 above.

3. In which of the following are the matrices conformable for multiplication?

(a) $\begin{bmatrix} 2 \\ 1 \end{bmatrix} \begin{bmatrix} 3 & 2 \\ 0 & 5 \end{bmatrix}$,

(b) $\begin{bmatrix} 2 & 3 \end{bmatrix} \begin{bmatrix} 4 & 5 \\ 6 & 1 \end{bmatrix}$,

(c) $\begin{bmatrix} 4 & 5 \\ 6 & 1 \end{bmatrix} \begin{bmatrix} 2 & 3 \end{bmatrix}$,

(d) $\begin{bmatrix} 1 \\ 0 \end{bmatrix} \begin{bmatrix} 5 & 6 \end{bmatrix}$.

4. Premultiply the matrix $\begin{bmatrix} 3 & -2 \\ -7 & 5 \end{bmatrix}$ by the matrix $\begin{bmatrix} 5 & 2 \\ 7 & 3 \end{bmatrix}$.

Comment on the matrix obtained.

5. Multiply the matrix

$$\begin{bmatrix} 2 & 3 & 8 & 1 \\ 0 & 5 & -\frac{1}{2} & 0 \\ -1 & 1 & 9 & 7 \end{bmatrix}$$

by the scalar 9 and transpose the resulting matrix.

6. If e is an $m \times 1$ vector, show that $e'e$ is a scalar, the sum of squares of e, and that ee' is an $m \times m$ matrix of squares and crossproducts of e.

7. If x is an $n \times 1$ vector and $D = [d_{ij}]$ is an $n \times n$ matrix $(i, j = 1, \ldots, n)$, show that

$$x'Dx \equiv \sum_{i=1}^{n} \sum_{j=1}^{n} x_i x_j d_{ij}.$$

Chapter 16

Economic Equilibrium and the Matrix Inverse

16.1 The Concept of the Matrix Inverse

We have learned that, in studying the properties of equilibrium in a static linear economic system, the set of equations comprising the model must be solved to find appropriate values for the unknowns or endogenous variables. Let us look at this problem of "solving the system" first in terms of the algebra of ordinary numbers. Consider the equation

$$wz = y \qquad (16.1)$$

where w, z and y stand for ordinary numbers.

If w and y are known, the unknown z can be determined by rearranging the equation to give

$$z = \frac{y}{w} \text{ or } w^{-1}y. \qquad (16.2)$$

The unknown is kept on the LHS, and the known number on the RHS (i.e., y) is multiplied by w^{-1}.

So, for example, when $w = 6$ and $y = 12$

$$z = w^{-1}y = \tfrac{1}{6} \times 12 = 2. \qquad (16.3)$$

Note that

$$w^{-1} \times w = 1. \qquad (16.4)$$

In ordinary algebra, we describe the quantity w^{-1} as the *reciprocal* of w.

We may define an analogous expression in matrix algebra. Take, for example, the typical matrix equation that we have studied in previous chapters,

$$\mathbf{Ax} = \mathbf{b}, \qquad (16.5)$$

where the matrix $\mathbf{A}$ multiplies a vector of unknowns $\mathbf{x}$ to give a vector of intercept terms $\mathbf{b}$. In our models, all the elements of $\mathbf{A}$ are known, and so are the elements of $\mathbf{b}$. Under certain conditions, we may find the values of $\mathbf{x}$ that satisfy the set of simultaneous linear equations by keeping the vector of unknowns on the left-hand side and premultiplying the vector of known intercept terms by a new matrix, called the *inverse of the matrix* **A**, which we shall denote $\mathbf{A}^{-1}$. Thus:

$$\mathbf{x} = \mathbf{A}^{-1}\mathbf{b}. \tag{16.6}$$

The process of calculating $\mathbf{A}^{-1}$, given **A**, is called *matrix inversion.*

16.2 Computing the Inverse Matrix
16.2.1 PRACTICAL ASPECTS OF MATRIX INVERSION

What form does $\mathbf{A}^{-1}$ take, and how can it be computed? First of all, it should be emphasised that $\mathbf{A}^{-1}$ is *not* obtained merely by writing down the reciprocal of each element of **A**. So, for instance, if we have the following matrix

$$\begin{bmatrix} 2 & 1 \\ 3 & 4 \end{bmatrix},$$

the inverse is most certainly *not*

$$\begin{bmatrix} \frac{1}{2} & \frac{1}{1} \\ \frac{1}{3} & \frac{1}{4} \end{bmatrix}.$$

It should be noted, nevertheless, that the inverse matrix will itself be a matrix. Further, as we shall see below, only a *square* matrix may have an inverse. If the number of rows in a matrix is not equal to the number of columns, the matrix inverse does not exist.

There are several ways in which the inverse of a matrix may be obtained, but except in simple cases involving small matrices of order, say, 2 × 2 or 3 × 3, the process of deriving the inverse is a time-consuming business. The easiest way is to carry out the operations using an electronic computer. Most computer units have a standard library programme for matrix inversion. The procedure is roughly as follows. First, we declare the order of the matrix to be inverted. If it is, say, a 20 × 20 matrix we instruct the computer to allocate us an array of 400 empty cells. We then prepare a set of data describing the elements of the matrix. The data are fed in, and each element takes its place in its appropriate cell within the array. The computer now possesses complete knowledge about the nature of the matrix, and is instructed to invert it. Normally, a special precedure will already have been written and stored in the computer's programme library. The computer can call in this procedure, perform the required calculations, and print out the inverse matrix. This is common practice in most areas of economics—in macro systems, linear programming, econometrics and input-output models. For any matrix of order 5 × 5 or greater, an electronic computer would almost certainly have to be used, although one does read reports that an experienced desk-calculator operator can invert a 10 × 10 matrix if he stays at it all day.

There are other methods of matrix inversion which emphasise computational efficiency and can be successfully employed to invert relatively small matrices by hand. Even though in practical work we will rarely have to invert a matrix by hand computation, it is necessary that we understand the process of matrix inversion if we are to appreciate what an inverse matrix really signifies. Fortunately, we can study matrix inversion using very small matrices; the methods used can be generalised to apply to larger matrices as required.

16.2.2 THE CONCEPT OF A DETERMINANT

As mentioned above, there are several different ways of inverting a matrix. For our purposes, the most relevant method is the traditional approach based on the theory of *determinants*. This is not a computationally efficient technique of matrix inversion. However, determinants are widely used in quantitative economics and are especially significant in theoretical analysis. Determinants were once referred to as "eliminants" because they originally arose in the course of solving simultaneous linear equations through progressive substitution and elimination of variables.

Consider the set of linear equations

$$a_{11}x_1 + a_{12}x_2 = b_1 \tag{16.7a}$$
$$a_{21}x_1 + a_{22}x_2 = b_2 \tag{16.7b}$$

or, in matrix notation

$$\begin{bmatrix} a_{11} & a_{12} \\ a_{21} & a_{22} \end{bmatrix} \begin{bmatrix} x_1 \\ x_2 \end{bmatrix} = \begin{bmatrix} b_1 \\ b_2 \end{bmatrix}. \tag{16.8}$$

The unknowns of the system, x_1 and x_2, can be obtained as expressions of the known coefficients and intercept terms. After appropriate substitutions, x_1 and x_2 emerge as

$$x_1 = \frac{a_{22}b_1 - a_{12}b_2}{a_{11}a_{22} - a_{21}a_{12}} \tag{16.9a}$$

$$x_2 = \frac{-a_{21}b_1 + a_{11}b_2}{a_{11}a_{22} - a_{21}a_{12}}. \tag{16.9b}$$

For both unknowns, there is a common denominator $a_{11}a_{22} - a_{21}a_{12}$. This expression is referred to as the *determinant* of the matrix **A**. The coefficients a_{11}, a_{22}, a_{21} and a_{12} are all known numbers. Thus the determinant is also a number.

There is a determinant associated with any square matrix. It is a number obtained by performing certain operations on the elements of the matrix. If the matrix is large, these operations become very tedious. For a 2×2 matrix, however, the process of finding the determinant is quite straightforward. We simply take the product of the pair of elements on the main diagonal and subtract from this the product of the other two elements. Thus, for example, for the matrix

$$\mathbf{A} = \begin{bmatrix} 4 & 2 \\ 5 & \frac{1}{2} \end{bmatrix}, \tag{16.10}$$

we find the product of the main diagonal elements ($4 \times \frac{1}{2}$) and subtract the product of the other two elements (5×2), giving

$$(4 \times \tfrac{1}{2}) - (5 \times 2) = 2 - 10 = -8.$$

Thus the determinant of the matrix $\mathbf{A}$ above is -8. We write this as

$$|\mathbf{A}| = -8 \text{ or } \det \mathbf{A} = -8.$$

In more general terms for a 2×2 matrix, if

$$\mathbf{A} = \begin{bmatrix} a_{11} & a_{12} \\ a_{21} & a_{22} \end{bmatrix}$$

then

$$|\mathbf{A}| = a_{11}a_{22} - a_{21}a_{12} \tag{16.11}$$

as we have already noted.

16.2.3 THE ADJOINT MATRIX

Let us return to Equations (16.9a and b), which showed the solutions for the unknowns x_1 and x_2 in our simple linear system. By substituting the more compact notation for the denominators of these two equations, we may write them as

$$x_1 = \frac{1}{|\mathbf{A}|}(a_{22}b_1 - a_{12}b_2) \tag{16.12a}$$

$$x_2 = \frac{1}{|\mathbf{A}|}(-a_{21}b_1 + a_{11}b_2). \tag{16.12b}$$

Now something quite remarkable can be observed. The above expressions for x_1 and x_2 correspond to the matrix equation

$$\begin{bmatrix} x_1 \\ x_2 \end{bmatrix} = \frac{1}{|\mathbf{A}|} \begin{bmatrix} a_{22} & -a_{12} \\ -a_{21} & a_{11} \end{bmatrix} \begin{bmatrix} b_1 \\ b_2 \end{bmatrix}. \tag{16.13}†$$

This equation shows the vector of unknowns to be a product of a scalar (the reciprocal of the determinant of $\mathbf{A}$), an odd-looking square matrix, and the vector of intercepts. What is the matrix

$$\begin{bmatrix} a_{22} & -a_{12} \\ -a_{21} & a_{11} \end{bmatrix} ?$$

We note that it contains the elements of the matrix $\mathbf{A}$, but with the positions of the main diagonal elements reversed (a_{11} and a_{22}), and with the other two elements (a_{12} and a_{21}) multiplied by -1. In fact this matrix is called the *adjoint* of $\mathbf{A}$, denoted $\mathbf{A}^+$ or adj $\mathbf{A}$. So, for example, for the matrix shown in Equation (16.10), we would have

$$\mathbf{A}^+ = \begin{bmatrix} \frac{1}{2} & -2 \\ -5 & 4 \end{bmatrix}.$$

---

† The reader who does not immediately understand the transition from Equation (16.12) to (16.13) should look back to Section 14.2, and compare, for example, Equation (14.4) with (14.8).

When **A** is only of order 2×2, the problem of finding $\mathbf{A}^+$ is, as we have just seen, a very simple matter. But, as in the case of determinants, the calculation of the adjoint for larger matrices becomes rather tedious. We will not concern ourselves here with the mechanics of these calculations for larger systems.

16.2.4 USING THE DETERMINANT AND THE ADJOINT TO FIND THE MATRIX INVERSE

Let us return at last to the question of finding the inverse of **A**. How can we use the notions of determinants and adjoints to find $\mathbf{A}^{-1}$? Equation (16.13) may be written more concisely as:

$$\mathbf{x} = \frac{1}{|\mathbf{A}|} \mathbf{A}^+ \mathbf{b}. \tag{16.14}$$

But from Equation (16.6) we know also that
$$\mathbf{x} = \mathbf{A}^{-1} \mathbf{b}.$$
From a comparison of (16.14) with (16.6) we deduce

$$\mathbf{A}^{-1} = \frac{1}{|\mathbf{A}|} \mathbf{A}^+. \tag{16.15}$$

The inverse of the matrix **A**, in other words, can be found by multiplying the adjoint of **A** by the reciprocal of the determinant of **A**.

Now let us illustrate the use of the general formula in Equation (16.15) to find the inverse of a particular 2×2 matrix. Suppose the matrix **A** is as shown in Equation (16.10). Then application of Equation (16.15) enables us to use our earlier results and to calculate its inverse as:

$$\mathbf{A}^{-1} = \frac{1}{-8} \begin{bmatrix} \frac{1}{2} & -2 \\ -5 & 4 \end{bmatrix}$$

$$= \begin{bmatrix} -\frac{1}{16} & \frac{1}{4} \\ \frac{5}{8} & -\frac{1}{2} \end{bmatrix}.$$

16.2.5 A MATRIX TIMES ITS INVERSE

We noted in Equation (16.4) that an ordinary number multiplied by its reciprocal equals unity. In a similar way, in matrix algebra, a matrix times its inverse equals the matrix equivalent of unity, i.e., the identity matrix. That is,

$$\mathbf{A}^{-1}\mathbf{A} = \mathbf{A}\mathbf{A}^{-1} = \mathbf{I}. \tag{16.16}$$

We may affirm from our numerical example that Equation (16.16) holds true. Premultiplying this particular matrix **A** (from Equation (16.10)) by its inverse gives

$$\begin{bmatrix} -\frac{1}{16} & \frac{1}{4} \\ \frac{5}{8} & -\frac{1}{2} \end{bmatrix} \begin{bmatrix} 4 & 2 \\ 5 & \frac{1}{2} \end{bmatrix} = \begin{bmatrix} -\frac{4}{16} + \frac{5}{4} & -\frac{2}{16} + \frac{1}{8} \\ \frac{20}{8} - \frac{5}{2} & \frac{10}{8} - \frac{1}{4} \end{bmatrix}$$

$$= \begin{bmatrix} 1 & 0 \\ 0 & 1 \end{bmatrix} = \mathbf{I}.$$

Likewise, postmultiplying $\mathbf{A}$ by its inverse gives

$$\begin{bmatrix} 4 & 2 \\ 5 & \frac{1}{2} \end{bmatrix} \begin{bmatrix} -\frac{1}{16} & \frac{1}{4} \\ \frac{5}{8} & -\frac{1}{2} \end{bmatrix} = \begin{bmatrix} -\frac{4}{16} + \frac{10}{8} & \frac{4}{4} - \frac{2}{2} \\ -\frac{5}{16} + \frac{5}{16} & \frac{5}{4} - \frac{1}{4} \end{bmatrix}$$

$$= \begin{bmatrix} 1 & 0 \\ 0 & 1 \end{bmatrix} = \mathbf{I}.$$

16.2.6 APPLICATION TO LARGER SYSTEMS

The results shown in Equations (16.6), (16.14) and (16.16) can be applied to systems of any size, even though we have demonstrated their application only in the 2 × 2 case. As we have seen, the set of equations can only be solved if we have the same number of equations as unknowns, that is, if the matrix $\mathbf{A}$ is square. Even then, a square matrix does not always possess an inverse. For example, if

$$\mathbf{A} = \begin{bmatrix} 3 & 6 \\ 2 & 4 \end{bmatrix},$$

we can see that $|\mathbf{A}| = (3 \times 4) - (2 \times 6) = 0$, and hence Equation (16.15) breaks down since the reciprocal of $|\mathbf{A}|$ will be infinitely large. A matrix such as this with a zero determinant is called a *singular* matrix.

As we have already pointed out, the calculations involved in applying these solution techniques to larger models will generally be performed for us by a computer. Appendix C, Sections 2 through 6, however, outline methods applicable to larger systems, should the reader wish to study the more advanced theory.

16.2.7 SUMMARY

We have discovered that, given any static linear economic system

$$\mathbf{A}\,\mathbf{x} = \mathbf{b}, \tag{16.17}$$

we can solve for $\mathbf{x}$ by means of the formula

$$\mathbf{x} = \mathbf{A}^{-1}\,\mathbf{b}, \tag{16.18}$$

that is,

$$\mathbf{x} = \frac{1}{|\mathbf{A}|}\,\mathbf{A}^{+}\,\mathbf{b}. \tag{16.19}$$

As a check for the inverse matrix we have

$$\mathbf{A}^{-1}\,\mathbf{A} = \mathbf{A}\,\mathbf{A}^{-1} = \mathbf{I}. \tag{16.20}$$

In the 2 × 2 case, the components of Equations (16.19) and (16.20) are:

$$\mathbf{A} = \begin{bmatrix} a_{11} & a_{12} \\ a_{21} & a_{22} \end{bmatrix}, \tag{16.21}$$

$$|\mathbf{A}| = a_{11}a_{22} - a_{21}a_{12}, \tag{16.22}$$

$$\mathbf{A}^+ = \begin{bmatrix} a_{22} & -a_{12} \\ -a_{21} & a_{11} \end{bmatrix}, \tag{16.23}$$

$$\mathbf{I} = \begin{bmatrix} 1 & 0 \\ 0 & 1 \end{bmatrix}. \tag{16.24}$$

16.3 Macroeconomic Equilibrium Once Again
16.3.1 A NUMERICAL EXAMPLE

Let us now apply the solution methods from the previous section to the determination of equilibrium values for the endogenous variables in one of our simple macroeconomic models. Consider the model

$$Y = C + I^* \tag{16.25a}$$
$$C = a + cY \tag{16.25b}$$

which we first studied in Equation (14.3) and, in matrix terms, in Equation (14.8). Suppose $I^* = \$50$ million, $a = \$100$ million and $c = 0.8$. In Chapter 4 we solved this model for these given values of the exogenous components using simple algebra. Now let us derive the solution using matrix methods.

Along the lines of matrix Equation (16.17) we write the system in the form:

$$\begin{bmatrix} 1 & -1 \\ -0.8 & 1 \end{bmatrix} \begin{bmatrix} Y \\ C \end{bmatrix} = \begin{bmatrix} 50 \\ 100 \end{bmatrix}. \tag{16.26}$$

Applying Equation (16.18) we have

$$\begin{bmatrix} Y \\ C \end{bmatrix} = \begin{bmatrix} 1 & -1 \\ -0.8 & 1 \end{bmatrix}^{-1} \begin{bmatrix} 50 \\ 100 \end{bmatrix}. \tag{16.27}$$

Proceeding to Equation (16.19) to obtain the inverse matrix, and making use of Equations (16.21) to (16.23) for the 2×2 case, we solve the system as follows:

$$\begin{bmatrix} Y \\ C \end{bmatrix} = \frac{1}{(1 \times 1) - (-0.8 \times -1)} \begin{bmatrix} 1 & -1 \\ -0.8 & 1 \end{bmatrix}^+ \begin{bmatrix} 50 \\ 100 \end{bmatrix}$$
$$= 5 \begin{bmatrix} 1 & 1 \\ 0.8 & 1 \end{bmatrix} \begin{bmatrix} 50 \\ 100 \end{bmatrix}$$
$$= \begin{bmatrix} 5 & 5 \\ 4 & 5 \end{bmatrix} \begin{bmatrix} 50 \\ 100 \end{bmatrix} \tag{16.28}$$
$$= \begin{bmatrix} (5 \times 50) + (5 \times 100) \\ (4 \times 50) + (5 \times 100) \end{bmatrix}$$
$$= \begin{bmatrix} 750 \\ 700 \end{bmatrix},$$

i.e., $\qquad Y = \$750$ million $\hfill$ (16.29a)

$\qquad\qquad C = \$700$ million, $\hfill$ (16.29b)

which is the same result as we found in Chapter 4.

As a check on the inverse matrix of the system—the 2×2 matrix in Equation (16.28)—we apply Equation (16.20):

$$\begin{bmatrix} 1 & -1 \\ -0.8 & 1 \end{bmatrix} \begin{bmatrix} 5 & 5 \\ 4 & 5 \end{bmatrix} = \begin{bmatrix} 1 & 0 \\ 0 & 1 \end{bmatrix}.$$

16.3.2 AN ALGEBRAIC EXAMPLE

As a second example, let us take the macromodel (14.11) and solve this system in general terms using matrix methods. Writing first the system in the form of Equation (16.17) we have

$$\begin{bmatrix} 1 & 1 \\ -p & 1 \end{bmatrix} \begin{bmatrix} Y \\ M \end{bmatrix} = \begin{bmatrix} C^* + X^* \\ s \end{bmatrix}. \hfill (16.30)$$

Solving for Y and M we apply the general formula (16.18):

$$\begin{bmatrix} Y \\ M \end{bmatrix} = \begin{bmatrix} 1 & 1 \\ -p & 1 \end{bmatrix}^{-1} \begin{bmatrix} C^* + X^* \\ s \end{bmatrix}.$$

Substituting for the determinant and adjoint matrix, making use of Equations (16.19), (16.22) and (16.23) we obtain:

$$\begin{aligned}
\begin{bmatrix} Y \\ M \end{bmatrix} &= \frac{1}{(1 \times 1) - (-p \times 1)} \begin{bmatrix} 1 & 1 \\ -p & 1 \end{bmatrix}^{+} \begin{bmatrix} C^* + X^* \\ s \end{bmatrix} \\
&= \frac{1}{1 + p} \begin{bmatrix} 1 & -1 \\ p & 1 \end{bmatrix} \begin{bmatrix} C^* + X^* \\ s \end{bmatrix} \\
&= \begin{bmatrix} \dfrac{1}{1+p} & \dfrac{-1}{1+p} \\[2mm] \dfrac{p}{1+p} & \dfrac{1}{1+p} \end{bmatrix} \begin{bmatrix} C^* + X^* \\ s \end{bmatrix} \hfill (16.31) \\
&= \begin{bmatrix} \dfrac{C^* + X^*}{1+p} - \dfrac{s}{1+p} \\[3mm] \dfrac{p(C^* + X^*)}{1+p} + \dfrac{s}{1+p} \end{bmatrix},
\end{aligned}$$

i.e., $\qquad Y = \dfrac{C^* + X^*}{1 + p} - \dfrac{s}{1 + p} \hfill (16.32a)$

$\qquad\qquad M = \dfrac{p(C^* + X^*)}{1 + p} + \dfrac{s}{1 + p}. \hfill (16.32b)$

As an exercise, the reader should multiply the original matrix in Equation (16.30) by its inverse in Equation (16.31) as a check to obtain the identity matrix.

Finally, it should be noted again that larger economic systems may be solved using the same techniques. The macromodel (14.15) clearly requires us to invert a 3×3 matrix to determine the equilibrium values of the endogenous variables, while for the system (14.18) inversion of a 4×4 matrix is indicated. The necessary techniques for solving these larger systems are considered in Appendix C.

Exercises

1. Find the equilibrium values of Y and C in the following model, using matrix methods:

$$Y = C + I^*$$
$$C = a + cY$$

where $I^* = \$200$ million, $a = \$440$ million, $c = 0.6$.

2. Repeat the procedure for the supply and demand model:

$$q = 15 - 2p \qquad \text{(demand equation)}$$
$$q = 10 + 3p. \qquad \text{(supply equation)}$$

3. Solve the following via matrix techniques:

$$Y = C^* + I$$
$$I = m + vY.$$

What is the relationship between changes in autonomous investment (m) and equilibrium income?

4. Take the original coefficient matrix from the system (16.30). Prove that postmultiplication of this matrix by the inverse matrix of coefficients in (16.31) yields a 2×2 identity matrix.

5. Compute the determinants of the following matrices:

(a) $\begin{bmatrix} -3 & -2 \\ -\frac{1}{2} & -1 \end{bmatrix}$,   (b) $\begin{bmatrix} 4 & 8 \\ -1 & -2 \end{bmatrix}$.

How would you describe the second of these matrices?

6. Solve the following pair of simultaneous equations using the methods of matrix algebra:

$$2x + 5y = 16$$
$$4x - 7y = -2.$$

7. Attempt to solve the following simultaneous equations using simple algebra:

$$2x_1 - 6x_2 = 5$$
$$x_1 - 3x_2 = 8.$$

Now try to solve the same set of equations using matrix algebra. Why does the procedure break down?

Chapter 17

Multiplier Analysis

17.1 The Concept of Macroeconomic Multipliers

We have seen that in the typical static linear macromodel, the equilibrium values of the system's endogenous variables can be determined as functions of various exogenous components. Just which elements in the system will be regarded as exogenous will depend to a large extent on the theoretical assumptions which are made in the course of constructing specific models. For example, in Chapter 14 we dealt with a simple system (14.3) where aggregate investment expenditure was assumed to be completely exogenous. On the other hand, in Equation (14.13) we extended this model to make aggregate investment an endogenous variable in the system. Furthermore, the introduction of government expenditure to the system in Equation (14.16) illustrates the arbitrary manner in which additional exogenous elements may be readily built into any model.

Of course, whether such rule-of-thumb procedures are sound from a methodological viewpoint will forever be open to debate. In reality, very few economic variables can be regarded as completely "exogenous". Even government expenditure, which is almost always treated as an exogenous component in elementary models, may be influenced by current economic activity. Again, the demand for exports, instead of remaining fixed, may be affected by various "feedbacks" among trading nations. For instance, a sudden decline in the United States demand for British exports may cause a severe recession in the United Kingdom, leading in turn to a decrease in the United Kingdom's demand for United States exports. Under these circumstances the United Kingdom's demand for United States exports could not be legitimately described as autonomous.

To the uninitiated, the obvious answer to these problems may seem to lie in treating all economic variables as endogenous. Unfortunately, this cannot be done in practice. Resultant models would be far too large and cumbersome to handle. In any case it is normally desirable to isolate, for policy purposes, certain variables which can be controlled—such as the money supply, taxes and government spending. More generally, it is usually necessary to regard some economic variables as exogenous to simplify the construction of a model, even though in the long run such variables may be more properly conceived as endogenously determined.

This chapter will show how changes in the exogenous variables of an economic model act upon the endogenous variables of the system. Because the relationships are of a multiplicative nature, this area of quantitative method is known as *multiplier analysis*. The techniques are particularly useful in tackling the practical problems of determining the economic repercussions of such phenomena as alterations in government policies or shifts of behaviour within the private sector.

17.2 The Simple Investment Multiplier

17.2.1 CALCULATION FROM A NUMERICAL EXAMPLE

The most elementary example of a static macroeconomic multiplier is the familiar Keynesian multiplier k, which the student of economics usually encounters early in his studies. He learns that k is the reciprocal of the marginal propensity to save or, identically, the reciprocal of 1 minus the marginal propensity to consume. This multiplier is sometimes referred to as the Keynesian investment multiplier because it is customarily presented as the mechanism by which a change in investment has a multiplicative effect on equilibrium income. In fact, the orthodox formula is valid only for a particular model, namely, one postulating that investment is entirely autonomous, and containing a consumption function that is linear. This model has already been encountered in equation system (14.3). It is:

$$Y = C + I^* \tag{17.1a}$$
$$C = a + cY. \tag{17.1b}$$

With given values of I^*, a and c, an equilibrium level of aggregate income will obtain. In the numerical example of this model (see Sections 4.4 and 16.3.1), given $I^* = \$50$ million, $a = \$100$ million and $c = 0.8$, we saw that equilibrium income was $750 million. Let us imagine that for some reason autonomous investment rises by some amount ΔI. Aggregate demand will clearly increase, leading to a higher level of equilibrium income. But by how much will income change? This is the question we are able to answer through multiplier theory. Assume an increase in I^* of $10 million. Initially, income will rise by $10 million, a direct result of the additional aggregate demand. However, this extra income will lead to additional consumption expenditure. With a marginal propensity to consume of 0.8, we know that aggregate consumption expenditure will expand by $10 million *times* 0.8, or $8 million. This $8 million will represent extra income to those supplying consumer goods and services, who in turn will spend $8 million *times* 0.8 on their own consumption of commodities. A third round of income generating and spending is thus created ... and so the process continues until the multiplier has fully worked itself out.

Mathematically, the ultimate increase in aggregate equilibrium income, ΔY, can be represented as the sum of a geometric progression:

$$\Delta Y = 10 + 10(0.8) + 10(0.8)(0.8) + \ldots \qquad (17.2a)$$

$$= 10(1 + 0.8 + (0.8)^2 + (0.8)^3 \ldots) \qquad (17.2b)$$

$$= 10\left(\frac{1}{1 - 0.8}\right) \qquad (17.2c)$$

$$= 10(5) = 50.$$

Thus, aggregate income will expand by \$50 million, and hence the new level of Y will be \$(750 + 50) million = \$800 million. The expression in brackets in Equation (17.2c) is the coefficient by which a change in investment is multiplied to yield the corresponding change in equilibrium income. Indeed it can be seen from Equation (17.2c) that this coefficient is the reciprocal of 1 minus the *MPC*, the simple Keynesian investment multiplier we encountered above.

Writing the relationship in (17.2c) symbolically, and reversing the order of the terms on the RHS, we have

$$\Delta Y = k\Delta I^* \qquad (17.3)$$

where $$k = \frac{1}{1 - MPC} \qquad (17.4)$$

or $$k = \frac{1}{MPS} . \qquad (17.5)$$

Thus, if *MPC* equals, say, 0.6, the multiplier k has the value 2.5.

A diagrammatic treatment of the multiplier process may further elucidate the concept. In Fig. 17.1, aggregate demand initially comprises autonomous investment expenditure I_1 and a consumption function C.

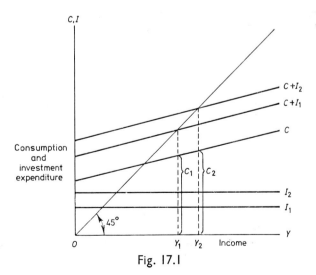

Fig. 17.1

The aggregate demand schedule is thus represented by the line $C + I_1$, which leads to the equilibrium income level Y_1. An increase in investment demand is shown by an upward movement of the investment line to I_2. This in turn yields a higher aggregate demand schedule $C + I_2$ which results in a new equilibrium income Y_2. Relating Equation (17.3) to the diagram, we see that $\Delta Y = Y_2 - Y_1$ and $\Delta I = I_2 - I_1$ so that

$$Y_2 - Y_1 = k(I_2 - I_1). \qquad (17.6)$$

The steeper the aggregate demand line, the greater will be the investment multiplier effect.

17.2.2 CALCULATION USING ORDINARY ALGEBRA

Another way of calculating the simple multiplier is to solve the original set of Equations (17.1) to obtain equilibrium income as a function of autonomous investment expenditure. It is then quite an easy matter to trace the impact of changes in I^* upon Y.

Substituting (17.1b) into (17.1a) we get

$$Y = a + cY + I^* \qquad (17.7)$$

which can be rearranged to give

$$Y = \left(\frac{1}{1-c}\right) a + \left(\frac{1}{1-c}\right) I^* . \qquad (17.8)$$

Equation (17.8) shows equilibrium income as a linear function of autonomous investment. The fixed coefficient associated with I^* is $1/(1-c)$, which is immediately recognisable as the multiplier k.

In fact, since this multiplier is by definition the change in Y per unit change in I^*, it falls out very easily as the derivative of the linear function (17.8):

$$\frac{dY}{dI^*} = \frac{1}{1-c} = k. \qquad (17.9)$$

Furthermore, since we are dealing with a linear function, the relationship in Equation (17.9) could be written for any finite change in Y and I^* as

$$\frac{\Delta Y}{\Delta I^*} = \frac{1}{1-c} = k, \qquad (17.10)$$

which we immediately see as being identical with Equation (17.3). Throughout, of course, we are presupposing no other change in the system.

17.3 The Impact of Changes in Autonomous Investment on Consumption Expenditure

For the macro system (17.1), there are two unknown endogenous variables, Y and C. The elementary Keynesian analysis in the preceding sections investigated the effects of changes in I^* on only one of these, equilibrium income. But we may also wish to predict the effects of the change in autonomous investment on the equilibrium level of consumption expenditure. Let us first find equilibrium consumption by substituting Equation (17.1a) in (17.1b):

$$C = a + c(C + I^*). \qquad (17.11)$$

Rearranging, we obtain

$$C = \left(\frac{1}{1 - c}\right)a + \left(\frac{c}{1 - c}\right)I^*. \qquad (17.12)$$

It is at once apparent that any change in autonomous investment must lead to a change in equilibrium consumption expenditure. Using the same reasoning as before, we can determine what change in C will eventuate per unit change in I^* by differentiating Equation (17.12) with respect to I^*. This gives

$$\frac{dC}{dI^*} = \frac{c}{1 - c} \qquad (17.13)$$

and since we are again dealing with a linear function we may write this, if we so wish, in terms of finite changes in C and I^*, as:

$$\frac{\Delta C}{\Delta I^*} = \frac{c}{1 - c}. \qquad (17.14)$$

The coefficient $c/(1 - c)$ in Equations (17.13) and (17.14) is the multiplier linking I^* with C. This multiplier is clearly quite different from the income-investment multiplier k.

To illustrate the use of the consumption-investment multiplier, we can calculate the effects on consumption if investment rises by, say, $10 million. With an MPC of 0.8 as before, Equations (17.13) and (17.14) show that the rise in consumption will be $0.8/(1 - 0.8)$ times the rise in investment. In other words, consumption will rise fourfold. Thus if I^* changes by $10 million, C will change by $40 million.

This can also be seen in Fig. 17.1. When investment demand rises from I_1 to I_2, equilibrium consumption increases from C_1 to C_2.

17.4 Changes in Autonomous Consumption Expenditure

We have now investigated the relationship between one exogenous variable (I^*) and the two endogenous variables (C and Y) of the macro system described by Equations (17.1a) and (17.1b). It is evident, however, that changes in autonomous consumption expenditure (a) will likewise have an impact on equilibrium income and consumption. In diagrammatic terms the consumption schedule and aggregate demand schedule will shift, leading to new levels of income and consumption, as can be seen by inspection of Fig. 17.1.

Consider the impact of a change in a on Y first. From Equation (17.8) we have:

$$Y = \left(\frac{1}{1 - c}\right)a + \left(\frac{1}{1 - c}\right)I^*.$$

To find the effect on Y of a change in a, we may differentiate this function with respect to a, as follows:

$$\frac{dY}{da} = \frac{1}{1-c} = \frac{\Delta Y}{\Delta a}. \tag{17.15}$$

Equation (17.15) shows that changes in autonomous consumption have the same multiplicative impact on income as changes in autonomous investment.

Next consider the impact on C of a change in a. From Equation (17.12) we have

$$C = \left(\frac{1}{1-c}\right)a + \left(\frac{c}{1-c}\right)I^*,$$

yielding the multiplier coefficient

$$\frac{dC}{da} = \frac{1}{1-c} = \frac{\Delta C}{\Delta a}. \tag{17.16}$$

This has the same numerical value as the multipliers in Equations (17.9) and (17.15).

17.5 Summary of Results

The preceding discussion has revealed that for our simple Keynesian macromodel with two exogenous expenditure components (I^* and a) and two endogenous unknowns (Y and C), there are four multipliers to be calculated. Multipliers of this variety measure the effects on the endogenous variables of changes in exogenous variables in a static equilibrium system. They are known as *impact multipliers*, and they play a very important role in practical endeavours by economists to study the quantitative significance of exogenous disturbances to an economy, such as changes in government policy, shifts in export demand or alterations in the spending habits of the community.

The four multipliers of the system (17.1) may be compactly described by a set of α_{ij} ($i = 1,2; j = 1,2$). Specifically, let us write:

$$\alpha_{11} = \frac{1}{1-c} \text{ for the multiplier linking } I^* \text{ and } Y;$$

$$\alpha_{21} = \frac{c}{1-c} \text{ for the multiplier linking } I^* \text{ and } C;$$

$$\alpha_{12} = \frac{1}{1-c} \text{ for the multiplier linking } a \text{ and } Y;$$

$$\alpha_{22} = \frac{1}{1-c} \text{ for the multiplier linking } a \text{ and } C.$$

Finally, observe how these results may be neatly summarised in the form of a square matrix

	I^*	a
Y	α_{11}	α_{12}
C	α_{21}	α_{22}

(17.17a)

that is,

$$
\begin{array}{c|cc}
 & I^* & a \\
\hline
Y & \dfrac{1}{1-c} & \dfrac{1}{1-c} \\[2ex]
C & \dfrac{c}{1-c} & \dfrac{1}{1-c}
\end{array}
\tag{17.17b}
$$

17.6 The Matrix Approach to Multiplier Analysis

17.6.1 APPLICATION TO THE BASIC KEYNESIAN MODEL

A great deal of time may be saved by using matrix algebra to calculate impact multipliers. With simple examples, of course, there is little to be gained by employing matrices, as multipliers may be derived quite readily via ordinary methods of substitution (as seen in previous sections). But with larger economic models the matrix approach is vastly superior. It will be appreciated that there is a macroeconomic multiplier corresponding to each possible relationship between an exogenous variable and an endogenous variable in a particular model. Thus in a 2×2 system there are usually four multipliers. For a three-equation model, up to nine multipliers may be involved. Generalising the concept, for a static system comprising n equations, we may be required to calculate as many as n^2 impact multipliers. Conventional methods of solution are obviously limited in such applications.

Even though our preceding 2×2 model may be a rather trivial example, it can nevertheless be used to demonstrate certain powerful characteristics of matrix algebra when applied to the problem of deriving impact multipliers.

Recall that the system (17.1) can be cast in matrix form $\mathbf{Ax} = \mathbf{b}$ as explained in Section 14.6. The system may be solved by finding $\mathbf{x} = \mathbf{A}^{-1}\mathbf{b}$, as shown in Section 16.2.

Working this through for our basic system in Equation (17.1) we have:

$$
\begin{bmatrix} 1 & -1 \\ -c & 1 \end{bmatrix}
\begin{bmatrix} Y \\ C \end{bmatrix} =
\begin{bmatrix} I^* \\ a \end{bmatrix}
\tag{17.18}
$$

which is solved for the endogenous variables Y and C as:

$$
\begin{bmatrix} Y \\ C \end{bmatrix} =
\begin{bmatrix} 1 & -1 \\ -c & 1 \end{bmatrix}^{-1}
\begin{bmatrix} I^* \\ a \end{bmatrix}.
\tag{17.19}
$$

Writing the inverse matrix in Equation (17.19) in terms of the determinant and adjoint gives:

$$
\begin{bmatrix} Y \\ C \end{bmatrix} =
\frac{1}{1-c}
\begin{bmatrix} 1 & -1 \\ -c & 1 \end{bmatrix}^{+}
\begin{bmatrix} I^* \\ a \end{bmatrix}
\tag{17.20}
$$

$$= \frac{1}{1-c} \begin{bmatrix} 1 & 1 \\ c & 1 \end{bmatrix} \begin{bmatrix} I^* \\ a \end{bmatrix} \qquad (17.21)$$

$$= \begin{bmatrix} \dfrac{1}{1-c} & \dfrac{1}{1-c} \\ \dfrac{c}{1-c} & \dfrac{1}{1-c} \end{bmatrix} \begin{bmatrix} I^* \\ a \end{bmatrix}. \qquad (17.22)$$

The matrix of coefficients in Equation (17.22) above is the inverse matrix of the system. To make this absolutely clear, we may write:

$$\begin{bmatrix} 1 & -1 \\ -c & 1 \end{bmatrix}^{-1} = \begin{bmatrix} \dfrac{1}{1-c} & \dfrac{1}{1-c} \\ \dfrac{c}{1-c} & \dfrac{1}{1-c} \end{bmatrix}. \qquad (17.23)$$

Now compare this inverse matrix, the RHS of Equation (17.23), with the table of results we compiled in Equation (17.17) after deriving the multipliers of the system via ordinary algebraic methods. It is identical. What we have discovered, in other words, is that for static linear macro-economic models, the relevant impact multipliers will always be neatly summarised in the inverse matrix of the system. Thus the inverse matrix in such models is useful not only because it is instrumental in determining the equilibrium values of the endogenous variables, but also because it contains a wealth of information directly applicable to a wide range of economic problems. To read off each multiplier, we may merely write the column of exogenous variables along the top of the inverse matrix and consult the relevant cell. Each *endogenous* variable's set of multipliers will appear in the corresponding *row* of the matrix, and each *exogenous* variable's multiplier coefficients will be read off down the relevant *column*. The following diagram explains this procedure:

$$\begin{bmatrix} Y \\ C \end{bmatrix} \begin{bmatrix} \text{multiplier} & \text{multiplier} \\ \text{for } Y, I^* & \text{for } Y, a \\ \text{multiplier} & \text{multiplier} \\ \text{for } C, I^* & \text{for } C, a \end{bmatrix} \begin{bmatrix} I^* \\ a \end{bmatrix}$$

inverse matrix of system

17.6.2 ANOTHER EXAMPLE

Take another simple model incorporating fixed consumption demand C^* and an endogenous investment function:

$$Y = C^* + I \qquad (17.24a)$$
$$I = m + vY. \qquad (17.24b)$$

Rearranging, we have

$$1Y - 1I = C^* \qquad (17.25a)$$
$$-vY + 1I = m \qquad (17.25b)$$

or

$$\mathbf{A}\,\mathbf{x} = \mathbf{b} \tag{17.26}$$

where

$$\mathbf{A} = \begin{bmatrix} 1 & -1 \\ -v & 1 \end{bmatrix} \qquad \mathbf{x} = \begin{bmatrix} Y \\ I \end{bmatrix} \qquad \mathbf{b} = \begin{bmatrix} C^* \\ m \end{bmatrix}.$$

Solving the system, we obtain, as before:

$$\mathbf{x} = \mathbf{A}^{-1}\,\mathbf{b}. \tag{17.27}$$

That is, in this case, we have:

$$\begin{bmatrix} Y \\ I \end{bmatrix} = \begin{bmatrix} 1 & -1 \\ -v & 1 \end{bmatrix}^{-1} \begin{bmatrix} C^* \\ m \end{bmatrix} \tag{17.28}$$

$$= \frac{1}{1-v} \begin{bmatrix} 1 & -1 \\ -v & 1 \end{bmatrix}^{+} \begin{bmatrix} C^* \\ m \end{bmatrix}$$

$$\frac{1}{1-v} \begin{bmatrix} 1 & 1 \\ v & 1 \end{bmatrix} \begin{bmatrix} C^* \\ m \end{bmatrix}$$

$$= \begin{bmatrix} \dfrac{1}{1-v} & \dfrac{1}{1-v} \\[2mm] \dfrac{v}{1-v} & \dfrac{1}{1-v} \end{bmatrix} \begin{bmatrix} C^* \\ m \end{bmatrix}. \tag{17.29}$$

The multipliers may now be read off from the inverse matrix of the system shown in (17.29) above.

		C^*	m		
Y		multiplier for Y, C^* i.e., $\dfrac{1}{1-v}$	multiplier for Y, m i.e., $\dfrac{1}{1-v}$	C^*	
I		multiplier for I, C^* i.e., $\dfrac{v}{1-v}$	multiplier for I, m i.e., $\dfrac{1}{1-v}$	m	

By consulting the bottom left-hand cell, for example, we know immediately

that $\Delta I = \dfrac{v}{1-v} \, \Delta C^*$.

17.6.3 MULTIPLIERS IN LARGER MACRO SYSTEMS

The preceding concepts extend readily to more general cases. Consider any macroeconomic system of the following linear form:

$$
\begin{bmatrix} a_{11} & a_{12} & \cdots & a_{1n} \\ a_{21} & a_{22} & \cdots & a_{2n} \\ \vdots & \vdots & & \vdots \\ a_{n1} & a_{n2} & \cdots & a_{nn} \end{bmatrix} \begin{bmatrix} x_1 \\ x_2 \\ \vdots \\ x_n \end{bmatrix} = \begin{bmatrix} b_1 \\ b_2 \\ \vdots \\ b_n \end{bmatrix}, \qquad (17.30)
$$

where a_{ij} are the fixed coefficients, x_j are the endogenous variables and b_i are the exogenous components of the model. The solution of the set of equations takes the form

$$
\begin{bmatrix} x_1 \\ x_2 \\ \vdots \\ x_n \end{bmatrix} = \begin{bmatrix} \alpha_{11} & \alpha_{12} & \cdots & \alpha_{1n} \\ \alpha_{21} & \alpha_{22} & \cdots & \alpha_{2n} \\ \vdots & \vdots & & \vdots \\ \alpha_{n1} & \alpha_{n2} & \cdots & \alpha_{nn} \end{bmatrix} \begin{bmatrix} b_1 \\ b_2 \\ \vdots \\ b_n \end{bmatrix} \qquad (17.31)
$$

where α_{ij} are the elements of the inverse matrix of the system. At the same time, each α_{ij} describes the multiplier coefficient linking the jth exogenous variable to the ith endogenous variable within the model.† In Equation (17.31), n^2 such multipliers are defined.

Exercises

1. (a) Given
$$Y = I^* + X^* - M, \qquad \text{(income identity)}$$
$$M = n + pY, \qquad \text{(import demand function)}$$
find the equilibrium values of Y and M.
(b) Calculate the relevant multipliers of the system when $p = \frac{2}{3}$.

2. (a) Given
$$Y = C + G^* \text{ where } G^* \text{ is government expenditure,}$$
$$C = a + cY,$$
find the equilibrium values of Y and C.
(b) What are the multipliers of the model?

3. With a value of 0.8 for c in Exercise 2 above, what increase in government expenditure would be required to raise consumer spending by $100 million?

4. Consider the model (14.18) in Chapter 14. How many multipliers are involved?

5. For the system in Equation (17.1) you are told that if exogenous investment rises by a given amount, consumption expenditure increases by one-and-a-half times this amount. What is the marginal propensity to consume?

6. What is the relationship between changes in autonomous investment (m) and equilibrium income in the model in Exercise 3, Chapter 16?

---

† Note that, after solving the system, it has become necessary to refer to x_i and b_j (instead of x_j and b_i) in order to read off the multipliers in the manner indicated.

Chapter 18

Input-Output Analysis

18.1 An Example

Input-output economics, or, as it is often called, interindustry economics, has emerged as one of the most useful and fascinating branches of the application of quantitative methods to economic problems. Economists working in many different fields find it an invaluable tool of analysis. Input-output tables are useful as a basis for economic planning in both developed and developing countries under both free-enterprise and centrally-planned systems. Macroeconomists are interested in input-output because of the wealth of sectoral detail it provides. The technique is a highly practical device and has been employed to study the effects of tariff policies, changes in wage rates, movements in consumer demands, the impact of foreign trade, regional income, employment and a host of other topics.

To gain some idea of what input-output is about, imagine that the economy can be disaggregated into a variety of different industries. In a large input-output system, several hundred industries may be postulated. Each industry sells its output to final consumers, and to other industries which use its output as a factor of production. At the same time, each industry will buy any such products of other industries as are required in its own production process. Each industry will thus be characterised by an inflow of inputs obtained from other industries and by an outflow of its own output that passes on to other industries and to final markets. In addition to inputs purchased from other industries, called *interindustry inputs*, factors of production such as labour and managerial skills will be directly used by each industry in the creation of its product; such inputs are called *direct* or *primary inputs*. It is from an explicit recognition of the interdependence of industries, based on the technological characteristics of modern production methods, that input-output derives such a high degree of realism in its view of how an economic system actually operates.

A fundamental assumption of input-output analysis is that each industry uses other industries' outputs (as well as primary inputs) strictly in fixed proportions. To see this, let us envisage a hypothetical economy comprising only two industries, coal and steel, and contrive an input-output representation of this system. Suppose that to make 1 ton of steel, 0.4 tons of coal are required as an input to production. Because a certain amount of steel is needed to install new plant within the steel industry itself, let us say that 1 ton of steel also requires 0.3 tons of steel in its own production. Simultaneously, assume that to produce 1 ton of coal, 0.9 tons of steel and 0.2 tons of coal are required. Primary inputs will, of course, be used by both industries but we shall disregard these for the moment so as to concentrate attention on our interindustry information, which reflects the interacting production processes of steel and coal. The numerical data given above can be set out in tableau form as in Table 18.1.

TABLE 18.1

Interindustry Coefficients for Hypothetical Economy

		Using Industries	
		Coal	Steel
Producing Industries	Coal	0.2	0.4
	Steel	0.9	0.3

The columns of Table 18.1 represent the two industries in the economy in their capacity as users of inputs, and have therefore been designated "Using Industries". The same two industries, however, may be thought of in terms of what they supply; the rows of the table are therefore designated "Producing Industries". The coefficients in the table show the number of units of output of the producing industries required to produce 1 unit of output of the using industries. Thus, reading across the second row of the table, we see that 0.9 tons of steel are required to produce 1 ton of coal and 0.3 tons of steel are used up in the production of 1 ton of steel. In other words, Table 18.1 may be seen as a 2 × 2 matrix of coefficients describing the per-unit physical relations between the coal and steel industries.†

Now suppose that consumers demand 20 tons of coal and 50 tons of steel. To produce the 20 tons of coal, the coal industry would require inputs of 0.9 × 20 tons of steel from the steel industry, and 0.2 × 20 tons of coal, which it would obtain from itself. Similarly, to produce its 50 tons of steel the steel industry would have direct input requirements of 0.4 × 50 tons of coal and 0.3 × 50 tons of steel. But the story does not end here. Due to the interdependence of the two production processes, the coal

---

† Input-output tables are more commonly drawn up in value terms, showing inter-industry *expenditure* flows rather than physical relations. The mathematical theory involved, however, is the same regardless of whether value or physical coefficients are employed.

industry must produce not only the 20 tons demanded by consumers, but also the coal needed by the steel industry to supply the steel required to produce coal. And because steel is needed to produce the coal to produce the steel to produce consumers' coal, further coal must be supplied to the steel industry ... and so on. The steel industry, in meeting the final demand for its product, would face a similar pattern of output require-ments. Thus we can say that each industry will be called upon to satisfy not only the *direct* requirements stipulated by consumers but also the *indirect* requirements generated by the interindustry use of its output as a factor of production.

Now, if we suppose that the output of each industry *must* be sold either to other industries (including itself) as an input or to final consumers, we can write:

$$\text{Total output} = \text{Interindustry sales} + \text{Final sales.}$$

In our example, let us denote total outputs of coal and steel by x_1 and x_2 respectively. Remembering that the final demands for coal and steel are 20 tons and 50 tons respectively, we may represent our hypothetical system algebraically as follows:

$$x_1 = 0.2x_1 + 0.4x_2 + 20 \tag{18.1a}$$
$$x_2 = 0.9x_1 + 0.3x_2 + 50. \tag{18.1b}$$

Thus, Equation (18.1b), for example, tells us that total output of steel (x_2) comprises the steel demand of the coal industry (0.9 tons of steel per ton of coal *times* x_1 tons of coal produced) *plus* the steel demand of the steel industry itself $(0.3 \times x_2)$ *plus* the consumers' final demand for steel, 50 tons.

Taking the analysis one step further, let us denote the final demands for coal and steel by f_1 and f_2 respectively. In addition, observe that in more general terms the 2 × 2 matrix of coefficients contained in Table 18.1 may be replaced by a set of elements a_{ij} $(i = 1,2,; j = 1,2)$, each of which describes the number of units of the ith industry's output required directly to produce 1 unit of the jth industry's output. Our two-industry input-output system may accordingly be represented in general terms by a set of two simultaneous linear equations:

$$x_1 = a_{11}x_1 + a_{12}x_2 + f_1 \tag{18.2a}$$
$$x_2 = a_{21}x_1 + a_{22}x_2 + f_2. \tag{18.2b}$$

Now let us write Equations (18.2) in matrix terms. We may define the x and f as the column vectors **x** and **f** respectively, where

$$\mathbf{x} = \begin{bmatrix} x_1 \\ x_2 \end{bmatrix} \qquad \mathbf{f} = \begin{bmatrix} f_1 \\ f_2 \end{bmatrix}. \tag{18.3}$$

In addition, the collection of a_{ij} coefficients may be written as the matrix **A** where

$$\mathbf{A} = \begin{bmatrix} a_{11} & a_{12} \\ a_{21} & a_{22} \end{bmatrix}. \tag{18.4}$$

Hence, Equations (18.2a and b) may be written compactly in matrix notation as

$$\mathbf{x} = \mathbf{Ax} + \mathbf{f}. \tag{18.5}$$

The derivation of the expression $\mathbf{Ax}$ on the RHS of Equation (18.5) from the RHS of Equations (18.2) should be clear to the reader from the analysis in Chapters 14 and 15. But the addition of the vector $\mathbf{f}$ requires further explanation.

18.2 Addition and Subtraction of Matrices

To add two matrices together they must be of the same *order* (see Section 14.5). This being the case, we simply take each element of the first matrix and add it to the corresponding element of the second matrix. Take a simple numerical example:

$$\begin{bmatrix} 14 & 3 \\ 0 & 5 \end{bmatrix} + \begin{bmatrix} 6 & 12 \\ \frac{1}{2} & -1 \end{bmatrix} = \begin{bmatrix} 14+6 & 3+12 \\ 0+\frac{1}{2} & 5+(-1) \end{bmatrix}$$

$$= \begin{bmatrix} 20 & 15 \\ \frac{1}{2} & 4 \end{bmatrix}.$$

Clearly, subtraction will follow a similar rule. To illustrate,

$$\begin{bmatrix} 14 & 3 \\ 0 & 5 \end{bmatrix} - \begin{bmatrix} 6 & 12 \\ \frac{1}{2} & -1 \end{bmatrix} = \begin{bmatrix} 14 & 6 & 3 & 12 \\ 0-\frac{1}{2} & 5-(-1) \end{bmatrix}$$

$$= \begin{bmatrix} 8 & -9 \\ -\frac{1}{2} & 6 \end{bmatrix}.$$

The following are examples of operations that *cannot* be performed because the matrices involved are of different orders:

$$\begin{bmatrix} 2 & 0 \\ 4 & 1 \\ 1 & 5 \end{bmatrix} - \begin{bmatrix} 1 & -8 & 16 \\ \frac{1}{2} & 7 & 0 \end{bmatrix};$$

$$\begin{bmatrix} 24 & 1 \\ 3 & 6 \end{bmatrix} + \begin{bmatrix} 4 \\ 5 \end{bmatrix}.$$

Now let us return to Equation (18.5) and demonstrate that it is indeed equivalent to Equation (18.2). We may write (18.5) in full as

$$\begin{bmatrix} x_1 \\ x_2 \end{bmatrix} = \begin{bmatrix} a_{11} & a_{12} \\ a_{21} & a_{22} \end{bmatrix} \begin{bmatrix} x_1 \\ x_2 \end{bmatrix} + \begin{bmatrix} f_1 \\ f_2 \end{bmatrix}. \tag{18.6}$$

Performing the premultiplication of the vector $\mathbf{x}$ by the matrix $\mathbf{A}$ we have:

$$\begin{bmatrix} x_1 \\ x_2 \end{bmatrix} = \begin{bmatrix} a_{11}x_1 + a_{12}x_2 \\ a_{21}x_1 + a_{22}x_2 \end{bmatrix} + \begin{bmatrix} f_1 \\ f_2 \end{bmatrix}. \tag{18.7}$$

The first term on the RHS of Equation (18.7) is in fact a 2×1 vector. To make this clearer, denote the scalar quantity $a_{11}x_1 + a_{12}x_2$ by the symbol X_1, and $a_{21}x_1 + a_{22}x_2$ by the symbol X_2. Then (18.7) may be written

$$\begin{bmatrix} x_1 \\ x_2 \end{bmatrix} = \begin{bmatrix} X_1 \\ X_2 \end{bmatrix} + \begin{bmatrix} f_1 \\ f_2 \end{bmatrix} \qquad (18.8)$$

and it is readily apparent that the vectors on the RHS of Equation (18.8) are of the same order. Therefore the appropriate addition can be performed, giving:

$$\begin{bmatrix} x_1 \\ x_2 \end{bmatrix} = \begin{bmatrix} X_1 + f_1 \\ X_2 + f_2 \end{bmatrix}. \qquad (18.9)$$

Replacing X_1 and X_2 in Equation (18.9) by their original expressions $a_{11}x_1 + a_{12}x_2$ and $a_{21}x_1 + a_{22}x_2$ respectively, and dropping the square brackets, gives:

$$x_1 = a_{11}x_1 + a_{12}x_2 + f_1 \qquad (18.10a)$$
$$x_2 = a_{21}x_1 + a_{22}x_2 + f_2 \qquad (18.10b)$$

which is, of course, Equation (18.2).

18.3 Solving the Input-Output System

18.3.1 BASIC PRINCIPLES

We have our general input-output system represented in the matrix equation

$$\mathbf{x} = \mathbf{A}\mathbf{x} + \mathbf{f}. \qquad (18.11)$$

Solution of this system entails determining the value of the vector $\mathbf{x}$— that is, the total outputs of the industries in the system, for known values of the matrix $\mathbf{A}$, and the vector $\mathbf{f}$.

Now suppose we had an equation in ordinary algebra of the form

$$y = by + g \qquad (18.12)$$

where y is a variable and b and g are constants. To solve for y we would go through the following steps.

(a) Subtract by from both sides:

$$y - by = g. \qquad (18.13)$$

(b) Take out the common factor y on the LHS of Equation (18.13):

$$(1 - b)y = g. \qquad (18.14)$$

(c) Multiply both sides of Equation (18.14) by the reciprocal of $(1 - b)$:

$$y = (1 - b)^{-1} g \equiv \frac{g}{(1 - b)}. \qquad (18.15)$$

Equation (18.15) provides the required solution for y.

A similar procedure may be followed in solving the matrix Equation (18.11) for the unknown vector $\mathbf{x}$. However, there are two important

differences. Firstly, we must be careful to write any matrix products with
the proper arrangement of the matrices to be multiplied (pre- or post-).
Secondly, we must make explicit the fact that, just as we understand "y"
on the LHS of Equation (18.12) to be "$1 \times y$", the vector **x** on the LHS
of Equation (18.11) is also "unity $\times$ **x**". To do this we may observe that
the matrix equivalent of "unity" is the identity matrix **I** (see Section
15.4.1). Hence, just as the scalar quantity y is equivalent to "$1 \times y$",
the vector **x** is identical with the matrix product **Ix**, where **I** has as many
rows and columns as **x** has elements. To illustrate, take a 3×1 vector **x**
and premultiply it by a 3×3 identity matrix. We have

$$\begin{bmatrix} 1 & 0 & 0 \\ 0 & 1 & 0 \\ 0 & 0 & 1 \end{bmatrix} \begin{bmatrix} x_1 \\ x_2 \\ x_3 \end{bmatrix} = \begin{bmatrix} 1(x_1) + 0(x_2) + 0(x_3) \\ 0(x_1) + 1(x_2) + 0(x_3) \\ 0(x_1) + 0(x_2) + 1(x_3) \end{bmatrix}$$

$$= \begin{bmatrix} x_1 \\ x_2 \\ x_3 \end{bmatrix}.$$

Thus in general we may say

$$\mathbf{Ix} \equiv \mathbf{x}. \tag{18.16}$$

Now return to Equation (18.11) and write **Ix** in place of **x** on the LHS:

$$\mathbf{Ix} = \mathbf{Ax} + \mathbf{f}. \tag{18.17}$$

Subtract **Ax** from both sides. This is possible because the matrix products
Ix and **Ax** and the vector **f** are all of the same order. In our two-industry
model, for instance, they are all of order 2×1. We obtain

$$\mathbf{Ix} - \mathbf{Ax} = \mathbf{f}. \tag{18.18}$$

We may now take out the common factor **x** on the LHS of Equation
(18.18), giving

$$(\mathbf{I} - \mathbf{A})\mathbf{x} = \mathbf{f}. \tag{18.19}$$

Now the matrix $(\mathbf{I} - \mathbf{A})$ is conformable for multiplication with the
vector **x**. For our two-industry example, $(\mathbf{I} - \mathbf{A})$ is of order 2×2, and
x is of order 2×1, hence the product $(\mathbf{I} - \mathbf{A})\mathbf{x}$ is defined. Note, however,
that the product $\mathbf{x}(\mathbf{I} - \mathbf{A})$ is *not* defined; thus, taking out a common
factor in matrix algebra requires careful consideration of the conforma-
bility of the resulting matrices.

Finally, we premultiply both sides of Equation (18.19) by the inverse
of the matrix $(\mathbf{I} - \mathbf{A})$, giving

$$\mathbf{x} = (\mathbf{I} - \mathbf{A})^{-1}\mathbf{f}, \tag{18.20}$$

which is our required solution. The solution vector **x** gives us the total
outputs of each industry in the system required, both directly and indi-
rectly, to satisfy a given bill of final demands, **f**. Again check that the
matrix product on the RHS of Equation (18.20) is defined. In the two-
industry case, $(\mathbf{I} - \mathbf{A})^{-1}$ is of order 2×2 and **f** is of order 2×1.

In input-output analysis, the inverse matrix $(\mathbf{I} - \mathbf{A})^{-1}$ which provides
the key to solving the system is frequently referred to as the *Leontief
inverse*, in recognition of Wassily Leontief, the founder of this important
tool of economic analysis.

18.3.2 SOLUTION TO THE TWO-INDUSTRY EXAMPLE

Recall that, in our example, the matrix **A** and the vector **f** were given as follows:

$$\mathbf{A} = \begin{bmatrix} 0.2 & 0.4 \\ 0.9 & 0.3 \end{bmatrix}, \quad \mathbf{f} = \begin{bmatrix} 20 \\ 50 \end{bmatrix}.$$

We may proceed directly to a solution for the unknown vector **x** by substituting these values into Equation (18.20). We obtain

$$\begin{bmatrix} x_1 \\ x_2 \end{bmatrix} = \left\{ \begin{bmatrix} 1 & 0 \\ 0 & 1 \end{bmatrix} - \begin{bmatrix} 0.2 & 0.4 \\ 0.9 & 0.3 \end{bmatrix} \right\}^{-1} \begin{bmatrix} 20 \\ 50 \end{bmatrix}. \tag{18.21}$$

Evaluating first the matrix $(\mathbf{I} - \mathbf{A})$ we have:

$$\begin{aligned} (\mathbf{I} - \mathbf{A}) &= \begin{bmatrix} 1 & 0 \\ 0 & 1 \end{bmatrix} - \begin{bmatrix} 0.2 & 0.4 \\ 0.9 & 0.3 \end{bmatrix} \\ &= \begin{bmatrix} 0.8 & -0.4 \\ -0.9 & 0.7 \end{bmatrix}. \end{aligned} \tag{18.22}$$

This matrix now has to be inverted. Applying our procedures from Chapter 16, we find first the determinant of $(\mathbf{I} - \mathbf{A})$ as:

$$\begin{aligned} |\mathbf{I} - \mathbf{A}| &= (0.8 \times 0.7) - (-0.9 \times -0.4) \\ &= 0.2. \end{aligned} \tag{18.23}$$

The adjoint matrix is

$$(\mathbf{I} - \mathbf{A})^+ = \begin{bmatrix} 0.7 & 0.4 \\ 0.9 & 0.8 \end{bmatrix}. \tag{18.24}$$

Hence the inverse matrix is

$$\begin{aligned} (\mathbf{I} - \mathbf{A})^{-1} &= \frac{1}{|\mathbf{I} - \mathbf{A}|} (\mathbf{I} - \mathbf{A})^+ = \frac{1}{0.2} \begin{bmatrix} 0.7 & 0.4 \\ 0.9 & 0.8 \end{bmatrix} \\ &= \begin{bmatrix} 3.5 & 2.0 \\ 4.5 & 4.0 \end{bmatrix}. \end{aligned} \tag{18.25}$$

Substituting Equations (18.25) into (18.21) we obtain

$$\begin{aligned} \begin{bmatrix} x_1 \\ x_2 \end{bmatrix} &= \begin{bmatrix} 3.5 & 2.0 \\ 4.5 & 4.0 \end{bmatrix} \begin{bmatrix} 20 \\ 50 \end{bmatrix} \\ &= \begin{bmatrix} 3.5(20) + 2.0(50) \\ 4.5(20) + 4.0(50) \end{bmatrix} \\ &= \begin{bmatrix} 170 \\ 290 \end{bmatrix}. \end{aligned} \tag{18.26}$$

Thus, in order to meet final demands of 20 tons and 50 tons of coal and steel respectively, the coal industry must produce a total of 170 tons of coal, and the steel industry's output must be 290 tons of steel. Reference back to Equations (18.1a and b) shows that the total quantities of coal and steel produced would be used up as follows:

Supply of *coal* to:

Coal industry	= 0.2(170) =	34 tons	} Interindustry demand
Steel industry	= 0.4(290) =	116 tons	} = 150 tons
Final consumers	=	20 tons	} Final demand = 20 tons
Total output of coal		170 tons	

Supply of *steel* to:

Coal industry	= 0.9(170) =	153 tons	} Interindustry demand
Steel industry	= 0.3(290) =	87 tons	} = 240 tons
Final consumers	=	50 tons	} Final demand = 50 tons
Total output of steel		290 tons	

18.4 Application to Larger Systems

The particular example we have studied above is a greatly simplified one. In practical applications of input-output analysis, the economic systems studied are often disaggregated into a very large number of industries. For instance, suppose n different industries are specified. Then Equations (18.2) may be extended in the following manner:

$$
\begin{aligned}
x_1 &= a_{11}x_1 + a_{12}x_2 + \ldots + a_{1n}x_n + f_1 \\
x_2 &= a_{21}x_1 + a_{22}x_2 + \ldots + a_{2n}x_n + f_2 \\
&\;\;\vdots \qquad \vdots \qquad \vdots \qquad\qquad \vdots \qquad \vdots \\
x_n &= a_{n1}x_1 + a_{n2}x_2 + \ldots + a_{nn}x_n + f_n.
\end{aligned}
\tag{18.27}
$$

This n-industry input-output model may be represented in matrix terms as in Equation (18.5), that is, as:

$$
\mathbf{x} = \mathbf{Ax} + \mathbf{f} \tag{18.28}
$$

where $\mathbf{x}$ = $n \times 1$ vector of total industry outputs;
$\mathbf{A}$ = $n \times n$ matrix of interindustry coefficients;
$\mathbf{f}$ = $n \times 1$ vector of final demands.

Solution of this n-industry model is, of course, by application of Equation (18.20). For most numerical examples where n is larger than, say, 4 or 5, the calculations involved in solving the system (i.e., finding the Leontief inverse and postmultiplying it by $\mathbf{f}$) would be performed on an electronic computer.

18.5 Some Further Ramifications of Input-Output Analysis

18.5.1 INPUT-OUTPUT AS A PLANNING DEVICE

Input-output can be applied at many levels. The most common use is at the national level, whereby input-output data may be pooled with other national-accounting information to provide a basis for economic planning. Final demands, for instance, are frequently disaggregated into the usual macroeconomic expenditure categories. The ith industry's final demand may be expressed, for example, as

$$f_i = C_i + I_i + G_i + X_i$$

where C_i = ith industry's output bought by consumers;
   I_i = ith industry's output bought by investment sector;
   G_i = ith industry's output bought by government authorities;
   X_i = ith industry's output bought by rest of the world.

Direct or primary inputs can also be treated in fine detail, and integrated with the national accounts system. Cost items appearing under this

TABLE 18.2

Costs of Production of Output for ith Industry

COSTS OF PRODUCTION	($ m)
Costs of inputs purchased from other industries	
Purchases from industry 1	25
Purchases from industry 2	6
$\vdots$	
Purchases from industry n	10
Total cost of interindustry inputs	150
Costs of direct inputs	
Wages and salaries	20
Profits	10
Taxes and subsidies	5
Imported materials	15
Total cost of direct inputs	50
Total cost of production	200
VALUE OF OUTPUT	
Value of sales to other industries	
Sales to industry 1	30
Sales to industry 2	45
$\vdots$	
Sales to industry n	4
Total value of interindustry sales	135
Value of sales to final demand sectors	
Consumers	38
Government	5
Exports	12
Investment	10
Total value of final demand sales	65
Total value of output	200

heading include wages and salaries, profits, taxes and subsidies, and the costs of imports used in production. That part of an industry's cost of production which is reflected in the costs of direct inputs can be related to the "value-added" method of evaluating industrial production and hence of calculating GNP.†

Overall, the total cost of production for each industry is equal to the total value of its output. The latter, as we have already seen, is equal to the value of interindustry sales *plus* the value of sales to final users. Similarly, total cost of production for the industry is equal to the cost of interindustry input purchases *plus* the cost of direct inputs. As an illustration, Table 18.2 shows the costs and value of production for the *i*th industry in an imaginary economy.

Input-output tables are used at other levels as well. International input-output systems, describing the industrial framework and trade flows of different countries, have been compiled and employed for planning purposes. Regional input-output analysis is commonly encountered as a method of studying such topics as localised unemployment, interregional trade and decentralisation. Again, the individual firm often finds value in input-output techniques. Multiproduct firms in the chemical industry, for example, may use an input-output table to describe interacting production processes. The flow of funds within a firm can also be represented by an input-output matrix. These are but a few of the many different uses to which input-output may be put.

18.5.2 MULTIPLIER ANALYSIS

In Chapter 17, we investigated the effect of changes in exogenous variables within static linear macroeconomic systems. Recall that the quantitative impact of a change in any selected exogenous variable upon a given endogenous variable can be calculated by means of a multiplier coefficient. More generally, the inverse matrix of the system provides a complete tabulation of the multiplier coefficients linking each exogenous to each endogenous variable within the model (see Section 17.6). The same concepts can be applied in input-output economics.

Let us consider the quantitative effect of a change in the final demand for a certain commodity upon the total outputs of all industries within an input-output system. Our previous discussion shows that interindustry repercussions must be taken into account, so that we must assess the resultant *direct* and *indirect* changes in outputs. Take a simple two-product example such as that considered earlier. Its solution is given by Equation (18.20). For convenience, let us replace the Leontief inverse matrix with a set of α_{ij} ($i = 1,2; j = 1,2$). That is, let

$$(\mathbf{I} - \mathbf{A})^{-1} = \begin{bmatrix} \alpha_{11} & \alpha_{12} \\ \alpha_{21} & \alpha_{22} \end{bmatrix}$$

† Imports would, of course, have to be excluded from the estimate.

Then we may write Equation (18.20) for this model as

$$x_1 = \alpha_{11}f_1 + \alpha_{12}f_2 \tag{18.29a}$$
$$x_2 = \alpha_{21}f_1 + \alpha_{22}f_2 \tag{18.29b}$$

which yields total equilibrium outputs, x_1 and x_2, as a function of final demands and the coefficients of the Leontief inverse.

Now observe the implications of, say, a finite change in the demand for the first commodity. Assuming all else constant, we have

$$\Delta x_1 = \alpha_{11}\Delta f_1 \tag{18.30a}$$
$$\Delta x_2 = \alpha_{21}\Delta f_1. \tag{18.30b}$$

It is evident that Equations (18.30a and b) can be rearranged to give

$$\frac{\Delta x_1}{\Delta f_1} = \alpha_{11} \tag{18.31a}$$

$$\frac{\Delta x_2}{\Delta f_1} = \alpha_{21}. \tag{18.31b}$$

A change in final demand for the first commodity thus has a multiplicative effect on the total outputs of the two industries in the model. The associated multiplier coefficients are described by Equations (18.31a and b). Thus, for instance, a change in the final demand for commodity 1 of Δf_1 will result in a change of $\alpha_{21}\Delta f_1$ in the total output of industry 2, as is apparent in Equations (18.30b) and (18.31b).

By similar reasoning we deduce that, given a change in the final demand for commodity 2, we will obtain

$$\Delta x_1 = \alpha_{12}\Delta f_2 \tag{18.32a}$$
$$\Delta x_2 = \alpha_{22}\Delta f_2, \tag{18.32b}$$

which yields the output multipliers

$$\frac{\Delta x_1}{\Delta f_2} = \alpha_{12} \tag{18.33a}$$

$$\frac{\Delta x_2}{\Delta f_2} = \alpha_{22}. \tag{18.33b}$$

Thus, a change in final demand for commodity 2 will, for example, alter the total output of industry 1 by the multiple α_{12}, as seen in Equations (18.32a) and (18.33a).†

Summarising the results, we find that output multipliers in input-output economics may be treated in exactly the same fashion as macroeconomic impact multipliers. Writing Equations (18.29a and b) in matrix form (remembering that the matrix of α_{ij} is identical with $(\mathbf{I} - \mathbf{A})^{-1}$) we get

$$\begin{bmatrix} x_1 \\ x_2 \end{bmatrix} = \begin{bmatrix} \overset{f_1}{\alpha_{11}} & \overset{f_2}{\alpha_{12}} \\ \alpha_{21} & \alpha_{22} \end{bmatrix} \begin{bmatrix} f_1 \\ f_2 \end{bmatrix}.$$

---

† These multipliers could equally have been derived by finding the first-order partial derivatives of Equations (18.29a and b) with respect to f_1 and f_2.

By moving the vector of final demands to the top of the inverse matrix we are at once able to read off the multipliers of the system. Each α_{ij} from the Leontief inverse is the multiplier linking a change in the jth final demand to the output of the ith industry. The method generalises to systems with n industries along similar lines to those outlined for macroeconomic multipliers.

An interesting extension of the above analysis is an evaluation of changes in final demands in terms of primary inputs. For example, we may wish to know how employment in, say, the steel industry will be affected if there is a decline in the demand for new cars. To find the result, we first calculate the multiplicative impact of the fall in demand for new cars on the total output of the steel industry, using the techniques discussed above. The answer may be, say, 100,000 tons of steel. We then consult the direct-input coefficients to see how many man-days are required to produce 1 ton of steel. Suppose the relevant coefficient is 0.01. Then a fall in steel output of 100,000 tons implies labour redundancy to the order of $100,000 \times 0.01$ or 1,000 man-days. The same estimation procedure can be applied to any final demand and any primary input in the system. The case we have just considered is an example of the operation of an *employment multiplier*.

Exercises

1. An economy is divided into three sectors—agricultural, manufacturing and transport. To produce a unit of agricultural output, 0.5 units of manufacturing, 0.8 units of transport and 0.1 units of agricultural output are required. A unit of manufacturing output uses up 0.1 units of its own output, 0.3 units of agricultural output and 0.9 units of transport. A unit of transport output needs only 0.1 units of manufacturing output. Consumers' final demands for the products of the three sectors are 50, 90 and 25 for agricultural products, manufactures and transport respectively. Set up this economy's structure in the input-output format $\mathbf{x} = \mathbf{Ax} + \mathbf{f}$.

2. Given that
$$
\begin{bmatrix}
0.9 & -0.3 & 0 \\
-0.5 & 0.9 & -0.1 \\
-0.8 & -0.9 & 1
\end{bmatrix}^{-1}
=
\begin{bmatrix}
1.460 & 0.541 & 0.054 \\
1.045 & 1.622 & 0.162 \\
2.108 & 1.892 & 1.189
\end{bmatrix},
$$
determine the levels of output of the three sectors that this economy should produce to meet the given final demands.

3. Show how the equilibrium levels of output are divided between inter-industry and final demands in the previous exercise.

4. Use the solution to Exercise 2 above to answer the following questions:
   (a) If final demand for manufacturing products increases by 5 per cent, what will be the effect on the output of the agricultural sector?
   (b) What would be the effect on agricultural output if the demand for transport services were to decline by 10 per cent?

5. Compute the following:

$$\begin{bmatrix} 3 & -2 \\ 1 & 0 \\ 0 & 4 \end{bmatrix} - \begin{bmatrix} 1 & -1 \\ 0 & 1 \\ 1 & 0 \end{bmatrix} + \begin{bmatrix} 2 & -2 \\ 3 & 4 \\ -\frac{1}{2} & 1 \end{bmatrix}.$$

6. Suppose the technical characteristics of production for an economy which produces only two commodities, x_1 and x_2, can be represented by the following matrix

$$\mathbf{A} = \begin{bmatrix} 0.1 & 0.8 \\ 0.4 & 0.2 \end{bmatrix}.$$

Compute the Leontief inverse.

7. In the preceding exercise, what total outputs of x_1 and x_2 must be produced to meet final demands of 50 and 100 units respectively for these commodities?

Chapter 19

Linear Programming

19.1 An Example

In Section 13.3.1 we considered the problem of maximising a linear function (a revenue function) subject to a nonlinear constraint (the product transformation curve). The application of Lagrange multipliers proved to be a satisfactory method of solving this constrained optimisation problem. In Section 13.3.3, a similar problem was solved in a like fashion: this time it was a problem of minimising a linear function (a cost function) subject to a nonlinear constraint (an isoquant).

Suppose instead that we imagine a problem involving the maximisation or minimisation of a linear function not subject to simply one nonlinear constraint, but subject to a set of linear constraints. Two things are different in comparison with the abovementioned examples: we are now dealing with problems containing *many* constraints; and they are *linear* in nature. Such problems fall into the realm of *linear programming*. To see how such problems might arise, consider the following numerical example.

19.1.1 THE OBJECTIVE FUNCTION

Imagine a small trading nation which is capable of producing two commodities—say wool and wheat. Let quantities of wool and wheat be denoted x_1 and x_2 respectively. International wool and wheat markets are assumed to be perfectly competitive, so that domestic producers of the two commodities must act as price takers. Imagine that prevailing international prices for wool and wheat are $5 and $3 per unit respectively. Thus for any output combination of x_1 and x_2, the international value of domestic aggregate income (z) will be

$$z = 5x_1 + 3x_2. \tag{19.1}$$

Geometrically, each value of z will be represented by an iso-income line, as shown in Fig. 19.1. As the line shifts outwards, higher values of z

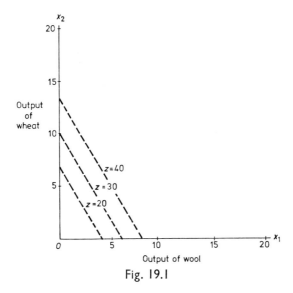

Fig. 19.1

are implied. The slope of the iso-income lines can be found by rearranging Equation (19.1) and differentiating x_2 with respect to x_1. Thus we obtain

$$3x_2 = z - 5x_1,$$

$$x_2 = \frac{z}{3} - \frac{5}{3}x_1,$$

and therefore the slope of the iso-income lines is

$$\frac{dx_2}{dx_1} = -\frac{5}{3}. \qquad (19.2)$$

All iso-income lines have the same slope, reflecting the fact that the relative international prices of x_1 and x_2 are constant.

An economically rational trading nation will endeavour to maximise its real income, or, in other words, to maximise the international value of what it is able to produce. Accordingly, the objective of our linear programming example is to maximise the function (19.1).

19.1.2 THE CONSTRAINTS

In our earlier constrained maximisation example (Section 13.3.1), the limit to which the isorevenue line could be moved outwards was set by the existence of the product transformation curve. This curve was smooth, continuous and differentiable, thus allowing a tangency equilibrium solution to be found.

However, in the application of the linear programming model to similar production problems, whether in the case of an individual firm or in the case of a whole economy (as in our present example), we presuppose the existence of a special kind of underlying production function. We assume that the short-run supplies of factors of production are fixed, and that these inputs are used in production in *fixed proportions*. Let us examine the implications of these assumptions in terms of our numerical example.

Suppose the country has two factors of production, labour and land, total supplies of which are 11 units and 16 units respectively. Suppose it takes 2 units of labour to produce 1 unit of wool (x_1) and 1 unit of labour to produce 1 unit of wheat (x_2). The total amount of labour used for wool and wheat production obviously cannot exceed the total supply of 11 units. In other words, labour inputs must be less than or equal to 11 units. Algebraically, this constraint may be written as an *inequation* or *inequality*, as follows:

$$2x_1 + 1x_2 \leqslant 11. \tag{19.3}$$

Turn to Fig. 19.2, which gives a geometric interpretation of the linear constraint (19.3). If all labour were directed to the production of x_2, output of x_1 would be zero. Substituting zero for x_1 in (19.3) we see that up to 11 units of x_2 could be produced. At the other extreme, there

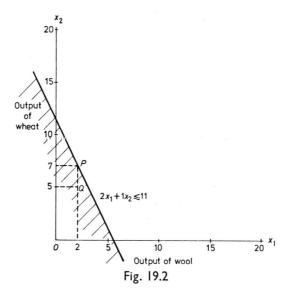

Fig. 19.2

might be complete specialisation in x_1. In this event, x_2 would be zero in (19.3), and up to 11/2 or $5\frac{1}{2}$ units of x_1 could be produced. When labour is being fully utilised, any combination of x_1 and x_2 lying on the line in Fig. 19.2 may be produced — for example, 2 units of x_1 and 7 of x_2 as at the point P. Indeed, this line, which reflects the maximum feasible outputs of x_1 and x_2 attainable from the available labour, corresponds to the equation

$$2x_1 + 1x_2 = 11. \tag{19.4}$$

Optimum technical efficiency in labour use is suggested by Equation (19.4). But our initial labour constraint (19.3) does not necessitate full employment of labour. Because an inequality sign appears in the constraint, labour inputs may be less than 11 units, resulting in less than the maximum feasible output of x_1 and x_2. Some of the country's labour supplies, in other words, may remain idle. Instead of producing an efficient bundle of wool and wheat as at P, for instance, the country may produce the combination at point Q with an output of 2 units of x_1 but only 5 of x_2. Clearly, in such a case the total input of labour would be $2(2) + 1(5)$ or 9 units, instead of the full 11 units of labour which are available. More generally, the linear inequality (19.3) implies that any output combination on or below the line in Fig. 19.2 may be produced. This is illustrated by the shaded region in the diagram.

Similar assumptions relate to the use of land. Let us imagine that 1 unit of land is required to produce 1 unit of x_1, and 4 units of land are used in the production of 1 unit of x_2. With these technical coefficients of production, and with a total land supply of 16 units, outputs of x_1 and x_2 attainable from the available land will be constrained by the linear inequality

$$1x_1 + 4x_2 \leqslant 16. \tag{19.5}$$

That is, the amount of land used by output x_1 (i.e., $1 \times x_1$) *plus* the amount of land used by output x_2 (i.e., $4 \times x_2$) must be *equal to or less than* the total of 16 units of land available. Figure 19.3 gives a diagrammatic account of the inequation (19.5). Again, the shaded region shows the feasible set of output combinations described by this constraint.

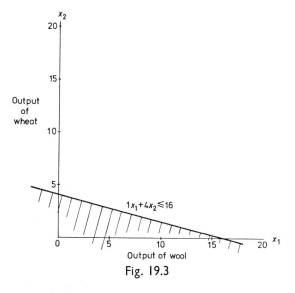

Fig. 19.3

Which output combinations simultaneously satisfy the constraints imposed by the labour and land restrictions (19.3) and (19.5)? Clearly, in diagrammatic terms, the relevant region will be where the two shaded regions of Figs 19.2 and 19.3 overlap. The outcome is illustrated in Fig. 19.4. The cross-hatched region describes all those combinations of x_1 and x_2 that can technically be produced. In fact, this set of points represents the country's production possibilities set. Technically efficient output combinations lie on the production possibilities (or transformation) frontier ABC which is itself composed of constraining linear segments stemming from the original labour and land restrictions. Inefficient output points such as J will be found inside, rather than upon, the production frontier. The segmented production possibilities frontier ABC in Fig. 19.4 is the counterpart in the linear programming model of the smooth continuous curved production possibilities frontier of the marginal analysis model which we have studied in earlier chapters.

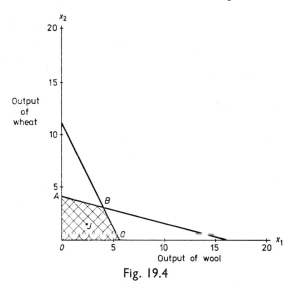

Fig. 19.4

In addition to the initial constraints (19.3) and (19.5), two further restrictions have been incorporated in Fig. 19.4. There is nothing in the inequations (19.3) and (19.5) which precludes negative values of x_1 and x_2. In (19.3), for example, one feasible set of values is $x_1 = 10$ and $x_2 = -9$. That is why the shaded region has been extended beyond the axes of each diagram in Figs 19.2 and 19.3. To overcome this difficulty and to ensure that only positive or zero outputs come under consideration, it is necessary to add non-negativity restrictions for x_1 and x_2. These can be written quite simply as

$$x_1 \geqslant 0 \tag{19.6a}$$

$$x_2 \geqslant 0. \tag{19.6b}$$

With the introduction of the last two inequalities, the axes of the diagram themselves assist in delineating the feasible set of output combinations. In Fig. 19.4, the constraining line segments OA, AB, BC and OC are *all* required to give a complete description of the restrictions imposed on x_1 and x_2. All feasible combinations lying within or on the boundary of $OABC$ in Fig. 19.4 comprise the so-called *feasible region*.

The significant point which emerges is that, in our linear programming example, factors of production are required *simultaneously* in *fixed proportions.* This is the same assumption as is made in input-output analysis. Indeed, an input-output system may be seen as a special variety of linear programming model.

19.1.3 SUMMARY

Collecting together the objective function and the constraints for our example, our problem may be summarised as follows:
Maximise

$$z = 5x_1 + 3x_2 \tag{19.7a}$$

subject to

$$2x_1 + 1x_2 \leqslant 11,$$
$$1x_1 + 4x_2 \leqslant 16, \tag{19.7b}$$
$$x_1, x_2 \geqslant 0.$$

In other words, we are required to maximise a linear function of two variables subject to a set of four linear constraints, i.e., two factor-supply constraints and two non-negativity conditions.

19.2 Solving the Linear Programming Example
19.2.1 GRAPHICAL SOLUTION

For very simple linear programming exercises, solutions may be readily found using diagrammatic techniques. Let us illustrate these methods by finding the outputs of x_1 and x_2 that maximise real national income in our example from the previous section. The logic of the graphical solution is identical with that used in solving the marginal analysis model by geometric methods in Section 9.3.2 (see Fig. 9.5); we simply combine Figs 19.1 and 19.4. The result is sketched in Fig. 19.5. Clearly, the highest attainable iso-income line passes through point B. We therefore conclude

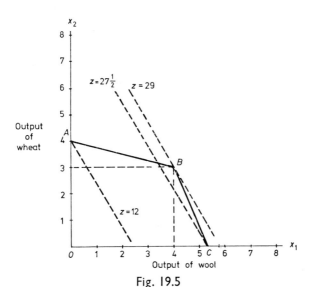

Fig. 19.5

that the maximum feasible value for the objective function will be reached when the country produces 4 units of x_1 and 3 of x_2. By substituting these output levels in Equation (19.1) we find that z equals 29 at this combination of outputs. No other output combination can lead to an improvement on this position.

19.2.2 ALGEBRAIC SOLUTION

The importance of algebraic solution methods in linear programming is at once obvious: the graphical technique is greatly limited by the number of variables it can handle. While we could add further constraints to the problem in Fig. 19.5, we are effectively limited to a production situation involving only two outputs. In real life, however, linear programming problems are set up containing large numbers of variables and constraints.

In applying ordinary algebra to the problem posed in Equation (19.7), we immediately encounter a difficulty: we are used to solving systems of simultaneous *equations*, but the constraints in (19.7b) are set up in terms of a set of simultaneous *inequations*. Thus, the first requirement in solving a linear programming problem by nongraphical means is to convert each input inequality into an equation. This is achieved by the introduction of a new set of variables, called *slack variables*. Let us illustrate this concept in terms of our example.

Consider a combination of outputs x_1 and x_2 where less than 11 units of labour are used. For instance, when $x_1 = 2$ and $x_2 = 3$, Inequation (19.3) tells us that total labour usage will be only 9 units, clearly leaving 2 labour units unemployed or "slack". At some other combination of wool and wheat production where only, say, 6 labour units are used, 5 labour units will be slack. In general, then, the amount of "slack labour" varies according to the levels of x_1 and x_2.

Define a new variable, s_1, to represent "slack labour". The inequality in (19.3) may now be rewritten as a strict equality as follows:

$$2x_1 + 1x_2 + 1s_1 = 11. \tag{19.8}$$

Equation (19.8) tells us that the amount of labour used by x_1 (i.e., $2 \times x_1$) *plus* the amount used by x_2 (i.e., $1 \times x_2$) *plus* any slack labour (i.e., $1 \times s_1$) must equal the 11 units of labour available. So if, as before, $x_1 = 2$, $x_2 = 5$, we immediately see that $s_1 = 2$ in order for (19.8) to hold. It should be apparent that we must also specify a non-negativity condition on s_1, just as we did for x_1 and x_2. That is,

$$s_1 \geqslant 0. \tag{19.9}$$

Without the condition (19.9), infeasible values of x_1 and x_2 would be possible. For example the infeasible combination $x_1 = 20$, $x_2 = 30$, $s_1 = -59$ satisfies Equation (19.8) but is ruled out by condition (19.9).

The same procedure may be followed to convert the land constraint (19.5) into an equality. Letting the non-negative variable s_2 denote units of slack land, we arrive at the equation

$$1x_1 + 4x_2 + 1s_2 = 16. \tag{19.10}$$

Equations (19.8) and (19.10) can now be combined to give a system of linear equations with x_1, x_2, s_1, and s_2 as "unknowns". Zero coefficients for s_2 and s_1 must be added to Equations (19.8) and (19.10) respectively. We obtain

$$2x_1 + 1x_2 + 1s_1 + 0s_2 = 11 \qquad (19.11\text{a})$$
$$1x_1 + 4x_2 + 0s_1 + 1s_2 = 16. \qquad (19.11\text{b})$$

Now consider the problem of solving a set of simultaneous equations in which there are more unknowns than equations. As a simple example, consider a system containing two unknowns and only one equation, such as

$$a + b = 5. \qquad (19.12)$$

It is obvious that there are many sets of possible values of a and b that will satisfy this system.

Returning to Equations (19.11), we see a system containing four unknowns and only two equations. Hence there will be many sets of possible values of x_1, x_2, s_1 and s_2 that will satisfy these equations. The way in which we proceed is to run a number of trials. In each trial we select two unknowns (corresponding to the number of equations in the system), assume that all other unknowns have a value of zero, solve the system as though it were a simple 2×2 example, and compute the corresponding value of z using Equation (19.1). We may then choose as the optimum that particular solution which yields the highest value of z. Thus, our solution procedure involves not just a single calculation, but a series of steps or *iterations*, corresponding to the series of trials just described.

The solution for the two chosen variables obtained in any such trial is called a *basic solution*; the two chosen variables are called *basic variables* and the two variables whose values are set to zero are called *nonbasic variables*. Of course, when we also introduce our non-negativity constraints, we must immediately reject any solution that contains negative values for any of the unknowns. Only *feasible* basic solutions will thus be considered. Interestingly enough, each basic feasible solution obtained by algebraic methods corresponds geometrically to a *corner-point*, or *vertex* (more correctly an *extreme point*)† of the feasible output set. In terms of Figs 19.4 and 19.5, the corner points at which basic feasible solutions lie are the points, O, A, B and C. Furthermore, the value of the objective function for each such solution is reflected in the iso-income line passing through the relevant extreme point.

Let us now see how this works in our elementary example. To begin with, let us set x_1 and x_2 at zero, and take s_1 and s_2 as our basic variables.

Equations (19.11) reduce to

$$1s_1 + 0s_2 = 11 \qquad (19.13\text{a})$$
$$0s_1 + 1s_2 = 16 \qquad (19.13\text{b})$$

---

† This terminology used in the jargon of set theory is related to, but should not be confused with, the extreme points of functions discussed in earlier chapters.

whence we obtain

$$s_1 = 11 \tag{19.14a}$$
$$s_2 = 16. \tag{19.14b}$$

Since in this solution x_1 and x_2 are zero (by assumption), the value of the objective function (Equation (19.1)) is zero. It should be apparent that this basic solution, involving no output of wool and wheat, and with both land and labour entirely slack, corresponds to the Point O on Fig. 19.5.

Point A is obtained when x_1 and s_2 are set at zero. In this case Equations (19.11) become:

$$1x_2 + 1s_1 = 11 \tag{19.15a}$$
$$4x_2 + 0s_1 = 16, \tag{19.15b}$$

from which we obtain the basic solution

$$x_2 = 4 \tag{19.16a}$$
$$s_1 = 7. \tag{19.16b}$$

Putting the values $x_1 = 0$ (by assumption) and $x_2 = 4$ (from Equation (19.16a)) into the objective function (19.1) yields the value of z at this point as $(5 \times 0) + (3 \times 4) = 12$.

In our next trial, set s_1 and s_2 as the nonbasic variables (i.e., zero), and solve (19.11) for x_1 and x_2:

$$2x_1 + 1x_2 = 11 \tag{19.17a}$$
$$1x_1 + 4x_2 = 16. \tag{19.17b}$$

Hence

$$x_1 = 4 \tag{19.18a}$$
$$x_2 = 3, \tag{19.18b}$$

and we calculate $z = 29$. This solution is at the point B in Fig. 19.5.

Finally, assume x_2 and s_1 are zero, and solve Equations (19.11) for the basic variables x_1 and s_2:

$$2x_1 + 0s_2 = 11 \tag{19.19a}$$
$$1x_1 + 1s_2 = 16. \tag{19.19b}$$

Hence

$$x_1 = 5\tfrac{1}{2} \tag{19.20a}$$
$$s_2 = 10\tfrac{1}{2}, \tag{19.20b}$$

and we calculate $z = 27\tfrac{1}{2}$. This solution corresponds to the point C on our diagram.

A comparison of the four basic solutions studied above shows that the one in which $x_1 = 4$, $x_2 = 3$, $s_1 = 0$ and $s_2 = 0$ (i.e., the solution corresponding to point B in Fig. 19.5) yields the highest value of z, namely, 29. This confirms our earlier graphical result.

In this series of trials we have examined only four feasible solutions, yet there are clearly many more possible feasible combinations of the four unknowns which would satisfy the constraints in Equations (19.11):

points lying within or elsewhere on the boundary of the feasible output set *OABC* in Fig. 19.5. How can we be confident that the solution found above is indeed optimum? A fundamental theorem of linear programming, which we cannot prove here, states that an optimal solution will always lie at an extreme point of the set described by the constraints, that is at a vertex of the feasible region.† Hence we are justified in considering only basic feasible solutions in our search.

Nevertheless, for larger linear programming problems a great deal of effort would be involved even if only basic feasible solutions were examined. Thus, more efficient methods have been contrived, all of which rely on iterative procedures. The most popular is the *simplex method*. Under this technique, basic feasible solutions are systematically worked through. In moving from one trial to the next, one variable is dropped from the solution and a new one added, always with the aim of obtaining a value for the objective function at least as great as in the previous trial. Each new step or iteration corresponds to a movement from one extreme point of the feasible region to an adjacent one. In terms of Fig. 19.5 we may imagine the simplex method leading us progressively from point O to C and finally to B.

19.3 Larger Problems

The same concepts extend to larger linear programming problems. In general, we may be dealing with n variables (called *activities*) and m constraints. The fixed coefficients of the model can be represented by a set of a_{ij}, where $i = 1, \ldots, m$ and $j = 1, \ldots, n$. Total supplies of inputs can be denoted by b_i where $i = 1, \ldots, m$. Finally, the prices of outputs can be represented by p_j where $j = 1, \ldots, n$. Such a programme may be written as:

Maximise

$$z = p_1 x_1 + p_2 x_2 + \ldots + p_n x_n \qquad (19.21a)$$

subject to

$$
\begin{aligned}
a_{11} x_1 + a_{12} x_2 + \ldots + a_{1n} x_n &\leqslant b_1 \\
a_{21} x_1 + a_{22} x_2 + \ldots + a_{2n} x_n &\leqslant b_2 \\
\vdots \qquad \vdots \qquad \qquad \vdots \qquad \vdots \\
a_{m1} x_1 + a_{m2} x_2 + \ldots + a_{mn} x_n &\leqslant b_m
\end{aligned}
\qquad (19.21b)
$$

and

$$x_1, x_2, \ldots, x_n \geqslant 0. \qquad (19.21c)$$

This system may be represented more compactly in matrix notation, as follows:

Maximise

$$z = \mathbf{px} \qquad (19.22a)$$

subject to

$$\mathbf{Ax} \leqslant \mathbf{b} \qquad (19.22b)$$

† In some problems the optimal solution lies at more than one vertex, but we shall not consider this case here.

and

$$\mathbf{x} \geq 0 \tag{19.22c}$$

where $\mathbf{x}$ = $n \times 1$ vector of activity levels to be determined;
$\quad \mathbf{p}$ = $1 \times n$ vector of prices attaching to the activities;†
$\quad \mathbf{A}$ = $m \times n$ matrix of fixed coefficients; and
$\quad \mathbf{b}$ = $m \times 1$ vector of input supplies.

To convert the inequalities in (19.21b) and (19.22b) to equations, we may add a set of m non-negative slack variables, $s_1, s_2, \ldots, s_m$.

The set of constraints (19.21b) therefore becomes:

$$
\begin{aligned}
a_{11}x_1 + a_{12}x_2 + \ldots + a_{1n}x_n + 1s_1 + 0s_2 + \ldots + 0s_m &= b_1, \\
a_{21}x_1 + a_{22}x_2 + \ldots + a_{2n}x_n + 0s_1 + 1s_2 + \ldots + 0s_m &= b_2 \\
\vdots \qquad\qquad \vdots \qquad\qquad \vdots \qquad \vdots \qquad \vdots \qquad\qquad \vdots \\
a_{m1}x_1 + a_{m2}x_2 + \ldots + a_{mn}x_n + 0s_1 + 0s_2 + \ldots + 1s_m &= b_m.
\end{aligned}
\tag{19.23}
$$

In matrix notation, the system of Equations (19.23) may be written

$$\mathbf{Ax} + \mathbf{Is} = \mathbf{b} \tag{19.24}$$

where $\mathbf{A}, \mathbf{x}, \mathbf{b}$ are as defined above;
$\quad \mathbf{s}$ = $m \times 1$ vector of slack variables; and
$\quad \mathbf{I}$ = $m \times m$ identity matrix.

19.4 Linear Programming Solutions in Matrix Terms

The mathematical aspects of linear programming become very complicated, and to cover them in any detail would take us far beyond our present scope. Nevertheless, to conclude our introduction to this topic, it will be useful to consider the notion of a basic solution in matrix terms.

In Equations (19.23) and (19.24) we have n "real" variables (i.e., x), and m slack variables (i.e., s) giving a total of $(m + n)$ variables altogether. Let us denote any variable in the system by the symbol y_k where $k = 1, \ldots, (m+n)$. Alternatively, we can identify $\mathbf{y}$ as the $(m+n) \times 1$ vector

$$
\mathbf{y} = \begin{bmatrix} x_1 \\ x_2 \\ \vdots \\ x_n \\ s_1 \\ s_2 \\ \vdots \\ s_m \end{bmatrix}.
$$

---

† Sometimes the vector $\mathbf{p}$ is written, like the other vectors in the problem, as a column vector. If so, it must be transposed in the objective function so that it can be post-multiplied by the vector $\mathbf{x}$. In such an event, Equation (19.22a) would appear: Maximise $z = \mathbf{p'x}$.

Now the coefficients of $\mathbf{y}$ may be seen from Equation (19.23) to be the $m \times (m+n)$ matrix

$$\begin{bmatrix} a_{11} & a_{12} & \ldots & a_{1n} & 1 & 0 & \ldots & 0 \\ a_{21} & a_{22} & \ldots & a_{2n} & 0 & 1 & \ldots & 0 \\ \vdots & \vdots & & \vdots & \vdots & \vdots & & \vdots \\ a_{m1} & a_{m2} & \ldots & a_{mn} & 0 & 0 & \ldots & 1 \end{bmatrix} \tag{19.25}$$

or more compactly

$$[\,\mathbf{A}\mid\mathbf{I}\,] \tag{19.26}$$

where the broken vertical line indicates a *partition*. In other words, (19.26) indicates that the columns of $\mathbf{A}$ and $\mathbf{I}$ are written side by side, just as is shown in (19.25). Make sure you understand that (19.26) is not the same as writing $\mathbf{A} + \mathbf{I}$ or $\mathbf{AI}$.

Now denote the matrix in (19.26) as $\mathbf{D}$. Then we can write the constraint set (19.24), using our new notation, as

$$\mathbf{Dy} = \mathbf{b}. \tag{19.27}$$

As we have seen, we may form a basic solution from any set of m variables in the vector $\mathbf{y}$. This leaves n variables remaining to be nonbasic and therefore set to zero. Let us denote a set of basic variables in $\mathbf{y}$ as a vector $\mathbf{y}_B$ and the corresponding nonbasic variables as a vector $\mathbf{y}_{NB}$. Now, the columns of the matrix $\mathbf{D}$ may be separated into those which correspond to the basic variables $\mathbf{y}_B$ and those which correspond to the nonbasic variables $\mathbf{y}_{NB}$. The columns of $\mathbf{D}$ corresponding to $\mathbf{y}_B$ may be collected together as a submatrix of $\mathbf{D}$, which we shall denote $\mathbf{B}$, and the columns of $\mathbf{D}$ corresponding to $\mathbf{y}_{NB}$ form another submatrix of $\mathbf{D}$ which we shall call $\mathbf{C}$. Hence Equation (19.27) may be written:

$$\mathbf{By}_B + \mathbf{Cy}_{NB} = \mathbf{b}. \tag{19.28}$$

In fact the matrix $\mathbf{B}$ is called the *basis matrix*, or simply the *basis*.

Now, since $\mathbf{y}_{NB} = 0$ by assumption, the second term on the LHS of Equation (19.28) drops out, leaving

$$\mathbf{By}_B = \mathbf{b}, \tag{19.29}$$

which may be solved for the values of the basic variables by premultiplying both sides by $\mathbf{B}^{-1}$. We obtain

$$\mathbf{y}_B = \mathbf{B}^{-1}\mathbf{b}. \tag{19.30}$$

The matrix $\mathbf{B}^{-1}$ is called the *basis inverse*,† and Equation (19.30) represents the concept we have already encountered, the *basic solution*.

We may illustrate these points with reference to our earlier example. Putting the numerical data from our example into Equation (19.27), we obtain

$$\begin{bmatrix} 2 & 1 & 1 & 0 \\ 1 & 4 & 0 & 1 \end{bmatrix} \begin{bmatrix} y_1 \\ y_2 \\ y_3 \\ y_4 \end{bmatrix} = \begin{bmatrix} 11 \\ 16 \end{bmatrix} \tag{19.31}$$

---

† To obtain $\mathbf{B}^{-1}$, it is clear that $\mathbf{B}$ must be nonsingular. Indeed, a basis can be formed only if this condition is met.

where $y_1 \equiv x_1$,
  $y_2 \equiv x_2$,
  $y_3 \equiv s_1$, and
  $y_4 \equiv s_2$.

Now let us determine a basic solution containing, say, x_1 and s_2. In terms of Equation (19.28), this means letting

$$\mathbf{y}_B = \begin{bmatrix} y_1 \\ y_4 \end{bmatrix} = \begin{bmatrix} x_1 \\ s_2 \end{bmatrix} \qquad (19.32a)$$

and

$$\mathbf{y}_{NB} = \begin{bmatrix} y_2 \\ y_3 \end{bmatrix} = \begin{bmatrix} x_2 \\ s_1 \end{bmatrix} = 0. \qquad (19.32b)$$

We can now write Equation (19.29) by forming the appropriate basis from the relevant columns of the 2×4 matrix $\mathbf{D}$ in (19.31), namely, the columns corresponding to the chosen basic variables x_1 and s_2. These are the first and fourth columns respectively. Hence Equation (19.29) becomes

$$\begin{bmatrix} 2 & 0 \\ 1 & 1 \end{bmatrix} \begin{bmatrix} y_1 \\ y_4 \end{bmatrix} = \begin{bmatrix} 11 \\ 16 \end{bmatrix}. \qquad (19.33)$$

The solution to Equation (19.33) is

$$\begin{bmatrix} y_1 \\ y_4 \end{bmatrix} = \begin{bmatrix} 2 & 0 \\ 1 & 1 \end{bmatrix}^{-1} \begin{bmatrix} 11 \\ 16 \end{bmatrix}$$

$$= \frac{1}{2} \begin{bmatrix} 1 & 0 \\ -1 & 2 \end{bmatrix} \begin{bmatrix} 11 \\ 16 \end{bmatrix}$$

$$= \begin{bmatrix} \frac{1}{2} & 0 \\ -\frac{1}{2} & 1 \end{bmatrix} \begin{bmatrix} 11 \\ 16 \end{bmatrix}$$

$$= \begin{bmatrix} 5\frac{1}{2} \\ 10\frac{1}{2} \end{bmatrix}.$$

Thus we see that the basic solution for a basis containing x_1 and s_2 is $x_1 = 5\frac{1}{2}$, $s_2 = 10\frac{1}{2}$ with $x_2 = 0$ and $s_1 = 0$. This confirms our earlier calculations (Equation (19.20)).

As another illustration, let x_1 and x_2 be basic variables. The basis matrix $\mathbf{B}$ is thus

$$\mathbf{B} = \begin{bmatrix} 2 & 1 \\ 1 & 4 \end{bmatrix}$$

and hence this basic solution, using Equation (19.30), is given as

$$
\mathbf{y}_B = \begin{bmatrix} y_1 \\ y_2 \end{bmatrix} = \begin{bmatrix} x_1 \\ x_2 \end{bmatrix} = \begin{bmatrix} 2 & 1 \\ 1 & 4 \end{bmatrix}^{-1} \begin{bmatrix} 11 \\ 16 \end{bmatrix}
$$

$$
= \frac{1}{7} \begin{bmatrix} 4 & -1 \\ -1 & 2 \end{bmatrix} \begin{bmatrix} 11 \\ 16 \end{bmatrix}
$$

$$
= \begin{bmatrix} \frac{4}{7} & -\frac{1}{7} \\ -\frac{1}{7} & \frac{2}{7} \end{bmatrix} \begin{bmatrix} 11 \\ 16 \end{bmatrix}
$$

$$
= \begin{bmatrix} 4 \\ 3 \end{bmatrix}. \tag{19.34}
$$

The values of $x_1 = 4$ and $x_2 = 3$ in this basic solution again confirm our earlier calculations (Equation (19.18)).

19.5 Some Further Ramifications of Linear Programming

As in the case of input-output analysis in the previous chapter, we have been able here only to scratch the surface of an important topic. In concluding our brief treatment of linear programming, we will consider some further ramifications of the technique.

Linear programming is equally applicable to problems involving the *minimisation* of a linear function subject to a set of linear constraints. The constraint set in such problems would doubtless contain *minimum* constraints in place of, or in addition to, the maximum constraints we have studied above. Conceptually, the procedures for setting up and solving such problems are the same as those outlined above, though computationally there are differences. An example of a minimisation problem amenable to solution by linear programming is the determination of the quantities of raw materials to make up a minimum-cost feed-mix for livestock, given certain minimum constraints on the levels of nutrients such as protein, starch, and so on, in the resulting mix.

Another useful feature of linear programming when applied to production problems such as the example used in this chapter is that it yields data on the marginal value products or *shadow prices* of the inputs. This information, which is made available to the analyst as a by-product of the use of the simplex method, is obtained via the so-called *dual* solution. Duality theory has come to play an important part in the analysis of general equilibrium systems in economics.

The application of linear programming to problems arising in the theory of the firm has led in recent years to important advances in microeconomic theory. Linear programming provides a model of the firm which is in many respects a more realistic representation of the structure of the modern firm than that derived from neoclassical theory, which is based on smooth-curved production functions.

At a practical empirical level, linear programming has been widely used in business and industry to solve warehousing, plant location, transportation, blending, resource allocation, scheduling, and a host of other problems. Mathematical developments such as integer programming and quadratic programming have been useful in overcoming some unrealities in the assumptions on which the method is based.

Finally, linear programming has been used at the aggregate national level in problems of macroeconomic planning and at the international level in the study of trade flows between countries. Indeed when one considers the range of problems studied by economists, it is surprising just how many can be formulated as problems of extremisation of a linear function subject to linear constraints. Little wonder, then, that the mathematical method of linear programming has had such a profound impact on theoretical and applied economics.

Exercises

1. Consider the set of linear constraints
$$1x_1 + 3x_2 \leqslant 15,$$
$$1x_1 + 1x_2 \leqslant 9,$$
$$x_1 \geqslant 0,$$
$$x_2 \geqslant 0.$$
Draw a graph of the feasible region for x_1 and x_2.

2. Suppose in Exercise 1 that the aim is to maximise z where
$$z = 7x_1 + 9x_2.$$
Find by graphical methods the solution to this problem.

3. Consider the linear programming problem:
Maximise
$$z = 2x_1 + 1x_2$$
subject to
$$1x_1 + 1x_2 \leqslant 5,$$
$$1x_1 + 2x_2 \leqslant 8,$$
$$3x_1 + 1x_2 \leqslant 12,$$
$$x_1 \geqslant 0,$$
$$x_2 \geqslant 0.$$
Draw a graph of the feasible region. Use the graph to find the values of x_1 and x_2 which lead to the maximisation of z. What is the value of z in the optimum solution?

4. For the set of constraints in Exercise 1, define appropriate slack variables and set the problem up as a set of simultaneous equations.

5. Given the set of constraint equations in Exercise 4, use matrix methods to find basic solutions to the problem when the following variables are in the basis:
   (a) s_1 and x_1,
   (b) x_1 and x_2,
   (c) s_1 and s_2.

6. A firm produces ladies' shoes and handbags using two inputs, leather and labour. Each pair of shoes sells for \$3 and each handbag for \$20. The labour required to make a pair of shoes is 4 man-hours and that for a handbag is 2 man-hours, while a handbag requires 8 units of leather, and a pair of shoes needs 2 units of leather. The firm has a daily delivery of 40 units of leather and its labour supply is 38 man-hours per day. The entrepreneur aims to maximise his sales revenue. Set up and solve this problem using linear programming.

7. How would the solution to Exercise 6 above be affected if the price of handbags fell to \$10 each, the price of shoes remaining as before?

Part V: Elementary Econometric Method

Chapter 20

Econometric Method and Simple Regression

20.1 Introduction

Throughout this book, we have used simple numerical examples of the functions we have been studying—demand and supply functions, consumption functions, utility functions, production functions, and so on. We have been careful to point out that these empirical functions in real life do not appear as if by magic. Rather, since they describe the behaviour of economic units (firms, consumers, industries, etc.) the functions must be obtained in practice from observation of real-world behaviour. The collection of data and the estimation of empirical functions takes us into the realm of the application of *statistical method* to economics, more particularly into the area of *econometrics*. It is impossible in the space of a few pages to go very far into this important subject. In any case, the serious student of economics will invariably take at least an introductory course in statistics and/or econometrics in its own right.

However, we regard an appreciation of the basic ideas and approaches of econometrics to be so important for an understanding of quantitative economics that we provide in these chapters an introduction to the fundamentals of this area. Our purpose is solely to give the beginning student some "feel" for the subject as a prelude to more detailed and rigorous subsequent study. All students should at least tackle the present chapter; however some will not be able to manage Chapter 21 (see footnote, page 283).

20.2 The Methodology of Econometrics

Before getting down to any mathematical or statistical detail, it is necessary for us to understand how an econometrician sets about his work. His approach should be based on a strict discipline of scientific method, otherwise he will end up aimlessly playing with numbers without useful result. To illustrate what is meant by "scientific method", a flowchart showing an idealised sequence of steps for any econometric investigation is given in Fig. 20.1. In fact, this type of scientific method is not confined to econometrics; a properly objective scientific approach should be applied to any sort of empirical economic analysis. Indeed, a "pure" econometrician may concern himself primarily with the step involving parameter estimation, and may be content to leave the other aspects to the more general economic theorist.

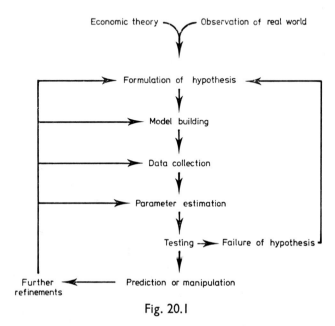

Fig. 20.1

Let us consider each of the steps in the sequence in turn.

20.2.1 THEORY AND OBSERVATION

The generation of ideas about how economic systems operate may come from theoretical consideration, from observation of economic behaviour in the real world, or from some combination of these two sources. To illustrate the latter possibility, consider a very simple example.

Observation of statistics for the economy as a whole might show that over some past period, imports of consumer goods and consumption expenditure have both risen. This observation might be formalised in an hypothesis that imports depend positively on consumption. But an alternative hypothesis might just as well be specified after observation of this set of data, namely, that consumption depends positively on imports. We may discriminate between these competing hypotheses on the basis of *theory*, which tells us that consumers satisfy their wants by choosing among the array of goods available on the basis of their tastes, incomes, etc. Part of their demand can be satisfied by domestically produced goods, and the remainder may be met only by imports from abroad. This very general "theorising" seems to suggest that imports are more likely to depend on consumption expenditures than the other way around. Hence we would be inclined to formulate the hypothesis in these terms for subsequent empirical investigation.

20.2.2 HYPOTHESIS FORMULATION

An hypothesis consists of a statement about reality that is derived from theory and/or from observation of real phenomena. In formulating a theory† it is very important to ensure that hypotheses are constructed which are capable of *refutation*. The emphasis on refutation and not on *proof* of hypotheses frequently puzzles students and deserves further explanation.

A theory that cannot be refuted cannot be meaningfully tested and tells us nothing about the world. Such a theory is called *empty*. Consider two examples of how empty hypotheses may arise. Firstly, consider the theory that the demand for bananas falls when the price rises, other things remaining equal (*ceteris paribus*). If the latter clause is left unspecified, the hypothesis is untestable. Suppose we observe the price of bananas rising and demand falling. We would conclude that our hypothesis is correct. On the other hand, suppose the demand for bananas *increases* when the price rises. We could conclude that our hypothesis is still correct, since other things must not have remained equal. In other words, while the *ceteris paribus* clause remains *unspecified*, any set of observations can be judged consistent with our hypothesis, which is therefore irrefutable.

A second example of an empty hypothesis is one which contains a variable whose definition is not independently given. For instance, consider the hypothesis that consumers allocate their income so as to maximise their utility. Unless we can provide an independent definition of "utility", this theory is irrefutable, since we may redefine "utility" to fit any set of observations of consumer behaviour.

What constitutes refutation of a theory? If the theory is *deterministic*, refutation may be very simple; for example, the hypothesis that all swans are white is refuted as soon as a black swan is observed (though note that the theory is not *proved* if our sample set of observations happens to produce only white swans). However, most economic theories are not formulated in such black and white terms. Rather, they typically say "if certain conditions apply, a given influence will tend to lead to such and such a result".‡ The cause-effect link is established theoretically, then a series of factual observations are made which are either consistent or inconsistent with the theory. Statistical method provides the means for

---

† We speak fairly interchangeably about "a theory" and "an hypothesis". In this sense "a theory" is contrasted with "theory" in general.

‡ Such an hypothesis admits the presence of *random* or *stochastic* influences in the system under study. In fact, econometric models (see Section 20.2.3) are always stochastic rather than deterministic in nature, in that they always contain random elements.

judging how many inconsistent observations can be regarded purely as statistical flukes, and how many would be required to refute the theory. Again we must stress that statistical analysis does not *prove* a theory, but merely shows that it is consistent or inconsistent with a given set of factual observations.

In the process of hypothesis formulation, great care must of course be taken to ensure that causal links between phenomena are properly established at the outset. If this is not done, the results of particular experiments may easily be misinterpreted. Too many economists have fallen into the trap of the famous professor of psychology who spent several years teaching a cockroach to walk on the command "Quick march!" In the next stage of the experiment, the professor removed the cockroach's legs. Now when ordered to walk, the poor creature remained motionless. All of which goes to show, the professor concluded, that removing a cockroach's legs interferes with its hearing.

20.2.3 MODEL BUILDING

An hypothesis makes a statement about how the world behaves. A *model*, as we have seen in earlier chapters, establishes the main variables involved in testing the hypothesis and connects them by means of verbal and/or mathematical statements. A model thus provides the mechanical or formal means by which an hypothesis is tested.

An econometric model is composed of one or more *structural equations*. The most important are *behavioural equations*, that is, equations such as consumption functions, investment functions, utility functions, and so on, which describe the behaviour of economic units. Another important type of structural equation, which we met in our study of macromodels in Chapters 14–17, is the *identity* or definitional equation.

We have already referred to the distinction between *endogenous* and *exogenous variables* in economic models. The reader should refer back to Section 4.4.2 to revise this important concept.

20.2.4 DATA COLLECTION

We are now at the stage in our sequence where we have constructed a theoretical model to test our particular hypothesis. The moment has almost arrived where we can confront our model with the empirical facts. However, we must first collect the empirical data we require.

Broadly speaking, there are two approaches to data collection in econometrics. On the one hand, we may observe the behaviour of an individual, a firm, an industry or the whole economy over a series of time periods; for example, over a sequence of months or years. The resulting set of observations is called a *time series*. On the other hand, we may at one particular point in time collect data from a number of individuals, firms or industries. Usually this procedure involves taking a *sample* from the whole population of individuals, firms or industries under study. Such an approach is called *cross-section analysis*. Occasionally it is possible to combine both time-series and cross-section methods in collecting data.

20.2.5 PARAMETER ESTIMATION

This step might be regarded as the heart of the econometric investigation. It is at this point that our theoretical model and our empirical data come face to face. For example, our model might consist of the hypothesised demand function:

$$q = a + bp \qquad (20.1)$$

where q and p are quantity and price respectively of some good. Our data consist of a set of observations on q and p. Our task in this step is to obtain numerical estimates of the parameters a and b.

A variety of methods may be used to make these estimates. One of the most widely used is *linear regression*, which we shall discuss in more detail in Section 20.3.

20.2.6 TESTING

Statistical tests applied to the parameter estimates obtained from the previous step help us to judge whether our hypothesis is consistent or inconsistent with our empirical observations. We shall look at some of these tests in the next chapter. If our hypothesis fails the empirical tests, we may wish to return to an earlier stage in the sequence, as shown on Fig. 20.1. For example, our estimates of a and b in Equation (20.1) may indicate that no linear relationship seems to exist between q and p. In such a case we may wish to rethink our hypothesis, perhaps introducing new variables in an attempt to explain the variation in q. This would necessitate recycling through all the stages from hypothesis formulation onwards.

20.2.7 PREDICTION

If the tests in the previous section support the hypothesis under consideration, and we can indeed take our model as a satisfactory empirical representation of the system under study, we may wish to investigate the behaviour of the model under different circumstances. In particular we may be interested in *predicting* the values of certain (endogenous) variables in the model for given levels of other (exogenous) components. For example, assuming an acceptable set of values for a and b in Equation (20.1), we may wish to predict the level of demand that we would expect to prevail at a variety of price levels.

It is important to appreciate the distinction between predictions and forecasts. A *forecast* or *projection* is a special case of prediction, that is, an explanation of *future* events. On the other hand, a prediction *per se* does not necessarily relate to the future. It is simply the process of deducing what would be expected to happen as a logical consequence of certain assumptions. For example, the theory of supply and demand predicts that, given constant demand, under certain conditions a fall in supply will lead to a rise in price. This prediction is *qualitative* in nature. Empirical models, on the other hand, provide *quantitative* predictions. Thus, given the structure of a particular model, certain values of the exogenous components will lead as a logical consequence to certain (predicted) values of the endogenous variables.

The end of this stage may mark the end of a piece of empirical economic analysis. On the other hand, the results obtained may be suggestive of further refinements that must be incorporated in hypotheses or models. Alternatively, the collection of further data may be indicated, or the re-estimation of parameters from existing data using different estimating techniques. Perhaps further testing of the model may be required. All of these possibilities are indicated by the arrows on the left side of Fig. 20.1.

In concluding this brief treatment of the methodology of empirical investigation in economics, we must stress again that the sequence of events portrayed in Fig. 20.1 represents a greatly simplified view. We have not discussed, for instance, the variety of economic, mathematical and statistical assumptions that must be made, critically examined, and possibly revised, during the process of an empirical study. Nor have we indicated the sorts of occasions where departure from the idealised sequence of steps would be necessitated. We have attempted simply to orientate the reader's thoughts towards the need for sound methodology before he plunges into the world of real data.

20.3 The Simple Regression Model

Let us now concentrate attention on the problem of estimating the parameters of a model using a given set of empirical data and employing the estimating technique of linear regression. We shall examine this problem in the context of an example.

20.3.1 AN EXAMPLE

Suppose a monopolist wishes to derive an empirical demand function for his product. He postulates a relationship of the form

$$Y = \alpha + \beta X \qquad (20.2)$$

where Y = quantity demanded in thousands of units per month;

X = price per unit in cents; and

α, β = unknown parameters to be estimated, known as the *regression coefficients*.

Suppose he varies the price for his product and notes the volume of sales that occur at different price levels. Over a six-month period, the set of observations may appear as in Table 20.1.

TABLE 20.1

Monopolist's Demand

Observation (i)	Month	Price (X) (cents)	Sales (Y) ('000)
1	Jan.	2	8
2	Feb.	4	3
3	Mar.	3	4
4	Apr.	1	7
5	May	3	8
6	June	5	0

A picture of the relationship between Y and X may be obtained by plotting the points from Table 20.1 on a graph. The observations numbered 1 through 6 on Table 20.1 are shown on Fig. 20.2. As a rough approximation to the relationship between Y and X the line that appears best to fit the data has been drawn by eye on Fig. 20.2. Using the graphical methods studied in Chapter 4, we could measure the slope of this line as being roughly -2 and the intercept as approximately $10\frac{1}{2}$. In other words, an approximate estimate of the parameters of Equation (20.2) is $\alpha = 10\frac{1}{2}$, $\beta = -2$, giving an equation that roughly describes this set of data as:

$$Y = 10\frac{1}{2} - 2X. \qquad (20.3)$$

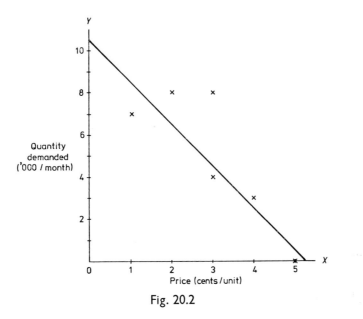

Fig. 20.2

It is clear, however, that graphical methods are only approximate. We need a more accurate method to find the line of *best* fit for this set of data. To do so we need to decide what we mean by "best" fit.

20.3.2 THE ERROR TERM

Let us denote the various observed values of Y and X by Y_i and X_i respectively. In our example, $i = 1, \ldots, 6$. Further, let $\hat{Y}_i$ denote the value of the dependent variable which is *predicted* by the (as yet undetermined) relationship between Y and X for a given X_i. In graphical terms, take a particular level of X_i, as shown on Fig. 20.3. The observed value of Y at that level of X is given at the point P. It is indicated by the level Y_i on the vertical axis. Now consider the downward sloping line in Fig. 20.3 representing a suggested relationship between Y and X. This relationship *predicts* a value of Y at the point Q for the given value X_i. This value of Y

is marked as $\hat{Y}_i$ on the vertical axis. Finally, let e_i equal the distance between the observed and predicted values of Y at the ith level of X. For the example in Fig. 20.3, the magnitude e_i is measured by the distance between P and Q.

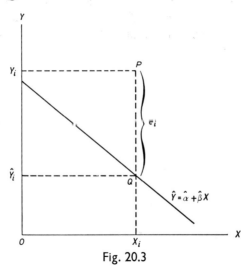

Fig. 20.3

Thus we can write the predicted values of Y as:

$$\hat{Y}_i = \hat{\alpha} + \hat{\beta} X_i \tag{20.4}$$

where the hats are placed on α and β to indicate that they are only *estimates* of the true regression coefficients α and β. We may also write the observed values of Y as:

$$Y_i = \hat{Y}_i + e_i \tag{20.5}$$

and, combining Equations (20.4) and (20.5), we obtain

$$Y_i = \hat{\alpha} + \hat{\beta} X_i + e_i. \tag{20.6}$$

The term e is called the *error term* or *residual*. If we have n observations of Y and X (i.e., if $i = 1, \ldots, n$), there will be a total of n values of the error term, one for each observation.

20.3.3 THE PRINCIPLE OF LEAST SQUARES

Take a scatter of points such as that shown in Fig. 20.2. It should be intuitively obvious that an acceptable definition of the "line of best fit" for these points will be that line for which the sum of the distances of all points from the line is as small as possible. Now the distance of the *i*th point from the line was defined in the previous section as the residual e_i. We note that e_i can be positive or negative depending on whether the particular observed value of Y falls above or below the line. Thus if we simply took the sum of the distances of points from the line, the positive and negative values of e_i would tend to cancel each other out. This problem can be overcome by squaring the e_i, since e_i^2 will be positive regardless of whether e_i itself is positive or negative. Now we may formally define the line of best fit as that placed such that *the sum of squared deviations of all points from the line is as small as possible*. This assertion is known as the *principle of least squares*. It is the basic principle of the technique of *linear regression*.

Mathematically, the sum of squared deviations is simply the sum of e_i^2 over observations $i = 1, \ldots, n$. Rearranging Equation (20.6) we obtain:

$$e_i = Y_i - \hat{\alpha} - \hat{\beta} X_i. \tag{20.7}$$

Squaring both sides of Equation (20.7) and summing over all the observations, i.e., over $i = 1, 2, \ldots, n$, gives:

$$\sum_{i=1}^{n} e_i^2 = \sum_{i=1}^{n} (Y_i - \hat{\alpha} - \hat{\beta} X_i)^2. \tag{20.8}$$

Our problem is to choose $\hat{\alpha}$ and $\hat{\beta}$ in Equation (20.8) such that $\sum e^2$ is minimised.† We may apply the straightforward methods of unconstrained minimisation from Chapter 13, namely, differentiate the function in (20.8) partially with respect to $\hat{\alpha}$ and $\hat{\beta}$, and set the partial derivatives to zero. We obtain:

$$\frac{\partial}{\partial \hat{\alpha}} \sum e^2 = -2\sum (Y - \hat{\alpha} - \hat{\beta} X) = 0 \tag{20.9a}$$

$$\frac{\partial}{\partial \hat{\beta}} \sum e^2 = -2\sum X(Y - \hat{\alpha} - \hat{\beta} X) = 0. \tag{20.9b}$$

On simplifying these two equations we obtain the simultaneous equations:

$$\sum Y = n\hat{\alpha} + \hat{\beta} \sum X \tag{20.10a}$$

$$\sum XY = \hat{\alpha} \sum X + \hat{\beta} \sum X^2. \tag{20.10b}$$

From any given set of data we can calculate $\sum Y, n, \sum X, \sum XY$ and $\sum X^2$.

---

† Note that from henceforward the subscript i is generally dropped from all variables simply for convenience. Thus, for example, $\sum e^2$ is understood to indicate the sum of e_i taken over the range $i = 1, 2, \ldots, n$.

Thus the only unknowns in (20.10) are $\hat{\alpha}$ and $\hat{\beta}$. Equations (20.10) are called the *normal equations.*†

20.3.4 SOLUTION TO THE NUMERICAL EXAMPLE

Let us use the normal equations to calculate $\hat{\alpha}$ and $\hat{\beta}$ for our example from Section 20.3.1. First we must calculate the sums of squares of X and Y and the sum of the cross-products, i.e., the sum of XY. The calculations are shown in Table 20.2.

TABLE 20.2

Regression Example Calculations

X	Y	X^2	Y^2	XY
2	8	4	64	16
4	3	16	9	12
3	4	9	16	12
1	7	1	49	7
3	8	9	64	24
5	0	25	0	0
$\Sigma X = 18$	$\Sigma Y = 30$	$\Sigma X^2 = 64$	$\Sigma Y^2 = 202$	$\Sigma XY = 71$
$n = 6$				

Now substitution of the values from Table 20.2 into Equations (20.10a and b) gives:

$$30 = 6\hat{\alpha} + 18\hat{\beta} \tag{20.11a}$$

$$71 = 18\hat{\alpha} + 64\hat{\beta}. \tag{20.11b}$$

The solution of these two simultaneous equations for the unknowns $\hat{\alpha}$ and $\hat{\beta}$ proceeds as follows:

Multiply (20.11a) by 3:

$$90 = 18\hat{\alpha} + 54\hat{\beta}, \tag{20.11c}$$

Subtract (20.11c) from (20.11b):

$$-19 = 10\hat{\beta},$$

$$\hat{\beta} = -1.9,$$

---

† In getting from Equations (20.8) to (20.10), the steps are as follows:

$$\Sigma e^2 = \Sigma(Y - \hat{\alpha} - \hat{\beta}X)^2 \equiv \Sigma[(Y - \hat{\beta}X) - \hat{\alpha}]^2$$

$$= \Sigma[(Y - \hat{\beta}X)^2 - 2\hat{\alpha}(Y - \hat{\beta}X) + \hat{\alpha}^2]$$

$$= \Sigma(Y - \hat{\beta}X)^2 - 2\hat{\alpha}\,\Sigma(Y - \hat{\beta}X) + n\hat{\alpha}^2$$

$$\frac{\partial}{\partial\hat{\alpha}}\,\Sigma e^2 = -2\,\Sigma(Y - \hat{\beta}X) + 2n\hat{\alpha} = 0.$$

Hence $-2\,\Sigma Y + 2\hat{\beta}\,\Sigma X + 2n\hat{\alpha} = 0$

whence $\Sigma Y = n\hat{\alpha} + \hat{\beta}\,\Sigma X$

which is Equation (20.10a). Calculations for (20.10b) are similar.

whence by substitution in (20.11a),

$$\hat{\alpha} = 10.7.$$

Hence our estimated regression equation is of the form

$$Y = 10.7 - 1.9X. \qquad (20.12)$$

This equation describes the line which best fits the data in Table 20.1. Comparison of (20.12) with (20.3) shows that our graphical guess at the line of best fit was fairly close to the mark.

20.4 An Alternative Way of Finding the Regression Coefficients

20.4.1 GENERAL METHOD

Another means of deriving the regression coefficients is given below without proof. Like the normal equations, it is based on the principle of least squares.

Let

$$\bar{X} = \frac{1}{n}\sum X \text{ and } \bar{Y} = \frac{1}{n}\sum Y \qquad (20.13)$$

where $\bar{X}$ and $\bar{Y}$ are the means of X and Y respectively. Let the deviation of any observation of X from its mean be denoted x; similarly for y. That is, for the ith observation,

$$x_i \equiv X_i - \bar{X} \text{ and } y_i \equiv Y_i - \bar{Y}. \qquad (20.14)$$

Then the regression coefficients may be found using the formulae

$$\hat{\beta} = \frac{\sum xy}{\sum x^2} \qquad (20.15a)$$

and $\qquad \hat{\alpha} = \bar{Y} - \hat{\beta}\bar{X}. \qquad (20.15b)$

It can be shown that

$$\sum xy \equiv \sum XY - n\bar{X}\bar{Y} \qquad (20.16)$$

and

$$\sum x^2 \equiv \sum X^2 - n\bar{X}^2. \qquad (20.17)$$

Thus Equation (20.15a) may be written alternatively as:

$$\hat{\beta} = \frac{\sum XY - n\bar{X}\bar{Y}}{\sum X^2 - n\bar{X}^2}. \qquad (20.18)$$

20.4.2 APPLICATION TO NUMERICAL EXAMPLE

The use of Equation (20.15a) to calculate $\hat{\beta}$ requires the computation of the deviation of each observed value of X and Y from the means of X and Y respectively. These are shown for our example in Table 20.3. Insertion of the results from this table into (20.15a) yields

$$\hat{\beta} = \frac{-19}{10} = -1.9, \qquad (20.19)$$

TABLE 20.3

Calculation of Deviations

X	Y	x $(= X - \bar{X})$	y $(= Y - \bar{Y})$	x²	y²	xy
2	8	−1	3	1	9	−3
4	3	1	−2	1	4	−2
3	4	0	−1	0	1	0
1	7	−2	2	4	4	−4
3	8	0	3	0	9	0
5	0	2	−5	4	25	−10

$\bar{X} = \dfrac{18}{6} = 3$ $\bar{Y} = \dfrac{30}{6} = 5$ $\Sigma x^2 = 10$ $\Sigma y^2 = 52$ $\Sigma xy = -19$

which confirms our earlier result. The same result is obtained yet again if Equation (20.18) is the preferred method of calculation. Using data from Tables 20.2 and 20.3 we quantify Equation (20.18) as follows:

$$\hat{\beta} = \frac{71 - 6(3)(5)}{64 - 6(3)^2} = -1.9. \tag{20.20}$$

Finally we calculate the value of $\hat{\alpha}$ by substitution in (20.15b). We obtain

$$\hat{\alpha} = 5 - (-1.9 \times 3)$$
$$= 10.7.$$

Again our earlier result is reproduced.

The method of calculation of the regression coefficients used depends simply on the preferences of the analyst and the circumstances of the calculations. For large problems, an electronic computer saves a lot of time.

20.5 The Applicability of the Regression Model

In this chapter we have seen the use of linear regression to estimate the parameters of a linear function of a single variable. From a consideration of the range and variety of functions we have studied in this book, it might appear to the reader that the *simple* regression model, involving as it does only *two* variables connected by a *linear* relationship, does not take us very far into the field of estimating the sorts of empirical relationships we are likely to encounter in economics. As we have noted, economists are frequently concerned with functions of *several* variables involving *nonlinear* relationships.

We may note first that the simple regression model may be extended readily to the case of linear relationships between several variables. For example, suppose we are considering the relationship between a dependent variable Y and a total of k independent variables $X_1, X_2, \ldots, X_k$. A linear function might be postulated, taking the form

$$Y = \alpha + \beta_1 X_1 + \beta_2 X_2 + \ldots + \beta_k X_k. \tag{20.21}$$

Extensions to our above estimating formulae for regression coefficients, which we shall not consider here,† enable us to calculate values for $\alpha, \beta_1, \beta_2, \ldots, \beta_k$ in Equation (20.21) for a given set of empirical observations on Y and the various X. When regression is applied to functions of two or more variables it is called *multiple regression*.

Secondly, when a nonlinear relationship is postulated between variables, there are several possible approaches to the estimation of the parameters of the appropriate model. On the one hand, a variety of *nonlinear estimation procedures* may be employed. On the other hand, it may be possible to adapt the basic data such that the ordinary methods of linear regression may be applied.

To illustrate the latter possibility, suppose we postulate a Cobb-Douglas function

$$y = AK^b, \tag{20.22}$$

where y = output; and
$\quad K$ = capital.

We have data on y and K, and wish to estimate the parameters A and b of this nonlinear function. In Section 5.3.2 we noted that taking logs of Equation (20.22) reduces it to a linear equation:

$$\log y = \log A + b \log K. \tag{20.23}$$

Hence if we *transform* our original y and K data into new variables, say Y and X respectively, we can in fact use simple linear regression to estimate the parameters of the relationship

$$Y = \alpha + \beta X \tag{20.24}$$

where $Y \equiv \log y$;
$\quad X \equiv \log K$;
$\quad \alpha \equiv \log A$; and
$\quad \beta \equiv b$.

As a further example, suppose a quadratic relationship is hypothesised between two variables z and w of the form

$$z = a + bw + cw^2. \tag{20.25}$$

For a given set of data on z and w we may use multiple linear regression to estimate the parameters a, b and c of (20.25) by again using *transformations* of the original variables. Let

$$X_1 \equiv w, \qquad\qquad X_2 \equiv w^2.$$

Then we may estimate the linear equation

$$z = a + bX_1 + cX_2 \tag{20.26}$$

where a, b, c are regression coefficients.

Not all nonlinear relationships can be estimated using linear regression on transformations of the variables. For instance the parameters a and b in the function

$$y = \frac{a}{x + b} \tag{20.27}$$

---

† In Appendix D, we formulate the linear regression model in matrix terms, enabling estimation of the parameters of a relationship such as in Equation (20.21).

could not be estimated using linear regression on transformations of a set of data on y and x. In the case of such a function, the nonlinear estimating procedures referred to earlier must be called upon.

Exercises

1. Write an essay on the way in which an econometrician might set about studying whether demand-pull or cost-push factors are significant in causing inflation.

2. Derive the formulae in Equations (20.15) for estimating the regression coefficients using the principle of least squares.

3. Show that
$$\sum y^2 = \sum Y^2 - n \bar{Y}^2.$$

4. Consider the following data relating the supply of beef to the export market over a ten-year period to the world price of beef measured in constant dollars.

Year	Export Price ($/unit)	Quantity Exported (million units)
1963	2	5
1964	4	4
1965	2	3
1966	3	1
1967	8	7
1968	7	9
1969	6	8
1970	8	10
1971	7	8
1972	3	2

(a) Draw a graph showing the scatter of these observations.
(b) Fit by eye a straight line which seems to describe these data. Use your line to compute approximate values for the intercept and slope terms in a linear relationship linking quantity with price.
(c) Use any method to calculate estimates of the parameters of the least-squares regression line of quantity on price from these data.
(d) Check your answer to part (c) above by recalculating the regression coefficients using any other method.

5. For the problem in Exercise 4, tabulate observed and predicted quantities supplied at the series of prices given in the original data. By subtracting predicted from observed values, calculate the value of the error term for each year. What is the mean of all the error terms?

6. How would you use linear regression to estimate the parameters of the following relationships:
(a) $y = AL^a K^b$,
(b) $C = a + b_1 W + b_2 Z + b_3 Z^2 + b_4 WZ$.

Chapter 21

Assumptions and Significance of the Simple Regression Model [†]

21.1 Assumptions of Linear Regression

21.1.1 THE GENERATION OF THE DATA

The example studied in the previous chapter involved a monopolist setting a different price for his product over a series of months, and observing the resulting quantities demanded. Over the particular six-month period he chose, the observations happened to be those shown in Table 20.1. Suppose he were to repeat this "experiment" over a subsequent six-month period, setting the same pattern of prices as before. We would be surprised if the quantities demanded turned out to be exactly the same as in the first six-month period. Other influences besides price affect the quantity demanded, and there is no reason to expect that these influences would be precisely the same from one six-month period to the next.

Suppose the monopolist were to repeat the experiment several more times, covering altogether a total of, say, five consecutive periods of six months. Assume the pattern of prices set in months 1,2, . . . , 6 of each period is the same as in the original experiment. The resulting quantities demanded might appear as in Table 21.1, where "Experiment 1" refers to the original set of observations which were analysed in the last chapter, and Experiments 2 to 5 refer to successive six-month periods.

Now suppose we apply the simple regression technique to each set of data in Table 21.1, i.e., to the results of each experiment taken separately. The regression coefficients relating the first set of values of Y (Experiment 1) to the set of values of X were obtained in the previous chapter as

---

[†] To follow this chapter fully, the student will require an elementary understanding of the concepts of mean, variance, standard deviation, degrees of freedom, levels of significance, simple distribution theory, and statistical hypothesis testing, such as is provided in the early stages of a basic statistics course or in the first few chapters of an elementary statistics text.

TABLE 21.1

Results of Repetition of the Monopolist's Experiment: Sales (Y) as a Function of Price

Month (*i*)	Price (X) (cents)	Experiment				
		1	2	3	4	5
1	2	8	10	6	9	8
2	4	3	2	6	6	3
3	3	4	5	4	6	4
4	1	7	8	8	7	10
5	3	8	8	2	5	8
6	5	0	0	2	1	3

$\hat{\alpha} = 10.7$, $\hat{\beta} = -1.9$. Repeating the estimating procedure and regressing the second, third, . . . , set of values of Y against the same set of values of X yields the results shown in Table 21.2. Each of these sets of data leads

TABLE 21.2

Estimated Regression Coefficients for Monopolist's Experiments

Experiment	$\hat{\alpha}$	$\hat{\beta}$
1	10.7	−1.9
2	12.7	−2.4
3	8.3	−1.2
4	10.2	−1.5
5	11.7	−1.9

to a different set of regression coefficients and thus to a different regression line. The five estimated regression lines corresponding to the five separate experiments are shown on Fig. 21.1.

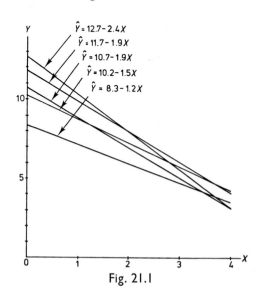

Fig. 21.1

We can explain the differences between these regression lines in terms of the extraneous influences mentioned earlier. These experiments are not so tightly controlled that the various other random influences affecting the quantity demanded in any month have been accounted for. Rather, these effects show up in "unexplained" variation in the dependent variable Y. In addition, such disturbances as errors of measurement may have crept into the data in some months.

It is therefore apparent that any single set of data, the results of any single experiment, must be regarded as a *sample* of price-quantity observations drawn from a much larger *population*. In fact the population of price-quantity observations in this example would be infinite because it would be possible to repeat the same experiment over and over again indefinitely, and each time a new set of observations would appear. Every now and then a set of data might crop up which was similar to an earlier set (for example, the results of Experiment 5 in Table 21.1 are quite like those of Experiment 1), but if the variables were measured in fractional terms and not just integer terms (as shown for simplicity in Table 21.1), we could never be sure we had exhausted all possible sets of data.

21.1.2 THE DISTRIBUTION OF Y VALUES

If we took repeated samples from this population, that is, conducted further experiments numbered 6,7,8, . . . , we would soon discover certain regularities in the results. For example, take any particular value of X, say $X = 2$, as shown for Month 1 in Table 21.1. Look at the corresponding Y values shown in the first row of the table. The mean of these five values is 8.2. We can observe, even in this very small set of five values, a tendency for the observed values of Y to cluster around their mean. If we were to run, say, one hundred experiments, we would see this tendency more clearly. To do this in practice would take us a total of one hundred consecutive six-month periods, i.e., fifty years. Instead of waiting this long, it is possible to "simulate" the behaviour of this system using an electronic computer. The computer is made to perform the experiments for us, and to generate the resulting observations in a matter of seconds. The mechanics by which this simulation is performed need not concern us here. Suffice it to say that Table 21.3 shows one hundred observations of Y "observed"

TABLE 21.3
One Hundred Values of Y when X = 2

8	10	6	9	8	8	7	7	6	10
6	9	3	5	5	4	9	7	11	6
8	8	7	8	7	4	7	10	6	6
6	6	4	7	5	8	10	4	4	11
8	7	10	6	8	8	9	7	7	5
7	4	6	7	7	7	6	10	7	10
5	6	7	6	5	9	6	7	4	6
6	5	2	8	5	8	11	5	5	5
10	7	5	7	10	5	5	5	10	7
5	8	10	5	5	5	11	7	6	8

when $X = 2$. In other words, the figures in Table 21.3 might be found by extending the first row of Table 21.1 across one hundred columns, corresponding to Experiments 1 through 100. The figures in Table 21.3 have been rounded to the nearest whole number.

The mean of the values of Y generated in this way is approximately 7. Table 21.4 shows the frequency of occurrence of every integer Y value from 1 to 12 over the one hundred experiments. We can see that the "observed" values of Y do tend to cluster around their mean value. Every now and then a value of Y is thrown up which for some chance reason is a long way from its mean; for example the values 2 and 3 both occur once in the 100 experiments, and a value of 11 happens to appear no less than four times. However, the majority of the Y values lie in the neighbourhood of 7.

TABLE 21.4

Frequency of Occurrence of Various Y Values when $X = 2$

Value of Y	Frequency of Occurrence in One Hunded Experiments
1	0
2	1
3	1
4	7
5	19
6	17
7	21
8	14
9	5
10	11
11	4
12	0

We might repeat this process for each value of X in Table 21.1. The various Y values corresponding to each X value would again tend to cluster around their particular mean.

Let us look at Table 21.4 in graphical terms. If we plot the frequency of the various Y values on the vertical axis against the values themselves on the horizontal axis, we obtain a picture of the *frequency distribution* of this variate. It is shown in Fig. 21.2. It so happens that our Y values

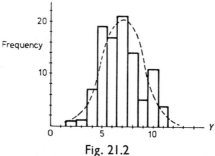

Fig. 21.2

approximately follow the *normal distribution*. A free-hand curve describing this distribution for this set of data is drawn on Fig. 21.2. If we were to perform several thousand experiments instead of just one hundred, the scatter of frequency points would lie much closer to a regular-looking normal distribution curve.

The characteristics of a particular normal distribution can be summed up in the *mean* and *variance* of the distribution. In the case of our observations on Y for $X = 2$ as shown in Table 21.3, the mean of Y is approximately 7 and the variance approximately 4. The distributions of the Y at other levels of X are also assumed to be normal and, furthermore, are assumed to have the same variance (though obviously different means) as that for the Y where $X = 2$.

21.1.3 THE DISTRIBUTION OF THE REGRESSION COEFFICIENTS

Suppose that one hundred complete sets of data were generated for the monopolist's problem. It follows that there must correspond one hundred sets of estimates of the regression coefficients, i.e., one hundred pairs of values of $\hat{\alpha}$ and $\hat{\beta}$. We could tabulate these values in tables similar to Table 21.3 and work out the frequency distributions of $\hat{\alpha}$ and $\hat{\beta}$ as we did for Y in Table 21.4. As a result, we would obtain a picture of the distributions of these coefficients.

These experiments have in fact been performed by our computer for the monopolist's problem. The distribution of the resulting $\hat{\alpha}$ is shown in Fig. 21.3 (a) and that of the resulting $\hat{\beta}$ in Fig. 21.3 (b). The distributions are roughly normal. The mean of all the $\hat{\alpha}$ is 10.8 and their variance 4.2. The $\hat{\beta}$ mean is -1.9, with a variance of approximately 0.4.

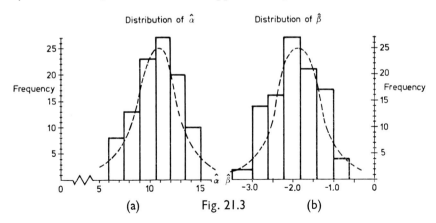

Fig. 21.3
(a)   (b)

We can, therefore, see that the various estimated $\hat{\alpha}$ and $\hat{\beta}$ tend to cluster around certain values which can be taken as the *true values* of α and β. These are the values which would be obtained if the whole population of price-quantity observations could be used in a single gigantic regression.

It is now possible to understand why the various values of $\hat{\alpha}$ and $\hat{\beta}$ obtained from single experiments are regarded only as estimates: they are estimates, obtained from *samples*, of the true but unknown *population* statistics α and β. In fact we use the term *least-squares estimators* to describe the statistics $\hat{\alpha}$ and $\hat{\beta}$. A great deal of effort in econometrics is spent in defining the properties of the distributions of these estimators.

21.1.4 THE DISTRIBUTION OF THE ERROR TERM

We may now translate the properties of the distribution of Y discussed above into the properties of the error term for the whole population of price-quantity observations. Let us suppose for simplicity that our group of one hundred experiments covers the whole population of price-quantity observations.† Hence we can specify the "true" relationship between the variables, i.e., that taken over the population as a whole, to be

$$Y = 10.8 - 1.9X \qquad (21.1)$$

as calculated earlier. Figure 21.4 shows this relationship. Figure 21.4 also shows the various observed values of Y for $X = 2$ taken from Table 21.3; we see them clustering about the "true" regression line. If we could measure the distance of each of these observed values of Y from the regression line, we would obtain an error term or residual for the whole *population* of these Y values corresponding to the error term e that was defined in the last chapter for our particular *sample*. Measure this residual, not just for Y where $X = 2$, but for all Y in the population. Call this residual u. It is referred to in econometrics as the *disturbance term*.

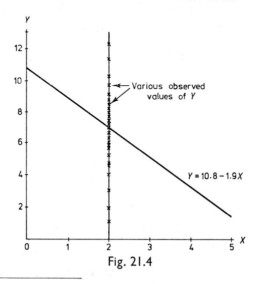

Fig. 21.4

---

† Usually in practice, however, the population from which our sample is drawn is assumed to be infinitely large.

It is clear from our knowledge of the distribution of the Y and from consideration of Fig. 21.4, that the distance of any point from the true regression line will be positive about as often as it is negative, and that overall, positive and negative values of u will tend to cancel each other out. In fact, given that the Y are normally distributed with a certain mean and a variance of σ^2, it follows that the u will also be normally distributed with a mean of zero and a variance of σ^2.

21.1.5 SUMMARY

We may now draw together the main results of this section. Combined they represent a set of assumptions on which the linear regression model is based. More specifically, they represent a set of assumptions as to how any given set of empirical data has been generated.

The values of the dependent variable in the population are related to the independent variable by the relationship

$$Y = \alpha + \beta X + u. \tag{21.2}$$

We assume that the disturbance term u is normally distributed with a mean of zero and a variance of σ^2. We have a sample of n observations of the dependent and independent variables Y_i and X_i respectively ($i = 1,2, \ldots, n$). The sample observations are connected by the relationship

$$Y_i = \hat{\alpha} + \hat{\beta} X_i + e_i \tag{21.3}$$

where the regression coefficients $\hat{\alpha}$ and $\hat{\beta}$ are estimators of the true but unknown population coefficients α and β respectively. As we shall see in Section 21.2.2, we may use the sample information to calculate also an estimate of the disturbance variance, σ^2.

Under the above assumptions, together with certain other assumptions which we cannot go into here,† our estimated values $\hat{\alpha}$ and $\hat{\beta}$ obtained from a set of data will be as satisfactory estimates of the true coefficients as we can hope for. Statistical procedures, some of which are discussed in the next section, are available for using the sample data to draw conclusions about the population from which the sample is drawn.

21.2 The Correlation Coefficient
21.2.1 INTERPRETATION

In performing a linear regression analysis, we are interested in "explaining" the variation in the dependent variable Y by connecting it via a linear equation with the independent variable X. Having fitted a particular regression, we would like to know how much of the variation in Y is "explained" by the regression model, and how much is "unexplained" or left over. In fact we may split up the variance of Y into two parts, that which is explained and that which is unexplained by the regression.

---

† See further in Appendix D, Section 3.

Accordingly we may write:

Variance of Y = Variance explained + Residual variance.   (21.4)

Denote the variance of Y, as measured over the sample observations of Y, as s_Y^2. Also let r^2 denote the proportion of the variance in Y which is explained by the regression. Then we may write Equation (21.4) as

$$s_Y^2 = r^2 s_Y^2 + (1 - r^2)s_Y^2 .$$ (21.5)

A formula for calculating r^2 from sample data is:†

$$r^2 = \frac{(\sum yx)^2}{\sum x^2 \sum y^2} .$$ (21.6)

The quantity r^2 is called the *coefficient of determination*. It indicates the "goodness of fit" of the regression line to the observations. Its value must lie between zero and one. A value for r^2 of one indicates a perfect fit, and a value of zero shows that there is no linear relationship between Y and X whatsoever.

The square root of r^2 is called the *correlation coefficient*:

$$r = \frac{\sum yx}{\sqrt{\sum x^2 \sum y^2}} .$$ (21.7)

In moving from Equations (21.6) to (21.7) we take the positive root of the bottom line.

The sign of the quantity $\sum yx$ on the top line of (21.7) indicates something about the relationship between Y and X. Suppose we divide a particular scatter of points into four quadrants using the means of Y and X as dividing lines as shown in Fig. 21.5. The quantities $x_i(\equiv X_i - \bar{X})$ and $y_i(\equiv Y_i - \bar{Y})$ are shown for a point P. It is apparent that at P both x_i and y_i are positive. However for another point Q, which happens to

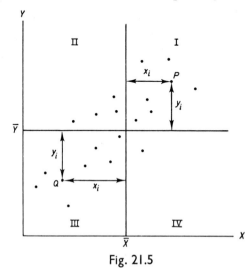

Fig. 21.5

---

† See Section 20.4.1 for a definition of y and x.

lie in the third quadrant, both x_i and y_i are negative. Thus we see:

- for a point in Quadrant I, the product yx is positive;
- for a point in Quadrant II, the product yx is negative;
- for a point in Quadrant III, the product yx is positive;
- for a point in Quadrant IV, the product yx is negative.

Hence, if there is a tendency for an upward sloping relationship between Y and X to exist, the majority of the points will lie in Quadrants III and I and hence $\sum yx$ will tend to be positive. On the other hand, if the relationship slopes downwards, most of the points will lie in Quadrants II and IV and hence $\sum yx$ will tend to be negative.

Thus the correlation coefficient r can range from -1 to $+1$ with the extremes of -1 and $+1$ indicating perfect negative and perfect positive correlation respectively.

21.2.2 SIGNIFICANCE TESTS ON r

Suppose we obtain a value of r^2 of 0.64 for a particular set of data. This tells us that 64 per cent of the variation in the dependent variable is explained by its linear relationship with the independent variable, leaving 36 per cent unexplained. How do we judge whether or not this is a satisfactory result? In particular, could some random statistical process have produced this value for r^2 purely by chance, meaning that there is in fact no relationship between Y and X? To answer these questions we may perform certain tests of significance on our calculated coefficients. Let us turn our attention first to the correlation coefficient r.

To examine the value of r calculated for a particular case, we form the hypothesis that there is no linear relationship between Y and X. This is called the *null hypothesis*, signified by the symbol H_0. Given this hypothesis, the statistic r may be expressed in terms of the "Student's" t distribution, as follows:

$$t = \frac{r\sqrt{n-2}}{\sqrt{1-r^2}}. \tag{21.8}$$

We consult tables of the t distribution at $n-2$ degrees of freedom and a given level of significance. The value of t so obtained is called the *critical value*. If our calculated value of t from Equation (21.8) exceeds the critical value in absolute terms, we reject the null hypothesis.

It can be shown that this t test is equivalent to an F test on the ratio between the variation in Y that is explained by the regression and the variation that is unexplained. There are many equivalent ways of writing the formula for F in this situation. A simple one is:

$$F = \frac{\hat{\beta}^2 \sum x^2}{\sum e^2 /(n-2)}. \tag{21.9}$$

The bottom line of the RHS of this equation is the variance of the error term e, usually denoted s^2. This latter statistic is an estimate of the unknown population variance σ^2 of the disturbance term u.

The F value from Equation (21.9) is tested against the critical value of F read from a table of the F distribution at a given level of confidence, for 1 and $n - 2$ degrees of freedom. If the calculated F value is greater than the critical F value, the null hypothesis is rejected.

21.3 Significance Tests on $\hat{\alpha}$ and $\hat{\beta}$

We have already seen a numerical example where the least-squares estimators $\hat{\alpha}$ and $\hat{\beta}$ followed a normal distribution. In fact we may now assert that, if certain assumptions are met—in particular if the error term is normally distributed with zero mean and constant variance σ^2—the estimators $\hat{\alpha}$ and $\hat{\beta}$ will also be normally distributed, with mean α and β respectively, and variance $\sigma^2(\sum X^2 / n \sum x^2)$ and $\sigma^2 / \sum x^2$ respectively. Of course, in calculating these variances, we do not know σ^2 and must replace it by an estimate of σ^2, namely s^2 as defined above. Having done so, we may take square roots to yield estimates of the *standard errors* of the two regression coefficients. We have, therefore,

$$SE(\hat{\alpha}) = s\sqrt{\frac{\sum X^2}{n \sum x^2}} \tag{21.10}$$

and

$$SE(\hat{\beta}) = \frac{s}{\sqrt{\sum x^2}}. \tag{21.11}$$

Our null hypothesis of no linear relationship between Y and X may be stated in terms of an hypothesis that $\beta = 0$. We can thus construct a t test on our estimate $\hat{\beta}$ by taking the ratio between the difference between estimated and hypothesised values of this statistic and its standard error. That is, we may write

$$t = \frac{\hat{\beta} - \beta}{s / \sqrt{\sum x^2}} \tag{21.12}$$

and since H_0 states $\beta = 0$, Equation (21.12) may be written as:

$$t = \frac{\hat{\beta}}{s / \sqrt{\sum x^2}} \tag{21.13}$$

where t has $n - 2$ degrees of freedom. Again H_0 is rejected if the calculated t exceeds the critical t found for the given level of confidence. In fact this t test is exactly the same as that performed earlier on the correlation coefficient r.

21.4 Significance Tests in Numerical Example
21.4.1 THE t TEST ON r

Let us return to the numerical data from Experiment 1 of the monopolist's problem, as studied in the last chapter. Using the results from Tables 20.2 and 20.3, we calculate first the value of the correlation coefficient, and the coefficient of determination. Using Equation (21.7) we obtain:

$$r = \frac{-19}{\sqrt{10 \times 52}} = -0.833. \tag{21.14}$$

Hence

$$r^2 = 0.694. \tag{21.15}$$

In other words, Equation (21.15) shows that 69.4 per cent of the variation in quantity demanded in this example is accounted for by its linear relationship with price.

From Equation (21.8) we have

$$t = \frac{-0.833\sqrt{6-2}}{\sqrt{1-0.694}} = -3.01. \tag{21.16}$$

From the tables for the t distribution we have a critical value of 2.776 for 4 degrees of freedom and a confidence level of 95 per cent.† Since our calculated t from Equation (21.16) exceeds the critical value in absolute terms, the null hypothesis of no linear relationship between quantity and price is rejected. In other words the chance that this calculated t value could have arisen due to random fluctuations is less than 5 per cent.

21.4.2 THE F TEST

To apply Equation (21.9) and calculate F, we need to compute the residual variance s^2. The sum of squared error terms, $\sum e^2$, may be calculated as:

$$\sum e^2 = \sum y^2 - \sum \hat{y}^2 \tag{21.17}$$

by squaring, summing and rearranging Equation (20.5). The quantity $\sum \hat{y}^2$ may in turn be computed using, say,

$$\sum \hat{y}^2 = \hat{\beta}^2 \sum x^2. \tag{21.18}$$

Applying (21.18) to our data we obtain

$$\sum \hat{y}^2 = (-1.9)^2 \times 10 = 36.09 \tag{21.19}$$

and substituting in (21.17) gives

$$\sum e^2 = 52.00 - 36.09 = 15.91 \tag{21.20}$$

whence

$$s^2 = \frac{15.91}{4} = 3.98. \tag{21.21}$$

Now applying Equation (21.9) yields:

$$F = \frac{36.09}{3.98} = 9.07. \tag{21.22}$$

---

† Here our alternative hypothesis is simply $r \neq 0$ (and thus also $\beta \neq 0$); hence a "two-tailed" t test is appropriate. The critical t value for an overall confidence level of 95 per cent is, therefore, that pertaining to a probability level of 0.025. Since our example relates to a demand function, however, we could have been more particular in formulating our alternative hypothesis, specifying it as $r < 0$ (and $\beta < 0$). In this case the critical t value would be that pertaining to a probability level of 0.05 ($= 2.132$ for 4 degrees of freedom).

From the F distribution tables we read that at 1 and 4 degrees of freedom the critical values are 7.71 for a confidence level of 95 per cent and 21.20 for a level of 99 per cent. Thus we would reject the null hypothesis at the former level of confidence, but we would not reject it if the higher level of confidence were required.

21.4.3 THE t TEST ON $\hat{\beta}$

The standard errors of the estimated regression coefficients may now be calculated. Using Equations (21.10) and (21.11) we obtain

$$SE(\hat{\alpha}) = 1.99 \sqrt{\frac{64}{6 \times 10}} = 2.059, \tag{21.23}$$

$$SE(\hat{\beta}) = \frac{1.99}{\sqrt{10}} = 0.631. \tag{21.24}$$

Hence, to test H_0 that $\beta = 0$, we apply Equation (21.13), obtaining

$$t = \frac{-1.9}{0.631} = -3.01 \tag{21.25}$$

which tallies with Equation (21.16).

Exercises

1. Using the numerical example from Exercise 4, Chapter 20, calculate the coefficient of determination and the correlation coefficient.

2. Test the significance of r as calculated in Exercise 1 above.

3. Calculate the standard errors of the estimated regression coefficients $\hat{\alpha}$ and $\hat{\beta}$ in the above example.

4. Use the above example to show that the t test on the null hypothesis $\beta = 0$ is identical with the t test on r under the same null hypothesis.

5. Compute the variance of the error term in the above example, using the formula given in the denominator of Equation (21.9).

6. A government department makes independent projections of the beef export price in future years. It is estimated that in 1974 the price will be \$8 per unit and in 1984 it will be \$12 per unit. Discuss the uses and limitations of the regression model fitted in Exercise 4, Chapter 20, in considering future exports of beef.

Revision of Some Basic Algebra

This appendix is included to enable the reader with a weak or faded mathematical background to revise some important operations of ordinary algebra. The techniques are presented in terms of simple numerical examples.

A.1 Solving Simultaneous Equations

Suppose we wish to find the values of the unknowns x and y that satisfy the following pair of simultaneous equations:

$$3x + 5y = 22 \qquad\qquad \text{(A.1a)}$$
$$-5(-3x + 2y) = 40. \qquad\qquad \text{(A.1b)}$$

To demonstrate a method of solving these equations we must make use of the following algebraic rules.

(a) When multiplying positive and negative quantities:
- a positive number *times* a positive number = a positive number;
- a positive number *times* a negative number = a negative number;
- a negative number *times* a positive number = a negative number;
- a negative number *times* a negative number = a positive number.

For example,

$$+6 \times +3 = +18,$$
$$+6 \times -3 = -18,$$
$$-6 \times +3 = -18,$$
$$-6 \times -3 = +18.$$

(b) Polynomial expressions may be added or subtracted by adding or subtracting like terms. For example

$$(3x^3 + 2x^2 - x + 1) + (2x^3 + 5x - 4)$$
$$= 5x^3 + 2x^2 + 4x - 3.$$

(c) Multiplication (division) of both sides of an equation by the same constant, or addition (subtraction) of the same constant to (from) both sides of an equation, does not alter the basic relationship expressed by the equation. For example, multiply both sides of the equation $x = 6$ by 2. We obtain $2x = 12$, which clearly represents the same relationship as does $x = 6$. Again, subtracting 4 from both sides of the same equation gives: $x - 4 = 6 - 4$, which again does not affect the values of the variable in the equation.

Now let us turn to the solution of the Equations (A.1). First we simplify (A.1b) by removing the brackets. Our pair of equations now reads:

$$3x + 5y = 22 \tag{A.2a}$$
$$15x - 10y = 40. \tag{A.2b}$$

Multiply equation (A.2a) by 2 to bring the coefficient of y in (A.2a) to the same numerical value as the coefficient of y in (A.2b). We obtain:

$$2(3x + 5y) = 2(22).$$

That is,

$$6x + 10y = 44. \tag{A.2c}$$

Now add the LHS and RHS of (A.2b) and (A.2c):

$$15x - 10y + 6x + 10y = 40 + 44.$$

Adding like terms gives

$$21x = 84. \tag{A.2d}$$

Dividing both sides of (A.2d) by 21 gives

$$x = 4. \tag{A.2e}$$

Substituting 4 for x in, say, (A.2a) gives

$$3(4) + 5y = 22. \tag{A.2f}$$

Subtracting 12 from both sides of (A.2f) gives

$$5y = 22 - 12 = 10. \tag{A.2g}$$

Dividing both sides of (A.2g) by 5 gives

$$y = 2.$$

The values of x and y which satisfy the simultaneous equations are $x = 4, y = 2$.

As an exercise, show that (A.2a) and (A.2b) may be equivalently solved by the following procedure.

(a) Divide (A.2b) throughout by 5;
(b) Subtract the resulting equation from (A.2a);
(c) Solve for y;
(d) Substitute for y in, say, (A.2a);
(e) Solve for x.

A.2 Solution of Quadratic Equations

In a quadratic equation

$$ax^2 + bx + c = 0, \tag{A.3}$$

the solutions for x are given by

$$x = \frac{-b \pm \sqrt{b^2 - 4ac}}{2a}. \tag{A.4}$$

For example, in the equation
$$x^2 - 5x - 2\tfrac{3}{4} = 0 \tag{A.5}$$
we have $a = 1$, $b = -5$, and $c = -\tfrac{11}{4}$. Hence the solutions to this equation, found by applying the formula from (A.4), are

$$x = \frac{-(-5) \pm \sqrt{(-5)^2 - 4(1 \times -\tfrac{11}{4})}}{2 \times 1}$$

$$= \frac{5 \pm \sqrt{25 + 11}}{2} = \frac{5 \pm \sqrt{36}}{2}$$

$$= \frac{5 \pm 6}{2} = \tfrac{11}{2} \text{ or } -\tfrac{1}{2}.$$

Thus the two solutions for x which satisfy Equation (A.5) are $x = 5\tfrac{1}{2}$ or $-\tfrac{1}{2}$.

If a quadratic equation can be expressed as the product of two terms equalling zero, the roots may be found by setting each term in turn to zero, since if $ab = 0$, either $a = 0$ and/or $b = 0$.

For example, the equation
$$x^2 - 5x = 0 \tag{A.6}$$
can be expressed as
$$x(x - 5) = 0$$
whence either $x = 0$, or $x - 5 = 0$, i.e., $x = 5$. Hence the roots of (A.6) are $x = 0$ or 5. Similarly, the LHS of
$$5x^2 + 7x - 6 = 0$$
may be factorised to give $(x + 2)(5x - 3)$. Setting each of these terms to zero gives
$$x + 2 = 0, \text{ or } 5x - 3 = 0,$$
whence $x = -2$ or $\tfrac{3}{5}$.

A.3 Indices

The integral *index* or *exponent* of a number or expression indicates the number of times the number or expression is to be multiplied by itself. For example:
$$x^5 = x \times x \times x \times x \times x,$$
$$(2x + 3)^2 = (2x + 3)(2x + 3).$$

The following are the more useful results involving indices:

(a) $x^n \times x^m = x^{n+m}$.
    For example,
    $$x^2 \times x^5 = x^{2+5} = x^7.$$

(b) $x^n \div x^m = x^{n-m}$.
    For example,
    $$x^8 \div x^3 = \frac{x^8}{x^3} = x^{8-3} = x^5.$$

(c) $(xy)^n = x^n y^n$.

For example,

$$(xy)^3 = x^3 y^3.$$

(d) $(x^n)^m = x^{n \times m}$.

For example,

$$(x^3)^2 = x^{3 \times 2} = x^6.$$

(e) $x^{-n} = \dfrac{1}{x^n}$.

For example,

$$x^{-3} = \frac{1}{x^3}.$$

(f) $x^{\frac{1}{n}} = \sqrt[n]{x}$.

For example,

$$x^{\frac{1}{2}} = \sqrt{x}.$$

(g) $x^0 = 1$.

A.4 Logarithms

The *logarithm* of a number is the power to which the base must be raised to give the number. For example, 10 must be raised to the power 2 to give 100, (i.e., $10^2 = 100$). Thus the logarithm of 100 to the base 10 is 2. This is written:

$$\log_{10} 100 = 2.$$

The two bases for which tables of logarithms are readily obtainable are 10 (called *common logarithms*) and $e = 2.71828 \ldots$ (called *natural* or *Napierian logarithms*).†

The following are the more useful results involving logarithms. For a given base greater than unity:

(a) $\log (x \times y) = \log x + \log y$,

(b) $\log \left(\dfrac{x}{y}\right) = \log x - \log y$,

(c) $\log (x^n) = n \log x$,

(d) $\log 1 = 0$,

(e) $\log_b b = 1$,

(f) To change the base of $\log_b x$ from b to, say a, we use the rule:

$$\log_a x = \log_a b \log_b x.$$

A.5 Expansion of $(x+y)^2$ and $(x+y)^3$

(a) To expand $(x + y)^2$ we write

$$(x + y)^2 \equiv (x + y)(x + y) \tag{A.7}$$

and form the products of all pairs of terms on the RHS of (A.7)

$$(x + y)(x + y) = x^2 + xy + xy + y^2$$
$$= x^2 + 2xy + y^2. \tag{A.8}$$

---

† Named after the Scottish mathematician John Napier (1550–1617).

(b) To expand $(x + y)^3$ we write
$$(x + y)^3 \equiv (x + y)(x + y)(x + y)$$
and noting $(x + y)(x + y) = x^2 + 2xy + y^2$ from (A.8) above we have:
$$(x + y)^3 = (x^2 + 2xy + y^2)(x + y). \tag{A.9}$$
We now form the products of all pairs of terms in the respective brackets on the RHS of (A.9):
$$\begin{aligned} (x + y)^3 &= x^3 + x^2y + 2x^2y + 2xy^2 + xy^2 + y^3 \\ &= x^3 + 3x^2y + 3xy^2 + y^3. \end{aligned}$$

Extensions of the Calculus

B.1 Maximisation and Minimisation of Functions of Several Variables

Consider the function $z = f(x,y)$. Denote the first derivatives of the function by $\frac{\partial z}{\partial x}$ and $\frac{\partial z}{\partial y}$. Denote the second-order derivatives by $\frac{\partial^2 z}{\partial x^2}$ and $\frac{\partial^2 z}{\partial y^2}$, and the cross-derivative by $\frac{\partial^2 z}{\partial x\,\partial y}$ (see Section 11.4).

(a) For a *maximum*, the necessary and sufficient conditions are:

$$\frac{\partial z}{\partial x} = \frac{\partial z}{\partial y} = 0 \quad \Big\} \; first\text{-}order\; conditions,$$

$$\left.\begin{array}{l} \dfrac{\partial^2 z}{\partial x^2} < 0 \quad \dfrac{\partial^2 z}{\partial y^2} < 0 \\[2ex] \dfrac{\partial^2 z}{\partial x^2} \times \dfrac{\partial^2 z}{\partial y^2} > \left(\dfrac{\partial^2 z}{\partial x\,\partial y}\right)^2 \end{array}\right\} \begin{array}{l} second\text{-}order \\ conditions. \end{array}$$

(b) For a *minimum*, the necessary and sufficient conditions are:

$$\frac{\partial z}{\partial x} = \frac{\partial z}{\partial y} = 0 \quad \Big\} \; first\text{-}order\; conditions,$$

$$\left.\begin{array}{l} \dfrac{\partial^2 z}{\partial x^2} > 0 \quad \dfrac{\partial^2 z}{\partial y^2} > 0 \\[2ex] \dfrac{\partial^2 z}{\partial x^2} \times \dfrac{\partial^2 z}{\partial y^2} > \left(\dfrac{\partial^2 z}{\partial x\,\partial y}\right)^2 \end{array}\right\} \begin{array}{l} second\text{-}order \\ conditions. \end{array}$$

To illustrate the use of these first- and second-order conditions in a maximisation case, refer to the example in Section 13.2.1. We have:

$$\left.\begin{array}{l} \dfrac{\partial y}{\partial L} = 3K + 3 - 6L = 0 \\[2ex] \dfrac{\partial y}{\partial K} = 3L - 2K \quad = 0 \end{array}\right\} \begin{array}{l} first\text{-}order \\ conditions, \end{array}$$

whence $K = 3, L = 2$.

$$\left.\begin{array}{ll} \dfrac{\partial^2 y}{\partial L^2} = -6 < 0 & \dfrac{\partial^2 y}{\partial K^2} = -2 < 0 \\[3mm] \dfrac{\partial^2 y}{\partial L^2} \times \dfrac{\partial^2 y}{\partial K^2} = 12 > \left(\dfrac{\partial^2 y}{\partial L \partial K}\right)^2 = 9 \end{array}\right\} \quad \begin{array}{l} \textit{second-order} \\ \textit{conditions.} \end{array}$$

B.2 Constrained Maximisation and Minimisation: First-Order Conditions in the General Case

Consider the following problem:
Maximise

$$y = f(x_1, x_2, \ldots, x_n)$$

subject to

$$g_1(x_1, x_2, \ldots, x_n) = 0,$$
$$g_2(x_1, x_2, \ldots, x_n) = 0$$
$$\vdots$$
$$g_m(x_1, x_2, \ldots, x_n) = 0.$$

The objective function is a function of n variables $x_1, x_2, \ldots, x_n$.
We also have m constraints in the form of a set of implicit functions $g_1, g_2, \ldots, g_m$.
To *maximise* y, introduce a Lagrange multiplier for each constraint and form the Lagrangean function:

$$L = f(x_1, x_2, \ldots, x_n) + \lambda_1 g_1(x_1, x_2, \ldots, x_n)$$
$$+ \lambda_2 g_2(x_1, x_2, \ldots, x_n) + \ldots + \lambda_m g_m(x_1, x_2, \ldots, x_n).$$

Now maximise the Lagrangean function by taking first-order partial derivatives of L with respect to $x_1, \ldots, x_n$ and $\lambda_1, \ldots, \lambda_m$ and setting these equal to zero:†

$$\frac{\partial L}{\partial x_1} = f_{x_1} + \lambda_1 g_{1x_1} + \lambda_2 g_{2x_1} + \ldots + \lambda_m g_{mx_1} = 0,$$

$$\frac{\partial L}{\partial x_2} = f_{x_2} + \lambda_1 g_{1x_2} + \lambda_2 g_{2x_2} + \ldots + \lambda_m g_{mx_2} = 0$$
$$\vdots \qquad\qquad\qquad\qquad\qquad\qquad \vdots$$
$$\frac{\partial L}{\partial x_n} = f_{x_n} + \lambda_1 g_{1x_n} + \lambda_2 g_{2x_n} + \ldots + \lambda_m g_{mx_n} = 0$$

$$\frac{\partial L}{\partial \lambda_1} = g_1(x_1, x_2, \ldots, x_n) = 0,$$

$$\frac{\partial L}{\partial \lambda_2} = g_2(x_1, x_2, \ldots, x_n) = 0$$
$$\vdots \qquad \vdots$$
$$\frac{\partial L}{\partial \lambda_m} = g_m(x_1, x_2, \ldots, x_n) = 0.$$

† For the notation of these partials, see Section 11.1.1.

We thus obtain $n + m$ equations in $n + m$ unknowns (i.e., $x_1, x_2,$ $\ldots, x_n, \lambda_1, \lambda_2, \ldots, \lambda_m$).

The set of equations may be solved to find the values of x and λ that maximise L, and hence that maximise y subject to the given constraints.

To *minimise* the objective function, an identical procedure is followed. Although the first-order conditions are the same in the case of both maximisation and minimisation, the second-order conditions are quite different. For a full treatment of this subject, however, the student is urged to consult a more advanced text.

Appendix C

Extensions of Matrix Algebra

C.1 Some Special Types of Matrices

C.1.1 SYMMETRIC MATRIX

A square matrix in which corresponding pairs of off-diagonal elements are equal is called *symmetric*. For example, the following matrix **A** is symmetric:

$$
\mathbf{A} = \begin{bmatrix} 15 & 0 & 3 & -1 \\ 0 & 2 & \frac{1}{2} & 8 \\ 3 & \frac{1}{2} & -4 & 5 \\ -1 & 8 & 5 & 1 \end{bmatrix}.
$$

To define a "corresponding pair" we note that in the above matrix **A** the element in, say, the third row first column (namely, 3) is identical with the element in the first row third column. That is, $a_{31} = a_{13}$ and, more generally in a symmetric matrix, $a_{ij} = a_{ji}$. In other words, the top and bottom triangular halves about the main diagonal are "mirror-images" of each other.

C.1.2 SKEW-SYMMETRIC MATRIX

A square matrix in which the corresponding pairs of off-diagonal elements are the negatives of each other is called *skew-symmetric*. For example,

$$
\mathbf{E} = \begin{bmatrix} 3 & -2 & -1 \\ 2 & 9 & \frac{1}{2} \\ 1 & -\frac{1}{2} & 4 \end{bmatrix}
$$

is an example of a 3 × 3 skew-symmetric matrix. We note that in such a matrix $a_{ij} = -a_{ji}$.

C.I.3. SUBMATRIX

A *submatrix* of a matrix **A** is a matrix obtained by deleting some of the rows and/or some of the columns of **A**. For example, if

$$\mathbf{A} = \begin{bmatrix} 9 & 0 & 5 \\ 4 & 2 & 7 \\ 1 & 3 & -8 \\ \frac{1}{2} & -1 & 2\frac{1}{2} \end{bmatrix},$$

all of the following are submatrices of **A**:

$$\begin{bmatrix} 9 & 0 \\ 4 & 2 \\ 1 & 3 \\ \frac{1}{2} & -1 \end{bmatrix}, \begin{bmatrix} 9 & 0 & 5 \\ 1 & 3 & -8 \end{bmatrix}, \begin{bmatrix} 3 & -8 \\ -1 & 2\frac{1}{2} \end{bmatrix},$$

$$\begin{bmatrix} 9 & 5 \\ \frac{1}{2} & 2\frac{1}{2} \end{bmatrix}, \begin{bmatrix} 0 \\ 2 \\ 3 \\ -1 \end{bmatrix}, [-8].$$

C.I.4 TRIANGULAR MATRIX

A square matrix in which all elements above or below the main diagonal are zero is called *triangular*. For instance

$$\mathbf{X} = \begin{bmatrix} 2 & 0 & 0 \\ 3 & 1 & 0 \\ \frac{1}{2} & -1 & 5 \end{bmatrix}$$

is a 3 × 3 *lower triangular matrix*, while

$$\mathbf{Y} = \begin{bmatrix} 4 & 2 & 0 & 11 \\ 0 & 1 & 8 & \frac{1}{2} \\ 0 & 0 & 10 & 3 \\ 0 & 0 & 0 & -1 \end{bmatrix}$$

is an example of a 4 × 4 *upper triangular matrix*.

C.I.5 DIAGONAL MATRIX

A square matrix which has zeros everywhere but on the main diagonal is called a *diagonal matrix*. For instance

$$\mathbf{Q} = \begin{bmatrix} 2 & 0 & 0 & 0 & 0 \\ 0 & \frac{1}{2} & 0 & 0 & 0 \\ 0 & 0 & 3 & 0 & 0 \\ 0 & 0 & 0 & -4 & 0 \\ 0 & 0 & 0 & 0 & 8 \end{bmatrix}$$

is an example of a 5 × 5 diagonal matrix.

C.I.6 SCALAR MATRIX

A diagonal matrix, as just defined, in which all the diagonal elements are equal, is called a *scalar matrix*. For instance

$$S = \begin{bmatrix} 5\frac{1}{2} & 0 & 0 \\ 0 & 5\frac{1}{2} & 0 \\ 0 & 0 & 5\frac{1}{2} \end{bmatrix}$$

is an example of a 3×3 scalar matrix.

C.I.7 NULL MATRIX

A matrix consisting entirely of zeros is called a *null matrix*. It is the counterpart in linear algebra of the single quantity zero in ordinary algebra. Usually a null matrix is denoted by the symbol **0**. Notice that whereas the identity matrix **I** must be square, no such restriction is placed on the null matrix. For example

$$0 = \begin{bmatrix} 0 & 0 & 0 & 0 \\ 0 & 0 & 0 & 0 \end{bmatrix}$$

is a 2×4 null matrix.

C.2 Cramer's Rule for Solving a Set of Linear Simultaneous Equations

Consider the set of linear simultaneous equations

$$Ax = b$$

where $A = n \times n$ matrix of coefficients;

$x = n \times 1$ vector of unknowns; and

$b = n \times 1$ vector of intercept terms.

An interesting method of finding **x**, given **A** and **b**, is *Cramer's rule*: To find x_1:

(a) replace the first column of the matrix **A** with the vector **b**;
(b) take the determinant of the matrix so formed, and divide this determinant by the determinant of the matrix **A**.

The value of x_2 can be found in the same way, but this time the vector **b** should replace the *second* column of the matrix **A**.

In general, the value of x_i can be found by replacing the ith column of the matrix **A** with the vector **b**, taking the determinant of the resulting matrix, and dividing this by the determinant of **A**.

Consider a 2×2 system

$$a_{11}x_1 + a_{12}x_2 = b_1,$$
$$a_{21}x_1 + a_{22}x_2 = b_2.$$

Applying Cramer's rule we have

$$x_1 = \frac{\begin{vmatrix} b_1 & a_{12} \\ b_2 & a_{22} \end{vmatrix}}{\begin{vmatrix} a_{11} & a_{12} \\ a_{21} & a_{22} \end{vmatrix}}, \qquad x_2 = \frac{\begin{vmatrix} a_{11} & b_1 \\ a_{21} & b_2 \end{vmatrix}}{\begin{vmatrix} a_{11} & a_{12} \\ a_{21} & a_{22} \end{vmatrix}}.$$

As an illustration, take Equation (16.26):

$$\begin{bmatrix} 1 & -1 \\ -0.8 & 1 \end{bmatrix} \begin{bmatrix} Y \\ C \end{bmatrix} = \begin{bmatrix} 50 \\ 100 \end{bmatrix}.$$

Using Cramer's rule, we obtain:

$$Y = \frac{\begin{vmatrix} 50 & -1 \\ 100 & 1 \end{vmatrix}}{\begin{vmatrix} 1 & -1 \\ -0.8 & 1 \end{vmatrix}} = \frac{150}{\frac{1}{5}} = 750,$$

$$C = \frac{\begin{vmatrix} 1 & 50 \\ -0.8 & 100 \end{vmatrix}}{\begin{vmatrix} 1 & -1 \\ -0.8 & 1 \end{vmatrix}} = \frac{140}{\frac{1}{5}} = 700.$$

C.3 A Method for Finding Third-Order Determinants

In Section 16.2.2 the concept of a determinant was explained. Equation (16.11) defined the determinant of a 2×2 matrix; such a determinant is said to be of *second-order*. The determinant of a 3×3 matrix is a *third-order determinant*.

Consider any 3×3 matrix of the form:

$$\begin{bmatrix} a_{11} & a_{12} & a_{13} \\ a_{21} & a_{22} & a_{23} \\ a_{31} & a_{32} & a_{33} \end{bmatrix}.$$

To find the determinant of the above matrix take the first two columns of the matrix and rewrite them to the right of the matrix, thus obtaining the 3×5 matrix:

$$\begin{bmatrix} a_{11} & a_{12} & a_{13} & a_{11} & a_{12} \\ a_{21} & a_{22} & a_{23} & a_{21} & a_{22} \\ a_{31} & a_{32} & a_{33} & a_{31} & a_{32} \end{bmatrix}.$$

Now draw in a set of six arrows as indicated below, each arrow forming a diagonal of the 3×5 matrix.

Take the product of the three elements on each arrow. If the arrow points downwards, attach a positive sign to the resulting term. If the arrow points upwards, attach a negative sign. The determinant of the original 3×3 matrix then comprises the collection of the six terms so obtained, as follows:

$$\begin{vmatrix} a_{11} & a_{12} & a_{13} \\ a_{21} & a_{22} & a_{23} \\ a_{31} & a_{32} & a_{33} \end{vmatrix} = a_{11}a_{22}a_{33} + a_{12}a_{23}a_{31} + a_{13}a_{21}a_{32} \\ - a_{31}a_{22}a_{13} - a_{32}a_{23}a_{11} - a_{33}a_{21}a_{12}.$$

As a numerical example, let us evaluate:

$$\begin{vmatrix} 2 & 1 & 2 \\ 0 & 3 & -1 \\ 4 & 0 & 5 \end{vmatrix}.$$

We have

giving the determinant as

$$(2 \times 3 \times 5) + (1 \times -1 \times 4) + (2 \times 0 \times 0) - (4 \times 3 \times 2) \\ - (0 \times -1 \times 2) - (5 \times 0 \times 1) \\ = 30 + (-4) + 0 - 24 - 0 - 0 = 2.$$

C.4 Determinants in the General Case

C.4.I FACTORIALS

Suppose a housewife has two kitchen canisters marked T for tea and C for coffee. Consider the number of ways she can place them in a row on a shelf. She can have two arrangements: TC or CT. Now suppose she has a third container marked S for sugar. The number of possible arrangements would be six: TCS, TSC, CST, CTS, STC and SCT. Each arrangement of objects in such a row is referred to more formally as a *permutation*.

The number of ways two objects can be permuted is 2×1. For three objects, the number of possible permutations is $3 \times 2 \times 1$. In general, n objects may be permuted in

$$n \times (n-1) \times (n-2) \times (n-3) \times \ldots \times 3 \times 2 \times 1$$

different ways. The number obtained by this multiplication process is known as *n factorial* and is usually denoted by $n!$

Thus $3! = 3 \times 2 \times 1 = 6$.

C.4.2 GENERAL FEATURES OF DETERMINANTS

(a) The determinant of a matrix $\mathbf{A}$ exists only if the matrix is square.

(b) If $\mathbf{A}$ is of order $n \times n$ then $|\mathbf{A}|$ will be an nth-order determinant.

(c) The number of different terms appearing in an nth-order determinant will be $n!$ Thus for a second-order determinant we have $2!$ (i.e., 2) terms (see Section 16.2.2), and for a third-order determinant we have $3!$ (i.e., 6) terms (see Section C.3 above).

(d) The number of elements appearing in each term will be n.
(e) Each term is taken as the product of one and only one element from each row and one and one only element from each column of the matrix $\mathbf{A}$. We obtain $n!$ permutations in this way, thus explaining (c) above.
(f) Half the terms will have positive signs, and the other half will have negative signs.

A method of expansion which ensures that the above features obtain and that each term is attributed its correct sign, is given in Section C.4.5 of this appendix.

C.4.3 MINORS

Take any element of a matrix $\mathbf{A}$. By crossing out all elements in the same row and column in which the chosen element appears, we are left with a submatrix of $\mathbf{A}$ (see Section C.1.3). Assume the submatrix is square and of order k. The kth-order determinant of this submatrix is referred to as a *minor* of $\mathbf{A}$. To illustrate, consider a 3×3 matrix $\mathbf{A}$. A minor of $\mathbf{A}$ may be found by eliminating the first row and second column as follows,

$$\begin{bmatrix} \cancel{a_{11}} & \cancel{a_{12}} & \cancel{a_{13}} \\ a_{21} & a_{22} & a_{23} \\ a_{31} & a_{32} & a_{33} \end{bmatrix},$$

and taking the second-order determinant

$$\begin{vmatrix} a_{21} & a_{23} \\ a_{31} & a_{33} \end{vmatrix}.$$

It is evident that

$$\begin{vmatrix} a_{22} & a_{23} \\ a_{32} & a_{33} \end{vmatrix} \quad \text{and} \quad \begin{vmatrix} a_{11} & a_{13} \\ a_{31} & a_{33} \end{vmatrix}$$

are also minors of $\mathbf{A}$. (In general, the matrix $\mathbf{A}$ need not be square for us to obtain a minor, for we are free to eliminate as many rows and columns as we wish in taking any submatrix. Thus the submatrix so obtained may be of any order as long as it is square and of smaller order than $\mathbf{A}$. The determinant of any submatrix so formed will be a minor of $\mathbf{A}$. For our present analysis, however, we restrict our attention to minors which are formed by eliminating just one row and column, as explained above. We assume that $\mathbf{A}$ is of order $n \times n$. It follows that the minors of interest to us must be determinants of order $n - 1$.)

C.4.4 COFACTORS

The preceding section showed how to take a minor of $\mathbf{A}$ by eliminating the row and column in which a selected element is situated. For the element

a_{ij}, in other words, we eliminate the ith row and jth column. Now suppose we attach a sign to the determinant of the submatrix so formed, such that the sign is that of the expression $-1^{(i+j)}$. For instance, the element in the second row and third column will take the sign of $-1^{(2+3)} = -1^5 = -1$; i.e., it will be negative. In general if $(i+j)$ is even, the corresponding term will be multiplied by $+1$; if $(i+j)$ is odd, the corresponding term will be multiplied by -1. The resulting signed minor is referred to as the *cofactor* of the element a_{ij}. Let us denote this cofactor by c_{ij}.

For example, take the following 3×3 matrix:

$$\begin{bmatrix} a_{11} & a_{12} & a_{13} \\ a_{21} & a_{22} & a_{23} \\ a_{31} & a_{32} & a_{33} \end{bmatrix}.$$

The cofactor of a_{11} is thus

$$c_{11} = -1^{(1+1)} \begin{vmatrix} a_{22} & a_{23} \\ a_{32} & a_{33} \end{vmatrix} \equiv \begin{vmatrix} a_{22} & a_{23} \\ a_{32} & a_{33} \end{vmatrix}.$$

We find the cofactor of a_{32} as follows:

$$c_{32} = -1^{(3+2)} \begin{vmatrix} a_{11} & a_{13} \\ a_{21} & a_{23} \end{vmatrix} \equiv - \begin{vmatrix} a_{11} & a_{13} \\ a_{21} & a_{23} \end{vmatrix}.$$

In general, for any $n \times n$ matrix there are n^2 cofactors, one corresponding to each element of the matrix.

C.4.5 EVALUATION OF DETERMINANTS VIA EXPANSION BY COFACTORS

The determinant of any square matrix $\mathbf{A}$ can be evaluated by taking *any* row or column of $\mathbf{A}$, multiplying each element in the row or column by its cofactor and summing the resulting products. To illustrate, let us work along the top row of the matrix of a 3×3 matrix $\mathbf{A}$. We have:

$$\begin{vmatrix} a_{11} & a_{12} & a_{13} \\ a_{21} & a_{22} & a_{23} \\ a_{31} & a_{32} & a_{33} \end{vmatrix} = a_{11}c_{11} + a_{12}c_{12} + a_{13}c_{13}$$

$$= a_{11}(+1) \begin{vmatrix} a_{22} & a_{23} \\ a_{32} & a_{33} \end{vmatrix} + a_{12}(-1) \begin{vmatrix} a_{21} & a_{23} \\ a_{31} & a_{33} \end{vmatrix}$$

$$+ a_{13}(+1) \begin{vmatrix} a_{21} & a_{22} \\ a_{31} & a_{32} \end{vmatrix}.$$

As an illustration, let us evaluate the determinant of the numerical example given in Section C.3, this time using the method of expansion by cofactors:

$$\begin{vmatrix} 2 & 1 & 2 \\ 0 & 3 & -1 \\ 4 & 0 & 5 \end{vmatrix} = 2 \begin{vmatrix} 3 & -1 \\ 0 & 5 \end{vmatrix} - 1 \begin{vmatrix} 0 & -1 \\ 4 & 5 \end{vmatrix} + 2 \begin{vmatrix} 0 & 3 \\ 4 & 0 \end{vmatrix}$$

$$= (2 \times 15) - (1 \times 4) + (2 \times -12)$$
$$= 30 - 4 - 24 = 2.$$

Note that we get the same result by expanding, say, down the second column:

$$\begin{vmatrix} 2 & 1 & 2 \\ 0 & 3 & -1 \\ 4 & 0 & 5 \end{vmatrix} = a_{12}c_{12} + a_{22}c_{22} + a_{32}c_{32}$$

$$= -1 \begin{vmatrix} 0 & -1 \\ 4 & 5 \end{vmatrix} + 3 \begin{vmatrix} 2 & 2 \\ 4 & 5 \end{vmatrix} - 0 \begin{vmatrix} 2 & 2 \\ 0 & -1 \end{vmatrix}$$

$$= (-1 \times 4) + (3 \times 2) = 2.$$

For larger matrices the same procedure may be followed, but each minor obviously must be separately evaluated by continual expansion, until broken down into cofactors comprising simple 3×3 or 2×2 determinants. This method is quite inefficient from a computational viewpoint. In practice, determinants of high order would be evaluated by using a computer or one of the techniques specially devised for desk calculation.

C.5 The Adjoint Matrix in the General Case

The adjoint of any square matrix A (see Section 16.2.3) is found quite simply by replacing each element with its cofactor and transposing the matrix so formed (for a discussion of transposition see Section 15.4.2). Denoting, once again, the cofactor of a_{ij} by c_{ij} we have

$$A^+ = C'$$

where C is the matrix of cofactors.
For example:

$$\begin{bmatrix} 2 & 1 & 2 \\ 0 & 3 & -1 \\ 4 & 0 & 5 \end{bmatrix}^+ = \begin{bmatrix} 15 & -4 & -12 \\ -5 & 2 & 4 \\ -7 & 2 & 6 \end{bmatrix}' = \begin{bmatrix} 15 & -5 & -7 \\ -4 & 2 & 2 \\ -12 & 4 & 6 \end{bmatrix}.$$

C.6 The Inverse Matrix in the General Case

As indicated in Section 16.2.4, the matrix inverse is given as

$$A^{-1} = \frac{A^+}{|A|}.$$

This formula applies to any nonsingular (see Section 16.2.6) square matrix. To obtain the matrix inverse, merely apply the techniques discussed in Sections C.4 and C.5 for calculating determinants and adjoints in the general case.

As a numerical illustration, we may calculate the inverse of the 3 × 3 matrix given in C.3. Taking the determinant of this matrix from Section C.4.5 and its adjoint from Section C.5, we have

$$\begin{bmatrix} 2 & 1 & 2 \\ 0 & 3 & -1 \\ 4 & 0 & 5 \end{bmatrix}^{-1} = \frac{A^+}{|A|} = \tfrac{1}{2}\begin{bmatrix} 15 & -5 & -7 \\ -4 & 2 & 2 \\ -12 & 4 & 6 \end{bmatrix}$$

$$= \begin{bmatrix} 7\tfrac{1}{2} & -2\tfrac{1}{2} & -3\tfrac{1}{2} \\ -2 & 1 & 1 \\ -6 & 2 & 3 \end{bmatrix}.$$

Applying the usual check we confirm $A^{-1}A = I$ as follows:

$$\begin{bmatrix} 7\tfrac{1}{2} & -2\tfrac{1}{2} & -3\tfrac{1}{2} \\ -2 & 1 & 1 \\ -6 & 2 & 3 \end{bmatrix}\begin{bmatrix} 2 & 1 & 2 \\ 0 & 3 & -1 \\ 4 & 0 & 5 \end{bmatrix} = \begin{bmatrix} 1 & 0 & 0 \\ 0 & 1 & 0 \\ 0 & 0 & 1 \end{bmatrix}.$$

The Linear Regression Model in Matrix Terms

D.I The Two-Variable Case

Consider the simple regression model relating a dependent variable Y with a single independent variable X. We may write

$$Y = \alpha + \beta X + u \qquad (D.1)$$

where α and β = population regression coefficients; and
$\quad\quad\quad\quad u$ = disturbance term.

We have a sample of n observations of Y and X. For the ith observation we may write:

$$Y_i = \alpha + \beta X_i + u_i \qquad (D.2)$$

where Y_i, X_i and u_i = ith observations of Y, X and u respectively.

The set of Equations (D.2) may be written for $i = 1, 2, \ldots, n$ in matrix terms as:

$$\mathbf{Y} = \mathbf{X}\beta + \mathbf{u} \qquad (D.3)$$

where $\mathbf{Y}$ = $n \times 1$ vector of observed Y values;

$\quad\quad\mathbf{X}$ = $n \times 2$ matrix whose first column consists entirely of ones and whose second column contains the n sample values of X;

$$\beta = \begin{bmatrix} \alpha \\ \beta \end{bmatrix}; \text{ and}$$

$\quad\quad\mathbf{u}$ = $n \times 1$ vector of disturbance terms.

To apply the principle of least squares, we define the error term or residual as:

$$\mathbf{e} = \mathbf{Y} - \mathbf{X}\hat{\beta} \qquad (D.4)$$

where $\hat{\beta} = \begin{bmatrix} \hat{\alpha} \\ \hat{\beta} \end{bmatrix}$, a 2×1 vector of estimators of the unknown population regression coefficients.

We note that

$$e'e \equiv \sum e^2 \qquad (D.5)$$

(see Exercise 6, Chapter 15). Hence to minimise the sum of squared residuals, we must minimise

$$e'e = (\mathbf{Y} - \mathbf{X}\hat{\beta})' (\mathbf{Y} - \mathbf{X}\hat{\beta}). \qquad (D.6)$$

Expanding, we have

$$e'e = \mathbf{Y}'\mathbf{Y} - 2\hat{\beta}'\mathbf{X}'\mathbf{Y} + \hat{\beta}'\mathbf{X}'\mathbf{X}\hat{\beta}$$

whence

$$\frac{\partial}{\partial\hat{\beta}} (e'e) = -2\mathbf{X}'\mathbf{Y} + 2\mathbf{X}'\mathbf{X}\hat{\beta}. \qquad (D.7)$$

Setting (D.7) to zero and rearranging gives:

$$\mathbf{X}'\mathbf{Y} = \mathbf{X}'\mathbf{X}\hat{\beta}. \qquad (D.8)$$

We can show that (D.8) is in fact the set of normal Equations (20.10), by observing:

$$\mathbf{X}'\mathbf{Y} \equiv \begin{bmatrix} 1 & 1 \dots 1 \\ X_1 & X_2 \dots X_n \end{bmatrix} \begin{bmatrix} Y_1 \\ Y_2 \\ \vdots \\ Y_n \end{bmatrix} \equiv \begin{bmatrix} \sum Y \\ \sum XY \end{bmatrix}$$

and

$$\mathbf{X}'\mathbf{X} \equiv \begin{bmatrix} 1 & 1 \dots 1 \\ X_1 & X_2 \dots X_n \end{bmatrix} \begin{bmatrix} 1 & X_1 \\ 1 & X_2 \\ \vdots & \vdots \\ 1 & X_n \end{bmatrix} \equiv \begin{bmatrix} n & \sum X \\ \sum X & \sum X^2 \end{bmatrix}.$$

Hence (D.8) may be written as

$$\begin{bmatrix} \sum Y \\ \sum XY \end{bmatrix} = \begin{bmatrix} n & \sum X \\ \sum X & \sum X^2 \end{bmatrix} \begin{bmatrix} \hat{\alpha} \\ \hat{\beta} \end{bmatrix},$$

that is,

$$\sum Y = n\hat{\alpha} + \hat{\beta} \sum X \qquad (D.9a)$$
$$\sum XY = \hat{\alpha} \sum X + \hat{\beta} \sum X^2, \qquad (D.9b)$$

which are the normal equations for the two-variable case.

Proceeding from (D.8) we obtain the formula for the least-squares estimator $\hat{\beta}$ as:

$$\hat{\beta} = (\mathbf{X}'\mathbf{X})^{-1} \mathbf{X}'\mathbf{Y}. \qquad (D.10)$$

D.2 The *m*-Variable Case

The above matrix equations may be equally applied in the general case of *m* independent variables by redefining $\mathbf{X}$ as having $m + 1$ columns (that is, *m* columns of observations of the explanatory variables, and a column of ones for the intercept term). Thus in Equations (D.4) to (D.10) the matrix $\mathbf{X}$ is of order $n \times (m + 1)$ and $\boldsymbol{\beta}$ is an $(m + 1) \times 1$ vector of regression coefficients including the intercept term.

D.3 Assumptions of the General Linear Model

The simplest set of assumptions governing the process which generates the observed data is as follows.

(a) The disturbance term *u* in Equation (D.2) is a random variable with a mean of zero and a constant variance σ^2.

(b) The covariance between u_i and u_j $(i \neq j)$ is zero. Assumptions (a) and (b) together mean that the variance-covariance matrix of the disturbances is assumed to be of the form

$$\begin{bmatrix} \sigma^2 & 0 & \dots & 0 \\ 0 & \sigma^2 & \dots & 0 \\ \vdots & \vdots & & \vdots \\ 0 & 0 & \dots & \sigma^2 \end{bmatrix} \equiv \sigma^2 \mathbf{I}.$$

(c) The *X* in (D.4) are a set of fixed numbers; that is, if repeated samples are taken, the *X* are the same in each sample (see the monopolist's problem, Chapters 20–21).

(d) The matrix $\mathbf{X'X}$ is nonsingular.

If the foregoing assumptions hold, the least-squares estimator $\hat{\boldsymbol{\beta}}$ in (D.10) has a mean of $\boldsymbol{\beta}$ and a variance $\sigma^2 (\mathbf{X'X})^{-1}$. Since σ^2, the population variance of *u*, is unknown, it must be estimated. The usual estimator is the sample variance of the error term, given as $s^2 = \mathbf{e'e}/(n - m - 1)$.

The consequences of the breakdown of some of the above assumptions are as follows.

(a) If the variance of the disturbance term is not constant, but varies with one or more of the explanatory variables, we have the problem of *heteroscedasticity*, which results in an increase in the variance of the ordinary least-squares estimator.

(b) If successive values of the disturbance term are not uncorrelated, the problem of *autocorrelation* or *serial correlation* arises. The effects of autocorrelation are again seen in the variances of the regression coefficients.

(c) Singularity of the matrix $\mathbf{X'X}$ may arise because, for example, there exists a perfect linear relationship between two or more explanatory variables. Thus the inverse of $\mathbf{X'X}$ does not exist, and the estimating Equation (D.10) breaks down. A more general problem is one where there is not a perfect but a high degree of association between two or more explanatory variables. This is the problem of *multicollinearity*,

which results in increases in the variance of the estimator $\hat{\beta}$, indicating that we can place less reliance on numerical results when this problem is present.

Answers to Exercises

Chapter 2

1. Suppose we choose the symbol S for savings, i for the rate of interest, and f for the function. Then we could write $S = f(i)$.
2. $i = f^{-1}(S)$.
3. Single-valued.
4. (a) $q - 5p = 0$,
   (b) two,
   (c) $q = 5p$; $p = \dfrac{q}{5}$.

Chapter 3

2.

y	AC
0 units	$150
2 units	$108
4 units	$ 82
6 units	$ 72
8 units	$ 78

4. (a) continuous,
   (b) nonlinear.
6. $\alpha_1 = 150$, $\alpha_2 = -25$, $\alpha_3 = 2$.
7. 75 units.

Chapter 4

2. $p_e = \dfrac{\gamma - \alpha}{\beta - \varepsilon}$.
3. $p_e = 23$, $q_e = 74$.
5. $350 million, $270 million.
7. $K = 50L - 100$, $y = 4 - \frac{1}{10}x$.
8. $q_4 = 6p$.
9. (a) the line is moved upwards, parallel to itself,
   (b) the slope of the line becomes less steep.

Chapter 5

2. (a) $16\frac{1}{2}$ thousand,
   (b) 53 thousand,
   (c) 260 thousand.

3. (a) rectangular hyperbola,
   (b) quartic,
   (c) linear,
   (d) cubic,
   (e) exponential.
4. $253.64.
5. $127.12.
7. $p = 2$, $q = 8$.

Chapter 6

2. $\dfrac{dq}{dp} = -4p^{-3}$, hence $\dfrac{dq}{dp} = -\tfrac{1}{2}$ when $p = 2$.

3. 9.

4. $\dfrac{dU}{dy} = 10y - \tfrac{3}{2}y^2$.

5. $\dfrac{dM}{ds} = -10s^{-2}$, hence $\dfrac{dM}{ds} = -1.6$ when $s = 2\tfrac{1}{2}$.

6. $\dfrac{dy}{dL} = \dfrac{238}{L^{0.15}}$.

7. $\dfrac{dq}{dp} = 3\alpha p^2 + \beta$.

Since α and β are positive by assumption, and p^2 is always positive, the value of the derivative is always positive, indicating that the original function slopes upwards at all levels of p.

Chapter 7

1. (a) -2,
   (b) -1.92.
2. 217.

3. $E_Y = -\dfrac{3}{2}\sqrt{Y} \times \dfrac{Y}{q} \equiv -\dfrac{3Y^{\frac{3}{2}}}{2q}$.

4. (a) $-\tfrac{3}{8}$,
   (b) Because its income elasticity of demand is negative, i.e., less of the commodity is bought as income rises.

5. 2.4 per cent reduction in meat consumption.

6. $MC = \dfrac{dTC}{dy} = y$.

Thus as y increases, MC increases. Since increasing MC indicates diminishing MP, the original production function must exhibit diminishing returns.

7. (a) $B = 500 + 5L^2 - \tfrac{1}{6}L^3$,
   (b) 50.
8. $L = 10$, $K = 31$.
9. -0.92.

Chapter 8

1. 8.75 litres.

2. $\dfrac{d^2U}{db^2} = -4 < 0$, hence the extreme point is a maximum.

3. Since $AC = y^2 - 10y + 40$, minimum AC is where

$\dfrac{dAC}{dy} = 2y - 10 = 0$, i.e., where $y = 5$.

Now $MC = \dfrac{dTC}{dy} = 3y^2 - 20y + 40$,

$MC = AC$ where $3y^2 - 20y + 40 = y^2 - 10y + 40$ from which $y = 0$ or 5. The latter is also the point of minimum AC as shown above.

4. Since $dy/dL = 238/L^{0.15}$ we can see that dy/dL will only approach zero (and therefore $f(L)$ approach a maximum) as L approaches infinity.

5. Since $AC = \frac{1}{2}y$, the AC curve is linear and has no global extreme point.

6. $y = 562\frac{1}{2}$.

7. Since $MP = dTP/dL = 10L - \frac{1}{2}L^2$, we calculate that $MP = AP$ where $10L - \frac{1}{2}L^2 = 5L - L^2/6$, which has the solution $L = 15$, the same input level for which AP is maximised (see the answer to Exercise 6 above).

Chapter 9

1. $4\frac{2}{3}$ units.

2. $NR = 180x^{\frac{1}{2}} - 9x$.

3. 100 units of leather.

4. 3 apples and $5\frac{1}{3}$ bananas.

5. Since the price ratio would be the same as before, the optimal combination would not change. However, the cost of purchasing this combination of goods would double.

8. (a) $0 \leqslant W \leqslant 2,\ 5 \leqslant B \leqslant 7$;
   (b) $W = 5,\ B = 2\frac{1}{2}$.

Chapter 10

1. (a) $D = \beta_1 + \beta_2\,GNP + \beta_3\,i$,
   (b) $D = \beta_1\,GNP^{\beta_2}\,i^{\beta_3}$,
   (c) $D = \beta_1 + \beta_2\,GNP + \beta_3 i + \beta_4\,GNP^2 + \beta_5 i^2 + \beta_6\,GNP(i)$.

3. $2x + 3y + z - 10 = 0$,

$x = 5 - \dfrac{3y}{2} - \dfrac{z}{2}$,

$y = 3\frac{1}{3} - \dfrac{2x}{3} - \dfrac{z}{3}$,

$z = 10 - 2x - 3y$.

4. A slice through the plane at $y = 2$ is taken yielding the equation $2x + z = 4$.

5. (a) constant,
   (b) increasing,
   (c) decreasing,
   (d) increasing.

7. The isoquants slope downwards and are convex to the origin.

8. The *MP* of capital declines as K increases, indicating the operation of the law of diminishing returns.

Chapter 11

1. $\dfrac{\partial y}{\partial L} = MP_L = \dfrac{3.5K^{0.3}}{L^{0.3}}$,

$\dfrac{\partial y}{\partial K} = MP_K = \dfrac{1.5L^{0.7}}{K^{0.7}}$.

2. Multiply both factor levels by $\lambda \neq 0$. The new output is
$$y_1 = 5(\lambda L)^{0.7} (\lambda K)^{0.3}$$
$$= \lambda^{0.7 + 0.3} 5L^{0.7} K^{0.3}$$
$$= \lambda y.$$
Hence constant returns prevail.

4. $MP_K = 1.993$.

5. $\dfrac{\partial y}{\partial L} = 3K + 3 - 6L$,

$\dfrac{\partial y}{\partial K} = 3L - 2K$.

6. They are downward sloping, indicating diminishing marginal product with respect to both factors.

7. (a) $E_L = 0.7$, $E_K = 0.3$;

(b) $E_L = \dfrac{3LK + 3L - 6L^2}{3LK + 3L - K^2 - 3L^2 + 25}$,

$E_K = \dfrac{3LK - 2K^2}{3LK + 3L - K^2 - 3L^2 + 25}$.

8. (a) $\dfrac{\partial y}{\partial L} = \dfrac{2.4K^{0.4}}{L^{0.2}}$, $\dfrac{\partial y}{\partial K} = \dfrac{1.2L^{0.8}}{K^{0.6}}$;

(b) $\dfrac{\partial y}{\partial L} = \dfrac{0.5K^{1.3}}{L^{0.9}}$, $\dfrac{\partial y}{\partial K} = 6.5L^{0.1} K^{0.3}$;

(c) $\dfrac{\partial D}{\partial GNP} = \beta_2$, $\dfrac{\partial D}{\partial i} = \beta_3$.

9. $y_1 = 16$, $y_2 = 22$, $y_3 = 0$.

Chapter 12

1. (a) nonhomogeneous,
   (b) homogeneous degree two,
   (c) homogeneous degree zero,
   (d) homogeneous degree 1.3,
   (e) homogeneous degree one.

3. Labour's share is 70 per cent, capital's is 30 per cent.

4. $x_1 = \$1.8$ billion,
   $x_2 = \$0.9$ billion,
   $x_3 = \$6.3$ billion.

5. $L = \$0.0336$ million, $K = \$0.0806$ million.

6. To maximise profit we must solve $MP_K = \dfrac{r}{p}$ and $MP_L = \dfrac{w}{p}$.

   In this case we must solve

   $$9 - \frac{L^2}{2K^2} = \frac{r}{p}$$

   and

   $$-3 + \frac{L}{K} = \frac{w}{p}$$

   simultaneously; these equations have no unique solution.

Chapter 13

1. $A = 2$, $B = 8$.
2. $y_1 = 4$, $y_2 = 3$.
3. $L = 300$, $K = 400$.
5. $y_1 = 14$, $y_2 = 28$, $y_3 = \frac{3}{8}$.
6. $L = 2$, $K = 3$.

Chapter 14

1. $Y = \$1600$ million, $C = \$1400$ million.

2. (a) Y rises to 1725 million,
   (b) The change in income is $2\frac{1}{2}$ times the change in investment. (See further Chapter 17.)

3. They may all be made endogenous in particular model constructions, if so desired.

4. (a) $a_{11}x_1 + a_{12}x_2 = b_1$
       $a_{21}x_1 + a_{22}x_2 = b_2$
       $a_{31}x_1 + a_{32}x_2 = b_3$.
   (b) The coefficient matrix is
   $$\begin{bmatrix} a_{11} & a_{12} \\ a_{21} & a_{22} \\ a_{31} & a_{32} \end{bmatrix}$$
   and is of order 3×2.

5. $4x - 3y - 5z = c - b,$
    $-2x - 4y + 1z = 0,$
    $-4x + 2y + 0z = -d.$

6. $$\begin{bmatrix} 4 & -3 & -5 \\ -2 & -4 & 1 \\ -4 & 2 & 0 \end{bmatrix} \qquad \begin{bmatrix} x \\ y \\ z \end{bmatrix} = \begin{bmatrix} c - b \\ 0 \\ -d \end{bmatrix}.$$

    3×3 matrix of 3×1 vector 3×1 vector
    coefficients   of unknowns   of intercepts

7. $$\begin{bmatrix} 1 & 2 \\ 1 & -3 \end{bmatrix} \qquad \begin{bmatrix} q \\ p \end{bmatrix} = \begin{bmatrix} 15 \\ 10 \end{bmatrix}.$$

    2×2 matrix of 2×1 vector 2×1 vector
    coefficients   of unknowns   of intercepts

8. $p = 1, q = 13$ at equilibrium.

9. (a) 2×2,
    (b) 5×1,
    (c) 1×2,
    (d) 1×1.

Chapter 15

1. (a) $2 \times 2, 2 \times 1, 2 \times 1$;
    (b) $2 \times 2, 2 \times 2, 2 \times 2$;
    (c) $2 \times 3, 3 \times 2, 2 \times 2$;
    (d) $1 \times 2, 2 \times 1, 1 \times 1$.

2. (a) $\begin{bmatrix} 23 \\ 37 \end{bmatrix}$,   (b) $\begin{bmatrix} 12 & 1 \\ 7 & -15 \end{bmatrix}$,   (c) $\begin{bmatrix} 12 & 10 \\ 32 & 28 \end{bmatrix}$,   (d) 2.

3. (b) and (d).

4. $\begin{bmatrix} 1 & 0 \\ 0 & 1 \end{bmatrix}$. This is a second-order identity matrix.

5. $\begin{bmatrix} 18 & 0 & -9 \\ 27 & 45 & 9 \\ 72 & -4\frac{1}{2} & 81 \\ 9 & 0 & 63 \end{bmatrix}.$

6. $\mathbf{e}'\mathbf{e} = [e_1 \ e_2 \ldots e_m] \begin{bmatrix} e_1 \\ e_2 \\ \vdots \\ e_m \end{bmatrix} = e_1^2 + e_2^2 + \ldots + e_m^2.$

    $\mathbf{e}\mathbf{e}' = \begin{bmatrix} e_1 \\ e_2 \\ \vdots \\ e_m \end{bmatrix} [e_1 \ e_2 \ldots e_m] = \begin{bmatrix} e_1^2 & e_1 e_2 & \ldots & e_1 e_m \\ e_2 e_1 & e_2^2 & \ldots & e_2 e_m \\ \vdots & \vdots & & \vdots \\ e_m e_1 & e_m e_2 & \ldots & e_m^2 \end{bmatrix}.$

Chapter 16

1. $Y = \$1600$ million, $C = \$1400$ million.

2. $p = 1, q = 13$.

3. $Y = \dfrac{C^* + m}{1 - v}$

$I = \dfrac{C^*v + m}{1 - v}$.

5. (a) 2,

(b) 0. The matrix is singular.

6. $x = 3, y = 2$.

7. There is no set of values for x_1 and x_2 which satisfies both equations simultaneously. In matrix algebra we recognise this by the fact that the coefficient matrix $\begin{bmatrix} 2 & -6 \\ 1 & -3 \end{bmatrix}$ is singular and hence has no inverse.

Chapter 17

1. (a) $Y = \dfrac{I^* + X^* - n}{1 + p}$,

$M = \dfrac{p(I^* + X^*) + n}{1 + p}$.

(b) $\begin{bmatrix} \frac{5}{7} & -\frac{5}{7} \\ \frac{2}{7} & \frac{5}{7} \end{bmatrix}$.

2. (a) $Y = \dfrac{G^* + a}{1 - c}$,

$C = \dfrac{G^*c + a}{1 - c}$;

(b) $\begin{bmatrix} \dfrac{1}{1 - c} & \dfrac{1}{1 - c} \\ \dfrac{c}{1 - c} & \dfrac{1}{1 - c} \end{bmatrix}$.

3. $\$25$ million.

4. $4 \times 4 = 16$ multipliers.

5. 0.6.

6. $\Delta Y = \dfrac{1}{1 - v} \Delta m$.

Chapter 18

1. $\begin{bmatrix} x_1 \\ x_2 \\ x_3 \end{bmatrix} = \begin{bmatrix} 0.1 & 0.3 & 0 \\ 0.5 & 0.1 & 0.1 \\ 0.8 & 0.9 & 0 \end{bmatrix} \begin{bmatrix} x_1 \\ x_2 \\ x_3 \end{bmatrix} + \begin{bmatrix} 50 \\ 90 \\ 25 \end{bmatrix}$

where x_1 = agricultural output;
$\quad\quad x_2$ = manufacturing output; and
$\quad\quad x_3$ = transport output.

2. $x_1 = 123.04$,
$\quad x_2 = 202.28$,
$\quad x_3 = 305.41$.

3. *Agricultural output*:
$\quad$ To: agricultural sector $\quad\quad$ 12.3
$\quad\quad\quad$ manufacturing sector $\quad$ 60.7
$\quad\quad\quad$ transport sector $\quad\quad\quad$ —
$\quad\quad\quad$ final demand $\quad\quad\quad\quad$ 50.0

$\quad\quad\quad\quad$ *Total* $\quad\quad\quad\quad$ 123.0

$\quad$ *Manufacturing output*:
$\quad$ To: agricultural sector $\quad\quad$ 61.5
$\quad\quad\quad$ manufacturing sector $\quad$ 20.2
$\quad\quad\quad$ transport sector $\quad\quad$ 30.5
$\quad\quad\quad$ final demand $\quad\quad\quad$ 90.0

$\quad\quad\quad\quad$ *Total* $\quad\quad\quad\quad$ 202.2

$\quad$ *Transport output*:
$\quad$ To: agricultural sector $\quad\quad$ 98.4
$\quad\quad\quad$ manufacturing sector $\quad$ 182.1
$\quad\quad\quad$ transport sector $\quad\quad\quad$ —
$\quad\quad\quad$ final demand $\quad\quad\quad\quad$ 25.0

$\quad\quad\quad\quad$ *Total* $\quad\quad\quad\quad$ 305.5

4. (a) It will rise by approximately 2.7 per cent;
$\quad$ (b) It would decline by 0.54 of 1 per cent.

5. $\begin{bmatrix} 4 & -3 \\ 4 & 3 \\ -1\frac{1}{2} & 5 \end{bmatrix}$.

6. $(\mathbf{I} - \mathbf{A})^{-1} = \begin{bmatrix} 2 & 2 \\ 1 & 2.25 \end{bmatrix}$.

7. $x_1 = 300$,
$\quad x_2 = 275$.

Chapter 19

2. $x_1 = 6$,
$\quad x_2 = 3$.

3. $x_1 = 3\frac{1}{2},$
$\ x_2 = 1\frac{1}{2},$
$\ z\ = 8\frac{1}{2}.$

4. $1x_1 + 3x_2 + 1s_1 + 0s_2 = 15,$
$\ 1x_1 + 1x_2 + 0s_1 + 1s_2 = 9,$
$\qquad\quad x_1, x_2, s_1, s_2 \geqslant 0.$

5. (a) $s_1 = 6, x_1 = 9$;
(b) $x_1 = 6, x_2 = 3$;
(c) $s_1 = 15, s_2 = 9.$

6. Optimal production is 5 handbags and no shoes per day, yielding a total revenue of $100.

7. The optimal production pattern would change to 3 handbags and 8 pairs of shoes, yielding a total revenue of $54.

Chapter 20

2. Given $Y = \hat{\alpha} + \hat{\beta}X + e$, we re-express this equation in deviation form:

$$y = \hat{\beta}x + e$$

or $\qquad\qquad e = y - \hat{\beta}x.$

Squaring and summing we have

$$\sum e^2 = \sum(y - \hat{\beta}x)^2$$
$$= \sum y^2 - 2\hat{\beta}\sum xy + \hat{\beta}^2\sum x^2$$

whence $\qquad \dfrac{d\sum e^2}{d\hat{\beta}} = -2\sum xy + 2\hat{\beta}\sum x^2.$

Setting this to zero in order to minimise $\sum e^2$ gives

$$\sum xy = \hat{\beta}\sum x^2$$

whence $\qquad\qquad \hat{\beta} = \dfrac{\sum xy}{\sum x^2}.$

Dividing the first normal Equation (20.10a) by n gives

$$Y = \hat{\alpha} + \hat{\beta}\bar{X}$$

whence $\qquad\qquad \hat{\alpha} = \bar{Y} - \hat{\beta}\bar{X}.$

3. $\qquad\qquad \sum y^2 = \sum(Y - \bar{Y})^2$
$\qquad\qquad\qquad = \sum Y^2 - 2\bar{Y}\sum Y + n\bar{Y}^2$
$\qquad\qquad\qquad = \sum Y^2 - 2n\bar{Y}^2 + n\bar{Y}^2$

since $\qquad\qquad \bar{Y} = \dfrac{\sum Y}{n}$ and $\sum Y = n\bar{Y}.$

Hence $\qquad\qquad \sum y^2 = \sum Y^2 - n\bar{Y}^2.$

4. (c) $Y = 1.0926 + 0.9815\,X.$

5.

Price	Observed Quantity	Predicted Quantity	Residual
2	5	3.06	1.94
4	4	5.02	−1.02
2	3	3.06	−0.06
3	4	4.04	−0.04
8	7	8.94	−1.94
7	9	7.96	1.04
6	8	6.98	1.02
8	10	8.94	1.06
7	8	7.96	0.04
3	2	4.04	−2.04

The mean of the residuals is zero.

6. (a) Take logs:

$\log y = \log A + a \log L + b \log K.$

Let $Y = \log y,$

$\alpha = \log A,$

$X_1 = \log L,$

$X_2 = \log K,$

$\beta_1 = a,$

$\beta_2 = b.$

Fit the equation:

$Y = \alpha + \beta_1 X_1 + \beta_2 X_2.$

(b) Let $X_1 = W,$

$X_2 = Z,$

$X_3 = Z^2,$

$X_4 = WZ.$

Fit

$C = a + b_1 X_1 + b_2 X_2 + b_3 X_3 + b_4 X_4.$

Chapter 21

1. $r^2 = 0.765,$

$r = 0.875.$

2. $t = 5.103.$ At 8 degrees of freedom and a 95 per cent confidence level, the critical t value (for a two-tailed test) is 2.306. Hence our null hypothesis is rejected at this confidence level.

3. $SE(\hat{\alpha}) = 1.060,$

$SE(\hat{\beta}) = 0.192.$

5. $s^2 = 1.998.$

Further Reading

In the Preface we pointed out that this book has been designed as an "easy" introduction to the use of mathematics in economic analysis. Hopefully the student who has mastered this text will feel sufficiently interested in the subject to proceed to some of the more advanced works in quantitative economics, or will at least have built up enough confidence to tackle books which provide a more rigorous treatment of ground we have covered here. We detail below some recommended books for the student who wishes to consolidate or extend his knowledge in the various areas of quantitative methods that we have studied.

I. General

The following six books look from different angles at the use of mathematics in economics. They are arranged in roughly ascending order of rigour.

ARCHIBALD, G. C., and R. G. LIPSEY, *An Introduction to a Mathematical Treatment of Economics*, Weidenfeld & Nicholson, London, 1967.

HUANG, D. S., *Introduction to the Use of Mathematics in Economic Analysis*, John Wiley, New York, 1964.

LEWIS, J. P., *An Introduction to Mathematics for Students of Economics*, Macmillan, London, 1959.

CHIANG, A. C., *Fundamental Methods of Mathematical Economics*, McGraw-Hill, New York, 1967.

ALLEN, R. G. D., *Mathematical Analysis for Economists*, Macmillan, London, 1938.

YAMANE, T., *Mathematics for Economists, an Elementary Survey*, Prentice-Hall, Englewood Cliffs, 1968, 2nd Ed.

The majority of modern "mainstream" economics texts use mathematical exposition and analysis to a greater or lesser degree. There are some, however, which provide a specifically mathematical view of modern micro or macro theory. Among books presenting a quantitative treatment of microeconomics, the following two stand out:

HENDERSON, J. H., and R. E. QUANDT, *Microeconomic Theory, a Mathematical Approach*, McGraw-Hill, New York, 1958.

NAYLOR, T. H., and J. M. VERNON, *Microeconomics and Decision Models of the Firm*, Harcourt, Brace & World, New York, 1969.

Quantitative treatments of macroeconomic theory may be found in the following:

BOWERS, D. A., and R. N. BAIRD, *Elementary Mathematical Macroeconomics*, Prentice-Hall, Englewood Cliffs, 1971.

KOGIKU, K. C., *An Introduction to Macroeconomic Models*, McGraw-Hill, New York, 1968.

A textbook which develops both micro and macro theory in a systematic and consistent way using a mathematical orientation is:

BREMS, H., *Quantitative Economic Theory: a Synthetic Approach*, John Wiley, New York, 1968.

2. Linear Algebra

Two books that develop linear algebra in the context of economics are:

MILLS, G., *Introduction to Linear Algebra for Social Scientists*, George Allen and Unwin, London, 1969.

PUCKETT, R. H., *Introduction to Mathematical Economics: Matrix Algebra and Linear Economic Models*, D. C. Heath, Lexington, 1971.

A more formal and extensive treatment of linear algebra is contained in the following text:

HADLEY, G., *Linear Algebra*, Addison-Wesley, Reading, 1965.

3. Input-Output Economics

Useful elementary treatments of input-output analysis may be found in the following introductory texts:

MIERNYK, W. H., *The Elements of Input-Output Analysis*, Random House, New York, 1965.

YAN, C., *Introduction to Input-Output Economics*, Holt, Rinehart and Winston, New York, 1969.

There is also a simple introduction to input-output analysis (and also to linear programming and some other aspects of mathematical analysis in economics) in:

BAUMOL, W. J., *Economic Theory and Operations Analysis*, Prentice-Hall, Englewood Cliffs, 1965, 2nd Ed.

To the student proceeding to a more detailed study of input-output, the following will prove useful.

LEONTIEF, W. W. (Ed.), *Studies in the Structure of the American Economy*, Oxford University Press, New York, 1953.

LEONTIEF, W. W., *Input-Output Economics*, Oxford University Press, New York, 1966.

CHENERY, H., and P. CLARK, *Interindustry Economics*, John Wiley, New York, 1959.

4. Linear Programming

A standard work dealing with the implications of linear programming for theoretical and applied economics is:

DORFMAN, R., P. SAMUELSON, and R. SOLOW, *Linear Programming and Economic Analysis*, McGraw-Hill, New York, 1958.

An elementary introduction to linear programming in economics is presented in non-matrix-algebra terms in:

THROSBY, C. D., *Elementary Linear Programming*, Random House, New York, 1970.

Textbooks providing more rigorous treatments of the subject with at least passing reference to economics include:

DANTZIG, G. B., *Linear Programming and Extensions*, Princeton University Press, Princeton, 1963.

GASS, S. I., *Linear Programming, Methods and Applications*, McGraw-Hill, New York, 1964, 2nd Ed.

HADLEY, G., *Linear Programming*, Addison-Wesley, Reading, 1965.

5. Econometrics

There are a number of introductory texts in econometrics, all of which adopt somewhat differing approaches. The following books should be accessible to the beginning student:

WONNACOTT, R. J., and T. H. WONNACOTT, *Econometrics*, John Wiley, New York, 1970.

KMENTA, J., *Elements of Econometrics*, Macmillan, New York, 1971.

KANE, E. J., *Economic Statistics and Econometrics: An Introduction to Quantitative Economics*, Harper and Row, New York, 1968.

KLEIN, L. R., *An Introduction to Econometrics*, Prentice-Hall, Englewood Cliffs, 1962.

WALTERS, A. A., *An Introduction to Econometrics*, Macmillan, London, 1969.

From these the serious student will progress through the following more advanced standard works in the field.

JOHNSTON, J., *Econometric Methods*, McGraw-Hill, New York, 1972, 2nd Ed.

GOLDBERGER, A. S., *Econometric Theory*, John Wiley, New York, 1964.

Index

Abscissa, 19
Adjoint matrix, 221-2, 310
Aggregate demand, 194, 196-8
Aggregate supply, 196
Alternative hypothesis, 293 n
Arc elasticity, 81-3
Argument, 174 n
Autocorrelation, 314
Autonomous consumption, 40, 231-2
Autonomous investment, 40, 230-1
Average cost, *see* Average total cost
Average fixed cost, 87, 112
Average product, 86-7
Average revenue, 88, 110-14
Average total cost, 87, 98, 112-14, 174-6
Average variable cost, 87, 113
Axis, 17-18, 49

Basic solution, 217, 261
Basic variable, 257
Basis, 261
Behavioural equation, 272

Calculus, 4, 70
Cardinal utility, 149, 181
Cartesian diagram, 130
Causality, 14-15
Ceteris paribus clause, 271
Chiang, A. C., 7
Cobb, C. W., 51
Cobb-Douglas production function
    elasticity of output, 156-7
    factor shares, 167-8
    general form, one input, 51
    general form, two inputs, 136

general form, more than two inputs, 148-9
homogeneity, 162-8
isoquants, 141-3
marginal products, 138-41, 152-8, 166-8
returns to scale, 143-8
Coefficient, 27
Coefficient of determination, 290, 293
Cofactor, 308-10
Column vector, 199
Computer, 6, 219, 280
Concavity, 50
Conformability, 213-14
Constant, 27
Constant function, 49
Constant returns to scale, 143-8 165
Constant term, 31, 133
Constraint, 109, 250-5
Consumer theory, 92-4, 121-2, 149-50, 181-6
Consumption function
    individual, 10, 25
    macroeconomic, 40, 94, 191-2
Continuity, 22-3
Convexity, 50
Coordinates, 19
Corner point, 257
Correlation coefficient, 289-93
Cost function, *see* Average total, Fixed, Marginal, Total, Variable cost.
Cramer's rule, 305-6
Cross elasticity, 81, 159

Cross-section analysis, 273
Cubic function
    defined, 48-9
    differentiation of, 75-6
    graph of, 50, 88, 101

d, 11, 70, 72-3
Data, 272
Demand curve
    firm, 89-90, 110, 113-14,
        119-21
    individual, 8, 25-6, 35, 44-5,
        127-33
    market, 35-6, 44-5
Demand function, 25-8, 127-33
Demand schedule, 8, 35-6, 44-5
Dependent variable, 9, 15, 18,
    127-8
Derivation, rules for, 72-7, 154-6,
    158-60
Derivative. See also Partial derivative.
    definition, 70
    first-order, 100
    of linear function, 72
    of nonlinear function, 72-7
    notation, 72-3, 100
    second-order, 99-100
Descartes, René, 130 n
Determinant, 220-1, 306-10
Deterministic theory, 271
Diagonal matrix, 304
Differentiation, 72-7
Diminishing returns to scale, 144-8
Direct inputs, 237, 245, 248
Discontinuity, 22-3
Disturbance term, 288, 312
Douglas, P. H., 51
Duality, 263

e, 11, 53, 298
Econometrics, 6, 26, 269-94
Economic variable, 9
Elasticity
    arc, 81-3
    definition, 79-80
    of linear function, 83
    of nonlinear function, 85
    partial, 156
    point, 80
    unitary, 84-5
Elasticity of cost function, 83
Elasticity of demand
    cross, 81, 159
    income, 81
    price, 80, 84, 159

Elasticity of output, 81, 156-7
Elasticity of supply, 81, 85
Eliminant, 220
Employment multiplier, 248
Empty hypothesis, 271
End point, 104
Endogenous variable, 42, 194,
    227-8, 234, 272
Equilibrium
    consumer, 121-2, 181-6
    firm, 110-21
    industry, 166-8
    international trade, 176-81
    macroeconomic, 40-3, 196,
        224-6, 228-36
    market, 38-40, 60-1
Equilibrium condition, 41
Equimarginal principle, 111
Error term
    definition, 276, 312
    distribution, 288, 314
    variance, 291, 314
Euler, Leonard, 167 n
Euler's theorem, 166-7
Exogenous variable, 42, 194, 227-8,
    234, 272
Expansion, 298-9
Explicit function, 15, 134-5
Exponent, 51, 52-4, 297
Exponential function, 52-4
Exponential growth, 53
Extreme point, 257
Extremisation, 96, 107
Extremum, 96

F test, 291, 293
Factor intensities, 166
Factor shares, 167-8
Factorial, 307
Feasible region, 254
Firm
    imperfect competition, 113-14
    monopolistic competition,
        119-21
    monopoly, 110-11
    perfect competition, 111-13
        117-19
First derivative, see Derivative
Fixed cost, 87-8
Forecast, 273
Frequency distribution, 286
Function. See also Consumption,
    Demand, Production, Supply,
    Utility function.
    addition of, 43-5

Function (continued)
algebraic representation of, 17, 26-7
constant, 48
continuous, 22-3
cubic, 48-9
definition, 12
discontinuous, 22-3, 67
explicit, 15, 134-5
exponential, 52-4
general form, 27
graphical representation of, 17-21, 130-3, 137-8
homogeneous, 162-8
implicit, 15, 134-5, 177-8
increasing, 150
inverse, 14-15
linear, *see* Linear function
linear homogeneous, 163, 165-8
logarithmic, 54-8, 77
multiple-valued, 15
nonhomogeneous, 164
nonlinear, *see* Nonlinear function
objective, 107-8
polynomial, 47-50, 128-35
power, 51-2, 135-68
quadratic, 48-9
quartic, 49
rational, 91
rectangular hyperbola, 58-60
of several variables, 127-86
single-valued, 14
of single variable, 8-122
value of, 13-14, 128

Global maxima and minima, 102-3
Gradient, *see* Slope
Graph
simple, 17-21
three-dimensional, 130-3, 137-8
Gross National Product, 23, 162
Growth processes, 52-8
Gruen, F. H., 7

Harpsichord, 176-81
Heteroscedasticity, 314
Homogeneous function, 162-8
Hyperbola, 58-60
Hyperplane, 133
Hypothesis
alternative, 293 n
empty, 271

formulation of, 270-2
null, 291-4

Identity, 40, 41, 162, 272
Identity matrix, 215, 242
Imperfect competition, 89-90, 110-11, 113-14
Implicit function, 15, 134-5, 177-8
Income determination model
in matrix terms, 194-8, 205-6, 224-6, 228-36
in simple terms, 40-3
Income distribution, 166-8
Increasing function, 150
Increasing returns to scale, 144-8
Independent variable, 9, 15-18, 127-8
Indices, 297-8
Indifference curve, 59, 92-4, 121-2, 149-50
Inequality, 252
Input-output analysis, 237-48, 255
direct inputs, 237, 245, 248
interindustry coefficients, 238
interindustry inputs, 237-9
multipliers in, 246-8
for planning, 245-6
primary inputs, 237, 245, 248
solution, 241-4
Integer, 22, 49
Intercept, 31, 133
Interindustry economics, *see* Input-output analysis
Interindustry inputs, 237
International trade, 166, 176-81, 250-9
Inverse matrix, 218-26, 310-11
Isocost line, 115
Isoquant, 91, 114-17, 141-3, 185-6
Isorevenue line, 117, 176-7

Keynesian model, *see* Income determination model

Lagrange, J. L., 177 n
Lagrange multipliers, 176-86, 301-2
Lagrangean function, 177-85, 301
Law of diminishing marginal utility, 93, 160
Law of diminishing returns, 87, 138-41, 148, 165
Law of variable proportions, 148
Leading diagonal, 215 n
Least-squares estimator, 288, 313

Leontief, W., 242
Leontief inverse, 242
LHS notation, 15
Limit, 70
Line of best fit, 275
Linear algebra, 193
Linear function
    definition, 21
    derivative of, 72
    in economic models, 191-4
    elasticity of, 83, 85
    general form, 35, 48-9
    in input-output, 237-48
    in linear programming, 250-64
    in macroeconomic models, 193-4
    maxima and minima of, 104-5
    properties of, 30-5
    of several variables, 133-4, 158-9
    slope of, 32-5
    of two variables, 128-33
Linear homogeneity, 163
Linear programming, 250-64
    activity, 259
    algebraic solution, 256-9
    applications, 263-4
    basic solution, 257
    basic variable, 257
    basis, 261
    constraints, 251-5
    duality, 263
    graphical solution, 255-6
    matrix solution, 259-63
    nonbasic variable, 257
    objective function, 250-1, 255
    shadow price, 263
    simplex method, 259
    slack variable, 256
Linear regression, 273
    assumptions, 283-94, 314-15
    in matrix terms, 312-14
    multiple, 280-1, 314
    significance tests, 289-94
    simple, 274-82, 312-13
Local maxima and minima, 102-3, 105
Logarithm
    common, 54 n, 55, 56, 298
    natural, 53 54 n, 55, 298
    in power function, 52
Logarithmic function
    defined, 54-5
    differentiation of, 77
    graph of, 56-8

Marginal cost, 87-8, 92, 111-14
Marginal product, 85-7, 92, 138-41, 148, 152-9, 166-8
Marginal propensity to consume, 40, 94, 192, 194, 228-33
Marginal propensity to import, 95, 196
Marginal propensity to save, 95
Marginal rate of substitution, 93-4, 121-2
Marginal rate of technical substitution, 90-1, 116-17, 186
Marginal rate of transformation, 91-2, 117-19, 178-9
Marginal revenue, 88-90, 92, 111-14
Marginal utility, 92-3, 181-4
Market demand, 35-6, 44-5
Market supply, 36-7
Matrix
    adjoint, 221-2, 310
    basis, 261
    conformable, 213-14
    definition, 195
    determinant of, 220-1, 306-10
    diagonal, 304
    identity, 215, 242
    inverse, 218-26, 310-11
    Leontief inverse, 242
    lower-triangular, 304
    notation, 194-5
    null, 305
    order of, 198-9
    partitioned, 261
    scalar, 305
    singular, 223
    skew-symmetric, 303
    square, 199
    submatrix, 304
    symmetric, 303
    triangular, 304
    upper-triangular, 304
Matrix operations
    addition, 240-1
    inversion, 218-22, 310-11
    multiplication, 205-15
    partitioning, 261
    scalar multiplication, 215
    subtraction, 240-1
    transposition, 216
Maximisation
    constrained, 117-19, 176-84, 250-63, 301-2
    unconstrained, 96-103, 110-14, 171-4, 300-1

Maximum, 96-105, 170-4, 176-84
Mean, 287
Minimisation
    constrained, 114-17, 120-1, 184-6, 263, 301-2
    unconstrained, 96-103, 174-6, 300-1
Minimum, 96-105, 170, 174-6, 184-6
Minor, 308
Model
    definition, 4, 37, 272
    income determination, 40-3, 194-8, 205-6, 224-6, 228-36
    linear, 191-4
    nonlinear, 60
    supply and demand, 37-40, 198, 206-7
Monopolistic competition, 119-21
Monopoly, 89-90, 110-11
Multicollinearity, 315
Multiple regression, 280-1, 314
Multipliers
    in input-output, 246-8
    Keynesian, 228
    Lagrange, 176-86, 301-2
    in macroeconomics, 227-36

Napier, J., 298 n
Natural exponential function, 53-4
Natural scale, 57-8
Net revenue, 111
Nonhomogeneous function, 164
Nonlinear estimation, 281-2
Nonlinear function
    definition, 21, 47
    examples, 47-61
    slope of, 65-77
Nonlinear model, 60
Normal distribution, 287
Normal equations, 278, 313
Null hypothesis, 291-4
Null matrix, 305

Objective function, 107-8, 170, 250-1
Optimisation. *See also* Maximisation, Minimisation.
    definition, 107-8, 170
    constrained, 109-10, 114-22, 176-86, 301-2
    unconstrained, 108, 110-14, 120, 171-6, 300-1
Ordinal utility, 150, 183-4

Ordinate, 19
Origin, 18, 131

Parabola, 49-50
Parameter, 27, 270, 273
Partial derivative
    cross, 160
    definition, 153-4
    first-order, 154
    graphical interpretation, 154-6
    of higher degree polynomials, 159
    of linear functions, 158-9
    mixed, 160
    notation, 154, 160
    second-order, 159-61
Partial elasticity, 156
Partition, 261
Perfect competition, 111-13, 117-19, 165-8
Permutation, 306
Plane, 131-2
Point elasticity, 80
Polynomial function
    definition, 47-9
    degree, 48-9
    differentiation, 76-7
    general form, 49
    graphs of, 49-50
    of several variables, 128-35
Population, 285, 288-9, 312-15
Postmultiplication, 215
Power, 51
Power function
    definition, 51
    differentiation, 76
    graph of, 51-2
    of several variables, 135-68
Prediction, 27-8, 273
Premultiplication, 215
Primary input, 237, 245, 248
Principal diagonal, 215 n
Product transformation curve, 91, 117-19, 176-7
Production function. *See also* Cobb-Douglas production function. 9, 25, 47, 171-4, 264
    derivative of, 85-7
    linear, 134-5
    linear homogeneous, 165-8
    phases of, 86-7, 112-13
Production possibilities frontier, 91, 117-19, 176-7
Production surface, 137

Profit
    definition, 111
    maximisation of, 111-21
Projection, 273

Quadrant, 18, 290
Quadratic equation
    definition, 48
    solution of, 296-7
Quadratic function
    definition, 48-9
    differentiation of, 73-4
    graph of, 49-50
Quantitative economics, 3-5
Quantitative model, 37

r, see Correlation coefficient
Random influences, 271
Rational function, 91
Ray, 146
Real number, 47 n
Real variable, 47 n
Reciprocal, 218
Rectangular hyperbola
    definition, 58-60
    graph of, 59
Regression, see Linear regression
Regression coefficients, 275,
    277-82, 283-94, 312-15
Relative maxima and minima,
    102-3
Residual, see Error term
Returns to scale, 143-8
Revealed preference, 150
Revenue function, see Average,
    Marginal, Total revenue
RHS notation, 15
Roots, 297
Row vector, 199
RTS, see Marginal rate of technical
    substitution

Sample, 272, 285, 288-9, 312-15
Scalar, 215
Scalar matrix, 305
Scale (in graphs), 18, 21, 57-8
Schumpeter, J. A., 4
Second derivatives
    definition, 99-100, 159-60
    notation, 100, 160
Second-order conditions, 100, 112,
    173-4, 300-1
Semilogarithmic graph, 57-8
Serial correlation, 314

Shadow prices, 263
Side condition, 109
Sigma notation, 202-3
Significance tests, 291-4
Simplex method, 259
Simulation, 285
Simultaneous equations, 39, 42,
    295-6, 305-6
Singular matrix, 223
Skew-symmetric matrix, 303
Slack variable, 256
Slope
    of linear function, 32-5
    of nonlinear function, 65-71,
    96-7
Social welfare function, 108 n
Standard error, 292-3
Statistical methods, 6, 269, 271-2
Stochastic models 271 n
Structural equation, 272
Submatrix, 304
Subscript notation, 11, 200-1
Supply and demand model, 37-40,
    198, 206-7
Symbols, 10-13
Symmetric matrix, 303

t test, 291-4
Tangent, 67-8
Time series, 272
Total cost, 48, 50, 87, 92, 111-17,
    185-6
Total fixed cost, 87, 111-12
Total product, 86, 92
Total revenue, 88-90, 92, 110-14
Total utility, 59, 92-3, 149-50,
    181-2
Total variable cost, 87, 111-12
Tradeoff, 109
Transformation, 281
Transposition, 216
Triangular matrix, 304

Unitary elasticity, 84-5
Utility
    cardinal, 149, 181
    ordinal, 150, 183-4
Utility function, 92-4, 121-2,
    149-50, 159-60, 181-4
Utility surface, 149, 160

Value judgment, 107-8
Value of a function, 13-14, 128

Variable
    basic, 257
    dependent, 9, 15, 18
    economic, 9
    endogenous, 42, 194, 227-8, 234, 272
    exogenous, 42, 194, 227-8, 234, 272
    independent, 9, 15, 18
    nonbasic, 257
    real, 47 n
    slack, 256
Variable cost, 87-8
Variance, 287
Vector, 199
Vertex, 257

Symbols

Σ 11, 202-3

$\equiv$ 20 n

Δ 11, 33

π 11

δ 11

∂ 154

$\gtrless$ 51 n

$\substack{\geqslant \\ \leqslant}$ 104 n

$\neq$ 52 n

σ^2 289, 291